THE MEDJUGORJE DECEPTION

THE MEDJUGORJE DECEPTION

Queen of Peace, Ethnic Cleansing, Ruined Lives

E. Michael Jones

Fidelity Press
206 Marquette Ave.
South Bend, IN 46617

You may be quite sure that in the last days there are going to be some difficult times. People will be self-centered and grasping; boastful, arrogant and rude; disobedient to their parents, ungrateful, irreligous; heartless and unappeasable; they will be slanderers, profligates, savages and enemies of everything that is good; they will be treacherous and reckless and demented by pride, preferring their own pleasure to God. They will keep up the outward appearance of religion, but will have rejected the inner power of it. Have nothing to do with people like that.

Of the same kind, too, are those men who insinuate themselves into families in order to get influence over silly women who are obsessed with their sins and follow one craze after another in an attempt to educate themselves, but can never come to knowledge of the truth.

2 Timothy 3: 1-7

A fierce frenzy has taken hold of the faithful who were good until now; they have become excessive and peculiar penitents. . . . One can look forward to a religious war here.

Pavao Zanic
Bishop of Mostar

CONTENTS

PROLOGUE

THE GHOSTS OF SURMANCI: 1941–1997

During the late afternoon of Wednesday June 25, 1997, a nondescript European rental car pulled off a narrow paved road at the far eastern end of the Brontjo plateau not far from the Neredva River in Bosnia-Herzegovina, driving onto an even narrower unpaved road that was no more than two tracks of red dust punctuated periodically by football-sized limestone rocks. The car proceeded slowly, perhaps because the track was so narrow. The thorn bushes, which encroached on the track, scratching occasionally against the car's roof like the fingernails of an ill-mannered child on a blackboard, seemed to grow to about two meters in height and then stop as if that were all the available nourishment and water allowed.

But the car proceeded slowly for another reason: both men in the car were looking for something. Both men were looking for the site of an atrocity committed against civilians in the early years of World War II. They were looking for something buried in the ground, something which had been buried over 50 years before, then exhumed and memorialized, then desecrated and abandoned. But the grave site, no matter how significant, especially in the light of atrocities which got committed even more recently, had symbolic value as well. The pit at Surmanci symbolized the dead hand of the past resting silently on the tiller of the present, steering a course of events which seem random when viewed in ignorance of the past, but only so in light of that ignorance. Both men's lives had been irrevocably changed by events which had taken place on the other side of the hill which now loomed to their west. Both men had been here before. Both of them were looking for something they had missed the first time around.

The driver of the rental car was a wealthy California business-man in his sixties. His face was tanned; his hair was silver gray and neatly combed, and he was dressed as if he had just wandered off a golf course. Sitting next to him on the passenger side was a younger man, roughly 20 years his junior, with darker, longer hair, the author of this account, and a journalist by trade, who had written a book about this region some nine years before.

I had made contact with Phil Kronzer, the driver of the car, in April of 1997, when he saw my name as one of a list of speakers at an anti-Call to Action Conference to be held in Lincoln, Nebraska, in May. Call to Action is a Catholic group, comprised mostly of liberal clergy or ex-clergy founded in 1976 as a way of updating or subverting—depending on your point of view— the Catholic Church in the United States. One person who felt that CTA was subverting rather than updating the Catholic Church was Bishop Fabian Bruskewitz, ordinary of the Diocese of Lincoln, Nebraska, who made national news in the spring of 1995 when he threatened to excommunicate anyone who belonged to Call to Action in his diocese. Phil Kronzer, who picked me up at the airport in Lincoln, was convinced that Call to Action had destroyed his marriage and was in the process of destroying his business empire and came to me as an expert to help him out.

Just where my field of expertise lay in this matter, however, was not immediately apparent. The more he talked, the more it be-came apparent to me that he was barking up the wrong tree. The source of Phil's marital problems was not Call to Action or radical feminism (although he made a plausible case for their connection in California); the source of Phil's problems was Medjugorje, the village we had just left, the site since June of 1981 of alleged apparitions of the Blessed Virgin Mary and since then the focus of a booming pilgrimage industry that had fallen on hard times but was now recovering because the civil war that had brought about the demise of Yugoslavia and its tourist industry during the four year period from 1991 to 1995 was now over. Phil and his wife Ardie had made their first pilgrimage to Medjugorje in the summer of 1987, and as a result of that trip became involved in Medjugorje prayer groups in California and then in the burgeoning and increasingly lucrative Marian conference industry, which took off in 1991 when the civil war put an end to tourism and left the Marian enthusiasts in the United States all dressed up with no place to go.

In early 1993, Ardie Kronzer met a fellow Medjugorje enthusiast by the name of Marcia Smith, a mysterious lady who frequented charismatic circles in San Francisco and had even been a lector at the pope's mass at Candlestick Park in 1986. Through Marcia Smith, Ardie became introduced to the tight circle of con men and felons who dominated the Medjugorje industry in the United States during the early 1990s. Through Smith, Ardie met Teresa Lopez, phony seer from Denver, and her handler at the time, Bishop Paolo Hnilica, of Rome and Slovakia, who had been convicted of trafficking in stolen goods in Rome. The good bishop had been wiretapped by the Italian police in conversation with underworld kingpin Flavio Carboni, whose notoriety became international when he was arrested in connection with the disappearance and death of Roberto Calvi, then president of the Banco Ambrosiano, whose failure in the early '80s was the biggest financial scandal to hit Rome and the Vatican in the post-World War II era. Bishop Hnilica was interested in buying Roberto Calvi's briefcase, which had disappeared reportedly full of Swiss bank account numbers around the same time Calvi was found dangling from Blackfriar's bridge in London on June 18, 1982.

Gradually the Smith-Lopez-Hnilica group became aware of the Kronzer family's financial resources and drew Ardie into a scheme which began with a series of retreats during which she was told that she and her money were to play a crucial role in the conversion of Russia and ended when Ardie moved out of her home in late June of 1994 after attending a Medjugorje conference at Notre Dame University. At that conference, Ardie and Marcia knelt down before Bishop Hnilica and, in a ritual that was bizarre even by Medjugorje conference standards, had offered up to him the 12 Bay area Mir groups, over which he was to preside as a way of bringing unity to a Medjugorje movement, whose main characteristic as of the early '90s had become battling over money from easily bilked pilgrims who had no place to go after the civil war broke out in Yugoslavia.

What this had to do with me would have been obvious to anyone who was familiar with these circles. In September and October 1988 I had published a series of articles on Medjugorje, later published in book form under the title *Medjugorje: The Untold Story*, which criticized the "apparitions" as a hoax and provided the world with one of the few sources on the phenomenon which wasn't written to serve the financial interests of tour guides, conference promoters, or rebellious Franciscans from Herzegovina. The revelations prompted a decline in the circulation of *Fidelity* magazine, where they first appeared, and in the esteem with which I was held in conservative, Marian circles in subsequent years. One perceptive reader wrote to me years later and at least partially in response to my stand on Medjugorje described me as "a one-legged man in an ass-kicking contest," a description which I saw as not without justification.

After their initial meeting in Lincoln, Nebraska, I joined Kronzer as the latter traveled back and forth across the country tracking down leads. One trip led to Reno, Nevada, where we met the husband of a seer, or better, the seer's ex-husband. Jeff Lopez met Tonie Alcorn in April of 1987 as the result of an affair they had had when both of them were working at a Wendy's in Denver, Colorado. In March of '91 Tonie, who was then known as Theresa Lopez, went to Medjugorje shortly after pleading *nolo contendere* to a charge of writing bad checks. By November of 1991 she was having her own apparitions and drawing thousands of people to the Cabrini Shrine near Denver, Colorado. Two years later, Theresa left her husband to become a full-time seer. The last time they were together Theresa told Jeff "if I get involved with this I can be somebody."

Phil Kronzer had lost his wife to Medjugorje around the same time Jeff Lopez had lost his, which is to say, over the winter of '93-'94. Both of these domestic tragedies began with Medjugorje; just where they were going to end was not clear. When I got back to my hotel room in Reno, I got a call from a man in England warning me that if I went back to Bosnia, the Franciscans were going to have me killed.

Proponents of the "apparition" like to talk about its fruits when they become uncomfortable with the behavior of the seers and their Franciscan handlers. Over the ten years since I had become involved in investigating Medjugorje, I had come up with my own list of fruits. The death threat I had just received in Reno was the beginning of a long list of bad things that had happened to the world since the Queen of Peace supposedly arrived in Yugoslavia in 1981. In addition to the broken families there were the broken vows, the pregnant nuns, the poor people bilked of their money, the division in the Church, the de facto schism, leading most recently to illicit confirmations in Capljina, the kidnapping of the local bishop, the ethnic cleansing, and, most dramatically, the worst fighting in Europe since World War II. All in all it was an impressive amount of malfeasance coming, as it did, from a group of people whose stated intention was prayer and following the instructions of the Blessed Mother. It was Bishop Pavao Zanic, then ordinary of Mostar, who wrote to Rene Laurentin, then Medjogorje's major promoter, and predicted that "one can look forward to a religious war here." Zanic, who predicted war in the mid-'80s, was more prescient than Our Lady of Medjugorje, who was saying at the time that she was the Queen of Peace and had come to bring peace to Yugoslavia and the world. Her promoters were saying that one of the signs of the authenticity of her messages was the fact that ethnic groups were living in peace in Yugoslavia.

Then came the break-up of Yugoslavia. The viciousness of the ensuing fighting is perhaps another reason why we peered so intently at the rusty red and white track in front of us as our car inched its way further into the scrubby thorn bushes. One year earlier, three journalists had died when their car had driven over a land mine on the outskirts of Mostar. As the car bumped its way slowly down the two tire-track path, I found myself remembering the incident and wondering just where the outskirts of Mostar began and ended.

At one point a farm appeared, the farmhouse, outbuildings, and fences all assembled out of the building material most readily at hand, namely, the chunks of limestone that littered the landscape. A toothless grandmother, clothed in the traditional black skirt and sweater favored by peasants of the region, raised a hand in either greeting or warning as we passed.

The object of our search was a geological formation peculiar to the area known as a "jama," translated roughly from the Croatian to mean pit or ravine. When the rains come to the Brontjo plateau, as they infrequently do, they percolate through the porous earth right to the limestone karst underneath where they erode caverns that lead directly to the Neredva river, which takes its luminous shade of blue-green from its journey through the limestone deposits.

During the spring and early summer of 1941, the Ustasha, a Croatian fascist group whose name means "insurgent," had created a short-lived but ferocious independent Croatian state by allying themselves with the Nazis. Local Ustasha did a little informal geological research of their own in the area between Medjugorje and the Neredva River, taking note of the largest jamas, the ones most suitable to their future purpose. Then in June of 1941 roughly two months after the creation of the NDH, the Croatian fascist state, on April 10, armed Ustasha functionaries showed up at the predominantly Serbian village of Prebilovci on the eastern side of the Neredva and at other Serb enclaves and announced to the villagers that they were all going to be deported to Belgrade. The Serbs were told they were going to be reunited with the Serbian fatherland, a prospect that took the edge off their anger and anxiety. So the Serbs showed up in their best clothes as they marched off to the train station, to become one more dislocated group in a Europe that seemed full of dislocation, and people who went off in trains and never came back. The Serbs of Prebilovci were herded together with other Serbs from the western part of Herzegovina and eventually six carloads of them were sent off on a train that was supposedly to take them back to Belgrade. The train ride proved to be much shorter than expected, at least as expected by the Serb passengers, who were ordered out of the six cars they occupied at a town called Surmanci, on the west bank of the Neredva, and marched off into the hills, never to return.

Roughly three months later, Bishop Zanic's predecessor, Aloysije Misic, ordinary of Mostar, the ornate Ottoman town a few train stations upstream from Surmanci, wrote to Cardinal Stepinac, primate of the once and future Yugoslavia, a man who would end up in prison at the hands of Tito's revolutionary justice, and told him of disquieting reports of atrocities perpetrated against the Serbs in his diocese. "Men are captured like animals," Misic wrote. "They are slaughtered, murdered; living men are thrown off cliffs.... From Mostar and from Capljina a train took six carloads of mothers, young girls, and children... to Surmanci.... They were led up the mountains and... thrown alive off the precipices.... In... Mostar itself they have been found by the hundreds, taken in wagons outside the town and then shot down like animals."

Eventually around 600 Serbs, including orthodox priests, women, and children, were thrown into the pit above Surmanci and then after throwing handgrenades in on top of them, the Ustasha thugs buried them, most probably still alive. Edmond Parris' account of the Surmanci massacre in his *Genocide in Satellite Croatia* corresponds in broad outline to Misic's account: "At Prebilovci and Surmanci, in Herzegovina, 559 Serbs, all of them old men, women and children, were led to a deep crevice called Golubinka, massacred and then thrown into space. And to do the job more thoroughly, hand grenades were hurled down upon the dying bodies." Parris then goes on to list the names of the perpetrators, a list which includes names like Ostojic and Ivankovic, names which are common enough in the area—names, in fact, of people still living in Medjugorje. Brian Hall wonders in his book on the break-up of Yugoslavia whether the Ostojic he stayed with while in Medjugorje was the Ostojic accused of the Surmanci atrocity.

The history of Yugoslavia, one quickly learns, is not something for those interested in a quick read. The more one delves into the issue, the more one comes away with the impression that there is no such thing as an impartial history of the region, certainly not concerning the period surrounding World War II. Parris, who is no exception to this rule, also claims that two priests took part in the massacre at Surmanci, one of whom also has a familiar name. Marko Zovko, it turns out, was a priest, but not a Franciscan like the more famous Jozo Zovko, the man who in many ways created the Medjugorje apparitions. Marko Zovko was the secretary to Bishop Cule, Misic's successor. I learned this from the current bishop of Mostar, Ratko Peric, who traces the Parris citation to Viktor Novak's book *Magnum Crimen,* which was written to accompany Tito's 1946 show trials. The purpose of both the book and the trials was to implicate the Church in the crimes of the Ustasha. As a result, Novak's book has to be viewed with caution, as does its claim that Father Marko Zovko was involved in murdering Serbs. This is the verdict not only of the current bishop of Mostar, but also Serb scholars as well. Miro Todorovich, editor of *Measure,* said no one, referring to the Serbs he knew, was willing to put his hand into the fire over Novak's book. Srdja Trifkovic, also a Serb, who now teaches at Rose Hill College, an Orthodox college in South Carolina, sees *Magnum Crimen* as "an attack on the role of the Catholic Church in Croatia, which Novak saw as the moving spirit behind the Ustasha atrocities." When Serb nationalism reawoke in 1988, a reissue of *Magnum Crimen* was a huge best-seller in Belgrade despite the book's high price. Bogdan Krizman called it, nonetheless, "a prominent Freemason's settling of scores with the clericals." Trifkovic has similarly unflattering things to say about Edmund Parris, claiming that his book *Genocide in Satellite Croatia* was ghost-written by Branko Miljus, a Serb emigre publicist, and dismissing Parris otherwise as the author of "several theological tracts critical of Roman Catholicism."

The religious situation is complicated by the fact that the Catholic Church in Herzegovina is split between two factions, one loyal to the bishop of Mostar and one loyal to the Franciscans, who have been in open rebellion against both the local ordinary and the Franciscan general in Rome since 1976 when they refused to hand over a number of parishes which they administered to the bishop of Mostar's jurisdiction.

Like his predecessors Misic and Zanic, Bishop Peric has had to deal with the rabidly nationalistic Herzegovinian Franciscans, the driving force behind the Medjugorje apparitions and collaborators in Ustasha atrocities during World War II. In January of 1997, roughly three months before I met with Peric at the chancery office in Mostar, Peric granted an interview to Yves Chiron in the French magazine *Present*, in which he admitted that Medjugorje was plagued with ecclesial disorders, which included Franciscans ministering at Medjugorje with no canonical mission, religious communities established without his permission, buildings erected without ecclesial approval, and parishes continuing to organize pilgrimages to a place where it had been determined there had been no apparitions. "Medjugorje," Peric concluded, "does not promote peace and unity but creates confusion and division, and not simply in its own diocese" (*Present*, 25 January 1997).

Peric found out first-hand just how bellicose the "Queen of Peace" and her supporters can be. In April of 1995 the bishop was attacked by a mob in his chancery, and his pectoral cross was ripped from his person. He was then beaten up, forced into a waiting car, driven to an illicit chapel run by the Medjugorje Franciscans, and held hostage for 10 hours. It was only when the mayor of Mostar showed up with UN troops that the bishop was released.

The Franciscan-orchestrated attacks on the bishop of Mostar are one indication that some things never change in this story. A drive through Medjugorje indicates the exact opposite. Perhaps the best way of resolving the conflict is to say that the more things change, the more they remain the same. The Catholic Church did end up in 1991 saying that there was nothing supernatural about Medjugorje, but St.

James Church continued to attract pilgrims. Even the war didn't stop that completely. The statement of condemnation issued by the Yugoslavian Bishops' Conference in Zadar in April 1991 was similarly fraught with ambivalence. It stated that there was nothing supernatural about the occurrences at Medjugorje, but then went on to add that the pilgrims should be taken care of, which prompted the Franciscans to claim that Medjugorje had been officially recognized as a shrine for pilgrims without specifying just why anyone should go there since officially nothing supernatural had ever happened there. Pilgrims to what? one is tempted to ask. Eventually, Rome stepped in and said, in effect, no, Medjugorje had not been recognized as a shrine.

As some indication of what Medjugorje was like during the dawn of its heyday, there is Mary Craig's book, *Spark from Heaven*, based on Craig's trip to Medjugorje in September of 1986 as part of the crew which made the Everyman film, which eventually ended up getting shown on the BBC and spread far beyond as a video. "Never," Craig tells us in no uncertain terms, "would the children accept money from well-wishers." The quote crosses my mind after I almost get run over by Ivan Dragicevic, a seer who is in a hurry to leave the church parking lot in his late model, gray BMW. The Franciscans may still hate the local bishop, but the lives of the seers have certainly changed dramatically since the mid-'80s when Ivan used to stand on a pile of rocks and address the pilgrims not far from his home at the far end of Bijakovici, the hamlet where all of the children were born and the site of the first apparition. Ivan is a lot heavier than he was in 1986, which indicates either that he is not following the three-day-a-week bread and water fast that he prescribed for the rest of the world (allegedly at the Blessed Mother's request) or that he is in urgent need of diuretics to alleviate water retention. In addition to being the proud owner of a BMW, Ivan also has a German-looking mansion now across from where he used to live and on pretty much the same spot where he used to address credulous pilgrims telling them that the Blessed Mother wanted them to spend two hours saying the rosary. In addition to all that, Ivan is also now married—to Loreen Murphy, formerly Miss Massachusetts. All in all this peasant boy from the poorest section of a poor country has done well for himself. His might be an inspiring success story were it not for the fact that his ostentatious lifestyle clashed so outrageously with the asceticism he preached to the rest of the world, the asceticism one associates with seers, or used to at any rate. Sister Lucia, the seer at Fatima, became a cloistered nun and disappeared from the world's view and only published a memoir of her encounter with the virgin at the request of her religious superior. Her two fellow seers died horribly painful deaths in childhood.

On the afternoon of June 25, 1997, Ivan spends his time mingling with the crowds outside St. James Church. His hair is thinner now; his gut hangs over the waistband of his expensive suit, but he still has the same false teeth, and the same aloofness if he doesn't know you and the same ingratiating obsequiousness if he does and thinks you can be of benefit to him.

St. James Church has undergone dramatic transformation as well. What used to be the muddy area surrounding it is now paved and decorated with statues. What used to be pasture and farmland behind it has now become a gravel parking lot, whose focal point is a hideous tent-like pavilion behind the church, which dwarfs the church itself, much as the apparitions and what they stand for have come to dwarf the Catholic parish which spawned them. Like the apparitions, the pavilion got the Franciscans in deeper trouble with the bishop for building it without permission, As I watch Ivan work the crowd, I remember the way people used to talk about the seers and their lives. Mary Craig wrote in 1986 that "it would be preposterous to say they've been telling lies for over five years, making fools of the whole world. They are too simple, too guileless, too unsophisticated for that. And anyway, why would they? For money? No, they resent being offered money. Fame? No, they shun publicity. A better life? Oh, theirs would be a miserable life indeed if they were living a lie. People have been besieging them, pestering them in their own homes for five years, leaving them no peace."

No peace, did she say? The words take on increasing irony with time. Medjugorje, it turns out, did not bring peace; it was an interlude between two wars. In fact, it was an incident that grew out of one war and led to another. This is one of the things that becomes apparent the second time around as Phil and I bump down the dusty track that leads to the hole in the ground where 600 Serbs were murdered almost to the day 40 years before the apparitions began. Ten years ago one heard rumors of the atrocity, but that all seemed part of the remote past then. One of the lessons one learns in this part of the world is that the past is never remote. It is always just beneath the surface, ready to emerge like a corpse from a shallow grave after a heavy rain.

The corpses of Surmanci did, in fact, emerge from the ground in 1989 when a delegation of Serbs arrived at the jama and broke through the concrete lid the Communists had fastened over it and exhumed the Serb remains and took them in ceremonial procession, in little coffins draped with Serbian banners, back across the river to be re-interred in Prebilovci, whence they had departed 48 years before. The disinterment took place in June, as does just about everything of significance in the Balkans. Politics didn't seem important back in 1988 when I had been here last. Politics never seemed important to Phil on any of the several trips he had made. But then the war broke out, and then he lost his wife, and suddenly both of us had the sense that we had missed something the first time around, something a careful search might reveal this time.

To link the *jama* with Surmanci, the village which gives it its name, is deceptive in a way. Surmanci is a village on the rail line that follows the Neredva River from Metkovic to Mostar. Surmanci is on the flood plain but surrounded by the cliffs which mark the beginning of the Brontjo plateau. It is from these cliffs that the Serbs were thrown to their death; it is on this plateau, which ends abruptly with the cliffs over the Neredva, that the village of Medjugorje is located. The drive out of Medjugorje is deceptive in this regard as well because the distance traveled is not in a straight line. The road from the place of the apparitions in Bijakovici to the *jama* above Surmanci is in effect a large U-turn around the hill called Crnica, now known as apparition hill. You begin the drive on the apparition side of Crnica, and you end up on the atrocity side of the same hill when you get to the *jama*, which prompts a thought: Were the atrocity and the apparition just two sides of the same coin?

What strikes you even more than the spatial propinquity of atrocity and apparition is the eerie coincidence of dates. Just about everything of significance in Balkan history seems to happen in June. The defining moment of Serbian history, the Battle of Kosovo Pole took place on June 28, 1389. The assassination of Archduke Ferdinand in Sarajevo, the event that led to the outbreak of World War I, occurred on June 28, 1914, as sort of weird symbolic commemoration of the Battle of Kosovo Pole. The Croatians declared their independence from Yugoslavia on June 25, 1991, which corresponded to the day to the tenth anniversary of the apparitions of Medjugorje, which took place on the fortieth anniversary of the Massacre at Surmanci.

The coincidence of dates struck Mary Craig too:

> Roger and I had seen, in the Orthodox Monastery at Zitomislic, a plaque that froze our blood. It commemorated the day, forty years earlier, 21st June 1941, when seven of the monks, from the Father Superior down to the youngest novice, were buried alive by the Ustasha in the pit at Surmanci. Three days after that plaque had gone up, the apparitions started a few miles away in Medjugorje. That weeping woman, could there be a connection? Was this why Medjugorje had been chosen? Had those six children absorbed the hopes, desires, fears-and guilts-of a suffering people?

The Orthodox monastery at Zitomislic is gone now, along with its plaque commemorating the slaughter at Surmanci, and gone too are the Serb sections of the town. The Serbs are gone too. In fact, the only thing that remains is history, which is a sophisticated kind of memory, which is all too prone to get repressed in the interest of wealth or power or convenience or guilt. This book is a history of Medjugorje and the lives of the people who were changed by it. It is the story of a very big lie and innumerable smaller lies, which taken together comprise, certainly in terms of money and numbers of gullible pilgrims, the biggest religious hoax of the twentieth century. But it is also the story of the connection between Surmanci and Medjugorje, the connection between the atrocity and the apparition. It is a story of how the repressed returns. Like the bones of the slaughtered Serbs on the other side of apparition hill, which the Communists tried to keep in the ground by placing a lid of concrete over them, the truth which got repressed eventually returned, in a form very few people recognized. This book is the story of that return.

E. Michael Jones
South Bend, Indiana
Ash Wednesday
February 25, 1998

-1-

THE CATHOLIC ANTI-COMMUNIST CRUSADE: 1945-1967

But cannot the Church which made a concordat with Hitler and kept it until he destroyed himself, compromise also with Moscow—at a price? That speculation seems idle now, but it should not be banished altogether from serious discussion of Vatican policy. There is so much basic kinship between the doctrinal absolutism of the Vatican and that of the Kremlin that the possibility of ultimate collaboration on a basis of mutual self-interest cannot be dismissed as unthinkable

Paul Blanshard
American Freedom and Catholic Power

At 9:00 in the morning of May 6, 1945, Professor Daniel Crljen, at this time an Ustasha colonel in charge of the education branch of the armed forces of the independent state of Croatia, wove his way through the clogged streets of Zagreb to St. Mark's Square, the location of the Ustasha parliament. Professor Crljen knew that the war was over; he knew that his side had lost, and now he was waiting for instructions on the role that he was to play in the evacuation of the city. Since April of that year Zagreb's population had swollen to three times its normal size—to almost one million people—as Croatian refugees bearing reports of Partisan atrocities poured in from the south.

One such incident occurred on February 7, 1945, when the Partisans stormed the Franciscan monastery at Siroki Brijeg in Herzegovina and killed 12 Franciscans. The details of the struggle are still disputed. The one thing that keeps the dispute still relevant and contentious is the connection between Siroki Brijeg and Medjugorje. Siroki Brijeg has been the center of Franciscan influence in Herzegovina ever since the Franciscans were invited into the area to combat the Bogomil heretics in the 13th century. Perhaps because of their isolated position as an island of Christianity in a sea of Gnostic heresy and then an equally hostile sea of Islam, the Franciscans have developed a peculiar attitude toward the state, ranging from truculent nationalism when it came to the Croatian people and any state con- trolled by them to underhanded docility when the state was not. Virtually all of the atrocity stories involving the Church's collaboration with the Ustasha are traceable to Franciscan priests. "Fra Satona," Father Miroslav Filipovic-Majstorovic, the butcher of Jansenovac, the Ustasha concentration camp, was a Franciscan. The only question which remains to be clarified was whether he had been excommuni- cated at the time he committed the atrocities attributed to him. In the period following World War II, the Franciscans went from being avid supporters of the Ustasha to being the first religious group to join *Dobri Pastir*, the communist-sanctioned priest's association. When Archbishop Stepinac was serving his term in jail at hard labor for not collaborating with Tito, the Franciscans had already become members of *Dobri Pastir* and were eligible for government pensions. Pius XII was so enraged at the behavior of the Franciscans in Herzegovina that he wrote an order excommunicating them, a decision which, for whatever reason, never got promulgated.

Reports over just what happened at Siroki Brijeg are still contested, like just about every other incident in recent Yugoslavian history, and still controversial because of the Franciscans' involvement in the alleged apparitions at Medjugorje, not far from the atrocity at Surmanci. In his pro-Medjugorje version of the incident, David Manuel claims that the Partisans' advance party murdered the 12 friars at the monastery and then put on their robes and deliberately fired on their own troops to defame the memory of the Franciscans as traitors. Richard West's account is less far-fetched and less flattering to the Franciscans. He claims that "the Franciscan Order played a leading role in the slaughter in Bosnia-Herzegovina" and that "the center of operations was the monastery at Siroki Brijeg, the Alma Mater of many leading Ustasha." One of the Siroki Brijeg alumni who had a leading role in the Ustasha government was Andrija Artukovic, head of the hated secret police. According to West, "the SS and Ustasha Franciscans fought side by side and literally to the last man to defend the monastery at Siroki Brijeg" (p. 191). Lending credence to West and refuting Manuel is a plaque at Siroki Brijeg commemorating the battle.

At the beginning of May, 1945, three months after the massacre at Siroki Brijeg, Josip Broz, now known as Tito, soon to be known as Marshall Tito, was in Belgrade anxiously awaiting news from the Slovenian border with Austria. Having declared himself ruler of Yugoslavia, where he had waged a moderately effective guerrilla war against the Nazi occupation forces and their Croatian collaborators, Tito told his lieutenant Milan Basta that the Croatian refugees under no circumstances should be allowed to cross the border, and at that time Tito's Partisan bands, which the Allies regarded with increasing contempt and concern as bandits, murderers, and thugs, were pressing northward for some final confrontation. The Partisans were bent on revenge not just against the Ustasha leadership, most of whom would escape anyway, but, in a pattern which would repeat itself tragically throughout the region, against the Croatian nation as well, which had picked up just about everything it could carry—man, woman, and child—and loaded it into horse drawn wagons or piled it on top of bicycles or packed it into suitcases and headed north, to Zagreb, to await its fate together.

The Ustasha army, a fully armed force of about 210,000 men, faced three options. They could take their stand in Zagreb and fight to the last man; they could retreat into the Croatian forests and wage a guerrilla campaign much as Tito had done, or they could retreat to the Austrian border, specifically to a town called Bleiburg, where they would surrender to the British forces. After some consideration the first option was ruled out because it would have resulted, most probably, in the total destruction of Zagreb. The Allies had already shown what they were capable of doing by leveling German cities. The firebombing of Dresden, which had no military significance and, like Zagreb, was flooded with helpless refugees from the Soviet army, had taken place less than a month before. The guerrilla option seemed equally pointless. Tito had achieved his legendary status as a guerrilla fighter not so much by dint of personal courage or tactical brilliance but by hanging on until the end of the war largely with the help of the British. The Ustasha leadership was clever enough to see that there was no one on the horizon left to champion their cause. To retreat to the forests, when Tito controlled all of the country's ports and could count on Allied air support and Soviet ground troops, seemed only a little less suicidal than taking a last stand in Zagreb, so the Ustasha leadership chose the third option.

When Professor Crljen finally arrived at Ustasha headquarters he was informed by Dr. Lovro Susic that the Croatian army and its dependents were withdrawing that day at 4:00 p.m. to the Austrian

3

border to surrender to the Anglo-American forces. The retreat came as the culmination of an eventful week. On May 2, Hitler had committed suicide as Soviet troops were advancing into Berlin. On May 5, the Poglavnik, Ante Pavelic, leader of the Ustasha government, had decided upon retreat to Klagenfurt in Austria. In addition to the options mentioned above, Pavelic understood the dynamics of history enough to realize that the alliance which brought about the fall of fascism was an unstable mixture that was not destined to last. A little over a year after the Poglavnik made his decision to retreat to the Austrian border, Winston Churchill would give a speech in the United States deploring the extinction of freedom in Eastern Europe as an "Iron Curtain" came down at the hands of Communist supporters of Stalinist imperialism. Churchill's speech, inaugurating what came to be known as the Cold War, would prove that Pavelic was right in general. Unfortunately, he was disastrously wrong in terms of timing. Pavelic was ahead of his time, a state not always rewarded by the opinion makers, a state that foreboded disaster, as far as the Croatian nation was concerned, as subsequent events would show. The world was still very much at war and the alliance that was forged to defeat fascism—no matter how unnatural, no matter how close it was to collapsing under the weight of its own self-contradictions—was still the order of the day.

"And so we set off down the Ilica," Crljen writes, describing the withdrawal of the Ustasha army and Croatian civilians during the evening of May 6.

> The journey was unforgettable. Disastrously unforgettable. The cars were halting all the time. Cars were merging with the countless numbers of passenger cars and transports. Peasants' wagons were merging with the other vehicles. At the sides were thousands of rows of marchers who bending from the weight were hurrying out of the city. At this moment a real damned City. There was a blackout. Only the lights of the cars were flashing. A very disturbingly sad night. The agitated citizens were following the unfortunate fugitives from their windows. They were co-participants in this general misfortune of the nation. I felt shame for leaving these people. After all, we were failing them, exposing them to the enemy. I cried my eyes out. And no less, the shame for my city hurt deeply! What an end! (Beljo, p. 99).

The column of Ustasha military and Croatian civilians gradually grew in size as it withdrew from Zagreb and headed toward Samobor and then the Slovenian border. By the time it reached Celje,

Crljen could only speculate on how long it stretched along both sides of the road. By the time he reached Dravograd, he would speculate that the column reached back 60 kilometers and was comparing the movement of the Croatian nation to the *Voelkerwanderung* at the end of the Roman empire. By then in addition to the 200,000 soldiers, there were also 200,000 civilians, all heading toward the small town of Bleiburg just on the other side of the Austrian border with Slovenia. Because the major part of the Partisan forces were still to the South, the Ustasha encountered only token resistance along their march. Nonetheless, the upheaval of war reached a staggering crescendo in this much-contested area of southeastern Europe, an area which was traditionally seen as the border between East and West. It seemed as if all of the various ethnic groups which had some connection to the area, were converging on the Slovenian border in one last effort to either surrender to the English or prevent that surrender, creating one huge polyglot mass of humanity, which seemed on the verge of hostility or despair. At moments of Partisan attack, the general confusion would intensify into panic and then subside, fraying further the nerves of the Croatian refugees and their military escort.

In addition to the fleeing units of the Ustasha regular army, there were *Domobranci* or home guards from both Croatia and Slovenia as well as units of the Bulgarian army as well as an entire Cossack division, which had fought on the side of the retreating German army and which now, like the Ustasha, had only one thing in mind, surrender to the Allies and escape from the Communists. Along with Cossack wagons pulled by Bactrian camels (soon turned into stew by the starving refugee hordes), groups of Mihailovic's Chetniks, the mainly Serbian supporters of the Yugoslavian Royal family, were also streaming toward the border in one huge logistics nightmare that threatened to explode into any number of battles which would have been pointless in terms of the outcome of the war but just as deadly nonetheless.

After Pavelic's hasty departure by car from Zagreb on May 5, he too became enmired in the columns of fleeing refugees, to the point where his car became useless and he took to fleeing on foot with his closest followers, slaking his thirst with snow and eating sugar cubes, the only food they had brought with them. Shortly before leaving Zagreb, Pavelic wrote hastily scrawled instructions on a sheet of checkered paper, a note which constituted his last communication with the Croatian nation. Under no circumstances were the Ustasha troops to surrender to the Communists. Instead they were to follow in his footsteps on "the path to Croatia's Calvary" and link up with him as he surrendered to the Anglo-American units just on the other side of the Austrian border. The word Calvary was to be more well-chosen than Pavelic probably knew at the time.

On the evening of May 10-11, the Poglavnik's note fell into the hands of Partisan troops, who quickly relayed it to Tito, who quickly dispatched a unit under Milan Basta to cut off the Ustasha retreat. Because Pavelic traveled virtually alone, he arrived at the border before the main Ustasha column and was able to cross over into Austria virtually unmolested. He even registered with the American troops stationed there, awaiting what he thought would be, if not a hero's welcome, then at least a political realism which took into account the new era of the Cold War. One hope drove the retreating Croatian forces, the hope that the West hated communism as much as the Croatians did. Joined to that hope was the belief that the West would need the Croatians in the new war that would start almost at the moment the old war ended. "At the border," Vinko Nikolic wrote, "the Anglo-American forces will accept us. There we will be reorganized, armed, supplied with all necessary means of modern warfare. And from there start a general national movement for the liberation of the whole territory. This should take place within a few days, some even think that the British could arrive in Croatia even earlier..." (Beljo, p. 96).

Colonel Crljen was of the same mind: "There is rumor that General Herencic made it to Dravograd, that the Croatian struggle continues: when those units reach our proximity, we will join them and prolong our battle, and then either return to the Croatian forests, or force the British to accept us as fellow-fighters (the greatest optimists thought that they would accept us as allies in the fight against communism which would take place shortly)."

What neither man understood is that things were much more complicated than they seemed. Just about all of the ethnic groups heading for the border or stationed to prevent a run to the border were riven by the internal divisions which would break out into the open with the start of the Cold War. When Crljen and the Ustasha found themselves blocked by the Bulgarian army outside of Dravograd, negotiations revealed that some of the soldiers were Communist and some anti-Communist, and negotiating safe passage meant playing one faction off against the other. The Ustasha column had encountered token resistance from the Partisans, but nothing that a 200,000 man army had difficulty overcoming. Both the Partisans and the Bulgarian communists told the Ustasha repeatedly that the war was over and that the defeated had nothing to fear. Actions, however, spoke louder than words, and the atrocities in central Bosnia and Herzegovina had created a determination to flee that no amount of propaganda could have created. The Partisans were willing to talk now, but only because at their current force levels they were no match for the Croatian army. As a result of the already mentioned divisions among the Bulgarians, one of the officers sympathetic to the plight of the Croatians mentioned that there was a wooden bridge upstream on the Drava just north of Dravograd. The Partisans had taken up positions in the hills surrounding the bridge, but their forces were no match for the Ustasha regulars, who drove them out of their positions on May 13. Once Partisan resistance had been removed, the passage was clear to Bleiburg, and gradually the fields surrounding that little town in a valley in the Karawanke Alps began to fill up with Croatian refugees.

The escape had succeeded. At least it seemed that way on the morning of May 15 when Crljen awoke to find himself surrounded by a hundred thousand refugees all milling around in a cloud of dust and noise. When he got to the headquarters of British General Keightley, he realized that things had become much more complicated than they seemed the night before. When they finally got into the general's headquarters in the castle overlooking the valley, they found that Partisan commander Milan Basta was already there, and that every request to Keightley was in effect immediately referred to the very group of Partisans the Ustasha was trying to escape. Instead of asylum, the Ustasha commanders were given an ultimatum. If they didn't surrender unconditionally within 20 minutes, both the Partisans and the English would commence attacking. Both Crljen and General Herencic were dumbfounded by the turn of events and could think of little to do other than stall for time and ask for a few concessions. Crljen said that it was impossible to communicate with the huge mass of people in the valley in so short a time and so asked for 24 hours, a request which was immediately vetoed by the Partisan Basta, with Keightley giving not the slightest objection.

Crljen and Herencic weren't the only people dumbfounded by the behavior of General Keightley. The Communist Partisans were bewildered as well. In 1979, more than 30 years after the fact, Milovan Djilas, Tito's former right-hand man, was asked if he felt the transfer of hundreds of thousands of innocent civilians to the Partisans was right. "No, it wasn't," Djilas answered without hesitation:

> The great majority of people the British forced back from Austria were simply peasants. They had no murders on their hands. They had not been Ustashis or Slovenian "Home Guards." Their only crime was the fear of Communism and the reputation of the Communists. Their sole motivation for leaving the country was panic.

At least part of the bewilderment Crljen and Herencic felt at the time grew out of their misunderstanding of the role the British had played in the war in Yugoslavia. Like the Bulgarians, the British were divided between Communist and anti-Communist factions but in a way that was much more clandestine and would in effect only become apparent years after the war was over. MI6, the British intelligence agency, had been infiltrated by Kim Philby, Anthony Blunt, and Guy Burgess—their names would appear in a series of revelations that rocked the British government during the post-war period. Taken together they formed a group of traitors who had met at Cambridge during the '30s and had dedicated themselves to the Communist cause. If Crljen and Herencic had been more perceptive they might have noticed that the British had withdrawn their support from Mihailovich and the Chetniks during the course of the war and placed it behind Tito and the Partisans. This was done largely as the result of reports that got falsified at MI6 headquarters after they arrived from the field. If Mihailovich's troops blew up a railroad line, the name got switched to Tito on the report, gradually inflating the reputation of the Communist leader and destroying that of Mihailovich, until finally, in a decision that would have long-standing repercussion, the British decided to throw their support behind the Partisans and abandon Mihailovich to his fate.

General Keightley most probably knew nothing of this at the time, but he did know that the Partisans, in addition to being a band of murdering thugs, were England's allies. Acting on the assurances of Milan Basta, therefore, Keightley handed the Croatian refugees over to the Partisan troops, who promptly slaughtered them. The massacre at Bleiburg was one of the greatest atrocities of World War II, a war not known for courteous treatment of non-combatants. Ustasha officers like Joseph Hecimovic were betrayed into thinking they were being moved into POW camps in Austria, when in fact they were simply driven across the border back into Yugoslavia, where they were forced into notorious death marches of the sort Stalin employed. Nikolai Tolstoy claims that the highly publicized death marches were a tactic to divert attention from the wholesale slaughter of groups like the Slovenian Domobranci, in a massacre which had all the earmarks of being done in the same manner of the slaughter of the Polish officers in the Katyn forest, even to the point of planting trees over the mass graves.

Tolstoy now claims that Keightley was acting under the express instructions of Harold Macmillan, later Prime Minister of Great Britain, who flew to Klagenfurt to deliver the order in person. Macmillan also ordered that the Czarist generals and the Cossacks be handed over to the Russians in addition to the Croatians, all of which was in violation of the Yalta accords because none of these people were Soviet citizens. Tolstoy clearly implicates Macmillan in a conspiracy that benefited Stalin and was probably coordinated by Kim

Philby out of MI6. When rumors of the slaughter reached England, another order countermanding that of Macmillan was issued on May 25, but by then the damage had been done. In a world grown numb over listening to atrocity accounts, what happened at Bleiburg beggars the imagination. Auschwitz at the height of Hitler's extermination campaign against the Jews in its grimly mechanized and efficient fashion claimed 6,000 victims a day. At its height, Bleiburg claimed twice as many victims a day. Following the British betrayal of the Croatians in mid-May, 15,000 men, women, and children a day were slaughtered in an orgy of killing that lasted over a month. If word had gotten out, the occurrences at Bleiburg would have jeopardized the Nuremberg trials, because everyone responsible for them, including the future British Prime Minister, should have been put on trial alongside Goering and the other Nazis. But word did not get out, at least not in the fashion that publicized the concentration camps run by the SS.

In retrospect, it's difficult to see how an atrocity of this magnitude could be suppressed, and in fact its existence was not suppressed, but denied access to the media controlled by the victors in the war, the story of Bleiburg was passed along by word of mouth among the victims. On May 18, after a long march through the mountains, the Poglavnik and a tattered remnant of his followers reached Langreith, and on June 1 he reported to the American authorities. Less than a week later, on June 6, news of the Bleiburg massacre reached the Croatian prisoners of war in Langreith, and a few days after that, when the American forces arrived to apprehend Pavelic, he was gone. Eventually Pavelic would surface in Argentina in the early '50s, but by then his prediction about the Cold War had come true, and no one was interested in arresting him as a war criminal any more. Pavelic was now a freedom fighter in the battle against Communism, and to be closer to the action he then moved to Spain, where he died on December 28, 1959.

Just how Ante Pavelic got from Austria to Argentina is, in a sense, the beginning of our story, for to say that no one had heard the story of Bleiburg and that no one was willing to support the Croatians in their hour of need, no matter how black their crimes, was not exactly true. In fact, at least partially as a result of massacres like Bleiburg, the world was waking up to the threat of Communist aggression, and the United States was beginning to fear another war and take preventative measures against the Communists and their intelligence apparatus throughout the world. Unlike the aftermath of World War I, when the United States disbanded its propaganda ministry months after the Versailles treaty had been signed, the aftermath of World War II showed little or no demobilization on the part of the Americans. The

Office of Strategic Services under William (Wild Bill) Donovan became the CIA and its funding levels increased under both the Truman and Eisenhower administrations as they attempted to use "science," in particular the burgeoning social sciences and communications theory as the backbone of their psychological warfare against the Communists.

The Americans weren't alone in their fear of Communists. In May of 1919 a Catholic priest by the name of Eugenio Pacelli, stood at the head of the stairs of the Vatican nunciature in Munich as a band of Red Spartacists surged toward him bent on revenge for their 300 comrades, who had just been killed by white forces in a battle that raged throughout the city. One Communist put a gun to Pacelli's head prompting him to smile ironically and say, "It is never wise to kill a diplomat." The revolutionaries were so dumbfounded by Pacelli's sang-froid that they decided to take his car instead, leaving the man who would become Pope Pius XII in 1939 with an abiding animus against communism.

As the fascist threat waned at the end of 1945, the old fear of communism grew. In May of 1943 Domenico Cardinal Tardini, the Vatican's secretary of state under Pius XII, predicted that "there is ground for fearing a) that the war will end in a preponderantly Russian victory in Europe and b) that the result will be a rapid diffusion of Communism in a great part of continental Europe and the destruction there of European civilization and Christian culture." Two years later, in the aftermath of the Soviet invasion of all of eastern Europe and almost half of Germany, it looked as it Tardini's prediction were coming true. Faced with this new enemy, Rome decided to take measures of its own. In August of 1943, a Croatian priest by the name of Krunoslav Draganovic arrived in Rome to take up residence at the ancient Croatian college of St. Jerome. His job was to coordinate the efforts of the Church and the Red Cross in alleviating the refugee problem, which the dislocations of war had brought about. What emerged from his efforts was either an extremely effective refugee organization or a way of smuggling ex-fascists to countries where they would avoid prosecution for war crimes. Indignation often comes with hindsight, but it just as often blurs the complexity of the situation at the time. To begin with, Bleiburg had convinced both the Vatican and the Americans that a fair trial for Ustasha refugees was impossible and that sending them back to Yugoslavia meant certain death for the innocent and the guilty alike. Incidents like Bleiburg and the subsequent squabble over the status of Trieste likewise convinced the West that Yugoslavia was an expansionist state with which war was imminent. As a result, people who knew the language and the terrain might be useful, no matter what their past sins. As a result, the policy of de-

Nazification came to an abrupt halt. The Americans were no longer interested in prosecuting potential allies who might be of use in the upcoming war with Communism, but they couldn't very well embrace their former enemies openly, and so a clandestine *modus operandi* involving the Vatican and its refugee relocation services came into being, as the first halting steps in a joint-venture anti-Communist crusade.

"Both Washington and London," write Arons and Loftus, "had entered into arrangements with the Holy See to assist many Nazi collaborators to emigrate via Draganovic's smuggling system. The Vatican was cynically being used as a respectable cover for the West's own immoral conduct."

The Vatican's worst fears about the intentions of the Communists were confirmed when Archbishop Alojsije Stepinac was arrested, put on trial, and convicted in 1946 to 17 years at hard labor. Tito's efforts at persuading Stepinac to create a national Church more congenial to the interests of the Communists failed with Stepinac just as dramatically as they had succeeded with the Franciscans. It was to prove a costly victory for Tito, as Stepinac, like Cardinal Mindszenty in Hungary, became a symbol of the very nationalism which the Communists hoped to extinguish. The heavyhandedness of the Communists also drove the Vatican into the waiting arms of the United States, as co-belligerents in the international anti-Communist crusade. The Vatican and the United States soon worked out their own *modus operandi*, collaborating in ill-fated resistance movements like the Krizari in Yugoslavia. Christopher Simpson claims that the failure of the Krizari derived from the fact that the anti-Communist movements had all been infiltrated by the KGB and that Giuseppe Montini, who ran the Vatican intelligence operation and would ascend to the throne of Peter himself in 1963 as Pope Paul VI, realized this in the late '50s.

But the alliance would prove fragile for other reasons as well, partially because of who was involved and partially as a result of the methods that got employed. Simpson make clear that the intelligence community in the United States was a very specific group of people with a very specific set of goals. Drawn largely from Yale University in general and often from secret societies like Skull and Bones in particular, the OSS drew much of its science of psychological warfare from studies funded by the Rockefeller Foundation in the '30s. Many of the OSS alumni stayed with the agency when it became the CIA, but many of its alumni drifted into the fields of communication theory, which was a euphemism for psychological warfare, in either the theoretical fields, as academics, or in more practical areas. In 1953 one OWI alumnus described how his colleagues became the publishers of *Time, Look, Fortune*, and several dailies, editors of such magazines as *Holiday, Coronet, Parade* and the *Saturday Review*, editors of the *Denver Post, New Orleans Times-Picayune*, and others; the heads of the Viking Press, Harper & Brothers, and Farrar, Straus and young; three Hollywood Oscar winners, a two time Pulitzer prizewinner, the board chairman of CBS and a dozen key network executives; President Eisenhower's chief speech writer; the editor of *Reader's Digest* international editions; at least six partners of large advertising agencies, and a dozen noted social scientists (Simpson, *Science of Coercion*, p. 28-9).

More importantly, OSS alumni also became the staff and oftentimes the directors of the major foundations—Ford, Rockefeller, Carnegie—which in turn funded most of the communications and social science research at the time. In 1939 the Rockefeller Foundation funded a series of secret seminars on ways to " find a 'democratic prophylaxis' that would immunize the United States' large immigrant population from the effects of Soviet and Axis propaganda." The use of vocabulary taken from the field of social hygiene is instructive. The psychological warriors all valued science highly and felt that the advances in physical hygiene might be matched by psychological advances that would help them win the war. In 1939, the Rockefeller Foundation organized a series of secret seminars with men it regarded as leading communication scholars to enlist them in a effort to consolidate public opinion in the United States in favor of war against Nazi Germany.

Although the end was noble, not everyone was enamored of the methods being proposed. Donald Slesinger, a dean of the social science department at the University of Chicago and participant at the secret conferences, felt that the democratic end did not justify essentially manipulative and coercive means. Slesinger saw in the new communications media, "a new form of authoritarianism." "We [the Rockefeller Seminar] have been willing, without thought, to sacrifice both truth and human individuality in order to bring about given mass responses to war stimuli." Slesinger contended. "We have thought in terms of fighting dictatorships-by-force through the establishment of dictatorship-by-manipulation" (Simpson, *Science of Coercion*, p. 23).

Although the members of the interlocking network of psychological warriors which staffed the CIA, the foundations and university communications departments came to be as fervently anti-Communist during the '50s as they had been anti-fascist during the '40s, this same group was equally suspicious of the Catholic Church. In fact, they often saw Rome as every bit as dangerous a foe to American freedoms as Moscow, and said so publicly no matter how severely it jeopardized the common front against communism. "To be honest," said Karl Barth a leading Protestant theologian who had a large following in the United States, "I see some connection between them." He was referring, of course, to Catholicism and Communism. "Both," he continued,

> are totalitarian; both claim man as a whole. Communism uses about the same methods of organization (learned from the Jesuits). Both lay great stress on all that is visible. But Roman Catholicism is the more dangerous of the two for Protestantism. Communism will pass; Roman Catholicism is lasting.

Thoughts like this made it clear that the anti-Communist alliance between the Church and the United States was just a fragile as the alliance between the United States and the Soviet Union against fascism. Americans, it was by now clear, were a diverse group of people who had to be mobilized in certain ways to achieve certain goals, the war against fascism being a good example. Alfred Hitchcock's film *Lifeboat* is a good example of the unity which comes from shared adversity, but once the war was over, the Catholics and the Protestants in the United States began to view each other suspiciously once again.

What emerged from the defeat of fascism in 1945 was a complex alliance involving three parties who were determined to fight a Cold War on two fronts. Each party got maneuvered into various *modi operandi* depending on the exigencies of the moment. So after the successful conclusion of the Great Patriotic War in 1945, the Soviet Union found itself at war with both the United States (and its allies) and with the Catholic Church, whose influence it sought to extirpate from Eastern European countries like Poland and Croatia. The Catholic Church for its part found itself in a two-front war as well, whose lines of battle could have been predicted by a close reading of the Church's social encyclicals beginning in 1891 with *Rerum Novarum*, but as recently as 1931 with *Quadragesimo Anno*. Leo XIII stated quite explicitly in the former document that both Liberalism, of the sort practiced in England in the 19th century, and Communism were antagonistic to a sound social order; in fact, the pope would claim Liberalism was the cause of Bolshevism. Pius XII's concern with a communism, a concern which went back to his days as nunc o n Mun ch n 1919 when he was almost murdered by a Bolshevist mob, led him to strategic alliances with the Liberals, but even he never confused their interests with those of the Catholic Church.

If the Communists were at war with both the Catholic Church and the capitalist powers—even if they conflated the two in the early days of the Cold War—the situation in the United States was even more complex because a large number—18 percent in the late '40s—of Americans were Catholic and had also fought in the war as patriotic Americans. The dominant class in America, the WASPs, which is to say the ruling elite which came from the mainline Protestant denominations, however, had never viewed Catholics without suspicion, and after the close of World War II, their suspicions reasserted themselves as the Catholic birthrate started to surge in what came to be known as the baby boom.

As a result, the rise of the CIA, with its penchant for psychological warfare, coincided with the rise of anti-Catholic animus on the part of the people who were staffing the intelligence community. A look at the personnel involved makes it quite clear that the intelligence community, the people running the anti-Communist crusade, were virtually the same people concerned about the "Catholic problem," as Paul Blanshard expressed it in his 1949 bestseller, *American Freedom and Catholic Power* . Blanshard was very aware of the communist threat, but he was far from willing to subordinate his animus against Catholics to bring about a common front against the Soviets. In fact, as even a superficial reading of his book makes clear, Blanshard regards the Catholics as every bit as dangerous to "American Freedom." Hence, his thoughts early on in the book:

> Some readers who accept every fact that I have recorded in these pages may still question the wisdom of discussing these matters in public at the present time, because of the critical international situation which finds the Western democracies pitted against a Russian communist aggressor. These critics would keep silent about the antidemocratic program of the Vatican until the present crisis is resolved, because they regard the Catholic Church, with all its faults, as a necessary bulwark against militant Communism. I respect the sincerity of this view and I share with most Americans the conviction that Russian aggression must be met with determined resistance. But I do not believe that fear of one authoritarian power justifies compromise with another, especially when the compromise may be used to strengthen clerical fascism in many countries. Certainly in this country the acceptance of any form of authoritarian control weakens the democratic spirit; and one encroachment upon the democratic way of life may be used as a precedent

for others. In the long run, the capacity to defend American democracy against a communist dictatorship must be based upon a free culture . . . (p. 6).

Blanshard misconstrued the Church's willingness to work under just about any form of government as "opportunism" and wondered if at some point in the future the Church might change its mind and decide to collaborate with the Communists. "If we are to judge by the writings of the outspoken apologists of Catholicism in Europe and America," writes Sidney Hook with Blanshard's obvious approval, "they are just as ready, if necessity arises, to baptize Marx as they once baptized Aristotle." Hook correctly predicted the rise of liberation theology in the '70s and '80s, but he failed to understand that the emphatic condemnation of Communism in *Quadragesimo Anno* would carry the day in terms of theory and eventually in terms of praxis as well.

But both Blanshard and Hook were right in their way. The Church was committed to no one form of government, and certainly not to democracy of the American variety, no matter how sacred that was in Blanshard's eyes. Nor was the Church committed to Fabian Socialism, where Blanshard's real political allegiance lay. What Blanshard failed to see was that his book was in many ways a self-fulfilling prophecy. The rising anti-Catholic animus among the elite, liberal classes in the United States almost guaranteed that the anti-Communist alliance would fall apart by the end of the '50s—and certainly by the mid-'60s— because the Church began to realize that the most pressing danger to its well-being came from its "friends."

Blanshard cheered on the Masonic persecution of the Church in Mexico, and he was galled by the Church's ability to impose a weapons embargo against Republican forces in Spain. He was likewise galled by the fact that "Archbishop Stepinac's martyrdom in a Yugoslav prison was dramatized by the hierarchy as undiluted religious persecution, although Stepinac had collaborated openly with rebel forces led by the notorious Croatian Fuehrer, Ante Pavelic." Doubly galling in this regard was the fact that Archbishop Fulton J. Sheen had a prime time TV show which allowed him "to broadcast, free of charge, innuendoes and pronouncements against political and religious liberalism, birth control, reasonable divorce laws, the government of Yugoslavia, and any other target that inspires his wrath." "Neither Monsignor Sheen nor the other Catholic speakers on this program are censored," Blanshard argued, evidently proposing the same sort of censorship he decried when it got practiced by Catholics.

Blanshard's book was prompted proximately by the *McCollum* and *Everson* Supreme Court decisions, which seemed to give aid to

Catholic schools, but his real concern was demographic, sexual, and moral. Catholics did not believe in artificial birth control, whereas their more established and better off Protestant countrymen did. The result was what people like Blanshard euphemistically referred to as "differential fertility." The ethnic Catholics were outprocreating the Protestants, and, if this state of affairs continued, the United States would soon become a Catholic country, a prospect which filled the dominant WASP class with dread.

"What are the actual prospects for Catholic control of the United States?" Blanshard wondered:

> Bertrand Russell said twenty years ago that he thought the Roman Catholic Church would dominate the United States "in another fifty or one hundred years" and "by sheer force of numbers." Many Catholic leaders have echoed that prophecy. Father James M. Gillis, editor of the *Catholic World*, predicted in 1929 that "America will be predominantly Catholic before the present younger generation dies."

Blanshard's fears of Catholic power came not just from the number of children they were having but from the fact that Catholics seemed so "monolithic," to use '60s cultural revolutionary Leo Pfeffer's term, when it came to values and organization, and that caused Blanshard concern because "in our individualistic nation a closely knit political organization does not need a majority of the people to control the government." That being granted, "the hierarchy's most substantial hope for transforming a Catholic minority into a majority lies in a differential birthrate." Blanshard then goes on to cite Catholics who seem to confirm his deepest fears:

> The Right Reverend John J. Bonner, diocesan superintendent of schools of Philadelphia, boasted in 1941 that the increase in the Catholic births in Philadelphia in the preceding decade had been more than fifty percent higher than the increase in the total population, and that Philadelphia "will be fifty percent Catholic in a comparatively short time." . . . If the disparity in birth rates which he claimed should continue indefinitely , it would not be long before the United States became a Catholic country by default (pp. 284-6).

After reading this sort of thing, McGeorge Bundy joined John Dewey, Albert Einstein, and Bertrand Russell in praising Blanshard's book, calling it "a very useful thing." Bundy was a professor at

Harvard at the time he made the comment, but he had been a member of Skull and Bones at Yale and would go on to head the Ford Foundation and, oddly enough, join the administration of John F. Kennedy, the first Catholic president of the United States. Bundy would eventually become responsible for investigating Kennedy's assassination and was a key figure in the interlocking circles that would make up the Liberal establishment in the United States that was at once at war with Communism and Catholicism as twin threats to American freedom.

During the early '50s, the United States government spent as much as $1 billion annually on psychological warfare. Christopher Simpson makes clear that much of this money was used illegally in "black" operations against American citizens. What he doesn't make clear, but what was obvious from an examination of the interlocking nature of the the groups which made up the CIA, foundation, and academic establishments, is that the psychological warfare community and the people concerned about the Catholic problem were effectively the same group of people. This meant that when Rome collaborated with the United States in the anti-Communist crusade, it also collaborated in its own demise in the United States as a political power. This became more and more obvious as first the Rockefeller controlled foundations, then the United States government, and then the United Nations got more heavily involved in the promotion of population control. By the mid-'60s, Catholics who had identified themselves as patriotic anti-Communists found themselves caught up in promoting something that was in direct contradiction to Church teaching. The only thing that made the contradiction less than obvious was the gradual way in which it had come about. Dr. Tom Dooley is just one example of the kind of anti-Communist Catholic who was being promoted by the CIA at the time. His connection with Notre Dame, another front for foundation money which was being used to subvert the Catholic Church's teaching on contraception, was memorialized in an engraved letter from Dooley to then-Notre Dame president Theodore Hesburgh at the Notre Dame replica of the grotto at Lourdes. On the other side of the coin, the same CIA which was involved in promoting Dooley was equally involved in the assasination of Ngo Dinh Diem, a man who was the president of Viet Nam but the wrong kind of Catholic. By the beginning of the '60s, anti-Communism had become in effect a way of managing the "Catholic Problem." As the United States became more aggressive in promoting population control throughout the world, Rome slowly came to the conclusion that it had more to fear from its friends than its enemies. The result was a change of heart. Rome got out of the anti-Communist crusade and got into *Ostpolitik*.

The anti-Communist crusade in eastern Europe may or may

not have been infiltrated by the KGB and directed by Moscow, but by the end of the decade, it was clear that it had achieved virtually no successes after years of effort. In Yugoslavia, the Krizari attempts at clandestine activity were routinely disastrous. It seemed that no matter what they planned the UDBA, the Yugoslav secret police, knew about it in advance and were waiting for them with open arms. This fact alone would have been reason to abandon the alliance, but there were other reasons as well, most of them having to do with the rise of America as the world's preeminent media power.

During the '50s a curious double bind arose in relations between the American and Italian film industries and their respective cultures. Hollywood was bound by the production code, largely a Catholic enterprise which came into being during the early '30s, not to portray nudity or profanity. In order to break the code, producers like Joseph E. Levine would bring over Italian films, by directors like Federico Fellini. One of his short films was part of a trilogy which provoked the *Burstyn* court case in New York in the early '50s, where the Catholics went to the barricades to defend the culture against what they saw as a deluge of degenerate films coming from Catholic Italy. Certain Italians, however, were equally upset by the effect that American films were having on Italy. One of the people most upset was Pius XII, who had much to say on the role of television and film. But as Pius XII slowly slipped into his dotage during the '50s, others took up his cause. Alfredo Cardinal Ottaviani was so concerned about the effect of film that he created his own chain of movie theaters, to insure that only films that had no detrimental effect on morals would be shown.

Writing in 1950, at a time when Pius XII and Cardinal Ottaviani were preoccupied with the Communist menace, W. W. Charters talked about the effect that film had on children in dark theaters:

> Watching in the dark of the theater, the young child sits in the presence of reality when he observes the actors perform and the plot of the drama unfold. He sees the actions of people living in a real world—not of actors playing a make-believe role. His emotions are aroused in ways that have been described. He forgets his surroundings. he loses ordinary control of his feelings, his actions, and his thoughts. He identifies himself with the plot and loses himself in the picture. His "emotional condition may get such a strong grip that even his efforts to rid himself of it by reasoning with himself may prove of little avail." He is possessed by the drama. (Berelson, p. 403).

The quote comes not from an indignant Catholic prelate but

from a collection of essays edited by Bernard Berelson, one of the prime psychological warriors of the '50s and eventually the head of John D. Rockefeller's Population Council. In many ways, Cardinal Ottaviani couldn't have framed the case against Hollywood better himself, and over the course of the '50s, as the threat of Communism waned, the threat from Hollywood grew in inverse proportion. Ottaviani became so concerned at the effect that Hollywood culture was having on Catholic life in Italy that he and Cardinal Tardini went to Pacelli's successor, Giuseppe Roncalli, during the very conclave which named him Pope John XXIII and told him that he must convene an ecumenical council to deal with the sclerotic state of Church administration, as it had evolved under Pius XII, and the threat to the Church from the outside, a threat just over the horizon but no less palpable for that. Ottaviani was responsible for the writing of all of the preliminary documents of Vatican II, most of which were scrapped by the Council, which was looking for new ways of dealing with the problems facing the Church. The issue of methodology, however, should not distract us from the intention that drove the convoking of the council. Ottaviani and Tardini were convinced that the Church was not prepared to face the onslaught against morals and family life that was being orchestrated through the media by their ostensible partner in the anti-Communist crusade. In his document on "The Moral Order," dated January 15, 1962, Ottaviani criticized the attempt

> to substitute the useful, the agreeable, the good of the race, the interests of a class, or the power of the state, as the criterion of morality. Thus, philosophical systems, literary fashions, and political doctrines have been created and propagated. These try to substitute for the Christian moral order the so-called morality of situation or individualistic morality, often condemned by Pius XII and finally condemned by a decree of the Holy Office in February of 1956. These also try to substitute the morality of independence (i.e. divorced from the Christian morality) for the idea of God, sanction and obligation.

The reference to those who elevate "the interests of class" seems clear enough. However, as one reads further, it becomes clear that Ottaviani's preliminary document on the moral order is best seen as an attack on both sides of the Cold War, and before long the attacks on the Church's supposed ally in the anti-Communist crusade take precedence over the attacks on their putative common enemy. Ottaviani attacked those who create "so-called conflicts. . . between art and morality, or between freedom of expression and conscience," an oblique reference to the increasingly beleaguered situation of the Legion of Decency in its efforts to uphold moral standards in cinema in the face of Hollywood's onslaught. Ottaviani attacked finally all "errors which degrade human dignity under the false pretext of freeing man from all bonds that would restrict his nature in some way. The moral order has the task, not only of leading man to his true end, but of defending him against all doctrines and practices that would enslave him to the minds, modes and passions that are contrary to the dignity of his intellect."

Enslaving the mind to passions which are contrary to the intellect was precisely the project that was being pursued by the psychological warriors throughout the '50s. The whole point of advertising was to elude the mind's rational control, to manipulate the customer into buying something he didn't need, or into buying something for reasons other than utility. Throughout the '50s the OSS alumni were putting their discoveries at the lucrative service of American corporations who were using them to coerce consumers into making choices that were not in their own interest. "Since World War II," Simpson wrote,

> the U.S .government's national security campaigns have usually overlapped with the commercial ambitions of major advertisers and media companies, and with the aspiration of an enterprising stratum of university administrators and professors. Military, intelligence and propaganda agencies such as the Department of Defense and the Central Intelligence Agency helped bankroll substantially all of the post-W.W.II generation's research in to techniques of persuasion, opinion measurement, interrogation, political and military mobilization , propagation of ideology and allied questions. The persuasion studies, in particular provided much of the scientific underpinning for modern advertising and motivational techniques (*Coercion*, p. 3-4).

As Ottaviani continued, the object of his ire becomes more apparent. After telling us that "the moral order defends the immutable principles of Christian modesty and chastity" he went on to say,

> we know the energies spent at the present time by the world of fashion, movies and the press in order to shake the foundations of Christian morality in this regard, as if the Sixth Commandment should be considered outmoded and free rein should be given to all passions, even those against nature. The council will have something

to say concerning this subject. It will clarify and eventually condemn all the attempts to revive paganism and all the trends that in the abuse of psychoanalysis tend to justify even those things which are directly contrary to the moral order.

Moscow was hardly known as a leader in the fashion world, nor was it known as a significant producer of movies. The attack here is against the West in general and Hollywood in particular. Ottaviani condemns "the modern world" just about *in toto,* along with its emphasis on "technical progress, its modes of life, and its growing means of propaganda and publicity" in a way that would have prompted Paul Blanshard to say "I told you so," even at the ecumenical council which had the reputation of opening up the windows of the Church to the winds of Liberalism.

At the same time that Hollywood was rising as the new menace to morals, the Church was faced with admitting that its collaboration with the United States in the anti-Communist crusade was a complete failure." It was a humiliating debacle," Arons and Loftus write. "By 1959, the United States had lost every courier, safehouse, and intelligence network behind the Iron Curtain. The intelligence scandal was swept quietly under the rug, just as the Vatican scandal before it. The Soviets kept quiet about the religious scandal because the Vatican's Nazi-smuggling provided a deadly method to infiltrate Western intelligence."

Propaganda and publicity, it should be remembered, were the stock in trade of the CIA, which was ostensibly the Vatican's ally in the war against Communism. But by the time of the Council in the early '60s, the alliance was over. And it was over primarily because it was becoming increasingly clear that the propaganda and publicity were being used more effectively against Catholics than against Communists. There were signs on both sides—*Ostpolitik* on the part of the Vatican, and the contraceptive campaign on the part of the Rockefellers—that a new era was dawning, an era which reached its culmination in 1974 at the United Nations' sponsored Bucharest Conference on World Population, where the Vatican forged an alliance with Communist bloc countries and the third world to block Rockefeller's attempt to institute Malthusian birth quotas throughout the world.

Twenty years earlier, Congressman Carroll Reece of Tennessee had become so alarmed at the power of tax-exempt foundations like Ford, Carnegie, and Rockefeller, that he convened Congressional hearings on the role these foundations were playing in undermining the democratic institutions of the United States. As anyone who knew the extent to which OSS alumni had taken over the media could have predicted, the press was all but universally unfavorable, attempting to tar Reece with the McCarthy brush. Senator Joe McCarthy, a Catholic from Wisconsin, held his hearings on Communism at around the same time Reece held his on the foundations. Reece had fallen victim to the very psychological warfare he sought to expose. By the mid-'50s it was clear that the CIA/Foundation/Anti-Catholic cabal was heavily involved in "black operations," i.e., operations against citizens of the United States, which clearly constituted illegal activity. The threat of communism had allowed this door to be opened and now anyone who opposed the goals of the above group or threatened to expose their methods were fair game to be targeted. Congressman Reece had to learn this the hard way. But he was only an individual. In terms of groups that were going to be targeted, the next victim after black operations were tolerated against domestic Communism was obvious. It was the Catholics, and the psychological warfare waged against the Church in the United States would be the battle over contraception, which reached its culmination in mid-'65 when the Supreme Court handed down its *Griswold v. Connecticut* decision, and Senator Ernest Gruening of Alaska started holding hearings about overpopulation and how the government meant to solve this problem.

Congressman "Reece," Simpson writes,

> took as his theme that major US foundations—including the Rockefeller Foundation, the Ford Foundation, the Carnegie Corporation and the Social Science Research Council—were engaged in a campaign to promote socialism and "one World" government through funding social science studies Reece regarded as critical of the US and the "free enterprise" economic system. He singled out John Dewey, Samuel Stouffer, and Bernard Berelson , among others as the purported ringleaders (p. 102).

Bernard Berelson was trained as a librarian but by the late '40s was considered an expert in public relations and the manipulation of public opinion. One year after the publication of Blanshard's book on Catholic power, Berelson co-edited *Public Opinion and Communication.* with Morris Janowitz, one of the seminal works on communications theory, and a good indication of how the psychological warfare techniques refined during World War II were now going to be turned on the American public as a way of controlling them through the manipulation of the new media, i.e., radio and television. Berelson establishes the book's major premise in his introduction:

> Growing secularization has meant that more and more

areas of life are open to opinion rather than divine law and to communication rather revelation. Growing industrialization has not only extended literacy; in addition, it has provided the technical facilities for mass communication. (p. ix).

The goal of secularization was the reduction of all of life's imperatives to "opinions," which is to say not the result of moral absolutes or divine law. Once this "secularization" occurred, the people who controlled "opinions" controlled the country. Berelson is equally frank about where the new science of public opinion originated:

Research in the field was accelerated during World War II by demands for studies on the effect of communications upon military personnel, adjustment to army life and attitudes toward military leaders, enemy propaganda, and civilian morale. After the war this growing interest led to the establishment of additional university centers for the study of public opinion and communication by the methods of social science. Together with the continuing activities of industry and government, they now represent a large-scale research enterprise.

Just how large scale would become clear before long. But before that happened some significant changes had to be made to the realm of what was communicable. In 1959 Berelson wrote that: "the 'great ideas' that gave the field of communications research so much vitality ten and twenty years ago have to a substantial extent worn out. No new ideas of comparable magnitude have appeared to take their place. We are on a plateau." (Simpson, p. 89). The way off this plateau was clear enough if one read Berelson's 1950 book carefully, particularly his claim that "there is a virtual pro-religious monopoly on communications available to large audiences in America today" (p. 457). Religious belief meant ipso facto the opposite of opinion, and therefore ideas not subject to the manipulation of the people who controlled the communications media. What needed to be done then was move large areas of thought from the realm of religion to the realm of opinion if any significant breakthroughs in political control through manipulation of the media were to take place.

And this is precisely what happened. During the 1960s, at the same time Hollywood was trying to break the production code and introduce nudity to the big screen, Berelson was hard at work for John D. Rockefeller, 3rd, running opinion polls whose purpose was to change the attitude of the American public toward contraception. Of particular interest in this regard were the attitudes of Catholics, whose opinions Berelson manipulated through a series of leading questions that were put to Catholics in the wake of Pope Paul VI's appearance at the UN in 1964. Question number eight of the survey Berelson was working on at the time asked: "The Roman Catholic Church does not approve many methods of birth control. Do you believe that the Church should change its position on this matter?" It didn't take a brain surgeon to figure out the right answer to this and other tendentious questions, whose purpose was to insinuate the idea that the Church should change her teaching into the mind of the population at large.

In keeping with their penchant for psychological warfare, the Rockefellers were always interested in clandestine ways of getting what they wanted. They stumbled across a major opportunity on July 6, 1962, when Cass Canfield, chairman of Planned Parenthood and a board member of John D. Rockefeller, 3rd's Population Council, wrote to Father John A. O'Brien, CSC, a theologian at the University of Notre Dame to say how impressed he was with Father O'Brien's enlightened views on contraception, views which had aired on the CBS documentary "Birth Control and the Law," on May 10, 1962. Canfield wanted to know if O'Brien would come to a Planned Parenthood symposium in New York, "to discuss fertility regulation in the context of responsible parenthood and population growth." When he got his answer, Canfield could hardly believe his eyes. O'Brien had passed the letter to George Shuster, assistant to Theodore Hesburgh, president of Notre Dame, and Shuster was suggesting that Planned Parenthood hold its conference at Notre Dame. The Rockefellers quickly exploited this opening by funding a series of secret conferences at Notre Dame from January 1963 to April 1965, when, as promised by Shuster and Hesburgh, the theologians obligingly issued a statement in which they claimed that they no longer found the Church's teaching on contraception persuasive.

If Pope Paul VI felt that this dissent would remain secret he was in for a series of unpleasant surprises, the most dramatic of which took place in mid-July of 1965 when Father Hesburgh showed up in Rome with John D. Rockefeller in tow. Not a man to beat around the bush, Rockefeller in the course of a private audience urged the pope to change the Church's teaching on contraception and even offered to write the pope's birth control encyclical for him. "As I see it," Mr. Rockefeller wrote to the pope the day after his private audience,

> if the Church does not supply this leadership, there will be two consequences: one, the present accelerating pace toward population stabilization will proceed, country by country, without overall guidance or direction, particularly on the moral side: on the other, if I may speak per-

fectly frankly, the Church will be bypassed on an issue of fundamental importance to its people and the well-being of mankind. The flooding tide cannot be stopped or even slowed, but it can be guided. Because I believe so keenly in the importance of the role which your church has to play in our troubled world of today, I am deeply concerned to see a situation developing which in the long run, it seems to me, inevitably will be harmful to the Church's position around the world.

Rockefeller's impromptu lecture made a deep impression on the pope, although probably not the one which Mr. Rockefeller intended. Paul VI issued *Humanae Vitae* three years later, an act which constituted *causus belli* in the eyes of the Malthusian Liberal establishment in the United States. But the Malthusians had been waging psychological warfare against the Church for some time by the time *Humane Vitae* came out. What came to be known as the sexual revolution of the '60s was in reality a black operation waged against the Catholic Church. The contraceptive was the solution to what Paul Blanshard was calling the "Catholic problem" in 1949, and it solved the Catholic problem in two ways. First of all, it brought Catholic fertility down to Protestant levels, thereby ending the demographic surge that was going to turn the United States into a Catholic country. Beyond that, however, it played an even more important psychological role by dividing Catholics into "liberal" or "conservative" Catholics, depending on where they stood on the contraception issue. *Divide et Impere* was an old motto whose effectiveness had not diminished with time. In 1976, Leo Pfeffer, the legal architect of the Cultural Revolution, could declare victory primarily because "monolithity," as he put it, was no longer a characteristic of the Catholic Church in America.

But Mr. Rockefeller's visit had other consequences as well. It convinced the pope that his main enemy lay now to the west and not to the east and brought about as a result the end of the anti-Communist crusade and the beginning of the Vatican's *Ostpolitik*. On June 26, 1966, less than a year after the pope's meeting with John D. Rockefeller, 3rd, Agostino Casaroli, the generally acknowledged architect of the Vatican's *Ostpolitik*, flew to Belgrade and signed an agreement normalizing relations between the Vatican and Yugoslavia (Hansjakob Stehle, *Die Ostpolitk des Vatikans* [Munich: Piper, 1975], p. 359). The reaction of the Yugoslavian episcopate was less than enthusiastic. Archbishop Frane Franic of Split, later the only Yugoslavian bishop who would support Medjugorje, gritted his teeth and said as diplomatically as possible that "the implementation of this agreement will be full of curves" (p. 360). The reaction of Cardinal Seper was so negative that he was criticized by name by the Central Committee of the Croatian Communist party and was eventually sent off to Rome, where he became head of the Congregation for the Doctrine of the Faith. The communists too began to have their own misgivings about the agreement which would eventually lead to the break-up of Yugoslavia. With hindsight it's difficult not to see a deadly combination here. The Croats, who had remained loyal to Stepinac, now felt betrayed by their own Church as Tito, the man who butchered hundreds of thousands of innocent Croatians at Bleiburg, was now received with full honors by Paul VI at the Vatican on March 29, 1971. The Croatians were snubbed and at the same time were told that they were now on their own by the Catholic Church and the United States, who were now in the process of getting a less than amiable divorce from the anti-Communist alliance which had driven politics since the end of World War II. It was a recipe for resurgent nationalism, and this is precisely what happened.

In the same year that Rockefeller met with Pope Paul VI, a retired 43-year-old Partisan major general by the name of Franjo Tudjman was elected to the Yugoslavian Parliament. Tudjman was a Croat but a Communist as well, and the two facets of his identity came into conflict one year later when Secret Police Chief Aleksandar Rankovic came to him to ask his help in planning the 25th anniversary celebration for the Partisan victory to be observed in 1966. Part of the celebration involved commemorating the "700,000 to 900,000" victims of the Ustasha who had died at Jasenovac, the Ustasha concentration camp. Tudjman, who was doing a Ph.D. in history at the time, knew that the figure had been inflated by roughly tenfold for propaganda purposes because his institute had collected the actual number of people who had died at Jasenovac for use in negotiations for war reparations with Germany. Tudjman wanted the real figures published; Rankovic and Tito did not, and so Tudjman lost his job as director of the Institute for the History of the Worker's Movement in 1967. In 1969 he lost his seat in Parliament. But by then he had become one of the leaders in the nationalist/liberationist movement known as the Croatian Spring. Eventually this movement suffered the same fate the Prague Spring suffered in 1968, the only difference being that Tito crushed the movement in 1971 without the aid of Soviet Tanks. The experience was to have a profound effect on Tudjman, transforming him from a Communist Yugoslavian internationalist into a Croatian nationalist who believed that Yugoslavia's experiment at equality had failed and that what called itself a country was really an empire in which the Croats had been subjugated by the Serbs, who used communism as a smokescreen to disguise their ethnic self-interest. With former Communist officials thinking thoughts like this, it was clear that the demise of the century's most rapacious ideology was only a matter of time. Yugoslavia was to learn the hard way that the Church's embrace was often more deadly than her opposition.

Right around the time that John D. Rockefeller was meeting with Pope Paul VI, Paul Vitz was a graduate student in psychology at Stanford University in Palo Alto, California. The nature of the work he was involved in required late nights at the psychology building, where Vitz struck up an acquaintance with the building's janitor, a Croatian immigrant now living in the Bay area. "He hated Tito," Vitz said, "which is not surprising I suppose. But he hated Churchill every bit as much, and I could never understand why." Vitz had never heard of Bleiburg. Vitz could also not recall the janitor's name.

Jure Ivankovic left his home in the hamlet of Bijakovici in the parish of Medjugorje in the region of Herzegovina before the war ended, probably around the same time that Father Draganovic arrived in Rome. Whether he traveled the Ratlines established by Father Draganovic, no one knows for sure. The one thing that can be known with certainty is that he was in Yugoslavia in 1941 because that is when his son Marinko was born. If he left before the war ended, Marinko was a very small boy when he saw his father for the last time in a long time. But Jure did not abandon Marinko when he became part of the Croatian Diaspora. When Jure got a job as a janitor at a college in the Bay area, he may not have earned much money by American standards, but he was paid in dollars, dollars he would send back to Yugoslavia, where their value was magnified in relation to the relatively worthless dinar and the general poverty in Bijakovici and all of Herzegovina, which as punishment for its support of the Ustasha movement was left to stagnate economically, an easy thing to accomplish in an economy run by the state.

The absent father was to become a prominent fixture of Croatian culture. Thousands of men departed for Germany as *Gastarbeiter* during the latter days of the *Bundesrepublik*'s economic miracle. In this regard, Medjugorje was similar to the equally bogus apparition site in Marpingen in Germany, another border region which was economically oppressed, forcing fathers to emigrate in search of work. Many of the emigrants from Marpingen left for America, but most of the men did not emigrate permanently, taking instead jobs at the coalfields nearby, which meant that the fathers were only there on weekends. The net result was an increasingly truculent attitude toward political authority. Absent fathers, paradoxically, were able to develop an emotionally closer relationship with their children because they were "no longer the ubiquitous delegator of work, but the cherished weekend visitor bearing gifts" (p. 57). The dichotomy between the absent but benign Catholic parent and the overbearing Prussian

Protestant political authority broke out in the open when Bismarck started to enforce the May Laws which signaled the start of *Kulturkampf* in the 1870s. Military resistance was impossible. Divine intervention seemed the only way out, and so when three young girls claimed to have seen the Blessed Virgin while collecting berries in the forest, the community accepted their statement and turned it into a grassroots protest against overbearing authority. Since oppression at home meant loss of a parent, it was psychologically coherent to see removal of the oppression as a sign that the absent parent was about to return. Or perhaps things worked the other way as well, the imminent return of the parent was a sign that the yoke of oppression was about to end. The appearance of the Virgin was the return of a parent, and the return of the parent meant that oppression was about to end.

-2-

VATICAN II AND ITS AFTERMATH: 1967-1978

In September 1967 Krunoslav Draganovic was reported missing in the Croatian emigre press, allegedly the victim of a kidnapping by the UDBA. The man who had helped so many other people disappear in the aftermath of World War II had now disappeared himself, in the aftermath of the Cold War, or at least the Vatican's involvement in it. The mystery surrounding Father Draganovic's disappearance was soon cleared up when it became clear that he was living in Zagreb, unmolested by the Yugoslavian government in spite of the role he had played in organizing the Ratlines. The clarification surrounding the mystery of his disappearance was followed by the more profound mystery surrounding the motivation for his departure and the motivation behind the Yugoslav government providing one of its major Cold War enemies with what amounted to political asylum. Almost from the moment his disappearance had been explained, rumors began circulating that Draganovic had been a double agent from the beginning. This explanation was in many ways more plausible than that being proposed by the Croatian nationalists because it could explain the failure of the Krizari and the fact that virtually all of their raids were known in advance. The fact that the resistance to Communism got nowhere in Yugoslavia could be explained by the fact that the UDBA had infiltrated Vatican intelligence sources, and who was more involved in those operations that Father Draganovic? Father Draganovic had been working with the 401st Counter Intelligence Corps, but he could have made even more money by double-crossing the Americans and collaborating with the Communists. Draganovic had no great commitment to American democracy, and if the Americans were no longer interested in supporting the Croatians, then he would have to look elsewhere for a better deal.

The most plausible explanation of Father Draganovic's disappearance is less arcane: the Vatican wanted to cut its losses and get out of the anti-Communist crusade. It was clear that sending Draganovic back to Yugoslavia in 1967 was much different than sending him back in 1947, an act that would have been tantamount to having him killed. And if his departure from Rome was the price of détente with the Communists, it was a small price to pay. Draganovic lived the rest of his life peacefully and unmolested in Zagreb until his death in 1983. By the summer of 1968, when Paul VI issued *Humanae Vitae* and set off a revolt in the Church in the United States and Western Europe, it was clear that Communism was no longer the major threat to the Church. *Ostpolitik* was simply a rational adjustment to this fact of life, and the departure of Father Draganovic to Zagreb was a sign that Rome was serious about the new course it was charting in the wake of Vatican II.

"The Vatican," according to John Loftus, co-author of *Unholy Trinity*, "got out of the anti-communism crusade in '67 when they sent back Draganovic. The UDBA had penetrated the Catholic Church in Yugoslavia during the '60s and '70s. They also penetrated the Ustasha networks and actually sustained them as boogie men to keep Tito in power. As part of the Vatican's deal with Tito in 1966, they agreed to shut down their anti-Communist crusade in 1966. As a result, Croatian nationalists and Franciscans needed another source of support, probably something like Medjugorje, which became a source of funds and national pride."

Right around the time that Father Draganovic disappeared from Rome a young man from California by the name of Denis Nolan arrived at Notre Dame University to begin his sophomore year of studies there. Nolan had gone back home for the "summer of love," the brief apotheosis of drugs and free love and rock music, and he came back to Notre Dame a hippie and found that the university, far from frowning on his adoption of the counter-culture ethos, seemed to coddle him as he walked the campus barefoot, sleeping in chapels, and eating out of cafeteria trash cans.

What he didn't know at the time was that Notre Dame had become an agent of the Rockefellers in promoting sexual liberation, particularly the promotion of contraception. Both Notre Dame and the Rockefellers were now engaged in a full court press to get the Church to change its teaching on contraception. The main agency of change was the papal birth control commission, which had been infiltrated by Notre Dame alumni and faculty who were getting money from the Rockefellers at the time.

In *Turning Point*, his account of the papal birth control commission, Robert McClory quotes commission member and Notre Dame sociologist Don Barrett a number of times. What he does not state is that Don Barrett at the end of his life was a fervent promoter of Natural Family Planning and the first one to maintain that he had been wrong when he voted to change the Church's teaching on contraception. What McClory also does not tell us is that Barrett, while on the Birth Control Commission, had applied for a grant from John D. Rockefeller's Population Council, a grant which was eventually passed on to the Ford Foundation, which approved it for around $500,000, big money at the time. In any other venue, this would be termed conflict of interest, a conflict which was shared by other members of the commission as well, but winners always write history, and so Barrett will be remembered now as a freedom fighter against papal tyranny and not a quisling who took money from people who were trying to weaken the Church and the political position of Catholics in the United States. McClory describes Commission member Thomas Burch as "scarred by his experience on the Commission." But then one line later, we learn that in 1970, Burch went to work for Rockefeller's Population Council in New York City. Are we to assume that Burch's views on contraception were somehow coincidental to the money he was receiving from the Rockefellers? Again McClory ignores the obvious conflict of interest.

And then there is the hero-couple of *Turning Point*, the Crowleys, who used their position as head of the Catholic Family Movement to lobby for change in the Church's teaching on contraception. McClory explains their change of heart as resulting from polling members of CFM, an explanation which makes it seem as if they are agitating for more democracy in the Catholic Church. Then McClory tells us that during the summer of 1968, the very summer during which Pope Paul VI issued *Humanae Vitae*, that "the Crowleys, *with a grant from the Rockefeller Foundation* [my emphasis], made plans for an international forum on the Christian Family in the World to be held in Italy." Even after citing evidence of this sort in his own book, McClory gives no indication of understanding that the intent of the papal birth control commission was being subverted by Rockefeller money. His commitment to contraception as a liberal Catholic evidently goes so deep that the thought never seems to cross his mind.

During the summer following Denis Nolan's sophomore year at Notre Dame, Pope Paul VI issued *Humanae Vitae*. The pope hadn't taken Mr. Rockefeller up on his offer, and the liberal theologians at Notre Dame who had were outraged. The theologians who signed the protest against *Humanae Vitae* gave the impression that they had been betrayed by their own Church, which was doing nothing more than reiterating its constant teaching on the matter, a teaching which had galled Paul Blanshard when it was articulated in Pius XI's encyclical *Casti Connubii* shortly after the Lambeth Conference approved contraception for Anglicans. The reasons are not hard to understand. Ever since John F. Kennedy had been elected president, Catholic intellectuals had been under the impression that they had been accepted as members of academe in good standing. *Humanae Vitae* meant that the deal was off. For ambitious young Catholic intellectuals like Michael Novak and Rosemary Ruether, who had collaborated on a tendentious tract called *What Modern Catholics Think about Birth Control* in 1963, the announcement was devastating. Once *Humane Vitae* hit the streets, Camelot was over for Catholic intellectuals. And, as if to emphasize that fact, Robert Kennedy was assassinated in the same year, making it clear that no Catholic would be president of the United States for a long time. What looked like a Catholic dynasty in 1960 destined to hold on to the presidency for the next 24 years, as John passed the baton to Robert and Robert the baton to Teddy, ended in a little over 1,000 days. The Catholic Problem was being solved in a dramatic way.

Leading the outraged theologians at Notre Dame was an up-and-coming young Holy Cross Priest by the name of James Tunstead Burtchaell, who announced to a cheering rally at Notre Dame that *Humanae Vitae* was worse than wrong; it was stupid. Twenty-three years later, Burtchaell was forced to resign from Notre Dame's theology department after being accused of homosexual activity in the liberal Catholic paper of record, the *National Catholic Reporter*. The outing of Father Burtchaell was an inside job. The information was supplied to the *NCR* by people at Notre Dame who wanted to get rid of him, because by the '90s when the outing took place, Burtchaell was known more for his opposition to abortion than for his support of contraception and had become a member of the board of directors of *First Things*, a journal known for it conservative, albeit neo-conservative, views. All of the evidence indicates it was Burtchaell's opposition to abortion and his plan to write a book about the secularization of Notre Dame that got him in trouble with the establishment at Notre Dame. In the mid-'70s Burtchaell was seen as Hesburgh's heir apparent. Then his views opposing abortion became known. In an interesting anecdote in his antiabortion book, *Rachel Weeping*, Burtchaell recounts being called into the office of John D. Rockefeller, 3rd, to explain himself. Just why a priest of the Catholic Church would have to explain his opposition to abortion never really gets explained, even though it is the most fascinating question which arises from the incident. Whatever the reason, shortly after facing down Mr. Rockefeller, Burtchaell was no longer considered Hesburgh's heir apparent, and eventually had to leave the university in disgrace.

All of this was far in the future in 1968 when Denis Nolan was falling under Burtchaell's spell. Nolan's life and subsequent involvement in Medjugorje reads like an illustrated history of the confusion that has reigned in the Church since the Council. Nolan entered Notre Dame in 1966, one year after the close of the Council. By the time he left Notre Dame in 1970 after majoring in theology and after being subjected to the intellectual currents that were to wreak so much havoc at Catholic campuses and seminaries over the next 20 years, he had lost his faith. In an autobiographical account of his education he wrote for publication, Nolan described his own spiritual odyssey:

> I lost my faith studying theology at a Catholic University in the latter 1960s. The more I came under the influence of the teaching of that time, the more convinced I became no one could know objective truth with any degree of certainty. Thus, for instance, Socrates was the wisest man in Athens because he knew that he knew nothing, whereas everyone else thought that they understood something. Only the weak must have answers. We each, rather, are left alone with our self. The challenge is to have the courage to recognize that and not allow the Church or anyone else to give you answers. Your only hope is to be true to yourself and face the darkness alone.

Needless to say, philosophical nihilism of this sort was to have practical consequences, not only for Nolan but for his generation of Catholic student as well. Nolan's family sent him to Notre Dame expecting him be strengthened in his faith by a Catholic education. What he and his cohort of the Baby Boom got was something more in line with Paul Blanshard's plan to solve the Catholic problem by weakening Catholic education.

> You can imagine the affect [sic] this had on my life. I became more and more lost. During my last two years I did not pay for room or board. I wandered around the campus sleeping in chapels, etc., and eating only when I could get a fee meal. I didn't wear shoes. I looked like a "free spirit" to others, with my long hair, untrimmed beard, and poncho over my shoulder. The chairman of the theology department would sometimes let me sleep on a

cot in his room. I remember him once declaring, "Denis, you're the only person I've ever heard of who was a legend at Notre Dame while he was still there."

The chairman of the department was to become legendary in his own way as well. Rev. James Tunstead Burtchaell, C.S.C., was known on campus at the time for his fiery rejection of *Humanae Vitae* when it appeared in 1968. At the time, Burtchaell was teaching in his Theology of Grace classes the theories which were eventually to emerge in his book *Philemon's Problem*. Nolan would later say that "fortunately an awful lot of what I studied in his class went over my head," but he still claims to remember the central assertion of *Philemon's Problem* (and even the page number), namely, in Nolan's words, that "Jesus is not the savior but the revealer of God's love."

Burtchaell is more polished in his prose, but the message is essentially the same. The message of the Catholic Church, according to Burtchaell in *Philemon's Problem*, is that it is not necessary for anyone's salvation: "It is time for the Church bluntly to disavow Cyprian's maxim," he writes,

> and to admit that extra ecclesiam there is plenty of salus. ... The Christian Church can claim no bonded franchise for salvation, no exclusive rights of distributorship for God's grace. It is perhaps one of the rare religious enterprises that confesses it is not necessary.

"Salvation," according to Father Burtchaell,

> occurs whenever any man emerges from his native selfishness and opens his heart to his neighbor.... And grace, like bacteria, is everywhere.... Grace is no monopoly of Christianity. The Church has been given no franchise on God's favor. The unbeliever and the believer are saved in exactly the same way: by loving and serving their neighbor. The difference is that the believer has been alerted to the fact that in this transaction eternity is at stake.

In a statement that would take on an especially ironic meaning in Nolan's life, Burtchaell claimed that "there are no direct transactions with the Father.... The only place one can find the Father is in one's brother and in the transmission of goods and services which will help that brother to become nourished and grow." The Church, according to Father Burtchaell's theory, becomes basically a social welfare agency surrounded by a lot of extraneous liturgical and doctrinal mumbo jumbo: "Thus, the most crucial activities of Christians are not peculiar to Christians. Christianity must be dedicated to what is not particular to Christianity.... It must be an agency of service with the understanding that, in washing the feet of the world, one is doing far more than would appear."

This corrosive rationalism had a predictable effect on the life of Nolan the undergraduate. He became alienated from the Church and its sacraments and as a result his moral life deteriorated. As a result of that his marriage later fell apart, and he hit rock bottom. At that point he turned to God for the forgiveness which he had learned at Notre Dame was unnecessary to request.

> Although I hadn't let anyone in college take away my personal relationship with Jesus, I had allowed pride to separate me from the Church, and without the Sacraments, even though I had the personal relationship with Christ, I began to die.... I remember the night the divorce papers came. The sheriff brought them to the door. I signed a form that was a promise to appear in court. After he left, I was overcome with grief. I knelt down on the floor praying as I gave free rain [sic] to my tears. It occurred to me that something I had done earlier that year was a sin. On my knees I asked God's forgiveness. I then heard an audible voice in the room above my head say, "Your marriage is healed. You are my son again." And it was at that moment that I experienced an outpouring of the Holy Spirit. I became filled with joy and started praying in tongues.

In 1973, Nolan became a Charismatic and joined the People of Praise, a South Bend charismatic community created by some of the movement's founders. Even though he was later to leave the community, feeling that "they had lost the Lord's anointing," he credits them with saving his marriage and saving his life. Being saved from the predations of the rationalists at the Notre Dame theology department by those who were now speaking in tongues and prophesying with words direct from the Holy Spirit caused Nolan's faith to take on a certain anti-intellectual character. From then on, the mind was more or less suspect as the mediator between God's law and his life. It was almost as if a large segment of the intellect's role in religious life had been cauterized by the traumatic effects of heresy at Notre Dame. It was a theme evident in the lives of other Charismatics as well.

Kevin Ranaghan, who was teaching at St. Mary's College and getting his Ph.D. at Notre Dame while Nolan was an undergraduate there and who eventually became one of the leaders of the People of Praise community, which was to play such a crucial role in Nolan's intellectual and moral development throughout the '70s and early '80s, wrote about the same type of malaise in his book *Catholic Pentecostals Today*. "In our age 'God is dead,'" he writes, citing the slogan that graced one cover of *Time* magazine in the late '60s and gave the name to a widely discussed, if short-lived school of theology:

> He is thought dead because He is "missing in action." The Christian looks within and around himself and sees only sin and weakness, an ineffective apostolate, and he hears only the pounding roar of God's silence. He looks to Scripture and sees what appears to be only the records of past prophets and past deeds which, though powerful, do not speak to him. Satellites, computers, and psychologists give us the answers to most of life's former riddles. It would seem that God, who was merely a crutch, is indeed dead. To this age of questioning, God has sent his prophets and his signs and wonders to call to men, "I the Lord am with you." . . . Results of the "Pentecostal Movement" might be summed up as one typically 20th-century student expressed it: "It works!"

Ranaghan is, of course, referring here and throughout his entire book to the spectacular growth of what has come to be known as the Charismatic Renewal, which was an inchoate response to the chaos in the Catholic Church which came about after the Council as a result of the Cultural Revolution. The numbers of those baptized in the spirit and willing to attend either small prayer groups or mass rallies, often at Notre Dame, rose dramatically during the '70s, but beneath the tone of exultation and the sometime crass pragmatism, one finds doubt and an unresolved intellectual conflict. Seeing secularism more as an inevitable historical force rather than a campaign of psychological *Kulturkampf* being waged against Catholics, Ranaghan pretty well concedes that that modernity is right on its own terms. Yes, he seems to be saying, science has all the answers if you want to be intellectual about the whole business, but the charismatics have, well, "signs and wonders" that will make mincemeat of all your powerful arguments.

The Charismatic Renewal didn't resolve the crisis of modernity; it simply tried to claim that modernity was irrelevant in light of the great signs that the Renewal was producing. Instead of doubt resolved, we have doubt postponed. In stating their case that way, the charismatics put themselves in a dangerous spiritual position. If signs and wonders are the only things that quiet their doubts, what happens, as is inevitably the case, when the signs and wonders cease? A crisis is what happens. A faith that is based on signs and wonders rather than on the "sign of Jonah," i.e., the resurrection as witnessed by the apostles, is an accident waiting to happen. As soon as attendance at the Notre Dame conferences is down, as soon as sales of cassettes drop, etc., the old doubts begin to reappear. One is faced with a choice. Either one grows into a mature faith—i.e., one not based on signs and wonders—or one looks for signs and wonders in ever-increasing doses in order to maintain the spiritual high one remembers from the past. There is evidence that the movement fragmented over the issue, and various groups took one or the other path.

Nolan was of course as oblivious to this behind-the-scenes maneuvering at the time as Ranaghan, but both men began to act out the ethos of the times nonetheless. The sexual constitution of a culture is so basic, so fundamentally important that it determines the broad trajectories of behavior in fundamental ways. Either a culture's sexual mores are congruent with the moral order or they are not. When a culture gets moved from the former to the latter state, when it gets moved from being congruent with the moral order to being a culture based on sexual liberation, the disruption is profound, but that does not mean that the results of that disruption are unpredictable. The foundations were now moving American culture off the plateau which Bernard Berelson described in 1959 because they understood that a sexually liberated culture was one which they could dominate through the powerful new media. If sex became a matter of opinion, rather than a function of decrees established by God, they could manipulate that opinion to their own advantage and turn sexual liberation into an instrument of political control. The lives of those who succumbed to the siren song of sexual liberation might seem disruptive when viewed up close, but from the point of view of the big picture, they would follow certain broad trajectories. The Charismatic movement was one of these trajectories, so were the cults. Plato and Aristotle had claimed that democracy always led to tyranny. In modern parlance, the sexual excess of the Weimar Republik was always followed by the totalitarian reaction epitomized the by the Nazis. The rise of the Moonies in San Francisco followed on the heels of the summer of love. People whose lives were out of control needed a dictator to create order. Denis Nolan became Notre Dame's most famous hippie. Then he became involved in sexual liberation; then when it looked as if his marriage was going to fall apart and he was overcome with a sense of sin, guilt, remorse and the sense that his life is out of control, he became a charismatic and joined the People of Praise, who took over his life and through the discipleship concept known as "headship" would tell him what to do down to the minutest detail and how to live his life in ways congenial to their goals. Since Denis was not alone in his experiences, since in fact his experiences were in many ways paradigmatic of the Catholics

of his generation, what followed was the rise of the charismatic movement throughout the world. Chaos creates a need for order, and if the
Church seems overcome by revolution itself, the faithful will look
beyond the Church for the stillpoint in the turning world not in ritual
and doctrine sanctioned by centuries of tradition, but in religious
ecstasy and prophesy directly from the mouth of the Holy Spirit—in
short, in religious enthusiasm which banishes the uncertainties of
everyday life in an orgy of intense if necessarily ephemeral experience.

Sexual liberation creates behavior patterns that are, if anything, more predictable than the pattern of normal family life lived
according to the moral order. The forces which were promoting sexual
liberation knew it would be destructive, but they were interested in
destruction—destruction of a social order based on the moral order
and destruction of the Catholic Church, which in the United States at
that time was the main support for traditional morals. They were
interested in destruction because they were engaged in a cultural civil
war over whose values would provide the default settings for the
culture, but also because they saw in sexual liberation a way of increasing their own power. Sexual liberation was a way off the plateau
Bernard Berelson described in 1959 because it provided more attractive bait and a much more powerful way to manipulate people. That
sexual liberation could lead to destruction has been a staple of horror
fiction since Mary Shelley wrote *Frankenstein*, but the warning is
always ignored by those who believe in the future by ignoring the past
and feel that one more invention or idea or law will tame the man's
sexual nature in the way that Ben Franklin tamed electricity. The law of
unintended consequences applies here in spades, and so as the '60s
became the '70s, it became clear that sexual liberation was leading to
religious enthusiasm.

Nolan was not alone; in many ways his life was like a cork
which bobbed along on the stream of spiritual pathologies which
afflicted the Catholic church in the period following the Second Vatican
Council. Father Philip Pavich was 18 years Nolan's senior and yet even
though he was technically old enough to be Nolan's father, he was
involved in essentially the same spiritual currents which deposited
them before long in the same spiritual place, a small village in Bosnia-
Herzegovina where six young seers would claim to have visions of the
Blessed Virgin Mary. Pavich became a charismatic in 1970, three years
before Dennis Nolan would, but for many of the same reasons.

Philip Pavich, an American of Croatian descent, was born in
America in Waterloo, Iowa, in 1930 to Croatian immigrants from the
Krajina, which was a Serb-dominated region and therefore to become
famous as one of the bloodiest battlegrounds of the 1991 Croatian civil

war. Pavich's father worked for the Southern Illinois Railroad, and he grew up at a time when someone who had a job like that didn't make much money but considered himself lucky to have a job at all. Philip learned English as his native language but heard Croatian at home, and when he and his brother felt the need to conceal secrets from non-Croatian neighbors, they would often use Croatian words, the way the Hardy boys might, but Philip never felt he had a grasp of the language.

Since they were part of the Croatian Diaspora, the Pavichs received the ministrations of the Croatian Franciscans who would travel down from Chicago and hold missions and retreats for the local Croatian population in Iowa. The purpose was to nurture the faith, but the visits also served to keep alive a sense of Croatian identity, and beyond that it allowed the priests to keep an eye out for Franciscan vocations. By the mid-'40s it didn't take a particularly sharp eye to discern that Pavich had a vocation to the Franciscans. His mother would tell him on the day of his ordination that she had consecrated him to God's service from the moment that she had held him in her arms, and now as Philip was getting ready to graduate from eighth grade it looked as if his mother's prayers were going to bear fruit.

As was often the case in the days before the Second Vatican Council, the seminary began with Philip Pavich on the day he entered high school. He left for Chicago and the Franciscan seminary and its 800-acre campus just west of Chicago in the early '40s and spent what he now recalls as an extraordinarily happy youth there roaming the grounds with the other seminarians and learning Latin and Greek. At one point during his seminary days, it suddenly occurred to Pavich that since he could learn languages like Latin and Greek by reading books, he might also learn Croatian that way too. When he mentioned this to the seminary rector, he was told bluntly that Croatian should be learned not by reading books but by talking to his mother.

It seems like a mild enough rebuke, if that is what one can call it, but it created a peculiar sort of trauma, perhaps because Pavich was at this point in his life so ambivalent about his status as a de facto binational. Pavich didn't see this ambivalence as rising from a political source. He claims to have had next to no contact whatsoever with Croatian nationalism at the time, even though the Croatian Diaspora in the late '30s was planning to return to its own country and was acting accordingly. Pavich remembers a picnic in 1938 organized by his uncle who was, according to him, into politics "big time." But as an eight year old, Pavich had little interest in politics and to this day knows little about the entire Ustasha period and claims that no one he knew at the time either in Iowa or the seminary knew anything about the Ustasha massacres. When asked about the citizens of Medjugorje, with whom he has lived for over ten years in his capacity as a

Franciscan friar and man of Croatian ancestry fluent in the language, he responds by saying that the natives are tight-lipped about the past.

The Croatian question came to a head for Pavich while he was in the seminary, which cost his family the princely sum of $220 per year—tuition, room and board— which modest sum his family could not afford, paying only half. Eventually Pavich was to go to the rector of the seminary and inform him that he didn't want to be a "Croatian Franciscan." He was a Croatian Franciscan whether he wanted to be or not simply because of his mother's blood and his decision to become a priest, but as he was to learn later on, being a Croatian Franciscan is a long complicated affair, something he was to learn about first hand much later in his life. When Pavich said he wanted out, the rector first mentioned the money, but that issue was quickly resolved. Philip had to resolve the other issue on his own going to the head of the Croatian section and telling the rector that the decision was completely his own and the American Franciscans hadn't been guilty of what the Protestants call "sheep-stealing."

So Philip was ordained as an "American" Franciscan in 1957, and it was as an American that he almost immediately began to experience problems. As anyone who knows the history of those times knows, the '50s were a booming time for American Catholicism. The baby boom was largely a Catholic phenomenon and was accompanied by a huge vocations boom and as a result Philip, who came from an older generation, was almost immediately promoted to the position of assistant novice master. After about four years of taking care of just about all the spiritual and psychological counseling that the young seminarians got at the time, Pavich began to feel somewhat inadequate to the task. What did he know about this sort of thing, he began to wonder and so as a result went to his superiors to ask them for permission to get a degree in psychology.

The times being what they were, Pavich was almost immediately granted permission, and almost just as immediately, introduced to the sort of psychology that was getting practiced at the time. Soon, he began to get into intellectual, then moral, and finally spiritual hot water. Pavich enrolled in the psychology program at Loyola, the Jesuit university in Chicago in 1962. He was one of a huge number of priests in the program, most of whom were parish priests from the Chicago area and most of whom were much older than Pavich, and as a result able to see that what was being taught was dangerous to both faith and morals. Pavich was taught by Eugene Kennedy, then a Maryknoll priest, and Charles A. Curran, then also a priest (the famous Curran was Charles E. Curran). Both Currran and Kennedy were devotees of Carl Rogers, who was on his way to becoming famous for inventing non-directive therapy of the sort that would ultimately destroy the

Immaculate Heart nuns in Los Angeles. Pavich remembers the William Coulson article on wrecking the Immaculate heart nuns in Los Angeles because he read it when it appeared in *Fidelity* in the early '80s and not because he knew Rogers or Coulson at the time.

Pavich, like so many religious at the time, like Bill Coulson, in fact, like Tony Massamini as described in *John Cardinal Krol and the Cultural Revolution*, was to learn first hand just how destructive this psychology could be for religious. The psychology of openness to anything (the *summum bonum* was being nonjudgmental, after all) combined with the Zeitgeist of sexual liberation being driven at the time at least partly by Hollywood's desire to break the production code and the foundations' promotion of contraception, combined with the new interpretation that Christian love, especially a la St. Francis, was getting at the hands of dissenting religious, was guaranteed to get people into sexual trouble, and Philip Pavich was no exception. In the course of his career as a counselor, Pavich became sexually intimate with one of his counselees. This led predictably to a crisis of faith and much agonizing. Pavich remembers rushing up to Eugene Kennedy at a conference, saying that he had to talk to him and then listening to Kennedy try to play the whole thing down. "Oh, Philip," he said, "You're just in love" as if it were no big deal after all for a man who had taken a vow of celibacy to be sleeping with a divorced woman. Kennedy eventually left the priesthood and got married.

Pavich, unlike his mentor, did consider it a big deal, big enough, in fact, to drive him to the brink of leaving the order. Pavich remembers the day when the crisis reached a head. The ladies' auxiliary for the seminary was having one of its fundraising events, and Pavich instead of circulating among his guests was up in his room in agony. Before him lay his laicization papers on his desk and there, head in proverbial hand, he engaged in a dialogue with God. "If I'm going to get married," he thought to himself, "why am I not happy?" Then—the next thought following naturally from the first—"maybe I shouldn't get married." Then the thought that the Lord was waiting to help him with this burden, if only he would ask! But then came another more chilling thought.

"I didn't want to ask," he said some 30 years later, "and that thought scared the hell out of me." So standing there tottering on the brink of damnation, Pavich, whether out of fear or some greater power outside himself for which one could use the shorthand term "grace," decided to ask and was immediately overcome by a sense of relief. The crisis was over—for the moment at least. Pavich decided during the course of that night that he was not going to ask for laicization, and the Franciscans, perhaps perplexed more by the fact that he wanted to stay rather than his decision to leave, took him by the hand and led him along step by step back to being a priest again.

Pavich still speaks about his brush with laicization with a combination of fear and anger. Fear of what have might become of him, but anger at how the Church was handling the issue. It was the era of revolving-door laicizations, and the only one who had anything to say anything against them was not one of his fellow Franciscans, not even a fellow clergyman, but Pavich's younger brother, who couldn't believe that the Church would simply throw away priests like that. His brother objected, and of course so did his mother. Pavich went to his mother and in the typically overheated rhetoric of the day told her that he had to leave the priesthood to save his soul. Pavich now feels that his mother was even willing to go along with that, so unconditional was her love, but now remembers her saying that "Satan is trying to destroy you."

In January of 1969 Pavich was transferred to a small Franciscan college to teach nursing students, and, although it sounds like the premise for a '60s era T & A film, the move allowed Pavich finally to break with his girlfriend and start over again as a priest. But the devil never sits still when it comes to the ruin of souls, and so just when Rogerian non-directive psychology was loosing its ability to corrupt Pavich, he ran into another movement that was just as corrosive but more subtle because ostensibly more religious. In May of 1970 Pavich was baptized in the Holy Spirit and so became a charismatic. Thus began an odyssey that was to prove just as traumatic as his venture into non-directive psychology. In many ways, the temptations were the same. Pavich found himself falling in love with another women in the mid-'70s, a woman he had met at a charismatic prayer group, many of which were under his direction in Cleveland at the time. As Monsignor Knox could have predicted, the charismatic movement became a front for lots of illicit sexual activity, and many of the priests who had resisted the siren songs of the secular '60s succumbed to the seductions of the charismatic spirit in the '70s. Pavich mentions the case of Francis MacNutt, whom he knew personally. He gives some indication that these seductions may have been planned by evangelicals as such as a way of getting Catholic priests out of the Catholic Church and into Protestant denominations. He remembers a woman by the name of Delinda who was a Baptist and kept telling him that she was going to get him out of the Catholic Church by getting him a wife, a tactic used by Luther among others, and remembers too that the woman who eventually ended up as Francis MacNutt's wife was a friend of hers.

Pavich eventually went on to become a leader in what came to be known as the Charismatic Renewal. He attended the mammoth Notre Dame Conferences in 1970, '71, and '72 as well as the famous Rome conference in 1975 in which Paul VI cautiously gave his blessing to the movement, along with a number of caveats which the movement promptly ignored. Then, perhaps because he could see the handwriting on the wall too, Pavich suddenly quit the charismatics in 1975. At the time he was working with an Assemblies of God minister in the Cleveland area and was head of a prayer group, but in retrospect he sees the Charismatic Renewal, especially its ecumenical aspect, as another form of seduction.

In 1975, right around the time Philip Pavich bailed out of the Charismatic Renewal, Marijan Pehar, a fellow Franciscan he had never met, was having spiritual difficulties of a different sort. Pehar had never heard of the human potential movement, Carl Rogers, sensitivity training or the Charismatic Renewal, but he had heard of prayer, and he knew that as a Franciscan priest he was supposed to do pray regularly and most probably with other Franciscans so he became involved in the prayer groups that were being formed in Herzegovina at the time. He was, however, troubled by the behavior of his fellow Franciscans at the prayer groups he was attending. Instead of just kneeling down and praying the Rosary or something traditional like that, Pehar's fellow Franciscans would wander around the room with their eyes closed bumping into each other and then confessing their sins, but not in the secrecy of the confessional. The prayer groups were led by two Franciscans a few years older than Pehar, Jozo Zovko and Tomislav Vlasic. Zovko was born in 1941, the year in which Croatia attained its independence. His family came from Siroki Brijeg, where both he and Pehar entered the Franciscan order. Pehar remembers doing brickwork at the monastery there in the late '60s.

By the mid-'70s, however, Zovko had become famous throughout Herzegovina for leading these groups, probably because of the pronounced effects they had on those who participated in them. Pehar was one such participant; however, did not like what he saw.

"There were about 20 people in the room," he said years later, "and Father Zovko and Father Leonardo [probably Orec] brought some music and we sat down and they read something from the Bible and later on they said, 'Okay, we walk through the room now. Just walk around.' And I said, 'Why?' [But they said,] 'Just walk around and look the other person in the eye, the partner.' We were supposed to go through the room and look some people in the eye and pick up a partner. I was going around and Father Leonardo went by me and I said, 'Oh, I know those eyes.' It was very funny. Then I left. Me and another guy, we went out and were playing ball.

Pehar left the "retreat" in disgust. When everyone else came out, however, Pehar noticed that a radical change had taken place.

"Later on, about two or three hours later, they come out, and there was some very good friends of mine, and they were different people. They were crying and everything. And I said, 'Well, what happened inside?' Well, it was some kind of public confession or something like that. Whatever happened in the past, whatever sins they had, they were talking openly.

Pehar walked out of a similar meeting in Zagreb for the same reason: he didn't like the manipulative atmosphere.

"They read some part of the Bible, and they were meditating about half an hour and praying alternately, and all of a sudden one guy in the middle, he start talking something like old Greek or Latin, and after him there were three or four guys talking in tongues. I left that meeting too because later on I found out that some of those people went in hospital, in mental hospital. That's what I said that time that I feel sorry for these people because there is something going on."

Something indeed was going on. Father Zovko was experimenting with an explosive mixture of charismatic prayer and sensitivity training. W. R. Coulson, who worked with Carl Rogers doing sensitivity training, recognized the techniques immediately.

"The exercise, for example, of milling around the room and looking in somebody's eyes, I mean that's been known for years that it works very effectively. It's been known since the mid-'60s, and it even has a name. It's the milling around exercise. It's probably found in the basic book of values clarification, practical strategies."

Coulson is right about the technique, but wrong about the book. However, it is mentioned in Will Schutz's book *Joy*. Schutz, who made encounter groups a household word while at Esalen in Big Sur, California, discussed not only the technique but the effect it had on people as well. "Blind milling," he tells us, "helps to open up the area of conflict between being alone and being together. . . . This can be done by having everyone stand up, shut his eyes, put out his hands and just start milling around the room. When people meet they explore each other in whatever way and however long they wish."

Anyone who has taken part in encounter groups can testify to the manipulation that takes place in them. The normal barriers between people fall in this artificial environment, and a synthetic euphoria which is much like being in love follows. According to Schutz, one 17-year-old girl who took part in an encounter group he staged, gave the following report: "I felt that I actually meant something to my teacher. . . . When I returned to school the next day, a period of constant high ecstasy followed" (p. 179). A Catholic priest who took part in Schutz's encounter group "vowed to go back and try to influence his Church to experience more of the warmth and humanness that he experienced." Another encounterer claimed: "I felt somehow that I was being swung from one end of the room to the other. . . . Tears flowed out of the sides of my eyes. I felt in complete ecstasy—totally beyond myself." One person, referring to her experiences in an encounter group, claimed, "I felt that the enactment of that ritual could exonerate me from the pressures of long-accumulated guilt."

By the time Schutz got around to writing his second book on the encounter movement, *Here Comes Everybody*, the religious undertone in the first book had become much more explicit. On p. 57, Schutz refers to the "encounter movement as a new religion," during which one comes to the following realization: "You know that you are God." Later on in the book, Schutz tells us that "many religious leaders have become involved with open encounter during the last few years. Some feel that the group offers a vehicle for parishioners to experience what religious service only talks about."

Coulson, who did encounter work with religious orders, including a group of Franciscans, in California in the late '60s, had seen the potent effect of combining sensitivity and religion first hand when he and Carl Rogers took part in what turned out to be the destruction of the Immaculate Heart Nuns in Los Angeles.

"Boundaries were broken," Coulson said. "In fact, there's another game in question called "Boundary Breakers." When boundaries are broken, you're open to all kinds of invasive maneuvers from God-knows-where. That's what can happen. If someone wants then to plant a suggestion, that's the right time to do it. Warm them up with a sensitivity exercise, and then suggest to them whatever you want.

The ability of encounter groups to magnify peer pressure and the often-subliminal directives of the group leader is legendary. Even Schutz himself has experienced it in the groups he has led, so much so that he feels obliged to defend the groups against the "right-wing" charge that they are nothing more than a form of brainwashing. The following anecdote of Schutz speaks volumes about the psychic power of the encounter technique:

> It seems clear that the frequent accusation that encounter groups are like brainwashing or group think could hardly be more mistaken. I have often held a firm belief, then gone to a group and, through the pressure of the group banding together against me, changed my mind. When I went home, I discovered that I still held my original view essentially. It is at this point that I have my choice of joining the right-wingers and agreeing that there is a strong brainwashing quality to these groups and that they are dangerous and that I was duped—in short feel it's their fault I've changed my mind. Or I can do what is in

keeping with the encounter mode, consider why I changed my mind under pressure. They didn't change my mind, I did. And why did I if I still believe my original thought? This line of pursuit turned out to be extremely fruitful. It revealed that I was conflicted. I wasn't sure of my belief; I wanted to be liked so much that I would allow their arguments to convince me even though I didn't believe them, or I didn't want to be seen as rigid, or I didn't have much confidence in my own reasoning ability.

When all is said and done here, Schutz is telling us that encounter groups are extremely effective ways to manipulate people. When combined with the normal charismatic tendency of praying for a passage or getting a word of prophecy, especially when this is done under an authority figure like a priest, they can be especially effective in producing what otherwise would be known as mystical experiences in the participants. In fact, Schutz, who can hardly be characterized as particularly well disposed toward things religious, has experienced the same sort of thing himself. "When the encounter gets more advanced," Schutz wrote, "say to include meditation, then mystical experiences begin occurring even more frequently. Combining the encounter group with the religious experience has helped me to elevate my aspirations for the encounter group." Michael Murphy, the founder of Esalen, saw the spiritual side of encounter groups almost immediately. In fact, according to Walter Truett Anderson's account in *The Upstart Spring*, a history of Esalen,

> Murphy found the workshop as much of a mind-blower as psychedelic drugs. In fact, he wrote an essay about the similarities between the group experience and the drug experience and concluded that, of the two, sensitivity groups were more powerful and effective. [Sensitivity] groups, he decided, would be one of the new American yogas—a path of union between the individual and the cosmos.

The impression that Father Zovko and his charismatic prayer-group-cum-sensitivity-session made on Pehar never really wore off. In fact, when Pehar heard that Zovko was the pastor at the parish where the alleged apparitions of Our Lady of Medjugorje were happening, he was immediately suspicious.

"Was Zovko doing this type of thing at St. James Parish in Medjugorje?" I asked Pehar.

"Yeah," he replied. "That's what I heard later on. And when I heard about that case, I said, 'Something must be wrong.'"

"So these girls," I said referring to the seers, "could have gone to one of these meetings like that?"

"That could happen."

"And he could have suggested something to them at one of these meetings."

"That's what I think. That's what my opinion is."

In 1976 Marijan Pehar was living in a sort of co-ed monastery in Zagreb with an number of nuns and fellow Franciscan priests, including Father Tomislav Vlasic. Then one day in late 1976, Sister Rufina, one of the nuns, just disappeared. Gradually it became clear that she had got pregnant and was living in Starnberg in Bavaria, West Germany, with a man in his nineties, a Herr Ott, who had a reputation for helping people out—usually students from Croatia. In a letter which Bishop Pavao Zanic, ordinary of the diocese of Mostar, received in 1984, Sister Rufina, who signed the letter simply as Manda, said that the father of the child was another resident of the monastery in Zagreb, Father Tomislav Vlasic, the man who along with Jozo Zovko was running the peculiar charismatic prayer sessions in Herzegovina.

After doing some detective work on his own, Bishop Zanic finally tracked her down and went to visit her. In addition to talking to Manda, the bishop got to see her son, who bore, he would later remark, a distinct resemblance to Father Vlasic. Manda, however, now denied that she had written any letters to the bishop, causing the bishop to believe that someone was manipulating her from behind the scenes.

The mysterious appearance of so important a person as the ordinary of Mostar at his house then got the aged Herr Ott wondering about the past of the woman who had been living with him for the past seven years, causing him to do some investigating of his own, in the course of which he discovered a series of letters between Vlasic and Manda discussing the birth of the child and how to deal with the whole incident.

In early December of 1976 Vlasic wrote to Manda, who was then nine months pregnant, from Zagreb. The letter is full of reassurances "Don't be so afraid. I am sure that God will help you and reward you. And we will also take care of you. I will not desert you even if all efforts fail." Vlasic also promises to send her $300, a dictionary and a cookbook. In another letter sent around the same time, Vlasic also talks about getting dispensed from his vows as a Franciscan. Although it is nowhere explicitly stated, the impression one gets is that Vlasic will soon leave the priesthood and marry Manda.

However, Vlasic is absolutely adamant about her not revealing the identity of the father. "Concerning the child's father," Vlasic writes, "no one can force you to tell his name. I think that it's best to say that you met someone passing by and he gave you a false name, and he told you he wants to marry you. Later he left and didn't call and you got pregnant. It's best to say you don't know him because they won't bother you then and it would be better for the child later. It's better for you that no one comes there."

In a letter dated January 9, 1977, which is to say, right around the time that the child was born, Vlasic continues in the same manipulative vein, but this time he adds a little theological embellishment to the story. "As to the child," he writes,

> it's better not to tell anyone. If you say it to even one person, even if it's your mother or sister, you already told it to the whole world. And you get no benefit from that, only more burden. But you will reap God's blessing if you keep it to yourself because you save a lot of sisters and brothers and the world in these unpleasant times. Then you will have more blessings than if you live as a nun. You will really be like Mary who accepted her particular destiny and went with her child wherever she had to, followed by Providence, and the child, despite her crosses, became the origin of the greatest glory.

It is an interesting statement from someone who was to become the chief propagandist for the most important alleged Marian apparition of our day. The letter shows a clearly manipulative and unattractive side to Vlasic. He shows no compunction about using religion, specifically an appeal to the Blessed Virgin, to save himself from the unpleasant consequences of his own selfish behavior. Manda, as one might expect from someone in her position, finds the advice a bit hard to accept. Apparently the appeal to the Blessed Virgin was a favorite line with Vlasic because she addresses it in one of her letters to him.

"It's not easy for me to bear all these things," she writes, "You're telling me to be like Mary, but I must tell you that she had Joseph with her in a strange land."

Manda's letter is also full of the confusion and pain that one might expect from someone who found herself in that situation. She prays that she will die in giving birth. "I would like 100 times more to be dead than to have all of mine see me have a child out of marriage. After 18 years of life as a nun, I still have to lie about myself and who the father is." It is clear that Manda is bothered about a number of things, not the least of which is that Vlasic is asking her to lie, not only to tell a lie but to live a lie as well. She wonders what effect the whole thing will have on her family.

"Tomo," she writes poignantly, "everybody wants to be honest. Even a fool wouldn't like to lie about himself. I nearly went crazy. I'm only one step away from being crazy. . . . I loved you so much and hoped you would come to Zagreb as a protector . . . . Still I have to hide from everyone like a snake."

Living in a foreign country whose language she would never master, but which, at this point, she couldn't speak at all, Manda fastens on Vlasic as her only hope and promises him the fidelity she should have kept to her vows.

"Don't worry, Tomo, I won't reveal your identity to anyone. . .." she swears, and then, as if the very idea gives her second thoughts, she adds, "At least for now."

On January 25, 1977, Manda gave birth to a baby boy and gave him the name Toni.

By late 1984 the second thoughts had become uppermost in her mind. We have no way of knowing now just what precipitated the letter to Bishop Zanic, but the general situation is clear enough. Manda, according to people who knew her, was not the type of person who could move easily to a foreign country and culture. She wasn't very bright, had never mastered the German language and, after seven years of being the housekeeper for a 90-year-old man, most probably was feeling lonely. Perhaps Vlasic and his Franciscan supporters had reneged on some specific provision they had agreed upon concerning the care of Manda and her child. More likely though is the fact that it was becoming clear to Manda that Vlasic was planning on staying a Franciscan and staying in Yugoslavia for good. Beyond that, by 1984 Vlasic was now a world celebrity. Herr Ott mentions having read his interview with Mirjana in German. Vlasic's new-found prominence as the spiritual advisor to the six seers in Medjugorje probably got Manda to thinking about her own relationship with him.

At any rate, once the letter got written, things started happening quickly. Ott found the other letters. Manda found out that Ott now knew and, either on her own or with the help of other Franciscans, moved out. Ott, who was 94 years old at the time and blind, felt betrayed after having taken in the two of them during what was a difficult period for them. He had also become in his own mind a grandfather to the child. As a result, Ott went public after a fashion with the letters. He published excerpts in a long rambling account of the affair in the newsletter of the student help organization he had founded in 1946. More importantly he sent copies to Cardinal Ratzinger, whom he had known from his days as ordinary in Munich. Ratzinger then relayed the material to Zanic, who confronted Vlasic in the presence of his

Franciscan superior. According to Zanic, Vlasic never denied that he was the father.

By now there were enough uncanny parallels between Vlasic and his contemporaries to create a sort of pyscho-sexual trajectory of the times. Like Denis Nolan, Tomislav Vlasic and Philip Pavich joined the charismatics either on the rebound from sexual sin or found the libidinous atmosphere of the prayer groups an inducement to sexual sin. In the instance of Nolan who joined the People of Praise community, it was a search for order in a disordered life of the same sort that led others of his generation to join cults like the Moonies, which sprouted in the fetid atmosphere after the sexual revolution like mushrooms after the rain. The charismatic movement was an expression of those disordered desires, being exploited after the fact, after repentance, but not after sufficient penance, and so as a result the same demons came back in even more dramatic form. Pavich escaped once again unscathed, but many did not. Enthusiasm reigned for a while as the dominant form of psychological compensation for ex-debauchees trying to make religious sense out of their lives, but then, as it always does, the enthusiasm faded, and people drifted off into other things, half conscious that the thrill was gone, and the crisis of faith got reported in articles in numerous charismatic publications, like *New Covenant* magazine.

The crisis hit the charismatic movement in the late '70s and early '80s. Adrian Reimers, writing in the February 1983 issue of *New Covenant*, the organ of the Charismatic Renewal in the United States, tells of how "for three years from 1979 through 1981, attendance at the Notre Dame conferences fell below 10,000. Some leaders began to wonder whether the Catholic Charismatic Renewal had peaked. . . . At the 1979 and 1980 conferences we saw no works of power, and we heard little prophecy." Reimers concluded his article by claiming that fellow charismatics were experiencing, not the demise of the movement, but rather a temporary lull. "I believe," he concluded, "that in 1981, when those 9,000 people agreed to embrace the cross, the Lord began a new work in the Charismatic Renewal. . . . It is my personal conviction that this movement has not peaked but that we are now seeing a new flowering of it." (For a later and more sober assessment, one should consult Reimers' subsequent article in *Fidelity* "Covenant Community: A Failed Promise," May 1986, pp. 30-41, which describes his subsequent expulsion from the People of Praise.) Even the perennially upbeat Ranaghan wrote an article, also in *New Covenant* (April 1980), entitled, "Has the Charismatic Renewal Peaked?" in which he broaches the question, only to reassure us that "reports that the Charismatic Renewal has peaked are exaggerated."

The leadership in the Charismatic Renewal would have done

better to read Msgr. Ronald Knox, who describes the natural trajectory of enthusiasm in his book in better prose: "Enthusiasm," he wrote in the early '50s, "does not maintain itself at fever heat; dance as you will, flap your hands as you will, you cannot conjure up the old days when people rolled on the floor in agonies of convincement and talked in strange sounds which might for all they knew be the language of the Hotmatots."

After a while, the articles on the crisis began to sound like so much whistling in the dark. Pro forma denials were not going to make the problem go away. One of the frankest treatments of the problem appeared in book form in 1981—the same year that the alleged apparitions in Medjugorje began. The book was *The Spirit and the Bride Say "Come!"* written by Revs. George Kosicki and Gerald Farrell. (One of the fascinating connections in the whole story is that Sister Briege McKenna, who was familiar with the arguments in the Kosicki book, prayed over an obviously troubled Father Tomislav Vlasic at the Charismatic leaders' conference in Rome in May 1981, one month before the apparitions began. McKenna told Vlasic that God would send him His mother.)

In their book, Kosicki and Farrell put their finger on one of the sore spots that had been dividing the charismatic movement, namely, the issue of "ecumenical sensitivity." Kosicki and Farrell felt that that sensitivity had degenerated into something perilously close to nondenominationalism. The charismatics had gotten their spiritual gifts from a Protestant minister and saw themselves as building bridges between the denominations. In such an atmosphere, reference to Mary or the rosary was seen as retrograde. As a result, all mention of Mary in the People of Praise was, according to Nolan's wife and other witnesses, discouraged. Kosicki and Farrell, who had been reading Father Stefano Gobbi's private revelations as collected in a book later censured by the Vatican, *Our Lady Speaks to Her Beloved Priests,* were struck by their apocalyptic tone and came to the conclusion that the Charismatic Renewal could only be saved by incorporating into itself this sort of Marian prophecy.

"It was our conviction," they wrote, "that Mary is to provide the new wisdom and new power that we do not yet have in order to understand the Lord and to accomplish his works." They then go on to explain "how we came to this answer ourselves. . . . The most influential factor in our coming to this answer was the acceptance of the message of the Marian Movement of Priests as a prophetic word to the Church in our time . . . ."

One reads *The Spirit and the Bride Say "Come!"* with mixed feelings, perhaps in the spirit of a good news/bad news joke. On the one hand, their indictment of the Charismatic Movement's truncation of the fullness of the Catholic faith and the simultaneous slide into nondenominationalism is compelling. On the other hand, the old, disconcerting thirst for signs and wonders still prevails. One gets the sense that the reason the movement has peaked is that it is no longer providing high voltage portents and messages of the apocalyptic variety the two priests now find in the writings of Father Gobbi. In addition to meditating on Father Gobbi, the two priests have also meditated on the message of Fatima and the promises the Virgin gave there. Given such ingredients, the final mixture takes on a decidedly apocalyptic tone, one which the charismatics were bound to find more bracing than the humdrum nondenominationalism that, in the name of ecumenical sensitivity, had come to dominate their prophesying as of late.

"We believe," Kosicki and Farrell wrote, "that the promise of our Lady concerning the final triumph of her Immaculate Heart, the conversion of Russia and the ensuing world peace is soon to be fulfilled. . . . Those who are spiritually attuned to the needs of our time agree that only a sovereign act of God can meet our present needs, an outpouring of the Spirit such as occurred at Guadaloupe."

Kosicki and Farrell, who claimed that "it can happen that some who pray the Rosary at this depth find that they shift unconsciously into the prayer of tongues," were convinced that the Charismatic Movement that had peaked was to be the prelude for an even larger movement on the scale of what happened in Mexico during the 16th century. This new movement would integrate Mary and the Holy Spirit and bring about the end of the modern age as was prophesied at Fatima. The conjunction of what up to then had been separate pieties and separate movements in the Church had an intoxicating effect on the two priests. It will be nothing more than the "dawning of a new age."

"Mary and the Holy Spirit working together," write Kosicki and Farrell, adopting the vatic tone themselves, "will provide you with these ingredients to help you hasten the sovereign act that ushers in the reign of Christ. Recall how she raised eight million Aztecs from the pagan practice of human sacrifice to Christianity in less than a decade. You well experience the truth of what the angel told Mary '. . . nothing is impossible with God' (Luke 1:37)." The importation of Mary into the Charismatic Renewal will bring about the "New Pentecost" which Pope John XXIII predicted at the beginning of the Second Vatican Council.

The Kosicki/Farrell book had a profound effect on Denis Nolan. It gave expression to the doubts which he had been having about the Charismatic Movement for quite some time. That the message was not popular with the People of Praise is evident from the fact that Nolan got his copy of *The Spirit and the Bride Say "Come!"* from the trash can of one of the community coordinators.

As with the book itself, one notices in Nolan a similar ambivalence at the time. One sees a new openness toward orthodoxy and the fullness of the Catholic faith after a long spell of spiritual dryness arising from being subjected to the community's version of "ecumenical sensitivity." Mary was to become both symbol and vehicle of a reawakened sense of the Catholic. However, at the same time, the Charismatic hunger for signs and wonders was almost certain to follow devotion to Mary off into one of this troubled world's many reported apparitions. Enthusiasm remained a constant in Nolan's life. However, now it was Marian devotion, specifically the alleged messages of people like Father Gobbi, which was providing the apocalyptic jolt that the People of Praise could no longer generate.

The fact remains, though, that the Charismatic Renewal was the conduit through which Denis Nolan found out about Medjugorje. The charismatics had a worldwide infrastructure, and Nolan was a part of it. Charismatics like Robert Faricy, S.J., Fr. John Bertolucci, and Fr. Michael Scanlon had all published or produced video material on Medjugorje. The University of Steubenville was a center for the specifically Kosickian brand of Charismatic Renewal—i.e., including devotion to Mary—and subsequently became a center for interest in Medjugorje. Video tapes on Medjugorje were shown in the university cafeteria, Sister Isabel Bettwy organized tours, and there is even a picture of the seer Marija Pavlovic wearing a University of Steubenville sweat shirt. In addition, the two most crucial players among the clergy in Medjugorje, Fathers Jozo Zovko and Tomislav Vlasic, were both charismatics and had organized Charismatic prayer groups. Something at Medjugorje spoke deeply to the Charismatic Movement, and Denis Nolan was affected by it. In fact, the former supplanted the latter as the focus of his spiritual life. By 1984 Nolan had become alienated from life in the People of Praise to the point where he had decided to leave. Whether by coincidence or not, this decision also coincided with the beginning of what would be a more and more passionate involvement in and attachment to the happenings at Medjugorje

After making his break with the charismatics, Pavich eventually ended up in Jerusalem where he continued to study the scriptures in Hebrew and functioned as a spiritual guide for the pilgrims who went there. Then one day in 1983 Pavich was handed a book which would change his life again. This was the story of six children living in remote Herzegovina, then a part of Yugoslavia, who claimed that the Blessed Mother had appeared to them. There is probably not a Catholic alive in this century who doesn't know of some apparition story. Either Fatima, occurring in 1917, which in terms of significant political movements if not for its precise date, probably inaugurated the century by focusing the world's eyes on Communism and the threat it posed or Lourdes, which took place in the mountains of Southern France in the mid-19th century. Then there was *The Song of Bernadette*, which a former revolutionary and Jew by the name of Franz Werfel wrote to fulfill a vow to the Blessed Virgin when he got interned in Lourdes on his way to Spain and eventually America during the middle of World War II. Werfel's novel got made into a film in 1941, a film which beat out *Casablanca* for that year's best picture and an academy award, when Philip Pavich was 11 years old.

Since the book Pavich picked up was written by a fellow Croatian and fellow Franciscan (this time it was a genuine "Croatian Franciscan") by the name of Ljudevit Rupcic, Pavich was favorably impressed. Eventually the book got translated into French by scripture scholar Rene Laurentin as *Is The Blessed Virgin Appearing at Medjugorje?* and that became the book that launched the entire Medjugorje phenomenon. Laurentin was to say in 1997 that he personally put a copy of that book into the hands of the pope in 1984, which may account for the mixed signals which have been emanating from the Vatican ever since on Medjugorje. On the one hand, the Church has never approved Medjugorje. The local bishop of Mostar/Duvno denounced it uncategorically as a fraud in 1987 and the Yugoslavian bishops conference followed suit on November 26, 1990, a statement that was "leaked" to the press on January 3, 1991. On the other hand, the Vatican has shown itself incapable of denouncing Medjugorje in anything approaching effective terms. I personally spoke with Cardinal Ratzinger in March of 1991, when he said that the Vatican was going to issue a statement on Medjugorje "soon." But nothing ever appeared. Later Ratzinger was taped at a conference in Austria as saying that the war had interfered with his plans. Whether it did or it didn't, the statement never came out, and perhaps as a result of the lack of clear guidance on the issue, Pavich arrived in Medjugorje to serve as a spiritual director to the dramatically increasing numbers of pilgrims that started arriving with lots of money and psychological and spiritual problems.

In December of 1976, the Vatican had had normalized relations with Yugoslavia for over 10 years, and the results were far from pleasing to the Franciscans of Herzegovina who had been quick to accommodate Tito's demands by joining *Dobri Pastir* and in many respects preferred the status quo ante. As members of the Good Shepherd organization, the rebellious Franciscans could carry on their feud with the local bishop with the tacit backing of the Yugoslav government. Ever since Bishop Cule was released from prison in 1956 the number of diocesan clergy began to rise, and as their numbers rose, so did the pressure on the Franciscans to return the parishes they administered back to the authority of the local bishop. Rome's agreement with Belgrade effectively removed the Franciscans' major support in their battle with Bishop Cule and, since 1970, his coadjutor Bishop Pavao Zanic.

On June 6, 1975 the situation reached a head when Rome issued the decree *Romanus Pontificibus* which gave the Franciscans a year and a day, until June 7, 1976, to hand over the contested parishes to the local bishop. In 1968 Cule had ordered the Franciscans to hand over five parishes, and they reluctantly complied by giving back two. Rather than concede anymore of their spiritual turf to the local bishops, the Franciscans in Herzegovina decided to rebel. Father Leonard Orec justified the defiance of *Romanus Pontificibus* by saying that the Croatians under their care would lose the Roman Catholic faith if their spiritual needs were met by anyone but Franciscans.

The argument seemed unpersuasive to anyone but the Franciscans of Herzegovina, and as a result Rome leveled certain penalties against the province, which lost its provincial and the right to elect a successor, who would now be imposed on them from the central Franciscan authority in Rome. In addition, the Herzegovinian Franciscans lost their votes to elect a new General of the Order. It was a terrible blow to the Herzegovina Franciscans, who had no difficulty outstripping all of the other provinces in Western Europe combined in the number of seminarians they attracted to the order. To add insult to injury, the new measures were a direct result of the Vatican's *Ostpolitik* under Paul VI and Agostino Cardinal Casaroli. First the Franciscans came out on the losing side of World War II and fatally implicated in atrocities and collaboration with the Nazis. Then the anti-Communist crusade gets nowhere as every Krizari insurrection is nipped in the bud by UDBA intelligence. Then Rome pulled out the anti-Communist crusade and invited the Butcher Tito to an audience with the pope. And then as a result of their conniving together and the normalization of relations which followed, the Franciscans lost their government support and were now being forced to relinquish parishes that they had administered for 400 years. The situation looked black; there seemed to be no help on the horizon to succor their rebellion. All they could do was pray to the Gospa and hope for a new pope.

-3-

THE REBIRTH OF THE ANTI-COMMUNIST CRUSADE: 1978-1989

In the early evening of October 16, 1978 Father Andrew Greeley was standing in a huge crowd in the Piazza San Pietro in Rome waiting, along with the rest of the world, to hear who would be the successor to Pope John Paul I, the charming Italian who had occupied the throne of St. Peter for one of the shortest tenures of the almost 2000 years of the papacy. It was almost as if the college of cardinals had made a mistake earlier that summer by choosing the wrong man for the job, a mistake which got rectified quickly enough by the Almighty but which had nevertheless cost the hapless John Paul I his life.

Father Greeley was probably at the apogee of his career as a Catholic social scientist at the time. His favorite message was that Rome had erred in 1968 when it declared the use of contraceptives immoral. Greeley had tried to parley this slim academic accomplishment, bolstered of course by any number of opinion polls which he conducted, into a position at the sociology department at Notre Dame. Unfortunately for his academic aspirations, Father Greeley arrived on the social science scene about ten years too late. John D. Rockefeller had failed to change Pope Paul VI's mind; the $500,000 grant which Ford had given to Don Barrett had gained them one additional vote on the papal birth control commission, which did vote to change the Church's teaching, but the pope had ignored his own commission, and by the late '70s, Barrett was a supporter of Natural Family Planning, the method approved by the Church. There seemed to be little reason to sink money into an effort to close the barn door after the contraceptive horse had long since escaped. When Greeley interviewed for the position, his arrogance so alienated the sociology department that they failed to make him an offer.

Greeley then went on to make a name for himself as the writer of steamy novels in Catholic settings, much to the dismay of clergy and Catholic laity across the country. In the interim, between peaking as sociologist manqué and taking off as best-selling peddler of soft-core Catholic smut, Greeley had the distinction of hatching the most famous American Catholic conspiracy of the late 20th century, when he conspired, without much success, to have then Archbishop Joseph Bernardin of Cincinnati elected pope. The plot blew up in Greeley's face and very nearly ended Bernardin's steady rise in the American hierarchy when an enterprising journalist went to Notre Dame and listened to Greeley's megalomaniac musings on tape and subsequently published an article on them in the *Chicago Reader.*

Greeley's prowess as a pundit and handicapper of papal elections was little better than his acumen as a social scientist, a fact which became apparent when Cardinal Felici appeared on the balcony of the papal apartments at St. Peter's Basilica and announced *"Habemus papam,"* followed by a string of syllables no one could understand. "Voyteewah," he seemed to be saying, a name that was on no one's short list of *papabili*, least of all Andrew Greeley's. Then suddenly it dawned on the crowd that the College of Cardinals has just elected the first non-Italian pope in over 400 years. Not only that, but this pope, Karol Wojtyla, cardinal archbishop of Krakow, came from Poland, a communist country. If Greeley thought that the new pope's relative youth and non-Italian heritage meant sympathy with Greeley's views on contraception, he was mistaken. "It was Wojtyla's arguments," Carl Bernstein wrote in his biography of Pope John Paul II, "and materials that proved decisive in helping the pope decide what his heart had been telling him all along: that the ban on artificial contraception must be upheld. After studying Wojtyla's submissions, [Paul VI] went ahead with his decision and issued *Humanae Vitae* in mid-July 1968." The election of John Paul II was deceptive in other ways as well. It seemed like a dramatic extension of Paul VI's *Ostpolitik*, but it wasn't that at all. In fact, the election of Pope John Paul II meant the end of the church's policy of détente and the rebirth of the anti-Communist crusade, the real anti-Communist crusade this time, the one that would do the job.

No one, of course, could have foreseen such a dramatic turn of events at the time, primarily because, as of the late '70s, Communism seemed to be on the rise. And, of course, it was. From the fall of Portugal in 1974 (and the subsequent loss of their colonies Angola and Mozambique in Africa) to the invasion of Afghanistan in 1979, to the fall of Samoza's regime in Nicaragua in the same year, Communism was making its most impressive geopolitical gains since the defeat of Germany in 1945. In addition to that, Soviet-sponsored terrorist groups like the Baader/Meinhoff gang in Germany and the *Brigatti Rossi* in Italy, who had just murdered Italian Prime Minister Aldo Moro, were wreaking havoc throughout Europe. Leader of the Free World, Jimmy Carter, the man Helmut Schmidt described as knowing everything and understanding nothing, seemed befuddled by the course of events and had taken to consulting his daughter Amy on foreign policy initiatives. "Nuclear Proliferation," was what Amy said when Jimmy asked her what he should concentrate on next, and bumper stickers started appearing at places like Notre Dame, which were normally sympathetic to Democratic presidents, asking "What now, Amy?"

On June 21, 1980, Jimmy Carter, who preferred morality of the Wilsonian sort over *Realpolitik* of the sort favored by Bismarck, met with the new pope along with his security advisor, the Polish émigré Zbigniew Brzezinski. Brzezinski came away from the meeting feeling that Woytyla should have been elected president and Carter elected pope. Brzezinski would soon get his wish—sort of. In 1979, the Labor Government was voted out in Great Britain and a pugnacious, anti-Communist Margaret Thatcher took its place. One year later, something similar happened in the United States when Ronald Reagan, former actor, former governor of California, notorious Cold Warrior, and the first prolife president since the Supreme Court handed down *Roe v. Wade* in 1973, moved into the White House. The stars seemed aligned for momentous change.

Within days of taking office in early 1981, Ronald Reagan dispatched CIA director William Casey on a confidential visit to the pope. Casey, a devout Catholic who attended daily Mass and had statues of the Virgin Mary throughout his house, brought with him a photograph taken by one of America's spy satellites of the open-air Mass which the pope had celebrated in his triumphal visit to Poland on June 2, 1979. When Pope John Paul II arrived in Poland, more than a million Poles showed up to greet him leaving the Communist authorities in his country visibly shaken. Now there was a man in the White House who felt that détente was the diplomatic version of the leisure suit and wanted to make the first move in what was to be one of the most significant meetings of the minds in this century.

Just what got said during this and subsequent meetings is a matter of dispute. Carl Bernstein claims that a "Holy Alliance" got forged uniting the Reagan administration and the Wojtyla papacy in a concerted effort to destabilize Communism in Eastern Europe. Jonathan Kwitny disputes the Holy Alliance thesis in his biography of Pope John Paul II, *Man of the Century*, claiming that the pope did it alone. Either way some radical change was afoot in Eastern Europe

Yugoslavia was about to do the same thing; however, the situation in Yugoslavia was complicated by the fact that the Franciscans, who would mount the Croatian equivalent to Solidarity, were simultaneously rebelling against a godless government and legitimate Church authority in the person of both the diocesan bishop, Pavao Zanic, and John Vaughn, the Franciscan General. The pope, as a result, was faced with the unenviable choice of quashing a nascent anti-Communist, Marian, Slavic Catholic grassroots movement or maintaining discipline in the Church.

In his analysis of the false apparitions in Marpingen David Blackbourne makes a number of comments on Pius IX and Marian devotion which are equally applicable to John Paul II:

> The pontificate of Pius IX showed that the church could successfully channel powerful currents of popular piety; that it could take up the fears and aspirations unleashed by the apparitions of the Virgin and give them institutional shape. In a period bounded by the anticlerical challenge of 1848 and the European wide church state struggles of the 1870s, Marian apparitions were a symptom of popular Catholic sentiment; they were also a potentially powerful weapon in the hands of the church. In these years the church domesticated a potentially anarchic wave of popular sentiment (*Marpingen*, p. 37).

Marian piety as a mass movement was always associated with a rejection of the French Revolution and the Enlightenment in the 19th century and, since Fatima, with a prophetic rejection of the Communist Revolution as well. However, as Blackbourne's use of the word "domesticated" implies, this free-floating, grass-roots Marian piety invariably posed a significant danger to Church authority as well. One might call it the Magnificat syndrome. Mary was the weak female who "deposed the mighty from their thrones." It was an image that could threaten Bismarck in Germany and Communism in Poland, but it could also threaten the authority of the local bishop in Mostar, especially if the apparitions were not genuine. It could also bring about a very different political consequences in two countries as different as Poland and Yugoslavia, a fact which Richard West noticed. West remembers well the euphoria that swept Poland when Wojtyla was elected pope; even the ostensibly Communist army was in tears as they listened on their transistor radios to the news that one of their fellow Poles has just been elected pope.

But West was troubled by the thought of the same thing happening in Yugoslavian because the situation there was so different.

Poland was 90 percent Catholic, and the Catholic population could provide a unified opposition to Communism, but Catholic Croatians constituted only a third of the population of Yugoslavia, a country which was deeply divided not only on political lines but on religious and ethnic lines as well. Including the Serbs in anti-Communist solidarity alongside the Slovenes and the Croatians in the list of captive nations the pope mentioned in his history-making sermon in June of 1979 seems a bit naive with hindsight. Including the Serbs in the anti-Communist crusade was wishful thinking, not because the Serbs were congenitally closer to Communism, but because they were on the other side of the east/west divide which antedated Communism by about a millennium. Communist internationalism hoped to erase the conflict, but as Franjo Tudjman, future president of Croatia and a former Communist, proved convincingly in a book which appeared in the same year that the apparitions began in Medjugorje, it only exacerbated it. Yugoslavia was different than Poland. Although West felt joy at seeing the workers kneeling in prayer in Gdansk,

> in Yugoslavia I had misgivings. In Poland the Roman Catholic Church represents almost the whole nation. In many respects it actually is the nation, having survived when there was no Polish state. Moreover the Polish Catholic Church has not tried to exterminate the Jews, Gypsies or Orthodox Christians. In Yugoslavia, however, the Croatian Catholic Church identifies with only a third of the nation, and it has blood on its hands (p. 210-11).

Implicit in Blackbourne's praise of Pius IX's ability to "domesticate" Marian piety is the possibility that it might elude another pope's grasp and become a rival to Church authority and fuel an anti-hierarchical movement like the Lollards in medieval England. The danger to Church authority that Marian apparitions posed should have been obvious to anyone who ever went on a pilgrimage. In 1988 on a plane back from Yugoslavia, I asked one lady from California what she would do if the Church disapproved of Medjugorje. The question provoked a diatribe against Archbishop Mahony of Los Angeles, presumably her local bishop.

"I'm going to pray for the Church," she said. "How many bishops have told me what I've learned here? They've turned the Bible around. They don't give us any consolation. They gave us dancing and singing and having skits instead of having devotion and adoration. After what they've done to the Mass, you can't trust them anymore. The Holy Spirit fills me with joy at Medjugorje."

"If the pope tells me it isn't true," the lady concluded, "then I'll

places.

In putting the emphasis on "fruits," as opposed to the simple truth of the matter, Ratzinger put a major weapon in the hands of Medjugorje's defenders, one which they would use from then on as the main weapon in their arsenal against the bishop. Bishop Ratko Peric, Zanic's successor as ordinary of Mostar, got so tired of hearing the "fruits" argument that he ran an article in his diocesan newspaper in 1997 entitled, "What kinds of Fruits Are These?" The article mentioned the fact that more than 40 Franciscans were celebrating the sacraments illicitly without faculties, that numerous religious communities had set up shop in Medjugorje without his permission, and that the Franciscans had even walled up the Church in Capljina to prevent the priest sent by the bishop from taking up residence in the parish as the "fruits" which never got mentioned in the original context established by Cardinal Ratzinger.

Father Jean Galot made a similar point in the definitive article on the subject, which appeared in the mid-'80s in *Civilta Cattolica:*. "It is not sufficient," he writes, "to use the spiritual fruits alone as the criterion to judge the authenticity of the apparitions. Cases are known in which conversions have been substantiated in which the pretended apparitions have later been rejected by the authority of the Church as without serious foundation."

Galot then goes on to list the criteria the Church uses in ascertaining whether an alleged apparition is genuine or not.

The frequency of an apparition, for example, is an argument against its authenticity because

> it would arouse the image of a Christian religion that was nourished much more by actual visions than by the revelation brought in the past by the coming of Christ on earth. Piety would develop more as a function of constant apparitions than by the leap of faith, or again faith would tend to become a faith in the truth of the apparitions and would be founded on the testimony of those who see.

According to Galot, one should also be skeptical if the messages entail "threats of revenge" if the message is not accepted or if the seers spread abroad a spirit of "denigration or revolt or disobedience to the authority of the Church." In addition, one should look for "progressive psychological formation . . . if the words of the apparition have not been suggested in a human manner by the surroundings, by preceding conversations, or by the hymns or songs of the crowd or by the seers themselves."

"Evidence of human manipulation" would also be a sign of inauthenticity, especially "when the beneficiaries of the apparitions determine themselves the place, the date and the frequency of the program of the apparitions."

Popular piety, however, is not driven by theological distinctions, no matter how relevant they may be, and the Church, more often than not, would rather err on the side of tolerance in matters like this, hoping not to quench the Holy Spirit, and hoping that it is indeed the Holy Spirit or the Blessed Mother who is speaking and not some diabolical counterfeit. Galot wrote his article in 1986 with Medjugorje specifically in mind. In 1980 in the early days of the pontificate of John Paul II, the dangers associated with Marian devotion seemed small and the benefits irresistibly large, especially in Poland, where Marian devotion was fast becoming the driving force behind the anti-Communist crusade there.

Tito died in May 1980. Three months later, in mid-August, Lech Walesa, the once and future electrician from the Lenin Shipyard in Gdansk, was in the midst of a strike that was making world news. Here, in the worker's paradise, Walesa had made the Black Madonna the unofficial symbol of Solidarity, the new non-government worker's union. "This," said one observer, "is a lesson for the whole world. Look at the contradiction: The workers are against communism." The workers, the world also noticed, were on their knees praying the rosary in front of pictures of the Polish pope and Black Madonna, which had been hung on the gates of the shipyard. In addition to the public recitation of the Rosary, the strikers were also flocking to outdoor confessionals, another aspect of Polish Catholicism which would become associated with Medjugorje, even though the necessity for outdoor confessionals outside a church was not apparent as it was outside a shipyard. Outdoor confessionals made for great political theater in Medjugorje and were a prominent feature of the early publicity shots emanating from there. From early on, Medjugorje was the Croatian version of Solidarity in Gdansk, a spectacle which was electrifying the world in 1980 with the possibility of the fall of Communism.

Slavic, grass-roots Marian devotion fueled both movements. On the same day Walesa was leading the strike in Gdansk, the Polish primate celebrated Mass in honor of Pilsudski's victory over the Russians sixty years before. Again it was the Virgin Mary to whom this victory over Communism was attributed. Frank Shakespeare, the Reagan administration's ambassador to the Holy See in the mid-'80s, remembers Walesa as "a man of unquestioned *gravitas*."

"When he walked into the room," Shakespeare continued, "you felt that all of Poland walked into the room. On his lapel he wore the

via and the rest of the world and as YUgoslavia's hunger for tourist-fueled hard currency increased, it became increasingly easy to travel back and forth from her new home in California to see her relatives in Split.

In July of 1981 Yelka was sitting in her sister's apartment watching television when they were visited by a woman who was visibly upset and wanted to talk, something which necessitated speaking *sotto voce*. Yugoslavia was still a police state at the time, and Yelka Tolaitch and her relatives were still under suspicion because of their ethnic, which is to say, religious, affiliation. The Gospa, Yelka was told, was in Herzegovina. As if to make her point the informant handed Yelka a Communist magazine which ridiculed the six seers and announced further that the local police were preventing pilgrims from coming to the hillside. The condemnation of the Communists was the only endorsement Yelka Tolaitch needed.

"This must be true," Yelka said. "How can I get there?" Yelka' conversion was instantaneous, and judging from the crowds that started converging on this hitherto unknown village in Herzegovina, typical as well. The announcement of the six children fell into the collective mind of Croatian Yugoslavia at the time like a crystal into a hypersaturated solution. Something jelled because the medium that received it was ready for change. Croatia was especially sick of Communism because it had so much contact with the West, and it knew that things could be better and that they didn't have to be the way they were. "The Communists promised paradise," Frank Shakespeare said, with the benefit of years of hindsight, "and then they didn't deliver. It made for an unstable situation."

Like so many people after her, Yelka Tolaitch became obsessed with going to Medjugorje. Her husband Joe was in France buying a Peugeot. When he arrived between 10 and 11 that night, he didn't even get a chance to shut the engine off. Yelka informed him that "we have to go to Medjugorje. The Blessed Mother is appearing there." When Joe and Yelka and their two boys finally arrived in Metkovic, they found that their relatives had already been to Medjugorje. The Tolaitches drove there the next day, over unpaved roads after they passed through Ljubjuski, through the blazing heat which afflicts that area in the summer. Yelka, who prided herself on coming from a sophisticated Roman city like Split, saw nothing but dirt and berries and ferocious thorn bushes six feet high on either side of the narrow unpaved road. Not knowing what to expect, she arrived at the foot of the apparition hill east of Bijakovici wearing high heels and a skirt and found people praying. Undeterred by the climb she finally arrived at the site of the apparitions and found there a big hole filled with money—real money, not Yugoslavian dinars but German Deutsch marks— and people milling around. The hole full of money was a symbol of what Medjugorje would become, as people from all over the world would gather there and throw millions of dollars of hard currency into what would soon become a bottomless pit of greed and deception.

Tony Tolaitch, Yelka's son, was ten at the time. He remembers Jakov, also his age, being mobbed by a group of bad-smelling toothless old women in black. Eventually, the Tolaitches went to Mass at St. James Church, about three kilometers north of Bijakovici, where the apparitions took place. The most significant event in the early history of the apparitions had already taken place by the time the Tolaitches arrived at St. James for Mass. The seers had been brought into the church and were now under the control of the Franciscans.

"I'll never forget Jakov kneeling behind the altar," Tony recounted later. "His head looked like a football sitting on top of it."

It wasn't the only unforgettable event of the day. Before Mass began, the Tolaitches looked at the altar and were stunned to see the Grb, the checkerboard Croatian coat of arms which had been banned as the symbol of the Ustasha state, on both candles on the altar.

"I remember that distinctly," Tony said. "It was illegal without a star."

Father Jozo Zovko, the pastor of the parish and the man responsible for its liturgies, had decided to push the envelope. If Communism was going to fall, it might fall faster with a little push from him. If the Poles could pray the rosary to the Black Madonna in front of the Lenin shipyard in Gdansk, then why couldn't he put the Grb on candles on the altar? That he saw some sort of equivalence between the two events boded ill for Yugoslavia, which would soon pass off the stage of history, but equally ill for the people who were to suffer and die as part of its passing.

but things had not been going well for him. Medjugorje was considered a good parish at the time, but Zovko had to face the fact that most of what he had undertaken there had been a failure. He had worked intensively with the young people of the parish, but found that the notion of prayer and penance was too much for them. During his stay with the nuns he asked them to pray that God would get this otherwise sleepy parish moving again.

The battle between Bishop Zanic and the Franciscans, now known as the Case of Herzegovina, was heating up every bit as much as the sleepy hamlet of Medjugorje seemed to be sinking deeper into spiritual lethargy. On September 14, 1980, Bishop Zanic created the cathedral parish in the city of Mostar, by taking away three-fourths of the parishes then administered by the Franciscans. A number of Franciscans from the Province of the Assumption disagreed violently with the bishop's action, and as a result two of the most vocal, Ivan Prusina and Ivica Vego were suspended *a divinis* on December 11, 1980. In April of 1981, two months before the apparitions began, Prusina and Vego, were ordered to leave Mostar. Craig implies a causal connection between the suspensions and the apparitions by describing the incident in the following way. "An extremely lucky accident saved them. Two weeks later, the apparitions in Medjugorje began—in a Franciscan parish in the diocese of Mostar. 'How very convenient for them,' wryly remarked an American Franciscan visiting Rome." On June 22, two days before the first apparition, Father Honororius Pontoglio, a special delegate from the Holy See threatened Prusina and Vego with expulsion from the order if they did not cease their ministry and leave Mostar.

During his absence, Zovko tried to contact his assistant pastor at Medjugorje, Father Zrinko Cuvalo, but in the course of a recent thunderstorm, both the local disco and the post office had been struck by lightning and set on fire, cutting the parish off from telephone contact with the outside world. Father Zovko then left the retreat and took a plane from Zagreb to Split. He then took a bus from Split to Imotski, then a taxi to visit his former parish at Posusje. It was there that he learned about the fire at Medjugorje, but he still remained ignorant of the apparitions and the crowds that were coming in increasing numbers to see the children.

On the following afternoon, Saturday, June 27, Zovko visited his mother in the hospital in Mostar and then went by car to Citluk, where he saw a woman from Bijakovici, bound hand and foot, who told him for the first time about the apparitions. He didn't take her seriously, however, assuming that she was mentally unstable. However, when he finally arrived at the parish, he found out that what she had been saying was true. Six children were claiming to have seen the

Gospa, and crowds from the entire area were pouring into Medjugorje parish. When Zovko arrived at the rectory, he found the space in front of the church full of cars and a huge crowd. Father Zovko was taken by surprise. According to Ljubic's account:

> Father Zovko didn't know any of them [the visionaries] personally. Only Vicka had been one of his pupils in religious instruction, but he didn't know her all that well. The families of the six young people were likewise unknown to him. It is worth noting that none of the visionaries took part in the charismatic prayer groups (*de groupes de renouveau charismatique*), neither those of Father Zovko, who directed such groups, nor those of anyone else. This demolishes the allegations of those who pretend that the apparitions were the fruit of such a practice.

Ljubic, who is obviously aware of the charges that Zovko was involved in manipulating the seers by using the same techniques that he had used on Marijan Pehar in Zagreb, airs the charges only to dismiss them, but one comes away from the exchange with the impression that he doth protest too much. Ljubic's denial involves the writer in a significant admission: that Zovko was in fact leading such groups and that he led them at Medjugorje.

In an earlier edition of the same book, Ljubic makes a similar disclaimer:

> None of the seers had ever assisted at any charismatic-meditation meetings (*n'avait jamais assistè á l'une ou l'autre réunion méditative-charismatique*), neither at those of the pastor [Zovko] nor any other priest. Therefore, certain assertions according to which the apparitions of the Gospa, instead of being authentic, were rather the result of the work accomplished by Father Zovko in this area are without foundation.

The atmosphere surrounding Medjugorje had been intensified significantly by the fact that six weeks earlier, on May 13, 1981, the anniversary of the apparitions at Fatima, the pope had been seriously wounded. He later attributed the fact that he did not die to the intercession of the Blessed Virgin, who had saved him, he came to believe, for some greater task. Since Our Lady of Fatima had announced in 1917 that "Russia would spread her errors," and that the pope would have much to suffer, it didn't take a genius to infer that the task at hand was the destruction of Communism. It has always been assumed that the

KGB was behind the assassination attempt, but an attempt to link the Bulgarian secret service to Ali Agca, the assailant, failed to convince an Italian court, and the ultimate perpetrator of the assassination attempt remains a mystery. The KGB was, however, very concerned with the effect the pope was having on Poland and kept urging General Wojiciech Jaruszelski to declare martial law, citing the example of Yugoslavia, which had done just that after an Albanian uprising in Kosovo, with no international repercussions. If anything, the fact that the assassination attempt occurred on May 13, with all of the mystical implications that involved, confirmed Pope John Paul II in his Marian devotion—dangerously so, some would say. One year after the assassination attempt, the pope went to Fatima to thank the Blessed Virgin for saving his life, and was almost assassinated again, this time by a sword-wielding traditionalist priest. Mary was becoming linked more closely with the struggle against Communism in the pope's mind. Bernstein accused him of "a systematic aggrandizement of the cult of Mary." President Reagan, meanwhile, had had his own brush with death. Like the pope he had been spared, and like the pope he began to wonder about the mystical significance of the fact that he had not died. Like the pope he began to feel that his life had been spared for a reason, and that that reason had something to do with the rise and fall of Communism, prophesied at Fatima in 1917. Four days after the assassination attempt on the pope in Rome, a convalescing Ronald Reagan arrived at Notre Dame University to make an emotionally charged appearance with Pat O'Brien, his co-star in *Knute Rockne: All American,* the '40s film based on Notre Dame's legendary football coach. Once again Our Lady seemed like an inevitable accomplice to dramatically unfolding contemporary events.

The Blessed Mother was on other people's minds as well. While attending a charismatic leaders' conference in Rome during the same month that the pope was shot, Father Tomislav Vlasic asked to be prayed over. Vlasic was a chaplain in Capljina at the time, about five kilometers away from Medjugorje, and he was obviously troubled about something. No one in Rome knew about his illegitimate child, but they could tell that some serious soul-searching was going on about his vocation, and so it was with a measure of relief we can imagine him listening to Father Emile Tardiff, O.P., announce in one of the prophecy sessions that invariably accompanied charismatic prayer meetings. "Do not fear, I am sending you my Mother." Six weeks later the Gospa had arrived in Medjugorje. Marija Pavlovic, one of the visionaries, once said that Father Vlasic knew about the apparitions one month in advance even though he did not know the place. It may have been Marija's reading of the prophecy incident, but it was coincidences like this that eventually led Bishop Zanic to conclude that

Vlasic was the mastermind behind the apparitions and that the seers were nothing more than his puppets.

Vlasic had gone to the charismatic leaders' conference in Rome, hoping for some resolution to his troubles not only with the local bishop but, most probably, to his personal troubles as well. The birth of his son in January of 1977 had precipitated a crisis in his life. Now, as he would write to Manda, his vocation was in doubt. Now he was torn between two sets of responsibilities with no possibility of finding a satisfactory resolution. If he remained faithful to his vows as a Franciscan, then he was turning his back on his child and the woman who had borne him. If on the other hand, he left the order, as Manda seems to have anticipated, then he was turning his back on solemn promises he had made to God. As with most people in situations like this, he couldn't bring himself to choose either alternative. He was just drifting with the current.

As a charismatic, he must have gone to the Rome conference with some sense of expectation. Then came the prophecy; then on June 24, the apparitions. For someone with the charismatic mindset, it must have seemed like a sure sign from God. Vlasic, who has the reputation for being a very persuasive guy, rushed to Medjugorje on June 29 and, we must assume, had lengthy discussions of the situation with Zovko. We have no record of these conversations; however, his psychological state would provide compelling motivation to accept the apparitions as genuine. In subsequent letters to Manda, Vlasic makes clear that the Gospa saved his vocation to the priesthood.

One can imagine the effect that this would have had on Manda. As soon as Vlasic's vocation to the priesthood is saved, he is lost to her as a potential husband and father of their child. Marijan Pehar, who knew both Manda and Vlasic in Zagreb, speculates that Manda's letter to the bishop was an attempt on her part to get him kicked out of the priesthood so that he would follow her to Germany and marry her. Whatever the reason, it didn't work. By 1984 Vlasic had resolved the issue through his attachment to the alleged apparitions. When confronted by Bishop Zanic, Vlasic did not deny being the father of the child, but by 1985 when the confrontation took place, he had already become a world-famous religious figure. He was, in a sense, beyond the bishop's power. Using the world press and the world-wide network of the Charismatic Renewal as a power base, he now effectively out-ranked the bishop in terms of de facto power. By turning the bishop's legitimate accusation into a charge of calumny, he and Laurentin had effectively checked the bishop's attempt to discredit the apparitions. Now, with millions believing that he had the Gospa on his side, he could do pretty much what he wanted to.

As of June 27, two days before Vlasic arrived in Medjugorje

with the prophecy from Rome, Jozo Zovko was pretty much in the dark. Judging from the first few tapes of his interviews with the seers, the apparitions took Zovko by surprise. However, his response to the seers is more surprising still. He begins with a certain amount of skepticism, and before long, he has the seers contradicting themselves and making what are obviously absurd statements. Often they simply can't answer his questions. For example, on the afternoon of June 30, Ivanka says that the lady doctor "gave us instructions to ask the Gospa if she could touch her. And we asked her and the Gospa said that there would always be incredulous Judases who come to her."

The statement takes Zovko aback.

"Judas wasn't incredulous," he replied.

"Incredulous," said Ivanka. "That means a traitor."

"A traitor is only an unbeliever if he hasn't received the gift of faith. Thomas was incredulous. How did you come to say Judas? Perhaps because he betrayed Jesus?"

"She said it. I didn't."

"Who?" Zovko asked.

"The Gospa," Ivanka responded.

"Who did she tell that to?"

"To us. Mirjana asked the question."

"I see. And who told you that?"

"I heard it. We all heard it."

"Why should it be Judas, since he had faith like the rest of the apostles?"

"What do I know? When the lady doctor touched her, the Gospa left. She also said she saw a cloud when the Gospa departed."

Ivanka is obviously becoming more defensive during the interview until finally she feels compelled to change the subject by adding the supernatural touch of the lady doctor seeing the cloud. (It is significant to note here also that Laurentin changed Judas to Thomas in his so-called definitive edition of the messages. Apparently he, like Zovko, considers it significant, as well as damaging to their case.) A little later Zovko warns her that "it's a terrible thing to play with religion." Zovko is clearly becoming more skeptical and, just as clearly, running out of patience with the children.

However, at the same time this is happening, one starts to notice something else in Zovko's attitude. In effect, instead of calling the whole thing off, he decides to take it over. He starts insisting over and over again that the children should ask the Virgin to appear in the church, a request they fulfill with some strange results.

The most crucial interview takes place at 6:30 p.m. on June 30. The date is significant. The alleged apparitions have been going on now for six days. Zovko has had a chance to talk things over with

Tomislav Vlasic, who has returned from Rome with his dramatic prophecy. With each day the crowds have gotten larger and, what is more important, more impatient. They want to know what is going on and when they are going to see something too. There are rumors circulating that the kids have been taking drugs. The pressure is mounting on everyone; it is becoming close to unbearable. The people think that the children are making fun of them. Vicka can't sleep at night; she spends the whole night calling out to the Virgin to leave a sign, which at this juncture seems to be the only thing that will get the kids off the hook.

Zovko himself is wondering how long the whole thing is going to last. In an interview with Mirjana, who is obviously the leader of the whole group, on the afternoon of the same day, he asks, "How many more days do you think you're going to see her?" to which he receives the peculiar reply, "Something just doesn't stop telling me: two or three more days." By that evening that something has set a much more definite date.

"I asked her," Mirjana says, "how many more days she would appear to us, exactly how many more days, and she said, 'Three more days.'"

"Three more," Zovko responds.

"Three more days. That means up until Friday. Then we asked her if she was mad at us because we left Podbrdo to come here, to the other place. She said that she wasn't mad."

"Where is that?"

"We left a mark there where we were."

"Was it by the road?"

"Yes. Then we asked her if she would be mad if we didn't go to Podbrdo anymore, but went instead to the church. She was rather undecided when we asked this question. It was as if she didn't like the idea, but finally she said that she wasn't mad."

Evidently the Blessed Mother was not only undecided; she was also wrong about how much longer the apparitions were going to last. Or perhaps she changed her mind, or perhaps the seers are not now telling us the truth. The story lacks consistency. But then again, maybe it doesn't. The psychologically consistent part is that the children have created an uproar beyond their wildest imaginings, and now, as the pressure mounts and the mood of the crowd turns ugly, they would like to call the whole thing off. So they announce that the Virgin says it will be over in three days. That much is certainly psychologically plausible.

One of the most disconcerting things about the 6:30 p.m. tape of June 30 is the laughter of the seers.

"It interests me to know," Zovko asks the visionaries, "if it isn't disagreeable for you to have these two girls [Ljubica Vasilj-Gluvic and Mica Ivankovic] with you."

"Not at all," they respond and then burst out laughing.

Then Mica says, "I forgot to ask them to ask the Blessed Virgin Mary if she was mad at us too."

Whereupon the children burst out laughing again. Zovko is hard pressed to get them to be serious.

"When did you agree to leave the village?" he asks.

"It was three o'clock."

"I find this very interesting. We've got a huge crowd of people here and you chose another hill. And now you're making fun of the people."

Zovko seems exasperated. The kids for their part are acting as if it's all a joke and that everyone knows that now. The relief becomes more palpable as the interview progresses and Zovko gets drawn into it as well.

At one point all of the visionaries say that they are hungry.

"Would you like some candy?" Father Zovko asks, "Let's see if there are any sandwiches? Bring three sandwiches."

"Let's make some for them," said Mica, "They're really hungry. I can help."

"What do you want to drink," Zovko asks, "Do you want some of the hard stuff?"

"Father, don't you know that we came by car?" Mica responds, and everyone laughs. "You have to watch out for those who drive."

"Don't worry," Zovko responds, "These are angels. Nothing affects them."

Everyone laughs.

"Nothing affects angels," Zovko repeats.

"I said, 'Ask the Gospa to make me fly in that fashion!'" said Ljubica.

"She would be very thankful," replied Jakov, whereupon everyone bursts out laughing again.

It seems that everyone is relieved because the key piece of business has been taken care of. It has been established that the visions will end on Friday and in the church, as Zovko wanted them to. Given the sort of tacit admissions that were taking place in the June 30 interview, Zovko should have had his suspicions confirmed. Yet the surprising thing about his reaction is that as his skepticism grew so did his desire to direct the apparitions. Instead of exposing them as fraudulent, he seems more interested in bringing them under his control, and in this regard, the children are by now only too happy to comply. They realize that Zovko has shot their story full of holes. At the same time, they realize that the crowd is increasing in size and impatience. Just to say that the apparitions had ceased is not enough. They need either a sign or someone to take them over. Since the Blessed Mother still hasn't come through on the first alternative, they would have to settle for the second. And as the tapes show, Zovko was only too willing to accommodate them.

Bolstering the evidence that Zovko's prime motivation in investigating the seers was not discovering the truth but rather bringing the apparitions into the church and then making them subservient to Franciscan ends is his suspicious rivalry with Marinko Ivankovic for the children's loyalty. Marinko was clearly in charge of the seers from day one of the apparitions until Zovko maneuvered them into the church, a fact that becomes clear in the course of the early tapes. In the June 30, interview Zovko wants to know how they get the messages.

Fr. Zovko: You must think up something. How long did it take you yesterday to think up what to tell the people? Did it take you 15 to 20 minutes, half an hour? How long did it take Marinko, for instance, to write up those questions, answers, and what you should say?

...You were with [Marinko].

A bit later he asks Ivanka:

Fr. Zovko: Does Marinko write up everything for you?

Ivanka: Marinko writes up everything. I memorize that, then I read.

He then asks Mirjana the same question:

Fr. Zovko: Did you ask Marinko what we should say to the people?

Mirjana: Marinko says that we should tell the people as if the Gospa had said that people shouldn't come anymore, that the Gospa will not come anymore.

At this point Zovko clearly feels that Marinko is manipulating the children:

Fr. Zovko: I would like to know what else Marinko thought up as to what people should be told....I do not know how you are imagining that. That's the big problem for me. I know that those who were misleading people or were transmitting wrong messages were severely punished. With the Israelites, and in the early Church such people were expelled from the Church, they were thrown out, God punished them terribly. Are you afraid of this? I am terribly afraid.

Fr. Zovko: Why won't he?

MIrjana: Because we aren't lying.

The main reason for the rivalry between Marinko and Zovko soon becomes apparent: Zovko wants the apparitions to happen in the church, where he, and not Marinko, can control them, because as things stand now, i.e., before they agree to have the Blessed Mother appear in church, Marinko is clearly in control and not Zovko.

Fr. Zovko: Absolutely. This interests me. What if the Gospa does not appear in the church? What do you think? Can you ask her to appear in the church?

Mirjana: We shall consult Marinko, see what he thinks; if it were not for him....

Fr. Zovko: What if Marinko disagrees with this, because it would be important to say the rosary in the church, that the entire community pray; if Marinko does not agree, you will obey Marinko, isn't that right?

Mirjana: It is interesting. Marinko is coming [from work] around 3 p.m.. If he doesn't agree, if he thinks differently, then we'll come over here. Are you going to be at home?

Fr. Zovko: I will. All right, then, you come with Marinko...

Later Zovko wants to know what the children discussed with Marinko:

Fr. Zovko: What did you talk about with Marinko?

Vicka: There is one question which Marinko gave us. What power does the Gospa have...that the Redeemer and Jesus help? Are we going to ask that since he told us?

Fr. Zovko: Did you read those questions [I gave you]?

Mirjana: We didn't have them with us.

Fr. Zovko: Why didn't you take them along? (sarcastically) Marinko most certainly told you not to take them along.

Marinko Ivankovic is Father Ivo Sivric's second cousin. Sivric spent a good deal of time with Marinko over the summer of 1986 as well as with his father Jure, who by 1986, thanks largely to the Gospa, was united with his son. Sivric suspected that his relative Marinko might be the "man behind the scenes." Zovko certainly thought he was and says so on the tapes. But for Father Sivric, the question remains, "What happened at the beginning?"

"Is it not possible," Sivric wonders, proposing his own hypothesis about what happened at the beginning,

> that the visionaries themselves might have mounted the whole affair of the apparitions? One day, they might have been at loose ends, looking for something to do to relieve their frustrations. They had neither movies nor a discotheque in the immediate neighborhood. They then thought of a worthy activity. On their own initiative they might have wanted to try something for the greater glory of God and the spiritual well-being of the people. They might have decided to try to shake the people up spiritually (p. 181).

The two original visionaries were Mirjana Dragicevic and Ivanka Ivankovic. Ivanka had just lost her mother. Mirjana was studying in Sarajevo and had the reputation of being a "Pankerica," i.e., a punk rocker who smoked dope. The allegations that the apparitions resulted from drugs dogged the seers during their early days. It seems that the priests were more concerned about the charges than the police. At some time between June 6, 1981, and June 27, when the apparitions began, Mirjana read *Lourdes: Heavenly Apparitions and Miraculous Cures* by Father Bozo Vuco, OFM, having gotten a copy from Zdravka Ivankovic. Jakov Colo mentioned reading the same book. In the BBC Everyman video, Mirjana claimed that she had never heard of Lourdes before the apparitions occurred.

In a conversation with a group of tour guides, Mirjana once related a vision in which the Virgin who appeared was then chased away by another Virgin, who announced then, "You see, even the devil can appear like me." The vision, which the tour guides are convinced was genuine, has a certain resonance with the religion of the Bogomils, which infested the area before the subsequent rise of Islam. Bogomilism was an essentially Gnostic heresy, which posited a rough equality of power between God and the devil. The region has been infected with it ever since. Even Yugoslav Communists like Milovan Djilas were, in a sense, Bogomil Marxists. "Djilas," according to biographer Stephen Clissold, " felt the appeal of the Manichaean concept."

> The Bogomils. . . held that the Devil had been given dominion over all material things; only a tiny elite, the 'Perfect', denied him earthly allegiance by embracing a life of extreme abstinence and austerity... a hyper-Puritanism which appealed to a spiritual minority as strongly as did the sect's uninhibited sensuality to the majority. The idealistic revolutionaries of his youth seemed to Djilas the heirs of the Bogomil 'Perfect' (West, p. 264-65).

Richard West writes that Djilas whiled away his time in prison translating Milton's homage to Satan's power, *Paradise Lost*, into Serbo-Croatian. Similarly, it is a rare message of Our Lady of Medjugorje which does not mention Satan. The texts are admittedly far more banal than Milton, but that is probably attributable to the guiding hand of the Franciscans, who try to eliminate theologically dubious passages from publication. The obscurity of the language provides a haven for the seers, whose solecisms and heresies usually get lopped off or corrected in the translation process. But it also acts as a veil over the darker aspects of Croatian culture, whose darker side manifests itself not only in periodic outbreaks of genocide but also in a penchant toward blasphemy in common speech. "F*** Jesus" is a common expletive, and one frequently mentioned in the confessional.

All of the seers came from families that were dysfunctional in one way or another. Jakov was raised by his grandmother. Vicka's father was a *Gastarbeiter* who never sent any money home. In this they were not unlike the "seers" of Marpingen, who were raised in a border land during a time in which Catholics were oppressed too. The children of Marpingen were often neglected by their parents too. Their fathers in particular had to leave the area to obtain work, a common occurrence in Croatia in the period following World War II.

There is reason to believe that the children were not in Zovko's prayer group; however, we know that 30 other young people were—a not inconsiderable number for a small place like Medjugorje—because they met on June 28 at Zovko's behest to pray to obtain the discernment of spirits to see if God was behind what was happening. Zovko, it seems, suspected that hallucinogenic drugs might have played a role in what was going on. The crowds were making the same sort of accusation and were especially suspicious of Mirjana.

At one point, Mica Ivankovic tells Father Zovko that a girl asked her, "Is it possible that the Gospa would appear to this 'Pankerica'?" She then asks Zovko if he knows what the word "Pankerica" means.

"No, I don't," Zovko replies.

"Then I'll explain it to you," Mica says, laughing. "It's a girl who is habitually immoral. The people can't identify with them [the seers] because they dress in a fashion that is very liberal. One woman said, "Is it possible that the Gospa would appear to this 'Pankerica'?" I said, "Girl, I beg your pardon. If Bernadette were living in our day, it's possible that she would have dressed in the same way."

The passage is instructive for a number of reasons. First of all, it gives some inkling of the position that the group of seers occupied in Medjugorje at the time of the apparitions. They were not what one would call part of the young people's in-crowd in the parish. Those people were most likely in Father Zovko's prayer group. Unlike those pious young people, the seers seem to have been viewed with some suspicion; they, especially Mirjana, were viewed as the small village version of the counterculture, of big city fashions, which probably just meant that they wore jeans and T-shirt-type tops instead of dresses. No one involved with the tapes seems to know what the word "Pankerica" means; however, after some reflection, I think, the etymology of the word becomes clear. The suffix "ica" is simply the feminine form in Croatian of "punker." In all likelihood, the seers probably had little to do with people like Sid Vicious. The term was probably appropriated by the typical small village culture as meaning citified, trendy, and, to some extent, at odds with traditional village culture. The fact is significant because it gives some inkling of the relation between the seers and Zovko and what he had been doing in the parish over the past nine months.

Ten years ago I proposed my own hypothesis of how the apparitions got started. Based on the laughter on the interview tapes and the flippant attitude of the seers toward Jozo Zovko, I surmised that the apparitions were a joke that got out of hand. This was Bishop Zanic's verdict, and that of Rev. Marko Orsolic, O.F.M., professor of theology at the theological faculty in Sarajevo. Ivan studied under Orsolic for three years, and so the professor claims to know him well (See Denis R. Janz, "Medjugorje's Miracles: Faith and Profit," *The Christian Century,* August 26-September 2, 1987, p. 724). The girls—specifically the two instigators, Mirjana and Ivanka—knew the type of thing that Zovko was doing in his young people's prayer group. Since they were not part of it, and perhaps sensing and resenting the manipulative elements involved in it, they decided to parody it. Mirjana had just read a book on Lourdes, so the vocabulary of apparitions was fresh in her mind. It could have been a way of livening up what looked like another hot, boring summer in the country.

In retrospect I think the explanation is too simplistic and that it does not take into sufficient account the personality of Mirjana Dragicevic, the girl who in effect created the apparitions. It was her idea. The others just went along for the ride. On June 24, Mirjana and Ivanka were doing something they weren't supposed to be doing. They originally said that they had gone up on the mountain to tend sheep, but when Ivanka was challenged by Bishop Zanic, who reminded her that it was a sin to tell a lie, she quickly backed down and said they had gone up the mountain to smoke. To smoke what never got explained, but the rumors surrounding the early apparitions were clear enough in implicating Mirjana as someone who smoked dope. The assumption at the time was that marijuana might produce hallucinations. A more plausible explanation might be that they were caught doing something they shouldn't have been doing by, say, Marinko Ivankovic, who lived right across the street from the site of the apparitions, and they tried to lie their way out of it. Either Marinko was taken in by the lie and believed them, or he used the lie against them as a way of controlling them. As is often the case in situations like these one lie leads to another and soon the children are too scared to admit the truth.

But did the seers actually see anything? The two bishops who have handled the case are divided on the issue. Bishop Zanic is convinced that the whole thing was a hoax cooked up by the Franciscans to best him in their battle over the contested parishes. Bishop Peric, the current ordinary, feels that the children may very well be seeing something. The only thing he is sure of is that whatever they are seeing, it is not the Blessed Mother. That leaves, of course, only one other option. Philip Pavich is convinced that the seers are trafficking in spirits. He bases his judgment on years of experience with New Age devotees who come to Medjugorje to him for confession and oftentimes exorcism and then leave their New Age/Occult literature behind. But there is a fourth possibility as well. Judging from the psychological evidence, Mirjana may very well be a "medium," i.e., a person who has an unusually sensitive relationship to the fears and hopes and sins and guilts which drive her community. It seems evident that she hears voices. In an interview with Tomislav Vlasic, which got suppressed, Mirjana talked about a woman who once heard tapping on her window and then heard the same tapping on a sixth floor window after moving to a new apartment far away. That woman could be Mirjana, who moved from the village to Sarajevo. But what was tapping at her window? The answer, according to the Gospa at least, was "souls in purgatory." They "were doing so because she has forgotten to pray for them and they are demanding her prayers."

What we are talking about here is not demons then but ghosts, the souls from purgatory who still haven't found the final closure of heaven or hell and who come back to remind us, therefore, of some unrighted wrong. Ghosts, such as Hamlet's father's ghost, invariably return to right some unrepented and unrighted wrong. The community of course is involved in the identification process, which proceeds according to cultural as well as personal lines. The seers of Marpingen saw some vague shape in the woods, and the meaning of that phantom was determined by a series of familial and cultural interactions with the elders in the village. In many ways, the needs of the times deter-mine what the children saw, and in Medjugorje an uncertain future demanded some sort of closure with the past. Communism had literally fastened a lid on the graves of the Serbs who had been mur-dered at Surmanci, and with Communism threatening to disappear, something they all wanted, the ghosts of the dead Serbs were threaten-ing to rise again. The fact that the bones of the Serb victims at Surmanci were quite literally repressed, along with the memories they evoked, by the hated Communists, became apparent in 1989, when with the fall of the Berlin Wall imminent and East Germans hemorrhag-ing to the West through Hungary, the Serbs came back to Surmanci to reclaim their dead. They exhumed the bodies and erected a monument in their memory. When I brought this up to the villagers eight years later, they claimed that the Serbs did this in preparation for war.

What the seers clearly hadn't counted on, however, was the reaction of the crowds. Instead of just fooling around and making fun of a few of the locals, or lying their way out of an embarrassing situation, or creating a pious fiction in the manner of aping Lourdes, the girls suddenly had the entire countryside as well as the police in an uproar over what they were claiming to see. The reaction of the crowds may very well have been the indirect result of Zovko's efforts. If his combination of charismatic prayer and encounter group therapy was getting convents of nuns in an uproar, why shouldn't it have the same effect on the general population in the parish? Having been primed by him to expect signs and wonders, the village exploded with fervor when they appeared. The times, it should be remembered, were apocalyptic anyway. The pope had just been shot on the anniversary of the first apparition at Fatima. Tito—the glue that held Yugoslavia together since World War II—had died a year before. There were rumors of civil war between the Albanians and the Serbs to the south. The village as well as the entire region had a reputation for Marian piety but also for cruel brutality as well. Local legend has it that once the huge cement cross was erected on Mount Krizevac in 1933, hail storms no longer destroyed the villagers' crops. In addition, there was the general atmosphere of the times. The millennium was approaching. The 2,000th anniversary of Mary's birth was at hand or, perhaps at the latest, a few years in the future. Apparitions pop up around the millennium—especially in times of general insecurity—the way toadstools spring up after a rain.

At any rate, judging from the transcripts of the tapes, both Zovko and the seers were shocked by the size and vehemence of the crowds. Once this shock settled in and the seers were faced with the possibility of admitting that they had made the whole thing up, they got scared. And in a sense the seers hadn't "made it all up"; the crowds had collaborated in making it up with them. But that fact did not remove them from danger. Indeed, until the government—quite wrongly, it turns out— became convinced that they had nothing to fear from the apparitions and that they were in effect a boon to the economy, a number of people were arrested. So the seers, at first shocked by the reaction of the crowd and then amused and finally fearful, were only too happy to have someone take the whole thing off their hands.

Which is just what Father Zovko did. The so-called apparitions went from being a teenage prank or whatever their mystical origin was to being on their way to becoming a world-wide religious phenomenon when Father Zovko brought them into the church. "Ask the Gospa if she'll appear in the church," Zovko kept insisting throughout his conversations with the children, and finally he got his wish. According to Ljubic's account, "The Gospa responded with hesitation and without enthusiasm according to the adolescents: 'I will appear in the church.'"

It happened on Thursday, July 2, 1981, the day on which the Gospa allegedly told the children her last apparition would take place. Toward 1:00 p.m., the place in front of the church was jammed with pilgrims, and the crowd grew larger with each minute. Before Mass began, the seers prayed the rosary, kneeling behind the altar. During the recitation of the rosary, the Virgin appeared in the church above the choir loft and bowed over the crowed. Some people claimed that Father Zovko saw her too.

By the time the sermon came around, the apparitions were firmly in Zovko's hand. The sermon was dedicated to the general theme of conversion with particular emphasis placed on penance, fasting, and prayer. The huge crowd gulped it all down as if they were hearing the word of God for the first time. That word fell on them, according to Ljubic's account, like torrents of rain on a parched earth, and it gave birth in them to a renewed spirit and a renewed heart.

Inspired by the reaction of the crowd, Zovko then took on the manner of a Pentecostal conducting a revival.

"Do you want to accept with love the divine grace and with joy fast on bread and water for three days as testimony to your conversion and to turn back the power of the demon?" he bellowed at the crowd.

Like a clap of thunder, the crowd roared back, "Yes, we do."

"Will you pray the rosary every day in your homes?"

"Yes, we will," roared the crowd, which was evidently finding emotional release from the tension and the insecurity of the past few days by responding to Zovko in the church. Their response was so thunderous that it seemed as if the walls and the roof of the church couldn't withstand its force.

"Will you have your families read the Bible every day?"

"Yes, we will." The response poured out of the hearts of the assembled faithful as a sign and confirmation of their definitive conversion to God and his word.

Then after Mass, the visionaries gave their testimony for the first time in public in the parish church. They described how the Gospa looked, and talked about the messages she had given them. Their testimony, according to Ljubic, was "convincing, lively and direct, as if Some Other had given it. It produced a tremendous effect among the assembled souls."

And, one might add, with Zovko as well, who seems more and more caught up in the revival-like emotional atmosphere which he himself created.

"The Gospa is here!" Zovko concluded. One imagines him shouting this over the roar of the crowd. "Here," he said, referring to St. James Church, "is where you can address to her your prayers and petitions. Here is where you must come to meet her."

The people, now emotionally drained, spent a long time after the service was over confessing their faults and praying. Zovko's afternoon service on July 2 was the crucial turning point in the history of the so-called apparitions. From now on, they would take place in the church, and it would be impossible to separate their alleged claims from the often genuine piety which surrounded them. Similarly, from that time on it would be virtually impossible for the average pilgrim to separate what the seers said from what the priests who watched over them wanted the world to hear. On one hot afternoon in June, something happened in a small village in Croatia; on a similar afternoon in July, the local church and community absorbed that event into itself by validating it as real. In effect, the latter event is the more significant. In a sense, the significant point in the whole story is not that certain adolescent girls would claim to have certain experiences, but rather how the population in general and the clergy reacted to these claims.

It's the type of thing that has happened before. In a similarly isolated village in Salem, Massachusetts, in the winter of 1692, a number of adolescent girls started to manifest similarly strange behavior. They had been—although the town fathers didn't know it at the time—consorting with the minister's black slave—Tituba, by name—who had been brought from Barbados and in all likelihood had picked up a passing knowledge of voodoo there, something which the Puritan girls found fascinating. Whatever else it was, it was also an interesting way to pass time during New England's long, dull winters. Soon they started showing signs of what may very well have been demonic possession. A doctor was called in, who quickly found himself out of his depth. What was going on here went beyond the medical expertise of his day. As a result, there was only one possible conclusion to draw: "The evil hand is on them," the doctor said, and from then on it was a matter for the clergy.

As Marion Starkey relates in his account of the affair in *The Devil in Massachusetts*, the town minister, Reverend

> Parris proclaimed a state of emergency and appealed for help to the ministers of the North Shore. When Dr. Griggs had relegated the affliction from the physical world to the spiritual, he had thrust the responsibility for its treatment upon the ministry. It was now plain that the devil was at work in Salem Village, and since even the devil cannot produce results on this scale without human accomplices, it was equally plain that he had commissioned witches here.

The girls were asked to discover the witches who were tormenting them, and the famous Salem Witch Trials came about as a result. Once the ministers got involved in the case and once the affair became public, the girls were put in a very uncomfortable position. They could either admit that they had been doing voodoo with Tituba, which would almost certainly warrant severe punishment for them and almost certainly death for Tituba, or they could start naming other people as witches. Human nature being what it is, they chose the latter course, and 20 innocent human beings—mostly that society's marginated—were put to death. Once the minister and the judges accepted the girls' testimony as true, their prestige was on the line as well. They had to go along every bit as much as the girls did lest they look even more foolish than the people responsible in the first place. According to Starkey, the significant thing about the Salem witch trials was not that it was initiated by crazed adolescent girls but that that behavior was continued and validated by the colony's adult population.

> In the long run what was remarkable here was less the antics of the girls than the way the community received them. It was the community—extended in time to include the whole Bay Colony—that would in the end suffer the most devastating attack of possession, and not only the ignorant, but the best minds.

Eventually one of the girls and two of the judges were to repent, but not before 20 people died. Starkey traces the hysteria to the baleful effects of Calvinism combined with a general sense of isolation in the colony and a feeling that with the turn of the century the millennium was at hand. "Similar examples of mass hysteria," he writes,

> and on a far more enormous scale had occurred repeatedly in the Middle Ages, and always like this one in the wake of stress and social disorganization, after wars or after an epidemic of the Black Death. There had been the Children's Crusades, the Flagellantes, the St. Vitus' Dance, and again and again there had been outbreaks of witchcraft. Sweden had recently had one, and on such a scale as to make what was going on in Salem Village look trivial.

In each case, though, the claims of the populace had to be validated with the authority of the clergy. If they were not, the whole incident would have been dismissed. If it hadn't been for the approval of Minister Parris, the whole thing might have ended with the girls getting a whipping and nothing more. Parris, since his own daughters were involved, found himself in an embarrassing situation, one in which he let his personal needs override the common good.

By now the parallels between Medjugorje and Salem should be apparent. Adolescent girls started both phenomena, but the crucial turning point came when the clergy, influenced by the general atmosphere and the pressure of the crowds which they had, in effect, helped create, validated the girls' experience as genuine. The girls, surprised by the reaction of the crowd, became too scared to back out. The only safe route was to press on with the assistance of the clergy, whose personal needs were also satisfied by the alleged supernatural phenomena.

But the situation wasn't quite that simple. If the external threat had been removed, there were still the unresolved internal pressures. As the number of pilgrims increased so did the clamoring for signs and wonders, specifically the promised sign, which was a long time in coming. How long was it possible to keep the whole thing going without fulfilling the apocalyptic promises and predictions that had fueled everyone's interest in the first place? Secondly, there was the issue of enthusiasm itself. Both Zovko and Vlasic, because of the type of prayer group spirituality they were involved in, were playing with fire. Could they continue to do so without being burnt themselves?

The forces which the Franciscans unleashed would soon take on life of their own. By July 11, 1981, the date which commemorated the socialist revolution in Yugoslavia, Father Zovko was riding the tiger along with the girls and no more capable than they anymore of getting off without getting hurt. Perhaps this is why he decided to up the ante. The Mass that day no longer just had the Grb on the candles. Now he decided to preach a sermon about the Church wandering in the wilderness for 40 years. He would claim later that the sermon had no political meaning but in the aftermath of the collapse of Yugoslavia and the rise of Croatian nationalism that sounds disingenuous. Either way, the sermon landed Jozo in jail. He was arrested on August 17. On August 8, Grgo Kozina, the village's unofficial chronicler of the apparitions, wrote that "In the Grand Hall in Citluk, young people and others accused Father Zovko of being the instigator of the incidents" [at Podbrdo, Medjugorje], which was precisely the opinion of party officials in Sarajevo. Brando Mikulic told a rally in Tjentiste in Bosnia that "clerico-nationalists" created the apparitions in order "to intimidate uneducated people and try to fool them; that is, to manipulate them politically and make them serve those who work against the interests of our nations and nationalities." The Communists obscured whatever truth there was to the matter by their heavy-handed propaganda, portraying the Virgin in cartoons as an Ustasha terrorist with a knife clenched between her teeth and a caption proclaiming, "The True Face of the Blessed Mother." They also expanded the conspiracy to include the Franciscans and the Bishop of Mostar, an improbable combination to anyone but a Serb.

Zanic, who was himself a Marian devotee and had conducted pilgrimages to Fatima and Lourdes, arrived at St. James Parish on July 25, 1981, and every early indication seems to show he was favorably disposed at least toward the possibility that the events might be genuine, and might even be a solution to the Herzegovina Problem of the rebellious Franciscans. Others were less favorably impressed. Father Tadija Pavlovic went to Medjugorje to visit his mother on the same day the bishop arrived for the first time since the beginning of the apparitions and watched the visionaries during Mass and communion. What he saw left him unimpressed. The visionaries made virtually no show of devotion to the Eucharist and spent their time during Mass talking and walking around. On August 6, Bishop Zanic, sensing he growing hostility of the government, issued a press release defending the clergy and the visionaries against the charges being published in the Communist press. Father Ivo Sivric now feels that Bishop Zanic himself was caught up in the apparition fever which swept the area during the summer of 1981, and claims that he "shares the blame for this painful, tense and dangerous situation" because "he too courted a desire to see Our Lady of Medjugorje appear. Quite probably, this is what motivated him not to stop the organized pilgrimages to Medjugorje earlier and not to create a commission of inquiry right away. Comparing Bishop Zanic's actions to those of other bishops in similar circumstances, he did not take the appropriate measures early enough." On August 12, the Communist authorities declared Podbrdo off-limits to pilgrims and anyone else. Years later, Zovko would claim in conversation with Mary Craig that the Communist authorities drove the seers into the church. That is clearly not true. Zovko wanted the apparitions to take place in the church almost from the minute he arrived back in Medjugorje on July 27, and that desire was always expressed in conjunction with taking control of the seers away from Marinko Ivankovic.

Once the seers became part of the religious services in the church, however, Zovko was swept up into the frenzy surrounding the apparitions as well. On August 15, 1981, Father Zovko said the evening Mass and announced to an enormous crowd of around 25,000 people that the Gospa was going to give a sign on Monday, August 17, 1981. Marinko was now saying that a huge church would suddenly appear on Podbrdo along with springs of running water and that the Zuzulj hill next to Krisevac would be miraculously swept away. Years later when Father Zovko appeared on *Mother Angelica Live,* a TV show broadcast over the Eternal Word Television Network, Mother Angelica confided to Zovko that she knew 1981 was significant because she had founded her network on August 15 of that year.

Needless to say, the miraculous sign did not appear, but another less miraculous sign appeared in its place. The police arrived at 8:00 a.m. and, after searching the rectory and church and strip-searching the nuns, they took Father Ferdo Vlasic and Father Zovko into custody. Eventually Zovko would be sentenced to three and a half years in prison.

One day after Father Zovko had been hauled off to jail, Father Tomislav Vlasic arrived in Medjugorje, now in an official capacity, to begin his duties as associate pastor of St. James Church. The children were now under the influence of the man whose wavering vocation had been saved by the appearance of the Virgin prophesied at the charismatic conference in Rome and would remain so until 1988 when Vlasic moved a group of young people and Marija Pavlovic to a palazzo near Parma in Italy to start a co-ed religious community with Agnes Heupel, a woman who claimed a miraculous cure as a result of coming to Medjugorje. That venture, which had all the earmarks of Vlasic's sexual problems, would become a major source of embarrassment to the Medjugorje supporters, but that event was still far in the future. Vlasic's influence over the seers at this point was crucial. In fact, so crucial that Bishop Zanic considered Vlasic and not Zovko the Franciscan who created Medjugorje.

At the same time that Medjugorje was shaken by the arrests and imminent trial of Father Zovko, a polyglot, former CIA agent by the name of Vernon Walters paid the pope a visit in Rome. Walters was now working for the Reagan administration and technically at least no longer working for the CIA, but his visit had everything to do with the reason the CIA was founded in the first place. Walters had come to explain to the pope why the United States was about to embark on a $340 billion defense build-up. It didn't take a genius to figure out that the purpose of the build-up was the final defeat of Communism, and it also didn't take a genius to realize that the Reagan Administration felt that the Polish pope had a crucial role to play in bringing that outcome about.

"We talked about the fact that the Church was the key to the emergence and survival of Poland as a free country." Walters told Carl Bernstein. "What we did about it is still classified" (p. 318).

Walters would later complain that Bernstein had inflated what was merely a courtesy call into a conspiracy, but the essential outlines of the situation remain the same no matter how one chooses to describe it. Walters saw in the pope a man who had made a fundamental break with Casaroli's *Ostpolitik* and was willing to work with anyone who was ready to bring about a fundamental change in the region.

"Wojtyla's analysis," according to Bernstein, "supported by American intelligence, held that Jaruszelski would come to resemble the late Marshal Tito of Yugoslavia rather than the typical Moscow puppet, particularly if the Church did not back him into a corner" (p. 351). As a result, the United States began secret transfers of money through papal accounts to the Solidarity underground in Poland, a fact which alarmed both Polish and Soviet intelligence sources, and moved Jaruszelski farther into the Soviet orbit and one step closer to martial law.

Meanwhile, the seers of Medjugorje under their new mentor, Tomislav Vlasic, were finding a new freedom of expression. At the beginning of September 1981, Vicka announced to Jure Ivankovic that Germany and the United States will be destroyed, that the pope will be exiled in Turkey, and that Bisce, the plain south of Mostar, would be covered "knee-deep in blood." On September 4, 1981, Vicka wrote the subsequently famous "bloody handkerchief" story in her diary about a "conductor," who

> met a man totally covered with blood and this man—it was Jesus—gave him a handkerchief soaked in blood and told him to throw it in the river. Before going very far, he met a woman and this woman was the Blessed Virgin Mary, who asked the conductor to give her the bloody handkerchief. The conductor offered to give her his own handkerchief, but the Gospa wanted the handkerchief soaked in blood. When the conductor gave her the bloody handkerchief, the Gospa remarked, "If you hadn't given it to me, that would have been the end of the world." The Gospa confirmed that this was the truth.

Gradually baroque folk tales in the Bogomil tradition like Vicka's account of the bloody handkerchief would drop out of the canon of Medjugorje messages as the Franciscans exerted more stringent control over the seers. Another layer of censorship was exercised by Rene Laurentin, who removed the bloody handkerchief story from his supposedly definitive and authoritative compilation of the messages, *Corpus Chronologique des messages* (Paris:O.E.I.L., 1988). Other embarrassing details would get dropped in the course of translation from one language to another. After passing through so many theological filters, it was no wonder that the apparitions' opponents could claim that there was nothing in the messages contrary to Catholic doctrine.

On September 1, Bishop Zanic wrote a letter protesting Zovko's arrest to Sergej Kreigher, president of the State Presidency of the Yugoslavian federal republic. Zovko would repay the favor by later accusing Zanic of collaborating with the Communist government in suppressing the apparitions. The slander eventually found its way into the feature-length film *Gospa*, starring Martin Sheen as Zovko and Morgan Fairchild as his sister. In the course of the film, Bishop "Pero Subic," the only character who doesn't have a real name, cuts a deal with the Communist government. The fact that Bishop Zanic was not mentioned by name was a tacit admission of the libelous nature of his portrayal in the film, a fact noted by Zanic's successor, Ratko Peric, who sent a withering critique of the film *ad multos*, but not before *Gospa* was shown under the official auspices of the Archdiocese of Los Angeles.

On October 21, 1981, Father Zovko went on trial in Mostar and, in the expeditious fashion typical of Communist courts, was convicted by 5:00 p.m. the following day and sentenced to three and one half years in prison. As of 1986 Secretary for Religious Affairs Simic still believed that the apparitions had at root a political purpose.

"It is a known fact," Simic told Mary Craig,

> that certain forces hostile to this country attempted to use this religious gathering, to exploit the apparitions for their own political ends. There were slogans like "Croats, arise," there were Nazi symbols up there on the hill ....Certain church people were writing articles to suggest that the Madonna was appearing in Yugoslavia just because the Communists are in power here....When people begin assembling in large numbers and claim that the Virgin Mary has come to bring liberation to one or the other of the nationalities in our country, it is difficult for a Yugoslav citizen who has suffered greatly through political division and strife, to believe that there is no political message here.

Craig goes on to add that fears of a political conspiracy behind Medjugorje were "heightened by awareness of events in nearby Poland, where Solidarity, supported by the powerful Catholic Church was beginning to look and sound like an alternative government." On September 14, a little over a month before Zovko went on trial, Pope John Paul II issued his first contribution to Catholic social teaching, *Laborem Exercens*, to coincide with the 90th anniversary of *Rerum Novarum*, but also with a Solidarity labor Congress being held in Poland. At around the same time that Jozo Zovko went on trial, Franjo

Tudjman was also convicted of conspiring against the state and was, like Zovko, sentenced to three years in jail and a loss of his civil rights for eight years. Before entering prison in November 1981, he was admitted to a Zagreb hospital with a heart condition. Despite a world-wide outcry that included the naming of Tudjman as a "Prisoner of Conscience" by Amnesty International, Tudjman was sent to the infamous Lepoglava prison in January 1982 where he suffered a series of four heart attacks.

On December 9, 1981, Robert Armao, an American business-man with connections to the Chase Manhattan Bank and representa-tive in the U.S. of the assets of the Pahlevi family, whose head was the recently ousted Shah of Iran, began conducting an evaluation of an Italian bank the Pahlevis were considering purchasing. The Banco Ambrosiano of Milan was a Catholic bank and one of the most repu-table in Italy, but recently its assets had taken a spectacular rise that was reflected in the fact that the Pahlevis as part of a consortium of Saudi, American, and Iranian interests were considering paying $1 billion to purchase it. At the time the consortium did not know that the bank's impressive assets were largely the result of an elaborate Ponzi scheme run by its director Roberto Calvi, who was only able to keep the bank afloat by getting ever-larger loans from an ever-shrinking pool of lenders. One of Calvi's ploys was showing potential lenders letters signed by Archbishop Paul Marcinkus, head of the IOR or Vatican Bank, testifying to Calvi's probity and trustworthiness and suggesting on vague terms that the Vatican stood behind the Banco Ambrosiano financially as well as spiritually. According to Rupert Cornwell's account of the Banco Ambrosiano scandal, "There is some evidence that towards the end Ambrosiano may have been linked with interna-tional arms trading; other rumors were that the bank's complex network could have served as a channel for financing Solidarity, the independent Polish trade union, close to the heart of a Polish Pope" (p. 21).

On December 12, General Jaruszelski declared martial law in Poland, partially as a way of forestalling a Russian invasion of his country. Solidarity was outlawed and its leaders rounded up and put in prison.

On December 15, 1981, Tomislav Vlasic wrote to Manda, who was now living in Germany with their almost five year old son, an-nouncing that he was now pastor of Medjugorje and wondering if she has heard of the apparitions. "I'm happy that I'm here, although there's a lot of work and I can't keep up. I'm happy that I'm a Franciscan and that I'm serving God." The events at Medjugorje seem to have resolved Vlasic's crisis of vocation. Instead of getting Vlasic as a husband and having his assistance in raising their child, Manda would now have to do that on her own, in a foreign land, largely as the domestic servant of the 90-year-old Herr Ott.

On December 21, 1981, Nikola Radic, provincial delegate for the Franciscans, arrived in Mostar and communicated a "final admonition" to Fathers Ivan Prusina and Ivica Vego. Two days before, however, the Blessed Mother had entered the case. In a notation in his diary, dated December 19, 1981, Vlasic wrote that "the Blessed Virgin told Vicka, she said to me, that the bishop had made false conclusions, but she could not repeat that literally." Just who all the "she's" refer to in the diary's entry's tangled syntax is not clear. The most plausible explanation is that the Blessed Virgin told Vicka that the bishop was wrong and that Prusina and Vego were innocent and that Vicka was to keep the information to herself. Information this momentous, however, is hard to keep a secret, and so when Ivica Vego returned from his visit to Medjugorje two days before Christmas, he unburdened himself to his diary too, with an obvious sense of relief: "I was in Medjugorje. They told me we were not guilty of anything. We can stay."

The Gospa was now involved in the internal politics of the Yugoslavian Federal Republic and the Catholic Church. The seers were proving to be an especially malleable group of people, especially Vicka, who takes on a prominent role at this point. Abandoning the apocalyptic nonsense about a miraculous sign and the pope being taken captive in Turkey, Vicka instead plunges into the Case of Herzegovina and situates the Blessed Mother firmly on the side of the rebellious Franciscans, a move that would have serious consequences. The bishop, it should be remembered, was the only person in the diocese with the power to approve the apparitions as genuine. Zovko's cry in St. James Church, "The Gospa is here," would need the ratification of the bishop, who seemed favorably disposed—initially, at least. In their haste to make use of the seers, the Franciscans under Tomislav Vlasic had just made a huge tactical error.

-5-

THE RISE OF MEDJUGORJE: 1982-1988

On January 14, 1982, Bishop Zanic met with Vicka, and for the first time since the apparitions had begun six months earlier, he began to have doubts about their authenticity. The doubts arose over the role the Blessed Mother was beginning to play in the case of Prusina and Vego, the soon-to-be-suspended Franciscans from Mostar. On January 3, 1982, Vicka evidently asked the Blessed Mother about the status of the two Franciscans because, according to the account she wrote in her diary on the same day,

> The Gospa answered: Ivica [Vego] is not guilty. Have him keep the faith even if the Franciscans expel him . . . . He is not guilty. The bishop does not see to it enough that there is order. It is his fault. But he will not always be bishop. I will show justice in the Kingdom.

Evidently Ivica Vego was present at the apparition because in an account dated the same day, he mentions the Gospa's message and his grateful reaction: "I was thankful, happy and exhausted. I returned to Mostar." Tomislav Vlasic was evidently also present, writing in his account: "Our mother wants it said to the bishop that he has made a precipitous decision." Taken together what emerges from the various diary entries is a picture of Vlasic orchestrating the visions for Vego's benefit and then insisting that Vicka carry the message to the bishop. The roles which the seers would play would change with time. They would become messengers of tolerance, to the point of religious indifferentism, fund-raisers, promoters of books on the Index, and finally advocates of Croatian nationalism, to the point of writing to President Bush and calling for air strikes against the Bosnian Serbs, but their first mission was getting the Blessed Mother on the side of the Franciscans Prusina and Vego in their battle against the bishop.

It is hardly surprising then that on January 14, Zanic's "doubts increased," according to his account, when Vicka announced that "the Gospa sent me to tell you that you have acted precipitously against the Franciscans." On January 20, Vicka persisted in her (or Vlasic's) plan to involve the Blessed Mother in Prusina and Vego's difficulties: "We asked [the Gospa]," she wrote, "what Fathers Ivica Vego and Ivan Prusina should do now that they had been expelled. The Gospa responded, 'They are not to blame. The bishop was hasty in his decision. They should remain, pray a lot and have the others pray for them.'" At the same time that Vicka is quoting the Blessed Mother on the friars' innocence, the canonical wheels in Rome were turning in the opposite direction. On January 29, 1982, a Vatican tribunal convened in Rome and issued an order suspending Prusina and Vego from the Franciscan order and relieving them of their vows and their jurisdiction. The fact that Zanic himself was not the author of the decree only increased his skepticism. If the suspension had been his idea alone, he might have been more amenable to criticism. But Vicka, clearly not understanding the jurisdictional distinctions in the case, involved the Blessed Mother in an attack on the governing structure of the Catholic Church.

Had the Franciscans and Vicka dropped the matter over the late winter and early spring of 1982, Zanic might have regained his originally favorable impression of the apparitions. But Vlasic was determined to press the issue, and Vicka was his willing accomplice in the matter. On April 4, Zanic, still favorably disposed but wavering, met with Vicka again, who now informed that "the last time that we were here, the Gospa reproached us for not having spoken about the two chaplains from Mostar." His suspicions reawakened, Zanic started to press Vicka with questions, which bespoke his suspicion that someone was manipulating her from behind the scenes. It was at this point that Zanic placed the blame on Tomislav Vlasic as the "*spiritus movens*" behind the apparitions. On January 11, 1982, at Vlasic's suggestion, the apparitions took place at the 6:00 p.m. Mass in St. James Church and remained a part of the Mass until Zanic ordered the practice stopped. However, in the meantime, the closer the seers became involved with the Franciscans, the more insistently the Gospa began interfering in the case of Prusina and Vego. Zanic began to suspect a connection and on April 4 began questioning Vicka accordingly.

"This message for the chaplains," he wondered, "when was it given to you? Before you came?"

"Yes, before," Vicka answered.

"That fact convinced me," Zanic wrote later, "that [the apparitions] did not deal with the Madonna, and that she could not defend the two priests expelled by the Order and released from their vows. That would be to destroy the hierarchy and the church, and I knew that Vicka spoke evil of her bishop."

Vicka, in the meantime, continued to come up with messages from the Gospa that confirmed the friars in their rebellion against the Church. "It is important," she said, "that you not leave Mostar." The Gospa couldn't stay out of the fight either, claiming that the Franciscans could celebrate Mass, "provided they remain inconspicuous"; they could function as priests, in other words, in direct disobedience to the bishop, "until everything returns to normal." "They are not to blame," the Gospa continued. "If they were guilty, I would tell them. They are not to be disturbed."

On April 16, the Gospa announced that Prusina and Vego "have not been expelled." She reportedly smiled when she said this. Two weeks later, on April 29, 1982, Father Honorio Pontaglio, the vicar general of the Franciscan order, presumably without a smile on his lips, announced that Prusina and Vego had been suspended from the order *a divinis*. By the time the suspension occurred, Zanic had come to the conclusion that the Franciscans were manipulating the seers from behind the scenes for their own benefit, and that the messages of the Gospa were tantamount to an attack on the hierarchical structure of the Catholic Church.

The credibility of the seers continued to decline apace. On May 10, 1982, Zanic sent two members of the commission he had formed to investigate the apparitions to interrogate the visionaries about the miraculous sign. When asked point blank to describe the sign, all of the visionaries refused. Zanic later surmised that Rev. Ivan Dugandzic, OFM, a Franciscan on the commission, had warned the visionaries in advance that something was afoot. Unfortunately for the visionaries and their Franciscan handlers, seer Ivan Dragicevic was *incommunicado* in the Franciscan seminary in Visoko at the time. When he was asked about the sign, he obligingly complied and wrote down something on two separate pieces of paper, which he placed in separate envelopes and then sealed, one copy being put in the seminary archives and another in the files of the chancery at Mostar. On August 3, 1982, Bishop Zanic invited all of the seers to Mostar to discuss "the great sign." On this occasion, he again asked all of the seers to write their version of the sign on a separate pieces of paper and put them in separate envelopes. All of the seers, including Ivan, refused, claiming that to do so was contrary to the Gospa's explicit instructions. Taken aback by Ivan's refusal to describe what he so willingly described at the seminary in Visoko in May, Zanic asked Ivan if the Gospa had reproached him for writing down the sign at Visoko, and Ivan answered, "No."

Almost three years later, on March 7, 1985, Zanic's episcopal commission was in session in Mostar, and three of its members went to Bijakovici to interview Ivan, who now under the impression that Father Vlasic had returned the envelope he had sealed in Visoko, insisted: "I put a blank piece of paper in the envelope; then I sealed it; then the Gospa appeared to me and she smiled." When the commissioners returned to Mostar, Ivan's envelope was retrieved from the chancery files and opened. The paper was not blank; in fact on it was a statement signed by Ivan and dated May 9, 1982, which stated that "the sign is: There will be a huge shrine in Medjugorje in memory of my apparitions and this shrine shall be [dedicated] to my person." The sign, Ivan also wrote, "will appear in June." Needless to say nothing happened in June of 1982 or any subsequent June either, prompting Bishop Zanic on January 17, 1985, to write in a letter to Rene Laurentin, the man who was by then the world's main promoter of the apparitions, that

> If the Madonna leaves a sign on the hillside as the seers and Father Vlasic have said and written innumerable times, which the whole world knows about and now awaits, I have already publicly announced and have also written that I would crawl on my knees from Mostar to Medjugorje, And I now add that I would beg the pardon of all humanity, of you, the seers and Father Tomislav Vlasic. If I see you after the gift of the sign, I will fall on my knees and kiss your feet. You have this on my oath, and you can publish wherever you please. This would be my indescribable joy and that of all the Church, the happiest day of my life.

One year later, Zanic again wrote to Laurentin. The knees of his trousers were still intact, but he was predicting that the "apparitions," which he now considered clearly a fraud, were going to lead to religious war in Yugoslavia.

On June 7, 1982, a little less than a month after Ivan had put the written description of the "miraculous sign" into the envelope at the Franciscan seminary at Visoko, President Reagan arrived at the Vatican for a meeting with the pope. The meeting took place between the two men without aides or interpreters present and lasted roughly 45 minutes. The two men would have many remarkable personal experiences to discuss; both had survived assassination attempts, and the pope attributed some mystical significance to the fact that the attempt on his life occurred on the anniversary of Fatima, whose warning about Russia spreading her errors had fueled Catholic anti-Communist sentiments for just about the entire century. Not surprisingly, no official account was given of the discussion, but Reagan afterward claimed that there would be "repeated explosions against repression in Eastern Europe." Bernstein claims that between Reagan's visit to the Vatican in 1982 and the fall of the Berlin Wall in 1989, the CIA would devote more than $50 million dollars to keeping Solidarity alive. Kwitny disputes the collaboration, claiming that the pope did it on his own, with the help of unions, who were unlikely to collaborate with Reagan, given what he had done to the air traffic controllers early in his administration, but Kwitny also gives some indication that the pope far from forging a "Holy Alliance," was wary of the intentions of the Americans and felt that they might be exploiting the anti-Communist situation for their own strategic benefit in Eastern Europe. The pope, according to Bohdan Cywinski, "was very distant from and distrustful of the United States."

"Are you aware of how politically interested the Americans are?" the pope asked Cywinski. "Are you aware they are always out to get what they want. Always trying to fulfill their goals?"

The exchange led Cywinski to conclude that the pope could not have been working closely with the Americans, but there are other, subtler ways to interpret the pope's outburst. All three major powers in the Cold War had been engaged in wars on two fronts since the end of World War II, and the fortuitous arrival of Reagan and Wojtyla on the world scene at the same time, along with their personal and philosophical compatibility, did little to change the broad geopolitical features of the conflict. The United States regime was wary of both Communism and Catholicism, and the popes since Paul VI, who saw the effect that Hollywood was having on morals, were wary of both Communism and the Malthusian clique that ran the State Department in the United States. Momentary alliances based on personal chemistry, no matter how momentous their results (and in this instance the results were truly momentous) could not hide the nature of the real forces which were at odds here.

At around the same time that Reagan was meeting with the pope, Roberto Calvi, head of Banco Ambrosiano, the Catholic bank in Milan which had shown such a spectacular rise in assets during the '70s and early '80s, felt that he had reached the end of his rope. In May of 1981, one week after the attack on the pope, Roberto Calvi had been arrested for fraud. The arrest had a direct bearing on the Vatican for two reasons: first of all, because Archbishop Paul Marcinkus, the hulking prelate from Chicago who ran the Vatican's bank, the Instituo Opere Religioso or IOR, had written letters of support vouching for

Calvi's honor and trustworthiness and implying that the IOR would guarantee Calvi's loans, and secondly, because Banco Ambrosiano was being used as conduit for CIA money to Solidarity in Poland. In terms of continuing the destabilization of Communism in Eastern Europe, the attack on Calvi was almost as serious as the attack on the pope, and both seemed to have the same motive. Calvi would tell his lawyers that he had channeled $50 million to Solidarity; and that there was more to follow. "If the whole thing comes out," he would say, "it'll be enough to start the Third World War."

For weeks after his arrest, Calvi's family importuned Marcinkus for financial assistance, but in vain. Calvi as a result was reduced to frantic scrambling to keep the Ponzi scheme that was his financial empire from collapsing. He was forced to borrow at an ever increasing rate to cover the debts that were coming due, and in spite of his efforts ended up $1.3 billion dollars short when the whole scheme collapsed in June 1982. Rebuffed by the Vatican, Calvi sought help from an figure out of the Roman underworld by the name of Flavio Carboni, who importuned his Vatican connections on Calvi's behalf with little effect. Calvi had shady connections of his own. Part of his debt resulted from buying his way into P2, the Italian Masonic lodge run by Licio Gelli. Access to P2's political connections allowed Calvi to borrow more money, but in the end the contacts cost more than his borrowing could cover. Carboni's services weren't cheap either. Swiss investigators eventually found $14 million of Calvi's money in Carboni's accounts. Another $6 million went to Carboni's girlfriend.

On June 13, 1982, Calvi fled the country with Carboni's assistance. On June 18, 1982, Calvi was found dangling from Blackfriar's Bridge in London in what was supposed to resemble a suicide but had instead all the earmarks of a Masonic-style execution. Calvi's death precipitated a severe financial crisis for the Vatican and turned Archbishop Marcinkus into a political prisoner there at precisely the moment when its anti-Communism crusade had reached a crucial phase, in the aftermath of the declaration of martial law in Poland in December of 1981.

There remained, moreover, one last mystifying circumstance, the disappearance of Calvi's briefcase. Calvi never let the briefcase out of his sight, and in the aftermath of his death and the spectacular collapse of Banco Ambrosiano, the briefcase took on a numinous quality, becoming for the Italian media a cross between the Holy Grail and the Maltese Falcon. Eventually, the briefcase got opened on Italian television, to much fanfare, but by then it was as empty as Al Capone's vault. Cornwell feels that many documents were apparently burnt that Sunday in Klagenfurt just before Calvi boarded a private jet for the trip to London, but other papers must have gone with Calvi to London.

"Like the key to the room at the Chelsea Cloisters and the rest of his address book," he continues, "they were never recovered. Did they depart on the private plane chartered by Kuntz which traveled from Geneva to Gatwick and back on the evening of June 18? Did Calvi destroy his most sensitive papers himself, or was their destruction the completion of the cover-up which began with his murder?" (p. 203).

On June 14, 1982, four days before Roberto Calvi was found dangling from Blackfriar's Bridge in London, Father Krunoslav Draganovic died in a hospital in Kosevo, Yugoslavia. If Draganovic's departure for Zagreb in 1967 meant that the anti-Communist crusade had outlived its usefulness to the Church, he died knowing that *Ostpolitik* had been superseded as well. If this caused him some satisfaction, he kept it to himself as he did with his other secrets and the diaries of Professor Crljen, the witness to the atrocities at Bleiburg.

Meanwhile in Medjugorje, the seers were coming up with a message of apocalypse which would prove more effective to the Croatian nation, abandoned by the Church in its struggle against Communism, than Draganovic and the Krizari and all of the other failed attempts at subversion during the '50s. On Christmas day 1982, Mirjana, the first to see the Virgin, announced that that the daily apparitions had stopped, except for one annual visit on March 18, her birthday. Mirjana was out of the apparition business and would remain so until February 1997, when financial pressures forced her back in again. Not one to leave quietly, Mirjana announced that on Christmas day she had received the tenth and last secret from the Blessed Virgin.

"As for the tenth," she announced dramatically, "it is terrible, and nothing can alter it. It will happen."

Just as the scenario for the original apparitions got borrowed from Lourdes, Mirjana evidently got the miraculous sign idea from Garabandal, another phony apparition, which took place in a remote village in northern Spain in the late '60s. First, there would be three warnings, which would be presented as three catastrophic events, then the miraculous, visible sign would appear. Three days before the first warning, Mirjana would announce what was going to happen to a priest of her choice, a Franciscan, it turns out, by the name of Pero Ljubicic. "It looks," said Fra Pero a bit glumly, "as though the first secret will be very disturbing." As the warnings were appearing, repentance would be possible, but once the great sign appeared, punishment was inevitable if repentance hadn't already taken place. Mirjana also announced that this was the last apparition of Jesus or His mother on earth, a claim that soon got refuted by subsequent history, as literally hundreds of tourists returning from Medjugorje became seers themselves.

As with the original apparitions, Mirjana's idea got embellished by the other seers, and the idea of the miraculous sign began to take on increasingly baroque permutations until it too was consigned to the collective memory hole when it became an embarrassment. Not to be outdone by Mirjana, Ivanka announced that she had received her secrets (which are not necessarily the same as Mirjana's) on a miraculous piece of "paper."

"It is of an indescribable material," Ivanka told a group of Italian pilgrims on June 25, 1985. "It seems like paper but it isn't; it seems like material, but it isn't. It's visible; you can touch it but not see the writing on it. My cousin, an engineer in Switzerland, has examined the stuff but can't identify it."

Like Joseph Smith's golden tablets, the paper seems to have disappeared, but not before the story changed. Later Ivanka told Rene Laurentin that she had not received a miraculous piece of "paper" from the Gospa but rather only a secret code which would allow her to write down the secrets so that only she and the Gospa could read them. Like Mirjana, Ivanka was to give the paper or the coded writing "to a specially chosen priest" of her choosing "when the right moment comes." This priest would then be "given the grace," which in this instance would function like a secret decoder ring and allow him to read secret number one. Both Mirjana and Ivanka then added that the time for revealing the first secret was, as of December 1982, fast approaching.

The general weirdness continued in December 1982 with the arrival of Dr. Ludvik Stopar, Slovenian parapsychologist and hypnotist from the University of Marbor. During an interview with Rene Laurentin, Stopar admitted hypnotizing Marija Pavlovic "because she appeared to me the most intelligent and the most mature of the visionaries and ... therefore the most suitable for the test, "obtaining from her in the process the ten secrets. Laurentin, who would administer his own "scientific" tests on the seers, was nonetheless a bit taken aback by the revelation, "But surely," he sputters, "this a violation of conscience. Now the secrets are no longer a secret."

Stopar, however, seems unconcerned about violating consciences or divulging secrets.

"You can trust my professionalism," he assures Laurentin blandly. "The secrets remain a secret for me as for Marija. I would not confide them, even to you. It is as serious as the confessional."

When Laurentin says that Marija said the procedure was done without her permission, the redoubtable Dr. Stopar is still unfazed:

"If I had asked," he replied, sounding more and more like the parapsychological version of Josef Mengele, "I am sure she would have refused. In therapy one does not ask permission."

The experiments of Dr. Stopar confirm a crucial transition as well. Mirjana had had enough; whether it is a result of libido, the theory of on priest, or not, the prime seer dropped out of the apparitions 18 months after they started and went back to her studies in Sarajevo. Here, as elsewhere, however, nature abhors a vacuum, and so within four days, on December 29, two new seers arrived on the scene. Ten-year-old Jelena Vasilj announced that she had seen a vision of Our Lady dressed in a white gown edged in gold, and beginning on Good Friday 1983, her friend Marijana Vasilj began seeing things too. Eventually, these two newcomers were demoted to the status of locutionists, i.e., people who just heard voices rather than those who heard and saw the Blessed Virgin.

The one who benefited the most from Mirjana and Ivanka dropping out of the apparition scene was Marija Pavlovic, who now under Father Vlasic's tutelage became the principal seer and the vessel through whom the messages, now confined to the 25th of each month, would arrive.

In February 1983, Father Jozo Zovko was released from prison and on the following day came to Medjugorje to offer a Mass of thanksgiving for his deliverance. Zovko, however, did not return to St. James Church as pastor. Instead he was sent to St. Elijah's Parish in Tihaljina; Zovko had been replaced by Tomislav Vlasic as spiritual director of the seers, and it was a role he was filling with increasing panache. Determined not to keep his light under a bushel basket, Vlasic wrote a letter to the pope on December 2, 1983, in which he gave the basic outline of the apparitions, including the bit about the warning and the miraculous sign.

"In addition to this basic message," Vlasic told the pope, "Mirjana related an apparition she had in 1982, which we believe sheds some light on some aspects of Church history. She spoke of an apparition in which Satan appeared to her disguised as the Blessed Virgin."

The pope's reaction to a missive like this is anyone's guess. To be sure it sounded a bit nutty and vaguely reminiscent of the condemned apparition of Garabandal. On the other hand, the pope's belief that the Blessed Virgin could intervene in human history had received dramatic reinforcement as he recovered from the assassin's bullets during the very time when the alleged apparitions were supposed to have begun. The pope was also less than three months away from fulfilling the request of the Virgin at Fatima, when on March 25, 1984, he would consecrate Russia to her Immaculate Heart. Either way, Karol Wojtyla was convinced that the Blessed Virgin had taken a direct hand in events in Eastern Europe and that he, as Pope John Paul II, was her instrument in some inscrutable way. Given this frame of mind, it is not far-fetched to imagine the pope feeling that Medjugorje was another manifestation of this divine plan, causing him, as a result, to overlook both the absurdities associated with the seers and the misgivings of the local bishop.

Those misgivings increased dramatically in 1983 when a Jesuit by the name of Radogost Grafenauer, *soi disant* expert in the discernment of spirits, showed up at the chancery in Mostar to see what was going on at Medjugorje. Zanic was so persuasive that Grafenauer almost returned home without stopping in Medjugorje to see what was going on. But he did go, and once there found Vlasic even more persuasive and became convinced that the apparitions were genuine. His abrupt conversion probably did little to convince Zanic of Grafenauer's discernment, but it did convince him that he had been lied to once again. Grafenauer had seen the diary with the anti-bishop messages in it, the diary which Vlasic swore did not exist. The stage was set for another confrontation, although it would come in a way that Zanic did not expect.

-6-

BISHOP HNILICA HELPS THE VATICAN

By early 1984, with Archbishop Marcinkus under virtual house arrest in the Vatican and public pressure mounting, the Vatican reached a decision on the Calvi case. Denying any legal responsibility for the $1.3 billion debt, but agreeing to a type of moral responsibility, the Vatican agreed to pay the Banco Ambrosiano's creditors $250 million. Many felt that the decision gave the Vatican the worst of both worlds. It cost them money, and it would be interpreted as well as an admission of guilt. Archbishop Marcinkus was one of the people who felt this way, and his premonitions turned out to be at least partially true. The settlement led to a whole new round of attacks in the press, linking the Vatican to the collapse of the Banco Ambrosiano.

One man who was especially concerned at the time about the Church's good name was a Slovakian émigré and bishop by the name of Paolo Maria Hnilica. Born in Unatin in Czechoslovakia on March 30, 1921, Hnilica suddenly appeared in Rome in the mid-'50s claiming to have been consecrated a bishop in 1951. The details of his consecration are still a matter of dispute. Concerning Hnilica there were two factions in the Vatican, those who accepted the consecration of the bishops behind the Iron Curtain, specifically places like Czechoslovakia, and those who rejected them. Some of the latter felt that Hnilica was a secret agent of the Communists whose goal was to infiltrate the Church.

Whatever his status, Bishop Hnilica was, according to his own account, increasingly concerned about the adverse publicity the Vatican was receiving in the Banco Ambrosiano case and determined to do something to counter it. As a result, in November of 1984, Hnilica along with Father Casimir Pryzadetek, the priest in charge of ministering to Polish pilgrims in Rome, met with Flavio Carboni at his apartment of the EUR section of Rome. At this meeting, Hnilica agreed to pay Carboni, the man who spirited Roberto Calvi to London in 1982, $3 million for the contents of Calvi's briefcase.

The crash of the Banco Ambrosiano created a financial crisis for the Vatican, but beyond that the crash also jeopardized the Vatican's efforts in eastern Europe at a crucial point during its struggle with Communism. The collapse of Banco Ambrosiano not only left the Vatican with a large debt, it also threatened its efforts to support Solidarity in Poland both financially and morally. If it could be shown that the Vatican was conspiring with the Reagan administration to bring about the collapse of regimes whose legitimacy it had recognized as a part of its *Ostpolitik*, then it would not only jeopardize any chance of success those efforts might have, it would also lose whatever leverage it had gained with those Communist governments over the past 20 years.

Perhaps thoughts like these were running through Bishop Hnilica's mind, perhaps not. According to his version of the story, Hnilica was concerned about the unfavorable publicity the Calvi affair had caused the Vatican and, therefore, decided to get these embarrassing documents by buying Calvi's briefcase and then using the documents to create a wave of publicity favorable to the Vatican at this crucial time in the anti-Communist crusade. But where did a bishop with no canonical assignment from a notoriously poor country get his hands on $3 million? Missing from Hnilica's largely self-serving account of his activities is the fact that Calvi's briefcase also contained account numbers and keys to secret Swiss safe deposit boxes, and that the charges that were eventually brought against him accused him of defrauding Calvi's heirs by taking possession of this property. But Hnilica could have gotten access to that money only after he had possession of the briefcase. Where did he get the money to give to Carboni in the first place, especially since the $3 million was evidently only the down payment.

At the end of 1985 Hnilica gave Carboni five blank checks. Several weeks later, Carboni made out the checks for a total which came to over $1 million. When the checks came to Hnilica's account at the IOR, the Vatican bank refused to honor them because Hnilica didn't have enough money in the account to cover them. Hnilica's embarrassment was severe and after several fruitless attempts to get the IOR to honor the checks, Hnilica wrote a letter to Vatican Secretary of State Agostino Cardinal Casaroli explaining his predicament and asking for financial assistance. "The events," Hnilica wrote on August 25, 1986, which followed the ruinous collapse of the Banco Ambrosiano and the tragic death of its president are well known to Your Eminence. The uproar in the press in Italy and abroad, treating the IOR with sarcasm and disdain and denouncing the alleged moral and juridical complicity of the Holy See . . . the accusations of arms trafficking in Latin America, support for opposition movements in the East and for *Solidarnosc*, money laundering and so forth caused a "noble priest" by the name of Virginio Rotundi to turn to Flavio Carboni, who had managed "to preserve the custody of documents that could be used in the interest of the IOR."

The letter goes on to confirm that Hnilica took possession of these documents and allowed him to carry out "an action" with great success. This action was a press campaign in favor of the Vatican which Hnilica conducted during 1985. The Italian prosecutor in the case eventually brought against Hnilica for trafficking in stolen goods produced evidence that Hnilica paid thousands of dollars to Italian and foreign journalists in exchange for favorable articles about the Vatican (*Fidelity*, February 1993, p. 29).

"You will understand," Hnilica then wrote, "that such a large operation, carried out in the circle of a few extremely reliable persons for more than a year and a half, has meant a quite limited financial expense in comparison to the quantity and quality of the results. Still, the cost has far surpassed our possibilities, forcing us to bear the weight, for the moment by heavy personal commitments which can no longer be deferred."

Hnilica then gets to the point. "I hope it is licit for me to think," he continued,

that the Holy See, whose welfare has been at the forefront of my constant concern, will deign to ratify choices and initiatives that seemed to me not to admit of doubt or hesitation and to unburden me, consequently of this insupportable weight. The delicacy of the matter advises against my indicating the names, places and ways regarding the financial relations which have taken place and are taking place, though I am ready, obviously, to give an accounting of this to Your Eminence, in a reserved and confidential audience, on the occasion that you would be willing to grant one to me. I limit myself to telling Your Eminence that the urgent—rather, extremely urgent—commitments made amount today to about 14.5 billion lire (about $10 million) in addition to the greater expenses already borne by those joined to me in making our own a cause which was that of the Holy See and the whole Church (p. 30).

Cardinal Casaroli began his response of September 9 to Hnilica's request for $10 million by first informing him that the "importance and the gravity of the situation" necessitated an immediate conference with the pope, and that Casaroli's response "comes in His Name as well." Preliminaries aside, the answer was short and to the point and unlikely to cheer up Bishop Hnilica. "Neither the Holy Father, in fact, nor the Holy See were aware of the activity that you briefly describe."

> It is therefore necessary, in the first place, that, to avoid any possible ambiguity, it be made totally clear that this activity has been carried out, and the relative decisions have been taken, without the slightest request, authorization or approval on the part of the Holy See (p. 30).

Hnilica, in other words, was on his own as far as the Holy See was concerned. He would have to cover his financial obligations as best he could from his own resources.

In 1989, Italian detectives investigating a drug smuggling ring stumbled across a tape recorded conversation between Giulio Lena, a Roman underworld figure and a man who was talking about making payments for the documents in Roberto Calvi's briefcase. That man, it turns out, was Bishop Hnilica, who was immediately interrogated and subsequently indicted for trafficking in stolen goods. What followed was more than a little ironical. The man who was ostensibly so concerned about restoring the good name of the Vatican in the press unleashed a whole new wave of anti-Catholic publicity. Much of it concerned the dubious status of Bishop Hnilica himself. Alceste Santini, a journalist for L'Unita, the Italian Communist Party's daily paper, wondered why Hnilica was not listed as a bishop in the Annuario Pontificio, the Vatican's official yearbook. "Today in the Vatican," Santini wrote on October 22 ,1989, "officials are asking themselves whether Monsignor Hnilica was ever consecrated a bishop, by whom and where. In the Annuario Pontificio, in the place where the date and place of Pavel Hnilica's consecration ought to be, there are only three dots."

The entry in the Annuario Pontificio changed subsequently, but the questions about Hnilica's credentials persisted. At around the same time he was involved in purchasing Calvi's briefcase and funding the subsequent publicity campaign, Hnilica's behavior at Medjugorje had come to the notice of Bishop Zanic.

"In about 1987 I forbade him to come into my diocese," Zanic stated in 1993. "In my diocese, he was arriving and conducting himself as if he were the bishop of the place, as if he were more important than I was, even though I was the rightful bishop. He allied himself with the rebel group of Franciscans and disobeyed my guidelines for Medjugorje. And he has also given problems to the Holy See, I was informed" (p. 34).

Zanic's successor, Ratko Peric, has had similar problems with Hnilica. In March of 1994 Hnilica showed up at the chancery office in Mostar and announced that he was on a special mission from the Holy Father to re-consecrate Russia to the Immaculate Heart and that he needed Peric's permission to say a Mass for that purpose on Mt. Podbrdo. When the bishop asked for a letter from the pope authorizing this mission, Hnilica said that he had been commissioned in person and had no supporting documents. Peric rolled his eyes at this point when recounting the incident. He also pointed out that in the current issue of *Annuario Pontifico*, Hnilica is listed as having been nominated 13 years after he was consecrated, a situation he could not explain. His curiosity piqued, Peric then went to Rome, where the Holy See explained to him some of the irregularities associated with Hnilica's case. The ultimate result was an article in *Cvrka na Kamenu*, the diocesan newspaper, denouncing Hnilica as "the pope's false delegate."

Hnilica's role as a major promoter of Medjugorje helps clarify some of the mystery surrounding his behavior in the mid-'80s. By May of 1985 after the Zanic Commission caught Ivan in his lie about the "great sign," the apparitions were in deep trouble. At the very point when the apparitions had begun to generate a significant amount of income from tourism, attracting much wealthier pilgrims from the United States, Medjugorje was threatened by the almost certainty that Zanic was going to come out with a negative judgment, thereby putting an end to the lucrative tourist trade and budding Croatian nationalism at a time when the anti-Communist crusade had reached a crucial phase.

By the mid-'80s the Yugoslavian government had decided upon a change of course in dealing with Medjugorje. Instead of trying to suppress it, the government decided to promote it, as long as they were the major financial beneficiaries. Room rates were fixed by the government and paid to the government. More importantly, all transactions had to take place in dinar, a currency that was worthless outside of the borders of Yugoslavia. As tourism increased, the Franciscans and their local supporters were faced with a new problem, namely, what to do with the money. If they deposited it in local banks, it became worthless as hard currency and subject to the government's draconian taxation policies. As a result, the promoters of Medjugorje were in urgent need of people willing to launder money for them, a process which involved getting it first out of the country.

Hnilica, according to one source close to the Franciscans in Medjugorje, was a major conduit of Medjugorje money out of Yugoslavia. The relationship was symbiotic in a number of ways. Hnilica was given access to money at a time when he was strapped himself and had just been turned down by the Holy See for a $10 million loan. He was also involved in a publicity campaign that could just as easily be turned to the benefit of Medjugorje as it was, at least according to his account, to the Holy See. And in the mid-'80s, Medjugorje was in desperate need of favorable publicity.

In November of 1984, at around the same time that Bishop Hnilica was meeting with Flavio Carboni in his apartment in EUR, the Franciscans, fearing that Zanic's discovery of Vlasic's illegitimate child in Germany would prove fatal to Medjugorje and the cover it afforded to Franciscan rebellion, launched a preemptive strike against the Bishop Zanic. Tacitly admitting the fact that the charge against Vlasic could no longer be ignored, they accused the bishop of calumny. In his book *La prolongation des apparitions de Medjugorje*, Rene Laurentin floated the rumor publicly, purged of all of the names, making it impossible either to confirm or to deny the story. According to the account in the French edition of Laurentin's book (the whole story was excised from the English translation published by the Riehle Foundation because, according to Bill Reck, the book's English editor, "We saw no purpose in putting it in"), "The presumed father of the child quit the order and went to the United States, where he is married after being reduced to the lay state."

The Franciscans were more specific. In private they were circulating the name of Marijan Pehar, who was indeed one of the Franciscans who had lived with Manda and Vlasic in Zagreb. He was, as Laurentin indicated, now out of the order and living as a married man in America. Indeed, he was the only Croatian ex-Franciscan in the world who fit Laurentin's description of the father. Pinning the paternity rap on Pehar was a clever move. It simultaneously got Vlasic off the hook and put the bishop in check by making it now look as if he were guilty of calumny. Laurentin even dragged the Blessed Mother into the story: "Let the Gospa defend you," the seers reportedly said. However, it was a dangerous move as well—all lies involve an element of danger—because it was based on the assumption that no one would contact Marijan Pehar.

Bishop Zanic had tried, but without success. Pehar had received his letter, but was put off by its tone. That and the residual animosity toward the local bishop of someone who had once been a

Franciscan caused the letter to go unanswered. The bishop made another mistake as well. In his private report on the matter, he claimed that "Franciscans from Herzegovina went to America to pursue ex-Franciscan Pehar to persuade him to take on the paternity of the child . . . but he didn't accept." In reality the Franciscans never approached Pehar, who was living at the time on the West Coast. Perhaps they knew better. Pehar was later to say that, if they had asked him to accept the paternity, he would have refused.

It was an effective, if nasty, strategy. The key to it all was to take the heinous and sensational story of a priest fathering a child and use that to smear the bishop. Laurentin and the Franciscans could use the normal reluctance of people to believe such things as the thrust that would drive their accusation of calumny home. That the charge was itself a grave calumny seems not to have given either the Franciscans or Laurentin pause, but this may simply be a result of the desperation they felt at the time. If it could be shown that the seers' spiritual advisor had fathered a child— by a nun, no less— the so-called apparitions at Medjugorje would be in serious danger in the public eye. Better to take the charge and twist it into a lie against the bishop than let something like that happen.

The strategy was not without risks, the main risk being that someone would eventually find Pehar and ask him for his version of things. Pehar's failure to respond to the Bishop Zanic's letter had thwarted any effort to deal with the calumny against him effectively. Without Pehar's testimony it was just the bishop's word against the entire Medjugorje propaganda apparatus, and in that struggle the bishop was clearly outgunned. In June of 1988, this author, while researching an article which eventually appeared in September and October 1988 issues of *Fidelity* magazine, reached Pehar by phone, and Pehar categorically denied that he was the father of the child. We then went through the names of the Croatian Franciscans who had left the order. None of them is named Tomislav or Tomo, and furthermore none of them had even been in Croatia in 1976. That coupled with the fact that Pehar, who knew both principals personally, confirmed that the letters were written by Manda and Vlasic respectively seemed to allow only one conclusion.

"So Laurentin's lying then," I said.

"That's right," Pehar replied. "There's no possibility that anybody here in America could be the father."

If the Medjugorjians felt that Vlasic fathering a child was a damning indictment of the apparitions, they were right. However, their attempt to cover that fact up is even more damning, and beyond that, their attempt to base the cover-up on a calumny of the bishop is worse still. When contacted to get his side of the story, Father Rene Laurentin was nervous and evasive. He began by explaining that "Monsignor Zanic does not hesitate before calumnies," but then asked me not to quote him on that. He then said that he could not give the name of the Franciscan who had been accused, apparently forgetting that he had mentioned Vlasic's name in a subsequent book, *Sept annèes d'apparitions*. When I brought that fact to his attention, he responded by saying, "But this book is not translated, yes?"

"Right," I said.

"You have this book in French?"

"Yes, I've seen it in French. You said that the accusation was made against Tomislav Vlasic in that book."

After getting caught in another lie, Laurentin lapsed first into incoherence and then fell back on his charge of calumny against the bishop.

"So you're saying that Vlasic is not the father?"

"Yes," Laurentin responded, if a bit incoherently, "for me."

Laurentin then claimed that the letters were forgeries, but stated his case in such a half-hearted fashion that it was clear that even he didn't believe it.

"I quote the letter of the mother of the boy. It's wrong, eh? She left her job because her master did this forged suggestion to the bishop. I think this seems to be clear, but you can judge what you want, eh?"

In the course of the conversation Laurentin confirmed that Manda was the name of the mother and that the old man, previously identified only as "M. O." in *La prolongation* was indeed named 'Ott." Given that sort of corroboration, there is only one avenue left by way of explanation—the one in fact Laurentin took, namely, that Herr Ott forged the letters. Even without Pehar's specific testimony that the letters are genuine, the accusation is preposterous. How is a blind 94-year-old German, who by his own admission speaks no Croatian, supposed to forge a series of letters in that language in two separate hands? The idea bespoke Laurentin's desperation in the matter and the desperation of the Medjugorjians in general.

I then asked Laurentin about the sentence he wrote explaining the whole thing, *"Le pére prèsumè de l'enfant quitta l'ordre et partit pour l'Amèrique, óu il s'est mariè, aprés rèduction á l'ètat laic."* ("The presumed father of the child quit the order and went to the United States, where he is married after being reduced to the lay state.")

Again he was evasive. He claimed not to know the name of the father.

"It is one of the hypotheses, one of the things that were said to me that probably the father would be this Franciscan which is now in America, but this I am not sure. It is a simple hypothesis. I could not verify. I want to be honest in this matter. I quote that like a hypothesis."

The word hypothesis, of course, never appeared in Laurentin's account, a fact which forced the perceptive reader to one of two conclusions. Either Laurentin knew the name of the "presumed father," but won't give it out for fear that someone will track him down, or he has based his accusation of calumny against the bishop on no solid information. The most probable explanation is the former. Laurentin got the story that Pehar was the father from the Franciscans and used the story and the concomitant calumny of the bishop as away of putting a favorable spin on the fact that the seers' spiritual advisor as of the early to mid-'80s had fathered an illegitimate child. The event took place before the apparitions, but one of the disqualifying factors was evidence of manipulation, and the letters to Manda made clear that Vlasic was a master of manipulation. His subsequent behavior with the seers would bear this unpleasant aspect of his character out as well.

As of 1985, the chance that the apparitions would get the approval of the Church was looking increasingly remote. The seers' spiritual advisor was involved in serious sexual immorality as well as lying, calumny and a cover-up (the latter involving Medjugorje's chief propagandist at the time, Rene Laurentin). The evidence against the seers was mounting as well. Vicka lied to the bishop about the existence of her diary; Ivan lied—as documented by Laurentin himself—about the alleged sign and when it was to appear (See Laurentin's *Derniéres nouvelles de Medjugorje: Vers la fin des apparitions*, O.E.I.L. Edition de Juin 1985, pp. 17-23).

During 1985 the negative evidence would continue to mount. During the early part of January 1985 a huge mass of arctic air roared into Western Europe, dropping snow and freezing pipes in even normally mild Rome. In the mountainous region surrounding Medjugorje, the conditions were even worse, forcing the few pilgrims there at the time to huddle in the few buildings available for warmth and fellowship. Jean-Louis Martin was one of these pilgrims. He had come as a believer months before, but living in close proximity to the seers had created doubts that he was now determined to resolve. One of the claims made about the seers at the time was that during the visions they were in a kind of ecstasy—out of contact with the normal realm of the senses. Martin, who was a frequent visitor to the apparition room, which was off to the side of the church sanctuary at the time, decided to test his hypothesis. During the apparition he lunged at Vicka and attempted to poke her in the eyes Three Stooges-style with his two fingers. Vicka's startled reaction was just what one might expect from a normal person but not from a seer who was reputedly out of contact with space and time. Perhaps realizing that her reaction gave her away, Vicka fled from the room.

Before long she returned, however, this time accompanied by a Franciscan priest who explained to Martin that what really happened had nothing to do with Martin's actions. Rather Vicka was watching the Blessed Mother, who looked as if she were going to drop the Baby Jesus, and so Vicka lunged forward to catch the falling Christ child. Martin remained skeptical, however. The motion Vicka made was clearly away from the vision and not toward it. We know this because the entire incident was documented on video by a parapsychologist from Montreal by the name of Louis Belanger and has subsequently appeared in British and Australian documentaries on Medjugorje. As with so many other incidents, the Martin incident gets mentioned in Mary Craig's book, only to be explained away by one of the seers' Franciscan handlers, in this instance Slavko Barbaric.

As the negative evidence mounted, so did Bishop Zanic's concerns about the consequences of so much mendacity. On January 25, 1985, Zanic wrote to Rene Laurentin, complaining that "A fierce frenzy has taken hold of many of the faithful who were good until now; they have become excessive and peculiar penitents...One can look forward to a religious war here" It was probably the only prophecy associated with Medjugorje which came true. One of the ironies, if one can call it that, associated with the apparitions is the fact that the chastisement which Medjugorje predicted for the world fell on its own head instead, largely as a result of the religious chauvinism spawned by the apparitions.

On March 7, 1985, three members of Zanic's episcopal commission caught Ivan in the lie about the Great Sign. Ivan was apparently devastated, at least for a while, by shame or at having been caught—so much so that on Mirjana's March 18 birthday apparition the Blessed Mother had to intervene, announcing that, "It wasn't Ivan's fault. I've scolded him enough now. Let him alone."

The role of the Franciscans in manipulating the seers was becoming more and more obvious. One day after catching Ivan in his lie, the commission announced that the most damning thing about the apparitions was the seers' making use of the Gospa to encourage the ecclesiastical disobedience of Prusina and Vego. Both suspended friars were regular visitors at Medjugorje, where they performed the sacraments in direct defiance of Church authority. Louis Belanger felt that their ministry went far beyond the sacramental functions of the Church and involved the occult. On March 17, 1985, Belanger wrote to Rene Laurentin, describing a video of Ivica Vego and children from another village nearby he had seen at Medjugorje on January 16 of that year. In it Ivica Vego claims that the children are seeing the Gospa. Or at least Vego, according to Belanger, is "encouraging them to think that."

For example, one scene shows two children on their knees in prayer. Ivica's insistent voice off camera asks a number of times, "Do you see her? Do you see the virgin?" In another sequence one of the children is lying motionless on his stomach. Ivica approaches him, feeling his legs and arms and then slips into his hand paper and pencil so that he can write down the messages of the Gospa. It was in the purest tradition of the occult. We know that those who induce automatic writing in young people can cause them more or less permanent damage in their identity formation.

According to Belanger, neither the psychotherapist priest Slavko Barbaric, who showed him the film, nor the suspended Franciscan Vego seemed concerned about the dangers involved in this sort of manipulation.

The same sort of manipulation becomes obvious in the case of Vicka, who was reportedly getting instructions on the life of the Blessed Virgin at the time, as well as "revelations about the future of the world." Vicka, pilgrims were told, was plagued by "violent headaches and sudden black-outs, though still smiling and saying she was perfectly all right." Eventually, the story of the headaches escalated into the announcement, made on the BBC/Everyman video, that Vicka had an inoperable brain tumor. Twelve years later, Vicka was still cranking out messages, and the story of her brain tumor had long since disappeared down the memory hole.

The manipulation of seers, however, continued apace. Just how it got done can be discerned by a careful reading of the interviews with Vicka which appeared in 1985 in the book *A Thousand Encounters with the Blessed Virgin Mary in Medjugorje*. The book is helpful because it consists of basically unedited transcripts of interviews with Vicka conducted by the Croatian priest Janko Bubalo. A good example of the type of manipulation we're talking about occurs on p. 54 of that book when Father Bubalo discusses with Vicka the type of clothing the Blessed Virgin wears during the apparitions:

> Bubalo: As long as we are speaking about it, you related to me previously that the Virgin is sometimes dressed in a special manner.

> Vicka: Yes, in a special manner, as it relates to color. Sometimes, (not often) she was in golden garments, but the style of her garments is always the same.

Bubalo: And why does she sometimes dress so richly?

Vicka: How should I know? It's not for me to ask!

Bubalo: [undeterred by Vicka's slightly rude response] That occurred, I suppose, for some formal occasions?

Vicka: Why yes, it occurred on some of the more important feast days.

Bubalo: And, do you recall any such occasions?

Vicka: I do recall, how could I not! One of her feast days is marked in my mind, one that occurs about the end of March or so.

Bubalo: That is the Annunciation?

Vicka: I don't know. She told us something about that day, but I don't remember.

Bubalo: And it's not clear to you what is commemorated on that day?

Vicka: It is and isn't. Don't let me jump off the deep end on that one.

Bubalo: Well, Vicka, that is the remembrance day of when the angel announced to Mary that she would conceive by the Holy Ghost, and that she would give birth to the Savior of the world.

Vicka: Really, I thought of that, but I wasn't sure. Then the Virgin had a right to be happy.

Bubalo: She was happy?

Vicka: I never saw her so happy, not even on Christmas. Why she almost danced with joy!

Bubalo: All right. Let's go on to something else now. Especially since, as you say, one cannot describe the Virgin's beauty.

The passage is significant for a number of reasons. First of all, it gives a good indication of the relation of the seers to those, specifically the priests, who are propagating the messages. The so-called revelations are the result of what seems to be unconscious prompting on the part of Father Bubalo, in which he fills in the lacunae of Vicka's knowledge with his own theological expertise. Beyond that, the dialogue gives some indication of Vicka's knowledge of the faith. This young lady—she is 21 years old at the time of the interview—apparently does not know what the Annunciation is. Now this would be strange to hear from anyone who prayed the rosary regularly, but even stranger to hear from someone who has had daily encounters with the Blessed Virgin.

But things get stranger still. On p. 222 of the same book, Father Bubalo writes:

Vicka informed me on the 11th of April, 1985, that the day before, the Virgin ceased narrating her life's story. Simple calculations tell that the Virgin narrated her story some 825 (!) days. She immediately began to tell Vicka of the fate of the world, telling her to keep a daily journal which, as far as I can tell, Vicka faithfully does.

In his book, Bubalo claims that Vicka has been receiving personal instruction on the life of the Virgin from the Virgin herself. Yet when confronted by clear evidence that Vicka doesn't know what the Annunciation is, Bubalo fills in the information himself rather than question Vicka's veracity. The apparition becomes as a result the overarching explanation which gives meaning to each of the events associated with it. Once a devotee like Father Bubalo commits himself to belief in the apparition, he becomes committed to protecting Vicka from her own inconsistencies and absurdities. The fact that Vicka knows even less about the life of the Blessed Virgin than even a cursory reading of Bible would reveal deters Bubalo's belief not in the least. In the following exchange it is interesting to see in just which direction the information is flowing:

Bubalo: Those of us who know a bit more about the happenings at Medjugorje also know that the Virgin, as you say, expounded on her life and asked that you keep notes on it.

Vicka: That is correct. And, what about it?

Bubalo: Well, tell me first off, to whom did the Virgin explain her life?

Vicka: As far as I know, to all except Mirjana.

Bubalo: And did the Virgin set forth her life to everyone at the same time?

Vicka: I don't know for certain. I think that she began to tell Ivan a bit before the rest. And, she handled it with Marija in a different way.

Bubalo: How do you mean?

Vicka: Well, when the Virgin appeared to her in Mostar, she didn't set forth her life's story, but only when she appeared to her in Medjugorje.

Bubalo: That's all right. I asked each of you separately about this. If you wish, I can clarify it a bit?

Vicka: Why of course! *I always like that you speak as much as possible* [my emphasis].

Given Vicka's track record on public statements, it's not hard to understand why. Here we have a 21-year-old young lady who has been getting daily personal instruction on the life of the Blessed Virgin for almost three years who cannot explain what the Annunciation is even though she supposedly meditates on it every time she prays the joyful mysteries of the Rosary. Given such an admission on Vicka's part, however, the significant thing about the dialogue is the willingness on the part of the priest to make up for Vicka's ignorance. Rather than concluding from this admission that the apparitions might not be authentic, Bubalo spends his time, depending on how you want to interpret things, either refreshing Vicka's memory or telling her what to say. So, as soon as Vicka says how much she likes it when Father Bubalo does the talking, Father Bubalo goes on to oblige by explaining to Vicka just how the seers have been getting the life of the Virgin explained to them:

The Virgin, as Ivan relates, began to expound on her life on the 22nd of December, 1982. He said that she explained her life to him on two occasions, and that she ceased telling her story on the 7th of January, 1983. She began to relate her story to the rest of you on January 7th, 1983. And, she did so to Ivanka every day up to May 22nd. She ceased telling of her life to little Jakov a bit sooner, but he, I don't know why, refused to give me that bit of information. She stopped telling her story to Marija on the 17th of July, 1983. With you, as we know, it was again, different. She began to explain her life to you as to the others, on the 7th of January, but as you say she continues to tell her life's story to you. But again she explained her story to Marija in a special manner.

Vicka: She said something about that, but it isn't too clear to me.

Given the preceding account of things, it does not seem unfair to ask just who is explaining the apparitions to whom? Is Vicka explaining things to Father Bubalo, or is she simply responding in a docile way to his leading questions and verbal prodding? The question is crucial if we are to understand what is going on there. Are the seers doing the leading or are they merely being led?

The situation for pilgrims who do not speak Croatian is even worse. In addition to the Franciscan handler, the interpreter/tour guides create another set of filters between the seers and their interlocutors. One tour guide explained that whenever Ivan would say something he would consider incredibly stupid, the statement would simply not get translated. This situation gradually resolved itself because the utterances of the seers became safely formulaic over the years as a result of sheer repetition, a fact which caused acute boredom and a tendency to substance abuse on the part of the translators.

In May of 1988 I attended a private meeting with Vicka in the bedroom of her home in Bijakovici. Present were Vicka, her interpreter, a priest on pilgrimage, and this author. In many ways the meeting was an uncanny replication of the Bubalo book. The priest had heard that Vicka had been taken up into heaven and so was intent on pumping her for information on the details. I began by asking her if the visions were coming to an end. Given the fact that Vicka speaks only Croatian, a private meeting means one with an interpreter present, in this case Draga Ivankovic, Vicka's cousin, who is also a tour guide and lives down the road from her. Vicka replied that, no, the apparitions were not coming to an end even though she had nine of the alleged ten secrets. When I asked her to explain the conflict with the local bishop, she replied that "the bishop doesn't know what he is doing," whereupon Draga said that it was getting late and that the interview was over. Access to the seers is a function of access to those around them, whether they be tour guides or priests. If the seers' managers dislike the drift of the questions, the meeting ends abruptly.

On May 23, 1985, the Vatican issued the first of its warnings on Medjugorje. Archbishop Alberto Bovone, undersecretary for the Congregation for the Doctrine of the Faith, sent a letter to the Italian Bishops in which he announced that the Church did not allow the faithful to organize pilgrimages to Medjugorje. He also condemned the publicity campaign surrounding Medjugorje, which at the time was making significant inroads among Catholics in Italy. These activities, he continued, only served to confuse the faithful. He deplored the propaganda on Medjugorje, the organized pilgrimages, and other similar enterprises which serve to stoke the confusion among the faithful.

Like two trains heading down the same track from opposite directions, the publicity campaign in favor of Medjugorje and the episcopal commission which would eventually condemn it collided in 1986, probably the most crucial year in the entire history of the apparitions. On May 2, 1986, Zanic's commission—in reality, his second commission—dissolved after presenting its unfavorable verdict to the bishop. One month later, in June, Zanic sent the report to Rome and presented it to the Congregation of the Doctrine of the Faith. What happened over the next six months is a matter of speculation. What we do know is that the negative findings of the commission were never published. Instead, on January 18, 1987, a front-page announcement appeared in *Glas Koncila*, announcing the formation of yet another commission, the third, this time under the auspices not of the ordinary of the diocese of Mostar but of the Yugoslavian Bishops' Conference. Cardinal Kuharic and Bishop Zanic, co-signers of the statement, explained that a third commission was necessary because "these events under investigation have appeared to go much beyond the limits of the diocese. Therefore, on the basis of the said regulations, it became fitting to continue the work at the level of the Bishops' Conference and thus to form a new Commission for that purpose."

The statement's third paragraph makes it clear that the new commission has been formed at the urging of the Congregation for the Doctrine of the Faith and not at the suggestion of either Bishop Zanic or the other Yugoslavian bishops. The statement concludes by urging "the practice of the usual prudence" in such circumstances.

For that reason, it is not permitted to organize either pilgrimages or other religious manifestations based on an alleged supernatural character attributed to Medjugorje's events. Marian devotion, legitimate and recommended by the Church must be in accordance with the directives of the Magisterium, and especially the apostolic encyclical *Marialis Cultus*.

The prohibition of pilgrimages, while in line with the warning of Archbishop Bovone a year earlier, strikes an odd note at the end of a document which, in effect, opened the gates for a flood of pilgrims, the most in the history of the apparition, which would last right up until the civil war made tourism impossible. The statement of January 1987 was the first of a series of statements, culminating in the April 1991 statement of the Yugoslavian Bishops' Conference at Zadar, which seemed designed to placate the interests of both sides in the conflict rather than put an end to the conflict by coming to a definitive answer about the truth of the matter. The strategy resonates with Ratzinger's statement in *Rapporto sulla Fede*, but whether it came from him is doubtful. In 1988 Zanic told me that Ratzinger did not believe in the apparitions and told him so in person.

Given the chain of command in Rome, that leaves just one other person which the authority to shelve a report by a bishop, namely, the pope. Did the pope intervene? Whether he did or did not, the issue seems to have been settled shortly after Zanic sent his report to Rome in June of 1986, which is to say, six months before the official statement announcing the formation of the third commission appeared in January 1987. In July 1986 Rene Laurentin wrote that "the threats which seems aimed at stifling or crushing Medjugorje" had been suspended, a claim echoed in an August 1986 article in *La Croix* of Paris with the headline: "Medjugorje: Rome Will Rule." More than anything else, the creation of a new commission effectively destroyed the authority of Bishop Zanic in the matter. Now proponents of Medjugorje could say that the issue had been taken out of his hands and could blithely ignore the caveat that pilgrimages were not permitted. If Rome had simply accepted the judgment of Bishop Zanic and published it as their own, it would have put an end to Medjugorje in 1986, before the huge mass of tourism arrived with huge amounts of hard currency, all of which fueled the self-confidence of Croatia and eventually led to the declaration of independence and subsequent war. That Rome did not accept the commission report indicates that it wanted that development to continue.

Father Ivo Sivric, who followed the events of 1986 closely as part of the research that eventuated in his book *The Hidden Side of Medjugorje*, confesses to being confused. While admitting that a negative decision would be easier to defend against a government avid for tourist money if it were issued by all of the bishops in Yugoslavia and not just one, Sivric feels that the January 1987 announcement not only undermined the authority of Bishop Zanic, but that it undermined Rome's previous positions as well. It "muddled the situation," leading Sivric to believe that Rome had an unspoken political agenda it was following rather than a simple desire to know and proclaim the truth:

"In the name of prudence," Sivric wrote, "Rome has persisted in delaying the final ruling from the very start. Whenever this ruling is scheduled, the Vatican makes a gesture which brings further delays and creates confusion. Are these deliberate politics? Does Rome nurse secret hopes? Is Rome really interested in having the truth known?" (p. 141).

In 1997 Father Rene Laurentin gave a talk at Medjugorje in which he announced that he had personally placed a copy of his book *Is the Virgin Mary Appearing at Medjugorje?* into the hands of the pope at what he termed a crucial moment. That moment was most likely the early summer of 1986 when the fate of Medjugorje hung by a thread. Not many people knew about it, certainly fewer than would know about it in five years when the official "condemnation" appeared. American tourists had not started coming by the planeload. The apparition would most probably have died in its infancy if Rome had accepted Zanic's negative report.

But it didn't, and the question remains, why? Sivric cites a book by Father Pier Angelo Gramaglia which denounces both Ratzinger's and the pope's sympathetic attitude toward the charismatic movement, which "which props up and inspires Medjugorje." The charismatics enjoy "sovereign protection" from the pope, who favors "big crowds who tend to show their faith in a theatrical way with spectacular devotional displays and apocalyptic predictions which seem to create the belief that the great Catholic renewal is shaping up for the early twenty-first century."

One gets the impression that the pope approved of the outpouring of Marian devotion emanating from Yugoslavia, and even if he wasn't sure whether the Virgin Mary was appearing there or not, he wanted to support the movement anyway. An article which appeared in the Italian periodical *La Vita del Populo* in February 1987 supports this view. "The Pope, "writes Bishop Mistronigo of Treviso, who discussed Medjugorje during his *ad limina* visit in early 1987,

> has shown that he knows and follows events in Medjugorje. He maintains there is nothing bad in them because people pray there, go to the sacraments and are given a chance to begin a more serious spiritual life. As

to the belief in the real presence of Mary there, caution is to be exercised, and of course, bishops' assessments as well as theologians' are still to be unanimous.

Again, the operative philosophy here seems to be the combination of consequentialism and agnosticism advocated by Cardinal Ratzinger in his famous 1984 interview. Who can know if the Virgin is appearing here? And as long as the people pray, what difference does it make? Zanic, on the other hand, was wary of the potential for scandal—he was thinking of how the Communists would exploit the situation—if it turned out to be false.

One priest closely associated with the apparitions for more than ten years gave his take on the crucial summer of 1986. He claimed that when Zanic arrived in Rome with a report that condemned Medjugorje in no uncertain terms, he found a willing collaborator in Cardinal Ratzinger who was ready to "blow it out of the water." The pope, however, was not going to let that happen for a number of reasons. The one which this priest mentions is the intervention of Rene Laurentin. But the pope was favorably disposed for other reasons as well. "The pope is an apparition nut," claimed the priest. "He had rehabilitated Sister Faustina in his diocese and he felt that the Medjugorje visionaries were just as real." So instead of condemning Medjugorje, the Vatican appointed another commission, which gave the impression that the whole thing was unsettled and that Zanic's authority got in the way. This state of affairs lasted for five years until the spring of 1991, when the Yugoslavian bishops finally condemned Medjugorje but in language that still seemed to allow for pilgrimages.

Frank Shakespeare was U.S. ambassador to the Holy See during the crucial summer of 1986. Perhaps because of his years in diplomatic service, he does not refer to the pope as "an apparition nut," but he does stress the role that Marian piety, particularly following the assassination attempt on the Fatima anniversary, played in the pope's life and in the collapse of Communism in eastern Europe. The pope felt that his life had been spared by Mary for a reason, and the reason had to do with Fatima, specifically the prediction about the conversion of Russia and the repudiation of Communism.

"The pope's role was central," Shakespeare said in an interview. "Without him, it wouldn't have happened," the *it* in question being the collapse of the Soviet Union. But Shakespeare feels that it wouldn't have happened without Ronald Reagan's military build-up either. Shakespeare refused to speak with Carl Bernstein, who called him repeatedly during his research for *His Holiness*, but Shakespeare disagrees with Kwitny's thesis that the pope did it alone without Reagan as well. Karol Wojtyla and Ronald Reagan were collaborating to bring about the demise of Communism. They met in 1982 and in 1987, and Shakespeare says the topic was discussed at the latter meeting because he was there and spoke with Reagan minutes later.

In June of '87 Reagan came to Rome to talk about the pope's visit to the United States that coming fall. The pope was going to spend nine days in the United States. It was understood that there would be a meeting of the two men beforehand, and that they would talk again when they met in the fall. About a month before the pope arrived, the American Ambassador to the Holy See [i.e., Shakespeare] got a cable, which said, "It is very desirable if you would inquire at the highest level if one individual could be with the president when the president meets with the pope." Shakespeare put the request in writing and sent it to the Holy See. The assumption, according to Shakespeare, was that the answer would be, "why, of course." The answer, however, was: "No, the pope feels that the meeting should be one-on-one."

"No one in the world would say that to the president of the United States," Shakespeare said. Then continuing, he described the meeting.

"During the June '87 visit to the Vatican, the president and the pope went into a room by themselves and stayed there from 11 to 12. When the visit to the Vatican was over, Nancy had to change her dress from black to something appropriate for meeting with the president of Italy. After the door closed on the antechamber where she was changing, there were just two people in that room, Ronald Reagan and Frank Shakespeare. While waiting the 20 minutes for her to change, Shakespeare said to President Reagan, "Sir, is there anything that occurred in the talk you just had that it would be appropriate to know to serve you better."

Reagan then mentioned a number of things to Shakespeare.

Shakespeare then said, "You know the value of secrecy. Only two people in the world know what you just told me. If it is agreeable I will never speak of what you told me. I will not tell my wife. I will not tell my aides."

And Reagan leaned over and said in a whisper, "Fine."

Three weeks later Shakespeare refused a request for a debriefing from the National Security Council. As of now he will say that the pope and the president talked "alone on the highest level. How their ideas got implemented I don't know. We're talking about an instinctive thing between two extraordinary men."

I then asked if Medjugorje played a role in destabilizing communism in Yugoslavia.

"Medjugorje," Shakespeare answers, "had a deep impact on the Croatian people, but not on the Serbs. Like Fatima, Medjugorje played a role in the lives of people committed to the Catholic faith."

Shakespeare then seemingly changed the subject to talk about his meeting with Lech Walesa, "a man of unquestioned gravitas."

Did the United States then support Medjugorje in the same way they were supporting Solidarity in Poland?

"No, not to my knowledge," Shakespeare answered obliquely. "For the people who dealt with eastern Europe, Yugoslavia was on the back burner. It was much less important that Poland.

"But, yes, you would support it," Shakespeare continued, "because Reagan, being Reagan, saw that the Soviet Union was an evil empire and that there was this extraordinary ferment there, and supporting something like this would increase the ferment. But this is not in neat columns. It's a matter of emphasis. There was ferment everywhere in eastern Europe and, yes, you would support something like Medjugorje but not as a matter of primary focus. Poland was the point of emphasis."

Shakespeare was then asked if the pope delayed condemning Medjugorje in 1986 because of what Sivric called "deliberate politics." The Zanic Commission Report was on the pope's desk at the same time he was being briefed about the Reagan administration's efforts to increase "ferment" in Eastern Europe. It was also clear that the Reagan administration considered Medjugorje an integral part of the ferment, even if it was not taking place in the primary theater of destabilization, namely, Poland.

Once again Shakespeare answered the questions obliquely, denying personal knowledge at first but then going on to give a general picture of what was happening.

"First of all, the pope had a sense of destiny. He was enormously conscious of the fact that he was the first non-Italian pope in 450 years. Secondly he was conscious of being a Slav pope. And third, the first thing he did after getting elected was identify himself as a Marian pope. He chose 'Totus Tuus' as his motto. Walesa is Marian too. In 1981 the pope was shot while driving around St. Peter's Square in the popemobile on May 13, the anniversary of Fatima. One year later he went to Fatima and said the Virgin played a role in sparing his life. These are things he has said in public. He knows that Fatima's message is specific to Russia, and that he's a Slavic pope at a crucial time though Mary's direct intervention. Being Marian, he is infused with Mary at the same time that events are going on in Yugoslavia."

In other words, several vectors were all converging toward one point during the crucial summer of 1986. The pope was being advised by the Reagan administration about their efforts to destabilize Communism, and he was personally inclined to see Ali Agca's assassination attempt as part of the message of Fatima. "The pope will have much to suffer," Lucia said, relaying the words of the Blessed Virgin. The bullets the pope took in the abdomen on the 64th anniversary of the first Fatima apparition seemed to fit that bill.

On the other hand, the details of the Zanic Commission report were too serious to overlook. The Church could never give its approval to something this scandalous. So instead of deciding, the pope temporized. He appointed another commission, which created a breathing space during which Medjugorje would continue to grow and along with it the Croatian nationalist pressure on Communism in Yugoslavia.

The best explanation of the strategy of delay and confusion which so troubled Father Sivric is that Rome's political aspirations interfered with its sense of Church governance and the truth. The pope was in the middle of the battle with Communism at the time. Ever since England and the United States conspired to dismember the Austro-Hungarian empire at the end of World War I, the Church was looking for a way to reinstitute what came to be known as Intermarium, a Catholic political bloc from the Baltic to the Adriatic, with Croatia as its southernmost bulwark against the East. The same Church that always wanted an independent Catholic Croatia knew that Medjugorje was an integral part of Croatian nationalism, and it knew as well that to condemn Medjugorje would have dealt a severe blow to Croatian identity and fundraising at the time.

On the other hand, the evidence against Medjugorje as documented by the local bishop, whose authority had been upgraded as a result of Vatican II, was so damning that anyone with a modicum of theological expertise knew it could never be approved. So Rome temporized and appointed another commission, which took five years to come up with a verdict. The years from 1986 to 1991 were, of course, five extremely crucial years, during which the forces of nationalism gained the upper hand in Yugoslavia and ultimately brought down the Communist regime there. But Yugoslavia was not Poland, and the religious forces which brought down Communism eventually set off a three-way religious war, as Bishop Zanic had predicted, between the Croatians, the Orthodox Serbs and the Muslims. So the apparitions of Our Lady, Queen of Peace set up the dynamic that led to the worst fighting in Europe since World War II and gave the world the new term "ethnic cleansing" as well. The promulgation of the Church's official position on Medjugorje coincided almost to the day with the dismemberment of Yugoslavia. In fact, one priest stationed at St. James says that the civil war saved Medjugorje because the outbreak of war prevented Bishop Zanic from ever implementing the guidelines of the Yugoslavian Bishops' Conference.

But if there was a geopolitical advantage in temporizing on the condemnation of Medjugorje, there was a ecclesial downside as well. It was a classic case of political goals in conflict with religious goals.

The Vatican wanted to bring about the fall of Communism; it wanted an independent Catholic Croatia as a bulwark against the East, and it knew that Medjugorje was the force driving Croatian nationalism at the time. The Vatican also knew that the local bishop considered it a fraud and that the Church could never approve it. The solution was to temporize, but that decision too was fraught with serious consequences in terms of Church governance, which was exploited by the pro-Medjugorje forces. It was during the period of the second commission's deliberations that the public relations campaign went into full swing. It was during this period that the Yugoslavian government changed its mind and got into the apparition business. The net result was a charismatic internal front in the Church, a group of people who would now be able to use Marian piety as a weapon against legitimate Church authority, specifically bishops. When it came to Medjugorje, the pope could attain his geopolitical goals only at the expense of his ability to govern the Church.

What was a dilemma for the pope, however, was a win/win situation for the CIA. Supporting Medjugorje corresponded to both long-term goals—anti-Communism and anti-Catholicism— established by Paul Blanshard and the faction he represented in the foundations and the State Department. Supporting Medjugorje brought about a simultaneous destabilization of Communism and the Catholic Church. The Herzegovina Franciscans were a Croatian nationalist group that agitated for the destabilization of Communism by attracting millions of pilgrims and their hard currency, but they also agitated against the local bishop, weakening the hierarchical structure of the Church, by creating a world-wide network of charismatic, Marian Lollards, an enthusiast fifth column, which would go home and spread not the faith passed on by the apostles but a sort of neo-Bogomil mumbo-jumbo that had all of the external trappings of traditional Marian piety but was in fact founded on disobedience and rebellion against legitimate Church authority.

In attempting to have its cake and eat it too, the Vatican played into the hands of the State Department types who had nothing to lose and everything to gain by promoting an essentially renegade movement like Medjugorje. Rome had to pay a steep price for the independence of Catholic Croatia while the United States paid nothing at all. And attempting to have its cake and eat it too is precisely what the Church was trying to bring about in Medjugorje. The ultimate solution, the bishops' statement of 1991, had already been adumbrated by Father Zivko Kustic in *Glas Koncila* on July 5, 1987.

"Perhaps," Kustic suggested in language that would be incorporated almost literally into the final statement of the Yugoslavian Bishops' Conference, a solution to the whole problem could be resolved if our bishops would publicly and strictly distinguish two aspects of the Medjugorje issue: the question of the apparitions from the question of the huge gatherings of the faithful in the Marian church or rather around the Virgin. Then the first question about the apparitions can be settled without a rush to the research of experts, and the second question should be accepted as a fact of our ecclesiastical reality to be supervised and directed. And nobody—not even the holiest, not even the pilgrims who yearn most for apparitions in various lands—will mind if we say that we, officially as the Church, do not know if Mary indeed has appeared in Medjugorje but that we do know very well what ought to be done and said where the faithful gather, longing for conversion and peace, eager to hear the word of God and to receive the sacraments under the protection of Mary and through her intercession.

Once the danger of condemnation had passed, the publicity campaign promoting Medjugorje as a site of pilgrimage took off in earnest. In September of 1986 BBC/Everyman producer Angela Tilby and John Bird of Westerhanger Productions arrived in Medjugorje with a film crew to produce the first full-length TV documentary on the apparitions. It would be shown on BBC and then sold as a video throughout the world, promoting tourism. In 1986 a Boston millionaire by the name of John Hill heard a tape on the apparitions and then decided to devote his fortune to promoting them. What followed were a series of expensive glossy magazines which began circulating throughout the United States. It was in 1986 that Mary Craig first noticed that the American pilgrims outnumbered the Italians for the first time. More Americans meant more money—for the Franciscans, the seers, and their families. It was also in 1986 that the government of Yugoslavia decided to abandon all opposition to the apparitions and concentrate on exploiting them financially instead.

In September 1986, Denis Nolan, who was now teaching religion at St. Joseph's Catholic High School in South Bend, Indiana, learned that his neighbor was going to Medjugorje, and what was previously an object of interest became an obsession. Teaching religion in the United States in the years following the Cultural Revolution of the '60s involved an ongoing struggle to preserve the integrity of Catholic teaching against liberal administrators and curricula. For a while, from 1984 until 1986, it looked as if devotion to Mary would be the opening into a fuller relationship with the Church and its concerns, but that openness was soon replaced with what one in all honesty would have to call an obsession with Medjugorje. One need only read the memos Nolan wrote to his principal to sketch out this trajectory of ever-increasing fanaticism. Given the influence that Notre Dame had on the high school, which is geographically, as well as ideologically, right across the street, it was an all but sure thing that Nolan was going to be an outsider because of his conservative theology. Yet in 1986 he was at least an outsider with an articulate and defensible position.

On March 16, 1986, Nolan wrote a memo taking the religion department to task for its sex-ed program after having been shocked to find a 14-year-old freshman girl writing about how to put on a condom in response to a question in a religion quiz. The course was taught by a Holy Cross Brother, who discussed penis size, among other things in classes of mixed freshmen. The sex-ed course was instituted under Bishop William McManus and continued by his successor Bishop John M. D'Arcy. It was called the Reverence for Life and Family Series and was, depending on the state of mind of the viewer, either scandalous or laughable. In early 1986 Nolan could mount an effective critique of the program based on both his own experiences and the teachings of the Church.

In 1986, however, two crucial things happened at the high school. In the spring the Theology Department chairman, who also doubled as the local front man for the Sandinista regime in Nicaragua, decided to leave South Bend to take a job working for Archbishop Marcus McGrath of Panama, and in the fall Denis Nolan went to Medjugorje. In a way, the two incidents are related. After the former department chairman left, there was a vacuum in the department that was just asking to be filled by someone who was willing to work toward bringing the theology department back in line with the teaching of the Church. Nolan was given just that opportunity when he was assigned to teach the so-called Justice and Peace course in the fall. Up until that time it had been little more than a primer in *Sandinismo* and liberation theology. Because of his newfound interest in Medjugorje, however, Nolan showed no interest in designing a course on Catholic social teaching, or in reading the papal encyclicals for that matter. He claimed that sort of thing didn't fit his teaching style. He preferred to be more anecdotal, which meant increasingly frequent anecdotes about Medjugorje. For whatever reason, the opportunity to teach a course on the Church's social teaching came and went.

Then in September of 1986 Nolan heard that his neighbor was going to Medjugorje. What had formerly been an object of interest now, for some reason, became an obsession. Even though the fall semester had just begun, and he had a 1,200-square-foot addition to his house, as well as an opening in his roof, unfinished and no firewood cut for the winter, Nolan became convinced that he had to go, so much so that he even went to his classes and asked his students to pray so that he would be given the $1,300 that he needed to get there. If he got the money, he reasoned, it must be a sign that he should go. In an account written after he returned, he gives some indication of his state of mind at the time:

> An incredible desire began to well up within me. I began to experience an overpowering desire to go to Medjugorje. I had never wanted anything so badly in all my life. The next day, Friday, as I closed the door to my classroom at the beginning of petitions in prayer I found myself literally roaring with emotion, "Pray with me that God will give me $1,300 by Sunday evening so that I can go to Medjugorje."

By Sunday he had the money. Evidently God or some other spiritual agent had heard his prayer.

When Nolan came back, he brought with him the crucifix from the apparition room at St. James Church, which now became a regular fixture in his classroom, along with the messages from the seers, which were written on the blackboard. Interestingly, Nolan said that when he first arrived in Medjugorje, he couldn't pray and had a deep spiritual sense that Satan was behind the whole thing. Nolan's approach to teaching had always been strongly anecdotal, but now the anecdotes were becoming increasingly fixated on what was happening in Medjugorje. Medjugorje had become the explicator of world events, and Nolan was evolving a theology based on the minutiae of its messages. What significance, for example, lay in the fact that Our Blessed Mother's real birthday was on August 5, and not September 8, the date fixed by the Church? He seemed willing to entertain any interpretation but the most obvious, namely, that this sort of thing was a subtle challenge to Church authority.

The reaction of the students was varied. Many at least at the beginning were stimulated by this combination of dire prediction and legitimate Marian devotion which had been so long suppressed by the clique who ran the Church's educational establishment. However, as with a diet that is high on sugar and low on substance, the Medjugorje phenomenon began to become cloying. With some, the emphasis on apocalypse had the effect of cutting the nerve of effort. Some, sensing this, began to react against Marian devotion in general.

Nolan's attachment to Medjugorje began to have its effect on his colleagues and the administration. By the end of the year, the principal asked Nolan, who had been there by then for 12 years, not to return the following fall. There are, I think, two ways of interpreting the announcement. On the one hand, Nolan had always been an embarrassment to the Notre Dame-dominated theological establishment at the school. One suspects that they had always been interested in getting rid of him because of this orthodoxy and opposition to things like the sex-ed program and that his new-found enthusiasm for Medjugorje gave them the excuse they had been looking for all along. On the other hand, one could say that, because of his involvement in Medjugorje, Nolan had finally gone around the bend and was no longer in contact with reality. The content of his courses did not correspond to the course titles; anecdotes and private revelations about Medjugorje were starting to take center stage.

Either way, he was clearly skating on thin ice when he began his summer vacation in 1987. By the fall of 1987, however, little had changed. Medjugorje had become, if anything, more of a fixation in his life. It became clear that he was involved in something like a vicious circle. As the threats around him grew, Nolan was more and more drawn to the apocalyptic messages of Medjugorje. Yet the more he became involved in the messages, the more he was accelerating the forces that were out to get him.

In September of 1987, with last year's warning still fresh in his ears, Nolan received a phone call from California. Someone whom he had met in Medjugorje the year before called and offered him a free ticket to Medjugorje. Nolan immediately accepted and gave the principal two days notice to get his classes covered. This time someone paid for a ticket for his wife Cathy. Someone's willingness to pay for a ticket had become synonymous in Nolan's mind for a direct call from God to go. A memo he wrote afterward gives a good indication of his state of mind at the time:

> During Mass I let my heart take the lead of my head for a moment, and I blurted out to the Blessed Mother, "If you have anything to give me that would necessitate my coming to Medjugorje, do a miracle and get me there. Open all the doors yourself and do miracles and get me there." Immediately what went through my mind were all the reasons Mary wouldn't want me to leave school. I know that when she appeared in Medjugorje, though her body was there, what was on her heart was right here in South Bend. My students were on her heart. And great miracles were happening with them. The "action," so to speak, was here. And I belong here with them. This is what my mind told me. But my heart is always there in the little

village that is made holy by the coming of Mary every evening. And so I just left the prayer with her and continued trying to respond to her call that day, which means to pray.

That same afternoon I received a phone call from a friend in California. I had met this lady last year in Medjugorje. She phoned to tell me that she was returning to Medjugorje that Friday, and she thought I should go too. She wanted to pay my way. Could I go? My mind told me "no," but my heart said "yes." My mind told me "no" because several weeks earlier the principal of the school where I teach forbade me to mention the Blessed Mother or Medjugorje in my classroom anymore. He cited the recent remarks of the local bishop assigning the Franciscans and visionaries there to the lowest place in Hell. And he told me to stop saying a decade of the rosary with my students at the beginning of each class.

> I knew he would not be very inclined to give me the permission to miss any teaching days of school in order to go to Medjugorje. But as I prayed about it, I could feel that the Blessed Mother was not going to let anything get in her way. Sunday night, as we were going to sleep, I remember whispering to Cathy, "They are going to let me go from school. I have a very strong sense that the Blessed Mother is not going to let anything get in her way." And sure enough. That Friday Cathy and I were on our way to Medjugorje together.

The trip was to last longer than they expected. On the day they were to return, Cathy Nolan had a miscarriage. For some time before the early fall of 1987 Denis, his wife, and his children had been observing the two-day bread and water fast recommended by the children at Medjugorje. During the summer of 1987, Cathy became pregnant with their eighth child. This, coupled with the fast, coupled with the prospect of a long trip to a foreign country whose language neither of them spoke, coupled with the fact that they didn't even have a place to stay, and coupled with the uncertain state of Yugoslavian medical facilities, prompted my wife and I to suggest that neither of them go. Since we had lived in Germany, and my wife had been in the hospital there and was not particularly happy with the care she had received, we reasoned that the situation in Yugoslavia could only be worse. It didn't seem to us, we told them, like a good idea.

The Nolans left for their week in Medjugorje, and when they didn't return at the appointed time, we began to fear that what we had warned them about had, in fact, happened. They were three days late in getting back. Cathy returned with a lingering intestinal infection.

More importantly, with the loss of a child, the psychological ante in the game that was Medjugorje had gone up. It became more imperative than ever to see the benevolent hand of God in actions that seemed on first glance the result of plain old imprudence.

The ante went up in the classroom as well, so much so that on September 14, 1987, the principal sent Nolan a memo. "It has been brought to my attention," it began,

> that you are spending an inordinate amount of time talk-ing about your personal experiences associated with Medjugorje and the Blessed Mother. Although I am most impressed with your faith and how you wish to share these experiences with your students, I must insist that you no longer spend classroom time talking about the Blessed Mother and Medjugorje. You have a curriculum, an outline, and textbooks that have been approved for these courses. I expect you to follow these as carefully and as closely as is necessary to teach the students these basic teachings of our Church.

Nolan was later to claim that he had never been given a curriculum in the years that he had been there, but that was to some extent beside the point. Perhaps the principal was just writing the memo to get one more piece of evidence against Nolan. Perhaps he was just building a dossier against him, but the fact remained that Nolan, by behaving the way he was, was putting an awful lot of ammu-nition in the hands of the administration if it was out to get him.

When Denis showed me the letter, I, in effect, agreed with the principal. He was not being paid to teach about Medjugorje, I said. It was a matter of simple justice. Beyond that, he ran the danger of making orthodoxy look ridiculous by his obsession with private revelation. It was something that he clearly did not want to hear. Now I was part of the conspiracy against him. Six days after he got the principal's letter, Denis sent a letter to me in which he took me to task for my lack of fervor.

"Your mind is very bright," Nolan wrote,

> but sometimes your spiritual senses are way off. . . . And I am most shocked by what I consider an incredible den-sity of heart, or just plain stubborn bullheadedness, your lack of zeal for what God is so obviously doing through Medjugorje. . . . Now I'm beginning to understand. You won't recognize the incredible thing that God is doing right now if you simply let your critical mind lead you

everywhere. . . . There is a fault among conservatives to see truth as flat things and to fail to see the dimension of depth sometimes, and a fault in the tendency, sometimes, to react to things and not to have the openness to follow the Holy Spirit. . . . God never works as people suppose. . . . I think the world (or at least this country) is going to go through a terrible time in the next two months.

"Michael," Denis concluded, "it is imperative that you recognize your weakness. It is a mistake to hide behind your intellect. You are not going to find what you need in books. You must listen to the 4th and 5th tape from the Marian Movement of priests Retreat."

After that, our correspondence descended into a sort of trench warfare, in which the sole purpose of his communications was to demonstrate without a doubt that the apparitions were genuine. On July 10, 1988, Nolan set off again but before leaving wrote to say that he had

received an excited letter from Gerry Faust [former Notre Dame football coach]. He had just returned from a pilgrimage to Fatima, Lourdes, and Medjugorje. He was excited about the power of God he experienced in Medjugorje. A friend of his had a rosary that turned gold there and when he got back to Akron, he found that the rosary that he keeps in his car in order to say it when driving had turned bright gold.

Almost immediately after getting the principal's note, Nolan asked his classes if they felt that he was imposing his views of Medjugorje on them. Almost to a man they said no, and it seems obvious from reading their responses that they were fascinated by his stories of God's doings in his life and the other signs and wonders associated with Medjugorje. However, as before, this sort of thing cloys quickly. By the end of the year, a different mood seems to predominate.

During the last week of February 1988 Nolan decided to show his classes the BBC/Everyman documentary on Medjugorje. His attitude toward the alleged apparitions remained unchanged. If anything, they had become more intense. "I sat on the edge of my chair," he said of a video he had seen many times before. "I didn't want anyone to miss one word. Especially, I wanted to include the last few minutes when Mary's messages are spoken. During several showings I found myself weeping in the back of the room. The familiar music and scenes put me back in Medjugorje, and the power of Mary's coming was sweeping though me again."

The attitude of the students, however, had changed radically from the enthusiasm of the previous September. According to the same memo,

> it was all I could do to try to keep everyone's attention. Some people put their heads down on their desks. (Out of fairness to them I must admit it was a Friday, and the afternoons do get long.) Several times I had to get up and stop people from talking. Once I had to take a game away from two fellows who were playing it back and forth between their desks. Several times I had to ask students not to do homework for other classes. Finally, by the end of the day I was kind of a wreck. My stomach muscles were in knots. I wanted so badly for this message to be shared with them.

However, if enthusiasm is starting to wane on the part of some, the signs and wonders, if anything, are increasing for others. One girl relates that

> she had seen the miracle of the sun several days before from her front porch in Jones, Michigan. Several days before showing the film, she had visited my home. She encouraged my wife to come outside and look at the miracle of the sun [in South Bend]. When I came home, I found my wife and six oldest children all praising God for what they were witnessing as they gazed into a very bright sun. . . . It was becoming more and more common to hear of people returning from Medjugorje after having witnessed this miracle there who were continuing to witness it here. But now my own family was seeing.

After debating with himself whether he should share this sign with his class, Denis finally does, whereupon the inevitable happens; the miracle of the sun begins happening during class time.

> As we were beginning the prayer Christy fell to her knees looking into the sun. She said, "I'm seeing it right now!" She said it was pulsating and colors were coming out from it. She also saw the face of Christ—a face full of pain and suffering in the middle of the sun. Several others tried to look at the sun but it was too bright. One fellow who sits in the back with Christy told me after class that he saw it too. Later he diagrammed on the board for the whole class what he saw. A number of other

students, eight or nine, in that class saw it too. I had forgotten to close the curtains as I usually do before class began and the sun was very bright that morning. The next day more children gazed into the sun. I had the blinds closed (and had told them not to do it) but they had come into class before the second bell rang and went to the window and stared with wide open eyes right into a very bright sun. They said there was something that at first was hard to make out. And then they all said what they saw in the middle of the sun was a dark cross.

It was a scene right out of *La Dolce Vita*. Nolan concludes by saying: "It strikes me that, in all the thousands of years of salvation history, from Abraham until now, never before has he [i.e., God] done what he's doing now. Never before have so many been given a sign. . . . What is happening now is totally unprecedented. And he commands us in the Gospels to pay attention to the signs of the times."

Given Nolan's spiritual trajectory, it was only a matter of time before the inevitable happened. On March 31, 1988, he received a note from the principal informing him that he had been fired. In this age orthodox religious educators are a rare commodity to begin with; now the local high school had one less, one who had made a significant contribution over the past 13 years. Although the principal didn't mention it in his letter, it's hard to believe that Nolan's increasingly fanatical involvement with Medjugorje wasn't the reason that he got fired. Perhaps he had always been an embarrassment to certain teachers; perhaps they had always been looking for a reason to get rid of him, but even given that, it seems that Nolan's fanaticism over Medjugorje presented them with an opportunity they couldn't turn down. Even if none of that were true, it would be hard to find any justification for the behavior that Medjugorje was causing in the classroom. Looking at the sun, in addition to being harmful to the eyes, is no substitute for learning Church history. If the devil were looking for a way to discredit Marian devotion in particular and Catholicism in general, he couldn't have found a better way.

Getting fired did little to dampen Nolan's enthusiasm for the alleged apparitions. Over the past few months he had become the de facto leader of an increasingly large Medjugorje prayer group which met at a local parish. Now he was talking about becoming a full-time "minister for Medjugorje." It wasn't exactly clear what that meant, much less how he was to raise a family of seven children on it, but that didn't deter him from looking into the possibility.

-7-

THE SPIN-OFFS BEGIN

O n a burning hot day in July of 1988, an American journalist by the name of Suzanne Rini arrived by taxi in front of a palazzo near Parma surrounded by a gold fence. In her possession were copies of the letters between Manda and Vlasic. She had come to the palazzo because *Fidelity* magazine was planning to run an article detailing the affair and wanted to get Vlasic's side of the story before it did. Vlasic was in Italy now because he had decided, with the encouragement of the Blessed Mother, to found a coed religious community there.

On March 25, 1988, Vlasic had published an open letter entitled "An Appeal in the Marian Year," from the same palazzo near Parma, in which he announced that "since the fall of 1985 Our Lord and Our Heavenly Mother spoke to me in my heart in a special manner. They kept giving me special communiques. They requested from me total self-denial and readiness for their plan." According to the same letter, God allegedly told Father Vlasic to form this community with a German woman by the name of Agnes Heupel, who was allegedly healed "in Medjugorje on the eve of the Lady of Fatima, May 12, 1986, after twelve years of partial paralysis." (If anyone is interested in seeing Frau Heupel, she is featured on the BBC/Everyman video handing her crutches over to Father Slavko Barbaric after discussing her miraculous cure and the spiritual problems which accompanied her ailments.) According to Vlasic's account, "On the eve of the Immaculate Conception, December 7, 1986, while we were praying the joyous mysteries of the rosary, Jesus gave a message to Agnes, in which he announced a new religious order in which both of us ought to offer ourselves to God like Sts. Clare and Francis. Both of us were surprised."

No doubt they were. The reference to St. Francis and St. Clare was especially surprising. As Vlasic goes into the particulars of how this community is supposed to look there are more surprises still. The community is to be comprised of a group of young people of both sexes. "Brother and sister," he continues, with apparent reference to himself and Frau Heupel,

> will always be the leaders of the community. While they are in charge, they will offer themselves as sacrifice for one another, then together for the community. This is an explicit wish of the Madonna. She wants this that the reconciliation might be realized in the roots of mankind. The war started in the world between two human beings which had been created in the image of God: between a male and female (Gen. 3). By offering themselves as propitiation for one another they realize the basis for reconciliation and harmony for all other human beings.

Vlasic then went on to relate the exact words of the Blessed Mother to him. "The Madonna says," he writes:

> Children, whatever you inflame with love in your vicinity, that you will set on fire in the entire world. And whatever you love in your sufferings, that will burn for the entire globe. My children, whenever you want to offer your sufferings through my hand to the eternal God, then you are going to become the fruit of salvation for entire mankind. Children, this is the mystery of God's love and His offer for all creatures.

The letter fairly radiated repressed sexual conflicts just beneath the surface of its devotional religious prose. In describing the community's alleged "sacrificial character," Vlasic tells of how the Madonna "demanded from Agnes and myself that the two of us offer ourselves together as a sacrifice so that we may carry the burden of sins of each other. Thereafter we ought to offer ourselves as a communal sacrifice for the community and the entire world."

Just what Father Vlasic was trying to tell his readers was unclear. It was difficult to tell whether his unresolved sexual conflicts had given rise to megalomania or vice versa. Either way, Marija Pavlovic, late of Medjugorje and now of Parma, endorsed the Vlasic/ Heupel community in a communiqué of her own dated April 21, 1988. Beyond that she went on to claim that the Blessed Mother had endorsed it as well and suggested that Marija should now follow the lead of Father Tomo and Agnes in joining their community. After Marija and her prayer group prayed for "a light that we might understand the program which the Madonna has given though Agnes Heupel and Fr. Tomislav Vlasic," things started happening:

> The Madonna arrived. She was joyful. She prayed over us all and said: "Dear children! Today I am offering you a special gift, a gift of freedom that you may opt for God. I am blessing the free decision of every one of you." In that way it became clear to me that I may accept this way since I have been waiting for an opportunity that I may withdraw into solitude and prayer. As you can see, the Madonna has given a program for the community "The Queen of Peace, We Are Completely Yours" [the name of the community] and leads this community through Fr. Tomislav and Agnes through whom the messages are coming for the community.

Rini did not have to knock at the gate and wait after she arrived at the palazzo. She arrived just as Vlasic and a number of young ladies were about to get into a car and head off for a day in the mountains. In spite of advertising itself as a community for men and women, there were precious few men on the scene. In fact, Rini saw only one, namely, Father Vlasic, who now seemed in a hurry to get away. Rini does not remember seeing Marija Pavlovic, but she does know that when she produced the Vlasic/Manda correspondence the young ladies crowded around to get a look. Vlasic denied everything, and before Rini could ask any more questions, the car and its inhabitants were gone.

The psychological dynamic behind the "Appeal in the Marian Year" is clear enough. The seers needed the Franciscans to get them off the hook in the first days of the apparition. As a result, the Franciscans carried the psychological burden from that time. Now it seemed that the priests— or Vlasic, at least— had the same psychological need to get off the hook themselves. In a way, Vlasic's situation was a lot like that of the Rev. Dimmesdale in Hawthorne's novel *The Scarlet Letter*. Dimmesdale, another minister who fathered a child out of wedlock, is simultaneously driven to confess and to cover up his moral failure, so he engages in ambiguous gestures like climbing up onto the scaffold in the public square, but only under the cover of darkness. He can't make up his mind whether he wants to confess or perpetuate the cover-up. Judging from his "Appeal in the Marian Year," Father Vlasic was in a similar psychological situation. Given his track record in sexual matters, how else are we to read statements like the Madonna's demanding "from Agnes and myself that the two of us offer ourselves together as a sacrifice so that we may carry the burden of the sins of each other"?

Commenting on that specific passage, Psychologist William Coulson said,

> I don't think he should write about that without telling us what his sins are or hers. I mean I would want to say, "Listen, Father, that's terribly imprudent of you to do unless you're prepared to tell us what sins you're talking about. My goodness, don't hint that you and Agnes have sinned—whether together or separately I don't know—unless you're willing to go a little bit further and tell us what it is so that we can judge for ourselves whether you're authentic. As it is, I don't need to know more about it because I'm prepared to dismiss it now. This is nothing like what I as a lay consumer of reports from Medjugorje have been led to believe. This stuff is coming to them through this couple, who do seem to be saying, at least Father Tomislav is saying, "We're romantically involved," whether sexually or not I don't know, but in a way that's irrelevant because they're romantic about one another.

The visit from Suzanne Rini provoked one of the major breaks in the Medjugorje story. Seeing the Manda/Vlasic correspondence in the hands of the press, Marija Pavlovic evidently panicked. A few days after Rini's arrival, on July 11, 1988, she issued a statement in both Italian and Croatian (the Croatian version bears her signature) which attempted to put some distance between herself (and, therefore, the apparitions) and Father Vlasic, whose past sexual derelictions threatened to drag the whole Medjugorje phenomenon into disrepute. On July 11, 1988, Marija Pavlovic stated that "my first declaration," referring to what she had written on April 21, 1988, "does not correspond to the truth." She went on to write: "I have never asked the Madonna for any approval for this undertaking begun by Father Tomislav V. and Agnes Heupel." Pavlovic then went on to claim that she had written the first statement as a result of pressure put on her by Vlasic. "I personally," she testifies in her July statement, "had no desire to give any sort of written declaration. Father Tomislav V. kept suggesting to me, stressing over and over again that I as a seer should write the declaration which the world was waiting for."

When the statement appeared, Rini was on the other side of

the Adriatic in Mostar meeting with Bishop Zanic. Zanic had stumbled across the affair between Manda and Vlasic but had never made contact with Pehar and so had no corroboration of the fact that he was not the father of Manda's child as the Franciscans had claimed. Rini arrived with documentation of that fact, plus letters which Zanic had never seen, plus a picture of Manda and Pehar and other religious from the convent in Zagreb in full habit. All in all it was an impressive pile of documents, and Zanic was determined to put them to good use by passing them on to the new commission now being conducted by the Yugoslavian Bishops' Conference. Ultimately, Zanic would add Marija Pavlovic's statement that she had not told the truth about the Blessed Mother's endorsement of Vlasic's community to the bulging dossier as well.

Perhaps it was his unexpected fortune that put Zanic in a good mood. He called his secretary in and showed the documents to him, and then, offering Rini a drink, he began to discuss the apparitions, which were starting to metastasize in Italy. At Pescara, a young priest by the name of Don Vicenzo became involved in pilgrimages to Medjugorje. As a result, he became a follower of a claimed visionary named Maria Antonina Fioriti, who announced a great miracle to occur on February 28, 1988. A sign in the sun as at Fatima was to occur by day, and then in the night sky, another sign was to occur around midnight. Needless to say, nothing happened. Pescara was significant, however, in that it was the first spin-off apparition of a whole slew which were to follow. Medjugorje, it was becoming increasingly clear, was contagious.

Rini opined that such things happened around the eve of each millennium, and Zanic agreed and went on to discuss Medjugorje in the light of other signs of the times. A few days before their meeting, in late June, Archbishop Marcel Lefebvre had been excommunicated after finally reneging on a deal that would have allowed him and the movement he led to reconcile with the Church. By consecrating four bishops, Lefebvre and his movement went into formal schism. Zanic felt that the Lefebvre schism might help Medjugorje gain Church approval because he felt that the pope didn't want any more division. The statement indicates that the disapproval of Medjugorje which eventually came in 1991 and which Zanic saw as his vindication was by no means a sure thing as of 1988. The statement about Lefebvre also led Zanic to comment on the pope, whom he described as a Marian enthusiast. Zanic had met with the pope in person, and in true Croatian fashion had bluntly called the apparitions a fraud. When asked what the pope's reaction was, Zanic said, "the pope said nothing."

The pope's silence was understandable, in a way, given his

psychological and spiritual make-up. The apparitions clearly put the pope in a bind. As an avid defender of Vatican II's rehabilitation of the bishop as a successor of the apostles, he could not very well demote Zanic to being a branch manager of the sort that bishops had been under Pius XII. At the same time, he knew that the evidence that Zanic presented posed insurmountable problems to the acceptance of the apparitions as genuine. On the other hand, there were the "fruits," fruits which he as a "Marian enthusiast," in Zanic's words, avidly desired for Eastern Europe. Marian devotion was the engine which pulled the anti-Communist train. It was a deep-rooted part of Catholic Slavic culture. It fueled the resistance to atheism in a way that intellectual theories could not, especially with the average citizen. And now on the crucial southeastern border of the Soviet empire, people were praying the rosary in droves and lining up to go to confession, in a public manifestation of piety that looked like the Croatian version of the Gdansk shipyard. The apparitions seemed like just the right event in the right place at the right time; it was tempting to see the hand of God in the matter, rather than listen to the disturbing reports of the bishop. The Church could never rule infallibly on something like this anyway. Infallibility was reserved for matters of faith and morals, which were based on the revelation handed down from the apostles. The Church's charism of infallibility extended to public revelation but not to private revelation, which could only be judged according to human prudence. The "fruits" argument seemed like the best way out. No one wanted to inhibit the actions of the Holy Spirit, and right now, it looked as if the Holy Sprit, through the Gospa, was converting the Communists themselves.

On April 18, 1988 a National Catholic News Service article under the headline "Yugoslavia Finds Tourist Gold at Site of Alleged Apparitions" appeared in Catholic newspapers across America. It seemed that the Communist government, after trying to suppress the apparitions as a disguised form of Croatian nationalism, had suddenly gotten religion and was now trying to cash in on the religious tourism which Medjugorje had spawned.

"The government made a big mistake in not recognizing the economic possibilities of Medjugorje. It's trying to catch up," said one Yugoslavian official who asked not to be identified. That official then went on to estimate Medjugorje's worth to the Yugoslavian economy at several hundred million dollars in badly need foreign currency annually. The government, as a result, decided in 1987 to cash in and promote Medjugorje, which became a feature of Yugoslavian tourist brochures a short time later.

A close reading of this and other accounts would lead the serious reader to conclusions other than that of religious conversion. If conversions were taking place in Yugoslavia among Communist officials, it was not to the Catholic Church but rather to capitalism. The pope would learn a bitter lesson in this regard in Poland, which used his leadership to overthrow communism but then ignored him when he demanded that they outlaw abortion. In this respect Medjugorje would bear similarly bitter fruits, all of the rosaries notwithstanding.

By 1988 the number of pilgrims had increased exponentially, but so also had the negative evidence surrounding the apparitions. In April 1988 Father Sivric's book appeared in French under the title *La Face Cachee du Medjugorje*. For the first time now, Zovko's initial interviews with the seers were in print with all of the damning evidence about the children saying that the Blessed Mother was going to appear for "three more days" as well as the joking and laughter and Zovko's insistence that the children have the apparitions in the church. All of this contradicted the official version of the initial apparitions, which was now spreading throughout the world on the BBC/Everyman video.

One month later, another scandal broke. In May of 1988, Ivica Vego, the priest which the Blessed Mother had defended in his battle with Bishop Zanic, announced that he had been having an affair with a nun stationed at Medjugorje and that the nun was pregnant.

"I turn to you," Vego wrote in an open letter that was causing severe consternation among the Franciscans at Medjugorje, "in the most difficult moment of my life. I have been a priest for 10 years. I was a punished priest for 10 years. Except for six weeks, jurisdiction has never been bestowed on me. Eight years ago I was punished by being expelled from my native land . For seven years I was punished with expulsion from the Franciscan order and suspended 'a divinis' [in 1981]. Our lives and our work were thrown in to the street. We died!"

Vego fails to mention that during this time he continued to function as a priest at Medjugorje, saying Mass and hearing confessions in direct disobedience to the Church. He also fails to make any connection between this disobedience and his subsequent sexual troubles, even if he does make a connection between his moral difficulties and spiritual laxity.

> I made a mistake because for an instant. I forgot God's warning through St. Peter that we must be watchful since our enemy, the devil, like a roaring lion, is trying to devour us. I made a mistake because I did not take seriously the message of the Virgin of Medjugorje. . . . It was during this time that I seldom prayed. The enemy used this, along with a series of unfavorable moments and cir-

cumstances, especially using my weakness and through me, injected in the body of the Church (in particular in God's work by means of the Virgin at Medjugorje) a poison which threatens to bring more harm than all the poisons thus experienced.. . . This is the reason why I committed a lustful sin with Sister Leopolda, a sin like other sins, but in the present circumstances, a sin that entails an avalanche of harm and scandal.

By the end of the summer of 1988, Medjugorje had suffered blows to its credibility from which it would never recover. One more priest associated with Medjugorje had gotten another nun, also associated with Medjugorje, pregnant. One more seer had been caught in a lie, this time admitting it publicly in writing. At the same time she had placed the blame on the Franciscan whom the world identified as the seers' spiritual advisor, accusing him of manipulating her for his own benefit.

In 1985 Jean Galot, S. J. had published criteria for evaluating apparitions in an article, "*Le Apparizioni Private Nella Vita Della Chiesa*," published in the *Civiltà Cattolica*, a journal which was the scholarly equivalent of *L'Osservatore Romano*, in conveying official Vatican views. Private revelation, by its very nature, always threatens to preempt the authority of the Church. Living by faith is difficult even in the best of times. The danger is that those who are bewildered by confusion in the Church or the world at large will become discouraged by what they see around them and go off seeking solace in signs and wonders, which, by definition, are always more tangible. In spite of what one is led to believe at Medjugorje, seeing and believing (or faith) are two separate things. They are, in fact, opposites, a point Galot makes clear. "Christianity," he writes,

> is not diffused in the world by means of apparitions, visions, or other similar supernatural phenomena. Men receive the message of salvation, not through a direct and miraculous intervention of God, who presents it to them from on high, but through an indirect attestation of witnesses who guarantee the truth that they preach. . . . Certainly the supernatural is not at all excluded in the transmission of truth, but it does not identify itself by means of these extraordinary or prodigious phenomena. It consists rather in the action of the Holy Spirit, who guides the activities of the Apostles and directs the development of the Church. This affirmation of the necessity of faith corresponds to the beatitude of those who

"believe without having seen" (John 20:28). In order to believe, one must not pretend to see. This testimony offers a sure base for faith.

Galot has similarly astringent things to say about the "fruits" argument. "It is not sufficient," he writes, "to use the spiritual fruits alone as the criterion to judge the authenticity of the apparitions. Cases are known in which conversions have been substantiated in which the pretended apparitions have later been rejected by the authority of the Church as without serious foundation."

Galot then goes on to list the criteria the Church uses in ascertaining whether an alleged apparition is genuine or not. The frequency of an apparition, for example, is an argument against its authenticity because it would arouse the image of a Christian religion that was nourished much more by actual visions than by the revelation brought in the past by the coming of Christ on earth. Piety would develop more as a function of constant apparitions than by the leap of faith, or again faith would tend to become a faith in the truth of the apparitions and would be founded on the testimony of those who see.

One should also be skeptical if the messages entail "threats of revenge" if the message is not accepted or if the seers spread abroad a spirit of "denigration or revolt or disobedience to the authority of the Church." In addition, one should look for "progressive psychological formation . . . if the words of the apparition have not been suggested in a human manner by the surroundings, by preceding conversations, or by the hymns or songs of the crowd or by the seers themselves."

"Evidence of human manipulation" would also be a sign of inauthenticity, especially "when the beneficiaries of the apparitions determine themselves the place, the date and the frequency of the program of the apparitions."

Given Galot's criteria, especially as expressed in a quasi-official Vatican journal, and given the events which occurred over the summer of 1988, it was clear that the Church could never give its approval to Medjugorje. However, at the same time that the negative evidence was mounting in the dossiers of the Yugoslavian Bishops' Commission, the public relations machinery was going into high gear, promoting tourism at the behest of what was still a Communist government and the financial interests surrounding the Herzegovina Franciscans. The dichotomy between what the Church knew and what it tolerated would remain up to the end when the dichotomy was expressed in the final judgment of the Bishops' Commission, which on the one hand denied that anything supernatural was happening in Medjugorje, i.e., asserted that the Blessed Mother was not appearing there, but at the same time seemed to encourage tourism by saying that the pilgrims who went there need to be taken care of. The ambiguity of the final document almost guaranteed that other documents would be necessary, explaining in effect that the Church was not encouraging pilgrimages, nor had Medjugorje become a "shrine."

In September and October of 1988, two articles by this author critical of Medjugorje appeared in *Fidelity* magazine, unleashing a storm of protest in the letters to the editor column that raged well into 1989. *Fidelity* had the reputation of being a "conservative" Catholic magazine, and as of the late '80s conservatism entailed a large amount of credulity when it came to private revelations, as well as a certain amount of antagonism toward bishops. By attacking Medjugorje, I was perceived as a traitor to my class and excoriated accordingly in the letters column. One reader wrote to say that he was praying daily to the Blessed Mother that I would have a massive heart attack and die. The incident illustrated a serious fault line in Catholicism at the time. I would write later that I felt the need to wage a war on two fronts— against heretics on the left who believed in reason without faith and lunatics on the right who believed in faith without reason. The Catholic Church found itself in the dangerous position of having two truths: an esoteric truth for those who knew the facts, which officially condemned Medjugorje, and an exoteric truth for those gullible enough to believe the travel brochures and ads for pilgrimages which got run regularly in diocesan newspapers. The history of the Church is full of dangers which came in pairs, and people who were willing to fall into one of the devil's traps in the process of avoiding the other. As Knox writes,

> The Church is always finding herself attacked from a new quarter just when she thinks her victory is assured. In the Middle Ages she raised a splendid fabric of argued belief against the Arabian philosophers; only to find herself cut off from the rear by the infiltration of Lollard simpletons, crying shame on her intellectualism.

Fueled by a massive publicity campaign, popular involvement with Medjugorje began taking off in the United States at the same time that the Yugoslavian Bishops' Commission was uncovering more and more evidence of fraud and manipulation. Then as the pilgrims returned home, something strange began happening. Not only was news of the apparitions at Medjugorje spreading, the apparitions themselves began to multiply. On August 15, 1988, the feast of the Assumption of the Blessed Virgin, body and soul, into heaven, 12,000 sweaty pilgrims gathered in front of a 52-foot altar built over the below ground church and its offices in Lubbock, Texas, for what was supposed to be a Mass which would fulfill the predominately Hispanic parish's obligation for that feast day. Rumor had been spreading for weeks that something spectacular would happen on the feast of the Assumption, and as with most predictions of this sort, it became a self-fulfilling prophecy. The Mass quickly took a back seat to the celestial theatrics. At one point a cloud passed in front of the sun, and almost immediately a howl went up from the crowd, "There she is," someone screamed, and the congregation gathered outside the church in the sweltering heat forgot the Mass for the moment and, with their hands half shielding their eyes from the blazing sun, attempted to get a glimpse of the Virgin appearing there.

The events at St. John Neuman Catholic Church in Lubbock were orchestrated by the parish pastor, Monsignor Joseph James, who, it turns out, had been a pilgrim to Medjugorje. The visions began in Lubbock after he returned from a pilgrimage there in February of 1988 after he claimed to have been cured of hypoglycemia. Since hypoglycemia can also be cured by eating doughnuts, it is doubtful that the medical bureau at Lourdes, the agency Bishop Zanic relied on for substantiation of miraculous cures, would have been much impressed. But scientific proof was not uppermost in the minds of the crowd that gathered in the hot Texas cottonfields that day. The people wanted a sign, and when they got what they thought fit the bill, they howled and fainted and rolled around in the dust, and Father James and his concelebrants at the Mass hugged each other at their good fortune. Then just as the howling died down and the Mass was about to resume, a woman who was in the courtyard where the wheelchair patients were assembled waiting for a cure, started crying, "My rosary is golden! My rosary is golden!" and pandemonium broke out again. One woman screamed that she saw the face of the crucified Jesus in the clouds, and once again heads turned and the TV news cameras and reporters holding their microphones turned with them adding to the general sense of religious frenzy. More women fainted.

The local bishop was less impressed. In a pattern that would repeat itself throughout the United States, Bishop Michael Sheehan urged first caution and then in October issued a statement saying there was nothing supernatural about the occurrences. The pattern of spiritual outburst followed by words of caution and ultimately disapproval had also been established at Medjugorje, and this, of course, meant that the faithful ignored their local bishops, every bit as much as the pilgrims to Medjugorje ignored the Bishop of Mostar. The underlying theme of Marian Lollardy was reinforced throughout the history of the apparitions and followed the pattern established in Medjugorje itself, when the Virgin appeared to the seers and told them the bishop was wrong. Psychologically, it appealed to the democratic sensibilities of American Catholics, who saw the seers as courageous underdogs in a struggle with a callous hierarchy. This attitude would reach its culmination in the film *Gospa*, where Bishop Zanic would be portrayed as a willing collaborator with the equally totalitarian Communist regime. Theologically, it fitted in with the pattern of rebellion against authority which began with the Franciscan rejection of *Romanus Pontificibus* in 1976. The seers became foot soldiers in that battle well before the first anniversary of the apparitions, and now the credulous in unlikely places like Lubbock, Texas, were being unwittingly recruited into the campaign, with similar consequences for Church authority in each diocese where a spin-off apparition occurred. The attack on Church authority was programmed into the story. The bishop was the villain.

On October 6, 1988, the visitation committee convoked by the local bishop issued its report calling the events at Lubbock and the messages of the visionaries "pious messages of good people and not private revelations miraculously produced." The report claimed that the people involved at St. John Neuman Parish were sincere and that there was no evidence of deception or desire for financial gain. "The limited phenomena we have been able to examine with sufficient analysis," the report concluded, "admit of natural explanations." If one takes, however, the ability to bring 15,000 people together in the dusty cotton fields of West Texas on a day in which the heat kept even the rattlesnakes in their holes and combines it with the greed that is part of fallen human nature, it didn't take a genius to predict that sooner or later people would be exploiting these crowds for financial gain. In fact it was only a matter of time before it happened. The Lone Star Lourdes, as it was named in one newspaper account, became a footnote in the history of Medjugorje, significant only by the fact that beginning in 1988 the chapters of that history were starting to take place in the United States as hordes of pilgrims returned from Medjugorje, fired up by their experiences, and looking for an outlet for their newly discovered religious enthusiasm.

In August of 1988, right around the same time that crowds were howling and passing out in the blazing heat in Lubbock, Texas, a landscaper by the name of Terry L. Colafrancesca took one of his lawnmowers and headed toward a lone pine tree in the middle of a 88 acre field near Starrett, Alabama. In 1986 Colafrancesco had founded Caritas of Birmingham to promote the messages of Our Lady, Queen of Peace, after having traveled to Medjugorje himself. A Mr. Tanner, who lives across the road from the field, thought Colafrancesco's behavior was a bit unusual at the time but didn't really understand its significance until that fall when thousands of pilgrims showed up in the field to witness an appearance of Our Lady of Medjugorje, who unlike previous apparitions, seemed content to follow the seers around the world and appear at their convenience. Marija Pavlovic arrived in Birmingham, Alabama, on November 18, 1988, to undergo medical tests to see if she could donate a kidney to her brother Andrija, who was 31 at the time and in need of an operation. While in Birmingham, Marija Pavlovic stayed at Colafrancesco's home and, as if to oblige him for his hospitality, promptly had an encounter with the Blessed Virgin in one of his bedrooms.

But Colafrancesco had bigger plans. Since he could not very well accommodate thousands of pilgrims in his bedroom, he asked Marija to have an apparition in the field adjacent to his house, at the base of a large pine tree, where he had been trimming the grass since mid-August. Colafrancesco, it turns out, had purchased the 88-acre field for $348,000 and was planning to build a chapel and Roman Catholic community on the grounds, an announcement he made after Marija Pavlovic went to the field on Thanksgiving and had her apparition. The increasingly skeptical Mr. Tanner was at Colafrancesco's house the night before Thanksgiving and heard him then ask Marjia if she would have her vision in front of the tree this time instead of in his bedroom. Miss Pavlovic obligingly agreed and a flood of pilgrims then descended on this predominately Baptist county to slog through the mud and rip bark from the tree. For a while in late 1988 and early 1989, the field near Sterrret was Alabama's third most popular tourist attraction. Motels in the area boasted a 75 percent occupancy rate, an unheard-of occurrence.

"This is huge," said Lisa Shivers, director of the Alabama Bureau of Tourism and Travel, "Southern Birmingham hotels and motels are doing quite well. We have not advertised this at all, " Mrs. Shivers continued. "I don't know how they find out about it, but they are finding out about it, and they are coming by the busloads."

As in Lubbock, Texas, the ordinary of the diocese, Most Rev. Raymond Boland, was skeptical and issued a statement warning potential pilgrims that the Yugoslavian Bishops' Conference had yet to reach a final verdict on the matter. But the pilgrims came anyway, undeterred by episcopal caveat. Marija Pavlovic was undeterred as well. On December 16, Marija Pavlovic arrived at University Hospital in Birmingham and had one of her kidneys removed, to be donated to her brother Andrija. During the operation, Miss Pavlovic made apparition history by having, as she announced afterward, a vision of the Blessed Virgin while under anesthesia.

On January 25, Marija was back in town for a medical check-up but also to have another apparition. This time the Blessed Mother's message for the world was, "God bless everybody and keep up the good work." In anticipation of that announcement, six busloads of pilgrims arrived from Miami along with other buses from Louisiana. Cars were parked a mile in each direction from the muddy field, formerly a cow pasture, where reporters gathered snippets of information from the pilgrims and tried to write stories on what motivated them. One lady in a fur coat opined that there had to be more than material possessions to life. Others were less articulate.

"At first I said to myself: 'you are stupid to be staring at this tree like it is some kind of different tree,'" said Gerlonde Perkens, a 42-year-old industrial seamstress for Lake Charles, Louisiana, "but I feel peaceful here; like this is something I've waited for my whole life. I could sit right here for the rest of my life. That must sound crazy to you."

Marija soon went back to Yugoslavia, but the apparitions in the field near Sterrett, Alabama, were not without lasting effect on many of the pilgrims. In early February 1989, a number of Birmingham ophthalmologists began reporting that they were treating people for "permanent eye damage to the retina of the eye" caused by looking directly at the sun. The ophthalmologists went on to warn that the damage was "permanent and that it could not be rectified by glasses or other means." Father Paul Rohling, Chancellor of the Diocese under Bishop Boland, took the warning to Terry Colafrancesco and "suggested that he should take precautionary measures regarding legal liability that might be incurred by Caritas."

In October of 1988, a wealthy California businessman by the name of Phil Kronzer went to Medjugorje for the second time with his wife Ardie. The Kronzers had been to Medjugorje for the first time during the summer of 1987. Kronzer had been born in Wisconsin to parents of Bohemian/German extraction and had traveled to California after World War II and together with his father, he cashed in on the economic boom there by first starting a tool and die shop and then buying up real estate. Until they had gone to Medjugorje, the Kronzers spent their time earning a living and raising their three children. Their involvement with the Catholic Church was confined pretty much to the Catholic parish they attended in Los Gatos. With Medjugorje all that would change. Both Kronzers became involved in Medjugorje prayer groups, but Phil quickly tired of their overheated atmosphere, a situation which allowed Ardie, now at the age where she was freed from the burdens of raising a family, to devote her time increasingly, and then almost exclusively, to activities which involved promoting the messages of Medjugorje. The Kronzers stayed with the Sivric family in 1988, relatives of Father Ivo Sivric, but who were also Communists. At least for the time being. The son would eventually become

Medjugorje editor for *Slobodna Dalmacija*, a Croatian paper with nationalist not internationalist leanings.

In January of 1989 Phil and Ardie decided to form a prayer group out of their home in Los Gatos, California, as a way of spreading the messages of Our Lady of Medjugorje and also as a way of meeting other like-minded people in the area. Once a week they would get together with eight or ten other people and pray the rosary. As part of her involvement in things religious, Ardie also worked at a religious bookstore at the time. Gradually, all of these individual activities began to fuse into an all-consuming concern for Medjugorje. At one point Phil was going to buy the store and let Ardie run it, but the deal eventually fell through because the parties concerned couldn't agree on a price. By then, Ardie was heavily involved in the conferences promoting Medjugorje, which took off in the Bay Area and elsewhere when the war broke out in Yugoslavia, making pilgrimages impossible and leaving the still growing apparitions audience in the United States all dressed up with no place to go. The Medjugorje conferences were good places to meet other enthusiasts, good places to sell things like books as well, and gradually Ardie shifted her focus from selling books through a store to selling books at conferences. It was during the preparations for the first Marian conference in Santa Clara, to be held at the Marriott Hotel there, that Ardie met a Bay Area woman by the name of Marcia Smith. Before long, Ardie and Marcia got along so well, they decided to go into business together. Instead of buying the book store, Ardie founded a book ministry called Two Hearts Alliance, which would supply books to the Medjugorje conferences in the Bay Area. Before long, Ardie and Marcia were spending a lot of time together, something which Phil, who was busy running his businesses, failed to notice.

-8-

THE SEER FROM WENDY'S

In April of 1987, a 27-year old woman by the name of Tonie Alcorn showed up at a Wendy's in Denver, Colorado, to begin her training as an assistant manager at the nationwide chain of hamburger fast-food restaurants. Tonie had long blonde hair and blue eyes and the earnest look of someone who wants to straighten out a messy life. Although she was only 27, Tonie was on her third marriage. As of mid-1987, her main goal in life was having a good time, a state of affairs which meant having enough money to buy the drugs that made her feel good while "partying." A salary of $17,219 per annum in weekly installments in a place like Denver, Colorado, allowed one to live the life of an ascetic monk but little else, and so the clash between Tonie's preferred lifestyle and her earning capacity left her perennially short of cash, which more often than not led her into temptation. Tonie's inability to handle money had been a factor in the failure of her past marriages, and it would be a factor in the failure of her future marriage as well.

Between 1989 and 1994, a period of time when she claimed to have reformed her life as the result of a religious conversion, Tonie had at least 24 different credit-card violations and debt recovery notices. This in addition to parking violations, court fees, and dunning notices from stores and video clubs made financial pressure a way of life and, since none of this impeded her spending habits, one must also assume that an ability to tune out bad news went with this lifestyle as well. Financial unreality was a way of life for Tonie, who grew up in no particular place in a family where the rules seemed made up as they went along. A sense that reality was a substance extremely malleable to her desires is what allowed her to ignore the bills that came in at the same time she was running up even more bills, buying her way to respectability, wearing expensive clothes, signing her name with an expensive pen. It was a weird combination of American consumerism and German idealism, and if these ideologies can be inherited, she came by them genetically, having been born in Fuerth of an American soldier and a German mother. Her birth name was Theresa Antonia Jones, daughter of Robert E. Jones and Waltraut Hillardt, and she was born on December 20, 1960. Her parents were most probably not religious because Tonie's baptism didn't take place until three years later.

Tonie seems to have followed in the religious footsteps of her parents, treating her marriage vows as seriously as the credit card slips she signed and then neglected to pay.

At age 20 she was living in Oklahoma and married to a man named Ames. Two years later she was living in Texas and married to a man named Christopher Hermey. On June 15, 1984, she married for the third time, a man by the name of Ernest Alcorn, in the town of Miami, Oklahoma. On August 11, she had a child by Alcorn, Natalie Nicole by name. Natalie was her second child; Tonie already had a son by the name of Arthur but the father of Arthur is unknown. It was to Ernest Alcorn that Tonie was married when she walked in the door of Wendy's in Denver to begin her internship. Mr. Alcorn was by all accounts no saint, but he was concerned about Tonie's behavior. "Please stay off drugs," he wrote in a postscript to a letter he sent her on September 20, 1987.

The manager in charge of her training was a slightly built soft-spoken man with a dark droopy moustache by the name of Jeff Lopez, who must have liked what he saw when Tonie walked in the door because before long the two of them were involved in an affair. Jeff was no saint either. Together Jeff and Tonie spent the rest of 1987 and 1988 getting high on drugs and alcohol. Tonie's spending habits didn't change as a result of her association with Jeff either. On June 9, 1987, Tonie bought a used but new year model 1987 Porsche 928S4, using the company name of Alcorn Acres, Inc. Shortly after buying the car, Tonie left Alcorn and moved in with Jeff Lopez, probably to stick her third husband with the car payments.

On August 31, 1987, Alcorn filed for divorce, and what ensued was the typical legal maneuvering complicated (or perhaps uncomplicated) by the fact that Tonie refused to cooperate with counsel. Answers to interrogatories were due on February 28, 1988, but Tonie never responded, and so her lawyer, in frustration, withdrew from the case, and Tonie lost the case by default for failure to appear. On August 18, 1989, the District Court of El Paso County, Colorado, finalized the divorce. In letting the divorce case go uncontested, Tonie also lost custody of her daughter Natalie Nicole, who was three years old at the time. According to court documents, Tonie showed no interest in either visiting or having custody of her daughter and in effect abandoned her by not contesting the divorce. She was awarded reasonable visitation rights by the courts.

Living with Tonie proved to be no bed of roses. In spite of taking Jeff's name and changing her first name—she was now known as Teresa Lopez (later, on the threshold of her 15 minutes of fame, she changed her name again to Therese, either because it seemed classier or was closer to the name of the Little Flower)—her commitment to the man who would eventually become her fourth husband was attenuated by frequent drug use, drinking, and the same financial irresponsibility which had brought an unhappy end to her three previous marriages. During their time together, Teresa went to jail for bouncing checks. After Jeff bailed her out, Teresa lost her checking account and had to write money orders instead. Therese also developed the bad habit of throwing out bills before Jeff got home from work, resulting one day in the unpleasant experience of hearing that their house was in foreclosure when he thought he had been making the mortgage payments all along. It seems that Teresa would cash the mortgage checks and then spend the money on other things. Alcorn, who had by now moved in with another woman, who ironically was named Lopez, warned Lopez about his ex-wife's bad habits. "Don't ever buy a house with her," he warned. It was a warning Lopez should have heeded but didn't. After learning that Teresa had diverted the mortgage payments, Lopez ran out and borrowed $5,000 to cover the missing payments but eventually lost the house anyway. Teresa seems to have been under the impression that she could create money by writing checks; it was a character flaw that would have spiritual ramifications before long.

In between Teresa's history as a petty criminal and her apotheosis as a seer, there were other difficulties as well. In the late spring of 1988, around one year after she began her training with Wendy's and her affair with Jeff, and around the same time she abandoned her daughter Natalie, Teresa discovered that she was pregnant with another child. Ignoring concerns about the unborn child's health, Teresa continued to take drugs during her pregnancy, which ended uneventfully on February 4, 1989 when Therese gave birth to a baby girl named Stephanie. Teresa had been using contraception during 1988 but had gotten pregnant with twins, a pregnancy which miscarried, and then she became pregnant with Stephanie. As if to make sure that that wouldn't happen again, Therese had her tubes tied while in the hospital to give birth and within a few days was back at work at Wendy's on February 15, leaving the child at home to be cared for during work hours by Patrick Lopez, Jeff's son from a previous marriage.

On March 24, 1989, both Teresa and Jeff were at work, and Patrick was baby-sitting for his younger siblings. At around 4:00 p.m., Patrick went into to Stephanie's room to see if she had awakened and needed to be changed. Surprised to find that the baby was still not awake, Patrick nudged her a bit in the crib and discovered that she had stopped breathing and had no pulse. He then called 911 and his father, who in turn called Teresa, who arrived home first since she was working only 15 minutes away. At some time during 1986 Theresa had received emergency medical training and so administered CPR to Stephanie before the ambulance arrived. It was too late to do any good; the baby was dead.

Although Teresa did not stop smoking dope until over two years later, Stephanie's death brought about a religious conversion of sorts. Bereft by the loss of what she had deliberately insured would be her last child, Teresa was overcome with grief and sought solace in the religion she had been baptized into as a child. The whole family seems to have been swept along in this direction by the same grief. Patrick was baptized a Catholic soon after Stephanie's death. Jeff, who had been baptized Catholic as an infant, started going back to church. There is no record of whether she went to confession, although that seems likely because Jeff was to say later that he thought Theresa's conversion sincere. "She's not a monster," he added as if offended by the question. "She's a human being," and one deeply affected by the loss of an infant daughter. Perhaps the new-found zeal accompanying her conversion left Therese with the impression that she wanted to do more than just attend Mass on Sunday, for, whatever the reason, she began attending prayer groups during the week as well, and prayer groups in this context usually meant one thing. As part of her contact with the parish prayer group, Therese heard about a village in Yugoslavia known as Medjugorje and the six seers there who claimed to be getting messages from the Blessed Mother. Before long Therese was avidly poring over the messages, and before long after that, as it inevitably does, the zeal and grief of the moment disappeared and, as often happens when remorse is unaccompanied by penance, the old habits started to reassert themselves. At some point Therese realized that a lot of money was changing hands in the circles surrounding Medjugorje in the United States, and when Therese understood that, the old con man in her awoke as well.

On June 25, 1987, shortly after Tonie had bought her late-model Porsche, Bishop Zanic arrived at St. James Parish in Medjugorje to do confirmations but also to express his latest feelings about the apparitions, on the day of their sixth anniversary. "Those who put words in the mouth of the Blessed Mother," he said in no uncertain terms, "deserve the lowest place in hell." As to the miraculous sign, which Marinko Ivankovic was saying would appear no later that August 15, 1986, it had finally arrived, the bishop announced. "It is your silence," he told the cowed crowd in the Church. "You are not here."

> I, Bishop of Mostar, before the multitude of your admirers through the world, discover and accept your big sign which has become certain and clear after these six years. It is your SILENCE. . . . I thank you, my Lady, because of your silence six years long. That's the way you show us whether you really spoke here, whether you appeared, spread messages. . . . Holy Virgin, Mother of Christ and our Mother, may you intervene for peace in this restless . . . diocese of Mostar. Especially may you intervene for this place, this parish where many times your name has been used in speeches not yours. May you stop a fabrication of your messages. May you accept, Holy Virgin, as satisfaction, sincere prayers of devoted souls who keep far from fanaticism and disobedience from the Church.

In a letter written to the author dated January 15, 1988, Bishop Zanic reiterated forcefully what had now become an unshakable belief. "For a long time I am convinced that the Blessed Mother is not appearing at Medjugorje, that the messages are not hers. There are no miracles, but all together is the fruit of fraud, disobedience to the Church and disease. Very important role in all these play money and personal interest. This is a new religion, a sect, a big division and real war in the Church."

The war in the Church was heating up, and waiting in the wings was another, less metaphorical war, based on the first.

At the conclusion of his homily on July 25, Zanic said, "A sober person who venerates Our Lady would naturally ask himself: 'Dear Mother of God, what are they doing to you'?"

Since Father Jack Spalding was in St. James Church on July 25, 1987, he most certainly heard Bishop Zanic's warning and denunciation, although the language barrier might have deterred him from hearing it from the bishop's lips directly. Father Spalding was there with a TV crew making a documentary to be shown on Mother Angelica's EWTN network out of Birmingham, Alabama. Mother Angelica would go on to become Medjugorje's major promoter in the United States in spite of her ups and downs with the seers themselves.

Spalding was in Medjugorje with Father Dale Fushek, who was also involved in doing a program for teenagers on the same Network, and now both men felt like Moses parting the Red Sea, the only comparison Spalding can find to describe the effect that a TV camera had on the seers and their promoters.

"I mean," he recounted later, "we could get in any place we wanted to and that's exactly what we did. We were able to be in the rectory at the time Our Blessed Mother was appearing to the kids in the rectory; in fact [we were able to get] in one of the priest's bedrooms, and we were able to be there for one of the apparitions."

Conspicuous by its absence from Father Spalding's account is any mention of Bishop Zanic's sermon, as well as its denunciation of the seers as liars and its warnings about the future, which is not surprising. In spite of masquerading as a TV reporter, Spalding was to say later, "We went over there not to find out whether we believed or not because we believed before we went." Instead of Bishop Zanic's warning, TV viewers got Father Spalding's enthusiastic account of the apparition which was taking place in defiance of the bishop's authority and a summary of what it all meant, which was "basically the message is an invitation to be people of peace."

Spalding's trip in June was so successful that he was back again in October, and as a result of that trip, upon his return, Spalding was asked on December 3, 1987, to form an adult Medjugorje prayer group at St. Maria Goretti Church in Scottsdale, Arizona. Initially there were 20 or 30 people who came to pray and discuss the messages of Our Lady of Medjugorje, but by 1991 the number had increased to over 500. Eventually a synergistic relationship would develop between prayer groups and pilgrimages. The returning pilgrims found in the prayer groups a way to download and prolong the spiritual high they had attained in Medjugorje, but this sort of activity generated a great deal of interest in pilgrimage among those who hadn't yet gone. So the one led to the other and the movement began to snowball into something really big during the five-year period between the summer of 1986, when the CDF appointed the third commission, and June of 1991, when Croatia and Slovenia declared independence and the civil war broke out in Yugoslavia.

As a result of this dynamic, Father Spalding was back in Medjugorje in March of 1988, this time with a film crew from CBS, and back again in June of 1988 with a group of pilgrims from the parish prayer group. By June of 1988, the emotional combination of prayer group and pilgrimage had become so intense that strange things started to happen. During the June 1988 pilgrimage, one member of the adult prayer group, a 31-year-old lady by the name of Mrs. Gianna Bianchi attended a talk given by then Lutheran Medjugorje promoter

Wayne Weible. Weible published a blue newspaper recounting how he had been touched by his experiences at Medjugorje, and the millions of copies he sent out gratis landed him on the Medjugorje promotion circuit. An avid golfer, Weible would spend the next several years playing at the world's most famous golf courses, while spreading the messages of Our Lady Queen of Peace. His daughter would also eventually make it on to the circuit, where she would give tearful talks about how Medjugorje healed her from guilt over aborting one of her children.

At this point in June 1988, Weible noticed Mrs. Bianchi in the crowd and finding her attractive went over to her and said, "You are going to play a significant role in Our Blessed Mother's Plan." Being a speaker on the Medjugorje circuit, Weible evidently had detailed knowledge of the Blessed Mother's plans. Gianna, who according to Father Spalding, is a "really sweet kid" and a pharmacist to boot, was taken aback by Weible's message, but not for along. The next day she announced to Spalding that she too was getting messages from the Blessed Mother. Undeterred by the proliferation of apparitions, Spalding decided to "employ the Church's criteria" to see if Mrs. Bianchi's messages are real or not. The criteria go something like this: "first of all if the person is married, is the person being drawn closer to their spouse because the Holy Spirit would never break up a sacramental marriage." The reference to marriage is especially interesting because at one point Spalding said that the Bianchis had no children although they were planning to at some point in the future, a statement which indicated that the absence of children was intentional and the result of contraception. It was also interesting because at one point Gianna got a message from the Blessed Mother that she was going to use the Bianchi marriage as an example to the entire world. "Your marriage is to be representative to all the world," the Blessed Mother allegedly said to Gianna in 1989, characterizing her marriage as one distinguished by "purity and gentleness." Two years later, the Bianchis were divorced. When Gianna filed for an annulment, she gave as grounds the fact that they had been living in a contraceptive marriage because husband Michael said he didn't want any children. Then to make matters worse, Gianna took to the seer circuit and eventually landed a doctor from Maryland as a husband. "This was a seer on the make," said one priest familiar with the story.

Soon another lady from the adult prayer group, Annie, came to Father Spalding and announced that she too was getting messages from the Blessed Virgin, and soon St. Maria Goretti Parish in Scottsdale, Arizona, was attracting pilgrims of its own. In each instance, the spiritual entity was telling the seers to follow their impulses. At least that is what whatever it was ended up saying to Father

Spalding, because before long he too was getting messages.

It seems that in November of 1988 Father Spalding was saying Mass in Scottsdale one Thursday evening. He remembers standing in front of the altar ready to give his homily when all of a sudden everything went blank.

"I didn't not only not remember what I was going to say in the homily," he recounted later, "but I didn't even remember what the gospel was."

Father "just stood there," wondering "what in the world is happening to me," when all of a sudden "this feeling came over me like I was being drained. And all of a sudden I heard myself speaking, and it wasn't me speaking. It lasted about 45 seconds and it was over. And I don't even remember hearing what it was. But I just remember when it was over I was so tired that I could hardly make it back to where I was sitting."

This experience needed explication from someone who was used to playing in the spiritual equivalent of the big leagues, and so after he finished saying Mass, Father Spalding decided to consult Gianna. After making it to the sacristy, Spalding asked Gianna, "Do you have any idea of what happened to me tonight?" and she said, "Yes I do."

"Well," Gianna told Spalding, "Our Lady told me that She doesn't want her children to have to wait for a week to hear what she has to say to them. If you will say, yes, she will use you like this every now and then." And so Father Spalding has been used ever since.

Mark Waterinckx was the first man from Belgium to make contact with Medjugorje and has made 24 pilgrimages there since 1984. He has raised thousand and thousands of dollars for Medjugorje In the summer of 1989 he had become friends with Jozo Zovko in Tihalina when an American woman came to him and told him that Zovko had sexually assaulted her. Waterinckx went to Zovko the next day, and Zovko denied everything but was pale and in a terrible sate. The incident precipitated a crisis of faith for Waterinckx, who had a conversion experience at San Damioano, which he now doubts. After praying in front of the Blessed Sacrament, Waterinckx decided to walk barefoot to Tihalinja to try to get to the bottom of the matter. When he arrived in Tihalijna, Zovko had regained his composure; he laughed at Waterinckx in spite of the fact that he had severe burns on his feet. Since that time, Zovko has pretended that he doesn't know Waterinckx.

Waterinckx now claims to know 12 women who Zovko has molested including a woman whose father still conducts pilgrimages to Medjugorje. One or two months after his first encounter with the American woman, Waterinckx, seeing that nothing was being done, went to see Leonardo Orec, then curate at Medjugorje. Orec seemed unconcerned about the whole thing. "If you don't do something," Waterinckx told Orec, "I'll go to the provincial in Mostar." Eventually Waterinckx had to write to Herman Schalueck, the Franciscan general, and it was he who finally brought about Zovko's suspension a few months later on August 23, 1989. Rene Laurentin mentioned the suspension in one of his books in '89 adding that the severity of the actions must have indicated that it happened for a good reason. In spite of being suspended, Zovko continued living at Tihalijna. Zrinko Cuvalo, one the Franciscans who was in Medjugorje on day one of the apparitions, was sent to keep an eye on him, but since Cuvalo had a drinking problem the eye was probably not all that observant. Zovko was disciplined a second time in 1994, this time under Bishop Peric for pertinacious disobedience.

Waterinckx had had a number of negative experiences which shook his faith beginning in 1986, but the events of 1989, particularly those associated with Jozo Zovko's behavior were so devastating that Waterinckx decided that he had to do warn people. However, when he tried to warn people in articles he had written, he suddenly found that his access to the Medjugorje publications which were previously so eager to print what he wrote had been cut off. It was a pattern which would repeat itself over and over again. Only "positive" articles got published. As a result, people were kept in the dark until the truth suddenly overwhelmed their defenses, at which point they became alienated from the Church and disillusioned. Vain credulity was quickly replaced by a general skepticism on the part of people who were having difficulty coping with changes they didn't understand in the first place.

The evidence against Zovko was particularly damning, not only because he had, in effect, created the apparitions by bringing them into the church and thereby conferring on them what seemed to be Church approval, but also because the Blessed Mother herself, at least according to the testimony of Marija Pavlovic on October 21, 1981, had said, "Jozo Zovko is a saint." By March of 1994, Marija had had enough experience with the Franciscans to convince her that Franciscans like Zovko and Vlasic were no saints, but apparently not enough to get her to admit that she wasn't seeing the Gospa. "We must not like only persons like Father Jozo," Marija said in March 1994, "or the seers themselves, since they can become a disillusion [sic] to you. They are not saints." Marija had by then forgotten that she, speaking for the Blessed Mother, had said the exact opposite 13 years before. By the time her caveat of 1994 was made public, Marija Pavlovic had been caught twice in lies involving the two Franciscans who had taken control of the apparitions over the summer of 1981, but by then the

Herzegovina Franciscans had shown that they were not interested in the truth—Father Barbaric had no difficulty inviting the twice-suspended Zovko to attend the International Youth Festival in August of 1997—and the pilgrims were too befuddled to know the difference.

-9-

THE FALL OF COMMUNISM

In September of 1989, with a modest amount of publicity and fanfare, a group of Austrian and Hungarian officials gathered on their common border and began, with the help of soldiers wearing thick gloves, rolling up the barbed-wire fence that demarcated the frontier between the two countries. The barrier between Austria and Hungary was by no means as formidable or as deadly as the one separating East and West Germany, but in many ways it was much more significant. By rolling up the barbed-wire fence, the first breach was made in the Iron Curtain which had descended in 1946 along a line stretching from the Adriatic to the Baltic Seas. But it meant more than that as well. It meant the de-facto regrouping of the nations which had once constituted the Austro-Hugarian empire, the southernmost border of which had been the Catholic nation of Croatia. The Catholic anti-Communist crusade inspired by the league of captive Catholic nations was on the verge of its greatest and final success. Intermarium was back in business.

On February 6, 1989, General Wojiciech Jaruzelski, the man who declared martial law in Poland (and according to his own claim later, saved Poland from a Soviet invasion) convened round table discussion involving Solidarity, the union he had outlawed when he declared martial law in December of 1981. Taking its cue from events in Poland, Hungary struck the leading role of the Communist Party from its constitution at around the same time, and after opening its border to the West in September stood by as tens of thousands of East Germans began streaming though its border to asylum in West Germany. East Germany had erected the Berlin Wall in 1960 precisely because its economy, based on low-paying jobs and police coercion, simply could not survive the competition from the West, whose "economic miracle" was causing a hemorrhage of workers so severe that it threatened to depopulate certain areas of the country. The same situation was *a fortiori* true 29 years later, as whole sections of the DDR shut down. Depopulation was now more than a threat; it was a reality. East Germany was in no position to weather a crisis like this, at this time, and, quite simply, it did not.

In October of 1989 huge crowds took to the streets in Leipzig, Dresden, and East Berlin, demanding the resignation of Erich Honecker. Honecker, knowing that he could not call up Soviet troops to quell the demonstrations as a result of Mikhail Gorbachev's decision cutting the Soviet satellites in Eastern Europe loose to fend for themselves, could not muster the will to have the Vopos and the East German army fire on its own citizens. As a result of this fact, Honecker was replaced by a younger Politburo functionary by the name of Egon Krenz, who took the helm of the DDR on November 9 and, faced with the inevitable, opened the DDR's border with the *Bundesrepublik* on the same day. On November 10, elated crowds surged through the border crossings in Berlin and began tearing down the wall that had divided that city for almost 30 years.

Soon the same thing started happening throughout Eastern Europe. On the same day that the wall came down, the 36-year-old regime of Todor Zhikov fell in Bulgaria, and crowds took to the streets in Czechoslovakia demanding elections and the resignation of President Husak. In all, it was a remarkably peaceful transition. The only Communist leader who lost his life was Romania's President Ceacescu, who provoked his own bloody demise by recourse to the military forces his fellow rulers avoided elsewhere.

Yugoslavia went though all of the same motions, but there the situation was significantly different because of the multi-ethnic nature of the country and the bellicose nature of the ethnic groups who lived there. Romania had a huge Hungarian minority living within its borders, but that minority seemed content to wait out the change rather than take up arms to form its own country. In Poland, the country which started the whole process in motion, the population was so homogeneous religiously that no changes were necessary. Czechoslovakia, however, another creation of the Versailles treaty whose purpose was to carve up the Austro-Hungarian empire, collapsed within a few years according to ethnic lines, even though it probably made more economic sense for Slovakians to remain in one country with the more affluent Czechs. In Yugoslavia, however, the situation was different. The only thing that held the country together was an ideology and a personality. Once Tito died the troubles began, and once the ideology he promoted died nine years later, the country died as well.

Nature abhors a vacuum, and the vacuum created by the departure of Tito and communism could only be filled by an appeal to ethnicity, which, in this instance, meant religion as well, the two forces the Communists had been so careful to suppress. There was no other option in the Balkans.

On November 29, 1989, a little less than three weeks after the fall of the Berlin Wall, Franjo Tudjman stepped forward as the head of the party he had just formed, the Croatian Democratic Union, or HDZ, and called on the Communist-controlled parliament of Croatia to form a new government. The new regime would end the Communist Party monopoly on power, guarantee direct elections, free political prisoners, and grant free travel to the Croatian community in exile. All of this was fine and in keeping with what was happening throughout the rest of Eastern Europe. Conspicuous by its absence from Tudjman's program, however, was any statement guaranteeing the rights of ethnic minorities, specifically Serbs, within Croatia's borders. As time went on the omission seemed more and more intentional and more and more ominous, and the Serbs became increasingly worried.

Unfortunately, the leaders of the other ethnic groups in Yugoslavia were caught up in the same nationalist vortex, an ironic state of affairs for a country which so assiduously promoted internationalism, brotherhood and unity. It was in many ways the political version of the return of the repressed, and Tudjman had predicted it, *expressis verbis*, in his 1981 book *Nationalism in Europe*. "It is an irony of history," he wrote, "that communism has triumphed only in countries where it championed the right of oppressed and colonial nations to self-determination and national independence, [but] an even greater paradox is that nationalism remains a most powerful force precisely in that part of Europe where communism has been established—communism, which was supposed to eliminate nationalism forever" (p. 3). Growing up in an area of the world where regimes came and went but the people with their ethnic identity remained, Tudjman would eventually repudiate his earlier belief in Marxism and become one of the world's leading proponents of nationalism. Once Communist internationalism disappeared from the scene along with Yugoslavia as well, Tudjman found himself locking horns with the post-Communist new world order and its mandarins, people like George Soros and the editors of the *New York Times*.

Franjo Tudjman wasn't the only former Communist who was promoting nationalism. Milan Kucan was doing the same thing in Slovenia, but Kucan would have less trouble implementing his program because Slovenia was the most ethnically homogeneous of all of the Yugoslav republics and geographically the most peripheral. It had only one internal border with Yugoslavia, with Croatia, which wanted out of the federation at the same time. It also had strong ties with Austria and the West.

Even though Serbia was the most Communist of all of Yugoslav republics, it too was caught up in the vortex of rising nationalism. In 1987 a then-all-but-unknown Communist official by the name of Slobodan Milosevic gave a speech at Kosovo defending the rights of ethnic Serbs against the predations of their Albanian neighbors, and suddenly everyone in Yugoslavia was defending a nationalist agenda that was at odds with the official ideology. Tudjman would claim that every multi-ethnic nation was an empire in which the dominant ethnic group exercises hegemony over subordinate groups in the name of national unity or some other internationalist ideology. Whatever the reason, each ethnic group was being maneuvered into ever narrower, oftentimes chauvinistic appeals to its constituents as its leaders attempted to hold onto power as Communism collapsed. Milosevic was in the curious position of being able to remain in power as a Communist only by appealing to the national feelings among the Serbs, a nationalism which Communism had attempted so assiduously to ban, and Tudjman was doing much the same thing, except that he no longer called himself a Communist. A close reading of Tudjman's book makes it clear that he had no real plan to deal with the lack of ethnic homogeneity within the various Yugoslavian republics or towns for that matter, nor did he consider Muslims an ethnic group in their own right. Yugoslavia may have been fatally tainted by its association with Communism and its totalitarian, police-state brutality, but Yugoslavia in and of itself is not such a far-fetched idea as a *modus vivendi* for the various ethnic groups living in the area. Taken together, the facts comprising the situation were a recipe for ethnic conflict. Since it is clear from the premises of his book on nationalism that the only thing that makes sense as the successor to Yugoslavia are ethnically pure republics, Tudjman had no way of adjudicating the conflicts when they inevitably arose within a republic like Croatia, which was theoretically supposed to be a nation but still had members of other nations living within its borders. The situation was that much worse in Bosnia-Herzegovina, which was even more mixed and even less a nation.

In January 1990, the Yugoslavian Communist Party convened in special session and tried to work out a solution that would hold the country together. Before it could reach a solution the Slovene delegates, supported by the Croatians, walked out, and the party for all intents and purposes ceased to exist after the Congress adjourned indefinitely. In February, the Croatian Parliament voted to legalize opposition parties and in April and May of that year, the first free elections in half a century were held, resulting in a landslide victory for Tudjman and the Croatian Democratic Union, which won 205 of 349

seats. The Communists could retain only 77 seats, and Franjo
Tudjman was elected President of Croatia, which was at least technically still part of Yugoslavia. Tudjman had a mandate, but he still
lacked a plan to deal with ethnic minorities within the newly sovereign
republics and so harassment of Serbs continued unabated, a fact
which played into the hands of Slobodan Milosevic and fueled his rise
to power in Serbia. Epithets like "Chetnik" and "Ustasha" flew back
and forth with increasing frequency. The war of words quickly escalated into physical violence. One group of policemen was ambushed
when responding to a call for help. In some instances the Serbs were
being harassed. In other instances, the federal troops would intervene
to protect ethnic Serbs and deliberately provoke what they were
ostensibly there to prevent as a way of cleansing an area of Croats.

The problem of ethnic minorities was minimal in Slovenia; it
was serious in Croatia, but it was catastrophic in Bosnia-Herzegovina,
which, Tudjman maintained persuasively, was never really a country to
begin with and could not be treated as such by the international
community without severe consequences. Before it got renamed as
Yugoslavia in 1929, the Balkan entity created by the Versailles Treaty in
southeastern Europe was known as the Kingdom of the Croats,
Slovenes, and Serbs. That was in effect the tripartite division that
Tudjman had in mind when the country disintegrated in the early
1990s. Muslims were not an ethnic group, according to this schema,
and Bosnia-Herzegovina was not a country—actually, potentially, or in
any other way. According to Tudjman's reckoning, Bosnia-Herzegovina

> should have been made a part of the Croatian federal
> unit. Bosnia and Herzegovina was declared a separate
> federal republic within the borders established during
> the Turkish occupation. But large parts of Croatia had
> been incorporated into Bosnia by the Turks. Further-
> more Bosnia and Herzegovina were historically linked
> with Croatia and they together comprise an indivisible
> geographic and economic entity. . . . The creation of a
> separate Bosnia and Herzegovina makes the territorial
> and geographic position of Croatia extremely unnatural
> in the economic sense and, therefore, in the broadest
> national-political sense, very unfavorable for life and de-
> velopment and in the narrower administrative sense
> unsuitable and disadvantageous. (p. 112).

What Tudjman failed to realize at the time is how his appeal to
nationalist self-consciousness was affecting not only the other traditional nations in Yugoslavia, the Slovenes and the Serbs, it was also

helping to bring into being a new "nation," the Muslims, who had traditionally identified themselves as Croats in places like Bosnia-Herzegovina, which had never been an independent nation. Given its ethnic make-up, its lack of access to the sea, and its terrain, it was hard to see how it ever would be, but that didn't stop a group of Muslim nationalists from asserting their case and taking it to the rest of the Muslim world for pan-Islamic support.

"An objective examination of the numerical composition of the population of Bosnia and Herzegovina," Tudjman wrote in 1981,

> cannot ignore that the majority of the Moslems is in its ethnic character and speech incontrovertibly of Croatian origin. Despite religious and cultural distinctions created by history, the vast majority of the Moslems declared themselves Croats whenever an opportunity arose. . . . The hegemonistic system in particular...has meant that the Bosnian Moslems in their aspirations and their views on the future completely identify themselves with the Croats. Any Serbian statesman who fails to take this fact into account cannot be considered seriously. On the basis of these facts we arrive at the conclusion that a majority of the population of Bosnia and Herzegovina is Croatian. On the other hand the geoeconomic connection of Bosnia with the other Croatian lands is such that neither Croatia in its present boundaries nor the separate Bosnia and Herzegovina possess the conditions for a separate, normal development.

Ten years later, the situation had changed, but, in principle at least, Tudjman's solution sounded plausible. There was no getting around the fact of ethnicity; it had prevailed after empires—the Ottoman, the Austro-Hungarian, and the Communist—had failed. The only problem lay in the fact that ethnic groups in Yugoslavia did not line up neatly according to the republics which represented them, and Franjo Tudjman had given no indication that the rights of Serbs would be respected in an independent Croatia. Given then the ethnic patch-quilt that was Yugoslavia and its constituent republics and the rise of nationalism and the absence of a plan to deal with minorities, ethnic conflict was an inevitable concomitant to the fall of Communism. Ethnic cleansing, if by that we understand not murder but rather the forced repatriation of ethnic minorities to the country of ethnic origin, was, in many ways, the only policy that made sense given the ideological state of mind in a rapidly collapsing Yugoslavia. In many ways, there were really only two alternatives in the Balkans: ethnic cleansing or Yugoslavia, and in 1981 the idea of Yugoslavia had been discredited by its association with Communism. Tudjman could cite Scandinavia as an example of a region where peace came only after each of the constituent nations relinquished its imperial aspirations and retired to clearly defined ethnic borders.

"Scandinavia," he wrote,

> quieted down only when all the forms of Scandinavian unions with Danish or Swedish hegemony were removed and when the establishment of the independent national states created the preconditions not only for lasting peace and harmonious Co-existence among the Scandinavian countries but also the kind of social progress which is not to be found where there has been no "Scandinavianization" at all or where it has been implemented only partially.

In 1981 Tudjman was hoping that the same thing would happen in Yugoslavia.

On July 26, 1990, the Croatian Parliament dropped the word "Socialist" from the official name of the Croatian republic and ordered the red star removed from the Grb, the checkerboard symbol which was the official crest of the Ustasha; it was the display of this crest on the altar at St. James Church which had gotten Jozo Zovko thrown into jail. Tudjman and the Croatian government continued to negotiate with Yugoslavia for a mutually beneficial *modus vivendi* but found the Serbs increasingly intransigent. The Serbs for their part felt betrayed and exploited financially, even if the Croats felt they held the upper hand politically. "Croatia," wrote Alex Dragnic, giving the Serb point of view, "with its large hard currency earnings from tourists, took little account of the fact that it fed its tourists on large quantities of food stuffs from other republics, mainly Serbia. This was reminiscent of the north-south situation in the United States at the time of the Civil War.... [I]n 1990 the average per capita income in Slovenia was $12,618; in Croatia, $7,179; in Serbia, $4,870. Serbians average a per capita income that was only one-third that of Slovenians."

The Serbs as a result felt betrayed and foolish and bewildered at being vilified for an arrangement from which the alleged victim benefited more than the victimizer financially. They were also taken aback by the rise of nationalism and anti-Serb animosity, which many said did not exist before the mid-'80s, and some traced directly to Medjugorje. In early 1990 the Serbs came in a formal little procession to Surmanci and, after cracking open the concrete seal which the

Communists had put over the mass grave, carried off the bones of their deceased comrades in little flag-bedraped coffins to be re-interred in Serbian cemeteries. The residents of Medjugorje saw this gesture as prefiguring the war to come, but the Serbs in the area said the same thing about the apparitions at Medjugorje. In 1992, AP religion writer June Johnson interviewed Serbian soldiers stationed near Medjugorje, who told her "that this war started heating up 10 years ago when the Virgin Mary started appearing in Medjugorje. This is when, they say, the government started losing control. The money that came in from the millions of tourists helped Croatians become more independent."

On August 17, 1990, Serbs near Banija and Kordun, an area of Croatia geographically remote from Serbia, declared their area, which was nonetheless 21 percent Croat, the "Serbian Autonomous Region Krajina" and began cutting down trees and blocking all significant roads and railroad lines with their trunks, actions which effectively cut off Croatia from its sources of food during the high point of its economically crucial tourist season and convinced the population that secession was inevitable. Now the Croats in "Krajina" were subjected to the same harassment that Serbs in Croatia had suffered. The economy was being strangled by ethnic conflict.

On April 3, 1990 at 2 o'clock in the morning, Teresa Lopez was awakened by a voice which told her to "Read the Word." Lopez would later claim that the voice was that of the Blessed Virgin and that this was the beginning of the visions that would later grant her fame on the Medjugorje apparition circuit. "What a special date this has become in my life," she wrote later. "The voice whom [sic] has led me for so long began on that night."

Later Jeff Lopez would say that Theresa started hearing voices shortly after Stephanie died. In her account, the voices started about a year after the death. Either way, they were related to the death of the child, and she started writing them down under the title "Stephanie: Is that you, God?" The death of Stephanie had brought Teresa back to the Church and there she made contact with Medjugorje prayer groups for the first time. Before long, she too was hearing voices associated with her dead child, which she took to a young priest at All Souls Parish in Denver, the church they were attending at the time. The priest, however, was unimpressed. He told her to keep her messages to herself, and the messages wouldn't become public until she went to Medjugorje, which was almost one year after they started and a little over two years after Stephanie died.

Since his days in junior high, Jeff Lopez carried a passage from Ephesians around with him in his wallet. When Teresa mentioned the same passage as coming from the mouth of the Blessed Mother, he became convinced that the apparitions were genuine. He now thinks that she found out about the passage the easy way, by going through his wallet.

"I believed her in the beginning because of that verse," Jeff said. "Now I think she's just a sneak and a liar."

Teresa would later claim that her encounter with the Blessed Mother changed her life. If so, the part that did not change was her appetite for drugs and expensive clothes. Nor did her inability to pay her bills change; nor did her eye for a way of making a fast buck by means less than honest change. On May 5, 1990, less than a month after her encounter with the Blessed Mother, Teresa was working at Wendy's and in her own words, taken from a legal deposition, "As I was putting away the delivery, I lost my balance and fell into a storage rack." Teresa alleged that the fall while working at Wendy's had dislocated her shoulder and as a result of that injury she filed a claim for compensation with the Denver division of the Department of Labor and Employment. In filing the claim, Teresa used one social security number, but she continued working during the same period under another social security number. In September of 1990 Teresa hired an attorney to take legal action against Wendy's, claiming permanent partial disability. The insurance agent for Wendy's made Teresa an offer of $6,000 in late October, right around the time she stopped seeing her doctor. In December 1990, the insurance company raised the offer to $7,500, and in January of 1991, she finally accepted Wendy's offer of $10,000. Her last day of work was officially December 27, 1990, but Teresa continued to work well into 1991 under the second social security number.

During the period of negotiations with Wendy's, Teresa's other bad habits began to catch up with her. On August 20, 1990, she pleaded guilty to a charge of second degree forgery and fraud. The charge had led to her arrest, but at the time of her pleading she was out on $5,000 bond posted by Jeff, who was soon to become her fourth husband. According to the final ruling in the case of *Valas Financial Corporation vs. Teresa A. Lopez*, Teresa had to pay back a sum of $1,598.43 at 22.45 percent interest beginning in December of 1990. Theresa negotiated a settlement whereby she could repay the sum in $100 monthly installments.

As part of her career plan as a seer, Teresa seems to have understood that she needed to rehabilitate her standing with the Catholic Church. And so one week before pleading guilty to check fraud, she applied for annulment with the metropolitan tribunal of the Archdiocese of Denver. Here as before, she was less than honest in what she said. Filing under the name Teresa Antonie Jones, she omitted her first and second marriage from the filing, giving the impression that she had only be married once and only to Ernest Alcorn, her most recent husband. At this time Teresa was a member of All Souls Catholic Church in Englewood, Colorado, and it was there that she and Jeff chose to be married, on October 13, 1990, the 73rd anniversary of the final apparition to the three peasant children at Fatima. Rev. Walter Jaeger presided at the ceremony. Teresa was also teaching religion to the children of the second grade at All Soul's Parish and involved in preparing them to make their first confession and Holy Communion. In 1991, Theresa was named Catechist of the Year.

On February 8, 1991, Teresa had more misfortune. While stopped at a stop sign, she was rear-ended by a car which pushed her forward into the car in front of her. Always one to see the silver lining in every cloud, especially if it involved a personal injury settlement, Teresa complained of shoulder pain, the same shoulder which had led to the Wendy's settlement and hired a lawyer. The insurance company eventually settled. The amount is undisclosed, but on January 2, 1992, Teresa bought a red Ford Probe for $16,415.70. Since her credit rating was as low as such things go, she had to pay cash for the car. To give some indication of her state of mind at the time, for by January of 1992, Teresa was famous as a seer, she applied for custom license plates for her car. Her first choices were "I.H.M., Rosary, M.I.R. (the Croatian word for peace) and PRAY. Unfortunately all her choices were rejected. The names had already been taken by other Marian-minded automobile drivers in Colorado.

On February 12, four days after the accident, Teresa and Jeff filed an application for tax-exempt status and trade-name registration for an organization called Rocky Mountain Project Peace, whose purpose was to collect money for prayer kits and Catholic literature for soldiers serving in the Persian Gulf. Jeff was later to testify that a significant amount of money came in as a result of television ads, but that none of it went to the soldiers in the Gulf War. Three years later, in the midst of acrimonious divorce proceedings, Jeff would testify to one of the interrogatories, that he "firmly believe[d] that Teresa attained the $30,000 car accident settlement fraudulently," that Teresa also "received her workman's compensation settlement fraudulently" by using a photocopier to change the dates on her medical reports, and that

> Teresa has defrauded tens of thousands of people to her own gain in making her claims that she has visions of the Virgin Mary. Through this, millions of dollars have been collected much of which one way or another ends up providing her with world-wide travel, all expenses, nu-

merous gifts and "stipends" paid directly to her in the form of cash or check. Including the attorney fees in this action.

Jeff went on to add that "Teresa during and prior to our marriage has completely destroyed my credit rating" and in addition had not paid any "federal taxes in her lifetime," but all of this acrimony was still in the distant future. In the immediate future as of early 1991, Teresa was planning a trip to Medjugorje, her first, which began on March 17, 1991, and lasted five days. In her own account of how she got there, Teresa said that she had been having medical problems during the fall of 1990 and that up until that October, she had never heard of Medjugorje, a statement contradicted by Jeff's testimony, which places her first contact a year earlier. According to her account, Teresa wanted to go but was looking for a sign that she should act on her desire, which was going to cost her money. She found the sign in church. In the pew in front of her, a woman had taken off her coat and there on the label, Teresa read "Made in Yugoslavia."

"I knew immediately," Teresa recounted later, "that that's how Our Lady was telling me, yes, this is what I want you to do, I want you to go, and I thought, I could hardly contain myself. I thought I was going to jump up in the church and just start screaming and just completely come unglued, and I couldn't stand it anymore. I said, 'Jeff, my sign, my sign! I received my sign! I know I'm supposed to go to Medjugorje,' and so that's how the trip to Medjugorje actually came about."

Teresa's account emphasizes the sanctity of marriage in general and her devotion to her husband Jeff in particular. "At this point in my marriage my husband was the one that was spiritual," she said modestly, but not without a certain element of truth. "He was the one who was into all the charismatic renewal, and he knew all the, you know, it wasn't me and if anything I would expect this to happen to him."

Be that as it may, Teresa goes on to assure us that "we have been called as a unit together" and that "Mary would never obstruct that" because "the sacrament of matrimony is very holy, and this [sacrament] is first and foremost our vocation . . . and from there wherever our lady wants to take us as whole, she will take us as a unit." Half the unit was back in Colorado when Teresa arrived in Medjugorje, where she was greeted by a Croatian lady who gave her a bouquet of violets. Judy Hill, wife (and soon to be ex-wife) of John Hill, the wealthy man who got into promoting Medjugorje from his private fortune, was the tour leader, and after seeing Teresa get the bouquet, she turned to Theresa and said, "you know there is not such thing as coincidence." Coincidence or not, shortly thereafter, Theresa was standing with her violets at the foot of the apparition hill when she suddenly felt impelled upward by an irresistible force. "I had no control of going up the hill whatsoever," she would say later. As a gesture of gratitude, Teresa just before leaving "put these violets between [Jesus'] feet on the cross there, and I had such a peace come over me, it was like, thank you."

Sensing that she had a hot property here, Judy arranged a meeting with Father Slavko Barbaric, who gave the stamp of approval to her apparitions after Teresa had an apparition while waiting in the St. James Parish rectory. The signs and wonders just kept on coming after that. On the way home, the Gospa appeared on the flight monitor (whether arrival or departure, she does not say) at Kennedy Airport, causing a crowd of people to assemble in front of it and say the Hail Mary on their knees.

On the next day of her visit to Medjugorje, a Croatian woman came running across the street and grabbing Teresa's blonde hair began shouting, "Lady's angel, Lady's angel."

"I said, 'thank you,' you know, and Judy next to me was just beaming, and she says, 'you really don't understand, do you?' and I said, 'understand what?'"

The whole thing was just one big surprise after another for Teresa, who also got to meet with Vicka, who perhaps suspecting that they were kindred spirits, or at least that they trafficked in kindred spirits, prayed over Theresa, causing "an intense and incredible electricity" to pass through her. "It was just like being completely jolted," she said later.

"We looked into each other's eyes," Theresa said later of her encounter with Vicka, "and it was just like an incredible bond, and she took me by the shoulders, and she turned me around, and she pointed up the hill, up Cross Mountain, and she says, 'Gospa, Gospa,' and next to the cross was Our Lady, and at this point I saw her as a silhouette in a glow that backlighted her, and that was the very first time that I actually saw her, and just cried and cried, and we cried together, and it was just so overwhelming."

"I could feel Our Lady coming in," Teresa said, getting more explicit about the feeling. "It started out as a very small feeling, if you will, and this feeling built and built and built in intensity to almost an ecstatic moment."

Later in comparing notes with another seer from the Denver area, Teresa would say that talking to Jesus was like having an orgasm.

One fellow pilgrim after hearing the tape of Teresa's talk wrote to dispute details of her account, but Teresa never answered her letter. On July 20, 1991, Mary Oakes began her open letter to her fellow pilgrims with a confession. In 1980, while single and a student at Catholic University, Oakes became pregnant and had an abortion. Like so many other women in this story, her life would become focused on voices which would rise up from the past on certain emotionally charged dates. In July of 1990, Oakes discovered that she was pregnant again, and, more significantly, that her due date was April 25, the same due date of the child she had aborted in 1980. "I took this to be a sign from God," she wrote to her fellow pilgrims, a sign "that I had been forgiven. He was giving me a second chance."

Nine weeks later Mary Oakes got another sign. The baby died in her womb, and she miscarried. It gave her another chance to think over her abortion.

"In the pain of those days and nights I had to admit that the things I aborted that baby for had never even come to pass. The man I married left me for another woman and since I had dropped out of school to support us I never received the degree I needed to be certified social worker."

Oakes then got pregnant again and lost that baby at 16 weeks. Two months later, Oakes left for Medjugorje and met Teresa Lopez. During the summer of 1992, in the year following her pilgrimage, Oakes enrolled at a course taught by Rene Laurentin, who now taught a course on Mary and Marian apparitions at the Notre Dame Institute in Northern Virginia. On July 20, one of her classmates handed her Lopez's book, *Our Holy Mother of Virtues*. When Oakes finally got a chance to read it, she was shocked at the misrepresentations Theresa made in it of the events of the pilgrimage.

"Teresa," she wrote, "this is not the way it happened. What is going on ? These paragraphs are very misleading."

According to Oakes' recollections, there was no locution during the meeting with Slavko Barbaric. That and other discrepancies lead Oakes "to wonder whet else is not as you say." There is no indication that Teresa ever answered Oakes' letter. Undeterred Oakes wrote back on October 28, 1992 with "a confession."

"On Tuesday afternoon of our pilgrimage, I returned to our room to take a shower. I noticed your journal there across the room. Without your permission, and without your being present, I went over to read it."

And again Oakes was struck by discrepancies between her recollection of the events of the pilgrimage and the account Teresa Lopez gave, specifically the scene where "Viska [sic] hugs you, points to the top of the mountain and indicates to you that she saw our Lady too, "And at that moment, I am filled with fear and dread, because for some reason I am certain that particular exchange never took place."

In order to "hash this out," Oakes asks Lopez to call her

collect, but there is no indication that Teresa ever responded to the letter either in writing or by phone. The exchange is significant because it points up the role that dead babies played in the minds of the mostly female protagonists in the apparition's history. Mirjana, who is "sensitive" and the originator of the apparitions, recounted the story of the woman who used to have the souls from purgatory come and tap on her window. Even when she moved away and her window was six stories above street level, the tapping continued. Many of the victims of the massacre at Surmanci were infants and children, helpless victims, who made the crime even more heinous. Similarly Mary Oakes went to Medjugorje for some sign that she had been forgiven for aborting her child. Teresa Lopez, according to the testimony of her fourth husband Jeff, began hearing voices shortly after the death of her child Stephanie, a death which may or may not have been hastened by the drugs she had been taking during the pregnancy. In each instance, women are seeking solace for remorse over the untimely or intentional death of innocent children, born and yet to be born. The arrival of the Blessed Mother seems to reaffirm the maternal nurturing protective behavior that these women found lacking in either themselves or the culture to which they respond as a medium.

In February of 1987, Sandy [not her real name] was sick in bed with a virus. "As Our Lady would have it," she says, she turned on the TV and saw Wayne Weible, the Lutheran Medjugorje enthusiast whose personally published newspaper account of events there has been distributed in the millions. He and two New Orleans journalists were describing their experiences. Something seemed to click immediately in Sandy's mind. "The second I saw it," she said, "I knew it was real." At the same time she learned about it she became in her own words "obsessed" with finding out all she could about it and with finding a way of getting there. She soon communicated her enthusiasm to her sister, who found herself under a similar compulsion.

Both Sandy and her sister had been raised Catholic but had fallen away from the faith. Both had lived what would have to be termed dissolute lives. Both had divorced and remarried, the sister a number of times; both had carried on a number of extramarital affairs besides; Sandy spoke of multiple partners and perversion at one point. Both were having trouble with drinking and/or drugs. The sister, who is older, had become seriously involved with the occult, so much so that she underwent an exorcism at the hands of Father Phillip Pavich, O.F.M., when she finally arrived at Medjugorje. Both attribute their conversion to finding out about Medjugorje. When Sandy went to her mother's house the summer following her introduction to Medjugorje, she found that she could no longer drink alcohol. "The Holy Spirit was preparing us," she said. She was no longer capable of "running around, drinking, and raising hell."

According to the two sisters' stories, however, the devil wasn't done with them yet. Having been apparently thwarted on the sex, drug, and alcohol front, he concentrated his efforts on screwing up their plans to get to Medjugorje. The sister had a young homosexual acquaintance all lined up to take care of her house and dog when the man suddenly turned on her and started beating her up, at one point throwing her suitcases through the window. Eventually she made it to the plane, but when she arrived at her sister's house, the kitchen stove caught on fire, causing her to exclaim that she had brought the devil with her.

According to the two sisters, their encounters with the devil only intensified when they arrived in Medjugorje. Sandy's sister got lost one night on the way down Crucifix Mountain and found herself pursued by demons, "horrible, disgusting animals," as she described them. She found herself running down some deserted road, banging on doors, screaming, and being, in general, "hysterical." At one point she had to go to the bathroom but became convinced that she was going to raped if she did. Any time she saw men, she became convinced that they were going to rape her. Eventually, still seeing devils, still afraid of being raped, she was found 10 kilometers from the house where she was staying.

In the meantime, Sandy was dealing with her own demons. One was telling her, "Surely you can run down the mountain," referring to the treacherous, rocky, and by now, pitch black path leading down Crucifix Mountain. Someone had died while attempting the same path in daylight the week before we had arrived. Sandy, who had already had visions of another sister who had been killed in an auto accident 17 years before, found herself in a cemetery, now obsessed with the fear of death. Hearing something behind her, she began running, praying Hail Marys for the Blessed Mother to get her through what was happening to her. She found herself feeling that there was no way out, that the devil was chasing her through the cemetery, as well as feeling certain that her dead sister was in the cemetery and would appear to her. Finally, she escaped from the cemetery, which she described as "like a maze," and made it to the church, but no one was there. By this time, she related, "I was hysterical, banging on doors, when a little Croatian woman found me and walked me across the street."

Eventually, she was taken back to the pensione where both she and her sister were staying, arriving there shortly before her sister. From then on she had to sleep with a light on. Her trip to Medjugorje convinced her that God was telling her, "Straighten out your act or you're going to Hell."

After hearing that friends of hers had seen the sun spin, Sandy was determined to see if God would favor her with the same sort of sign. The next day she stared at the sun at 12 noon until, as she says, "an arrow of pain" hit her eyes and "everything went orange."

"I knew instantly that I shouldn't have done what I did. My eyes hurt so bad. I knew right then and there that I had permanent damage and was afraid that I was going to be blind."

Sandy then called her husband, who is a doctor, and asked what she should do but knew instinctively that it was already too late. She spent the next 24 hours praying and asked her husband, who is an atheist, to pray too.

"I fought with demons all night long," Sandy said. "Satan spent the entire night screaming at me. It was the worst battle of my life. It was the first time I ever had chest pains like that. I felt that I was gong to die."

Eventually she did not die; she did not go blind either, not totally anyway; however, she does have permanent eye damage as a result of what she did. She has a black spot at the center of her vision where the sun scarred the retina but is thankful, given what she did, that she has any vision left at all. She attributes that to her prayer to the Blessed Mother.

Now both women are charismatics as a result of Medjugorje. Sandy's sister now claims to have the gift of healing. She also claims to have seen the Blessed Mother twice on her VCR.

"I have been absolutely obsessed with Medjugorje and Jesus Christ," she says of the period following her conversion.

In the face of such intense personal testimony, one finds oneself at a loss for words. Can anyone say with any amount of certitude that another fellow human being has not been wrestling with Satan, that he or she has not been hearing demons' voices? Given the way that these two women described their personal lives, it would seem that a fairly rigorous conversion was in order. If they had continued committing adultery, taking drugs, and trafficking in spirits, then it does not seem impossible that, had they died unrepentant, they would have gone to Hell. If Medjugorje or a Lutheran minister or two journalists from New Orleans were instrumental in their conversion, then that is all to the good. However, one does not have to be an expert in the discernment of spirits to detect certain spiritual dangers in the radical swings that characterize these women's lives.

The most sensible thing one can say about the matter is that it has happened many times before in the history of the Church. As a matter of fact, St. Paul, according to Msgr. Knox, found something very similar going on in the Corinth of his day. "Corinth," according to Knox, "was a city well known in a world of sufficiently lax standards as the paradise of the prostitute." No one, so far as I know, is disputing that the Holy Spirit was at work in Corinth; however, we should be sophisticated enough to know that the fruit of the Spirit is conditioned in many ways by the ground upon which the seed falls. Like Greece at the time of the Apostles, our culture has been living out its own licentious fantasies for long enough to have had a profound effect on many of the men and women who have been involved in them. According to Knox's reading of St. Paul, the sudden conjunction of God's grace and a previously licentious life was bound to produce strange spiritual effects: "The sudden conversion accompanied by violent emotional experiences of souls hitherto sunk in debilitating vice, might give rise, without difficulty, to a kind of enthusiasm, which would need regulation by an expert in the discerning of spirits."

So just as no one would deny that the spirit was at work in Corinth, no one should deny that certain dangers were associated with that work as well. The crucial issue is what role these gifts, if one wants to call them that, these charismata, are to play in the life of the Church. Just as no one should overlook the gifts, no one should overlook the dangers associated with them. The perennial spiritual danger associated with enthusiasm, according to Knox, is "to drive a wedge between the Christianity of Christ and the Christianity of the Church. It meant that you were appealing away from ecclesiastical authority to the validity of private revelation. And once you have done that, you have set your feet on the perilous slopes of disunion." The devil has a strategy ready for everyone, even, perhaps especially, the most zealous of converts.

The Catholic finds himself in a bit of a dilemma at points like these. As a firm believer in the ability of God to intervene in his life, he wants to do nothing to impede the actions and inspirations of the Holy Spirit. At the same time, however, he is smart enough to realize that everyone who claims to have received some sort of direct inspiration may not necessarily be telling the truth or in full contact with the spiritual reality he claims to convey. The devil, we know, can counterfeit such things. And beyond that, there is always mental instability, hysteria, and all of the other myriad foibles of human nature that the credulous tend to ignore in situations like these.

However, faith and credulity, no matter how things seem to merge at Medjugorje, are two separate things. And St. Paul, faced with the twin dangers of stifling the spirit or destroying the Church by surrendering to the primacy of every man's private revelation, chooses a middle course. In Knox's words:

> That devout women, in this as in every other age, were
> sometimes granted revelations in the course of their pri-

vate devotions cannot be doubted. . . . It was a different matter, whether they were free to communicate these revelations to others at times of public worship.

The danger is clear: "The unfettered exercise of the prophetic ministry by the more devout sex can threaten the ordinary decencies of ecclesiastical order." Private revelation is fine, one might say, but it carries with itself a constant danger. In addition to the women themselves, there are the "furtive hierophants," to use Knox's term, who "make their way into house after house, captivating women whose consciences are burdened with sin" (2 Tim. 3:6). Taken together, they became the hidden subtext of Medjugorje. Women, burdened by the psychological sequelae of the sexual revolution, transposed the sexuality of their earlier years into the sensual sprituality of visions, locutions, and all of the accompanying signs and wonders that typified Medjugorje. Preying on them in turn were the "furtive heirophants" who could turn a profit by exploiting these women's need for forgiveness. Taken together, the two groups formed a powerful block within the Church which was constantly attempting to subvert the Church's authority. To see all these people as simply wanting to say the rosary was to miss a deeper point. These suddenly pious, guilt-ridden ladies were not only easy prey for groups like the Herzegovina Franciscans or Mother Angelica; like the seers, they were potential footsoldiers in an ecclesial civil war that threatened to break out as soon as the Church asked them to give up their gold rosary beads. Nurtured on the opiate of religious consumerism, the pious ladies had become a fifth column within the Church. The threat of schism was never far beneath the surface.

Shortly after her return from Medjugorje, Teresa started having visions near Grand Lake. Then she started frequenting the Mother Cabrini Shrine in Denver, probably because she realized the she was getting nowhere with the priest at All Souls parish. Then in November of 1991 first the local newspaper and then CNN did a story on her, and the phone started ringing off the hook. On December 9, 1991, the Denver archdiocese appointed a commission to look into the apparitions.

On April 10, 1991, less than a month after Teresa Lopez became a seer, the Yugoslavian Bishops' Conference published its findings on Medjugorje at Zadar. There was little surprise surrounding the statement that they found "nothing supernatural" about the events there because a copy of the document had been leaked to reporters from the Catholic News Service in late 1990. The Yugoslavian bishops were determined to be pastoral on this one, perhaps in reaction to the brusque denunciations of fraud which Bishop Zanic had gotten used to issuing to anyone who would listen. Later Zanic would claim to be vindicated, but other reports had him complaining that the document was the best one could expect from a committee. Perhaps what bothered him was the fact that over half of the short document was devoted to instructions on how to care for pilgrims, in spite of the fact that the first half had just demonstrated that there was no reason to go there on pilgrimage because the Blessed Mother wasn't appearing there. In January of 1991, shortly after the BCY Commission statement got leaked to the press, Auxiliary Bishop Djuro Koksa of Zagreb was quoted as saying that the Yugoslavian bishops were concerned that "they were going to lose Medjugorje to the sects" if they came out with a negative statement. The CNS news account fails to mention that the final statement parallels exactly the agnosticism of Father Zivko Kustic's July 5, 1987 article in *Glas Koncila*: "Nobody—" Kustic wrote then

> not even the holiest, and the pilgrims who yearn most for apparitions in various lands—will mind if we say that we, officially as the Church, do not know if Mary indeed has appeared in Medjugorje, but that we know very well what ought to be done and said where the faithful gather, longing for conversion and peace, eager to hear the word of God and to receive the sacraments under the protection of Mary and through her intercession.

The bishops' statement wasn't that bad. It did say that the Blessed Mother wasn't appearing in Medjugorje, if one deduced that fact from the official verdict that "nothing supernatural" had occurred there, but the second half of statement about caring for pilgrims seemed to undercut the first. If the Blessed Virgin were not there, why was the Church spending so much time talking about pilgrims?

On February 8, 1991, the pope, according to a CNS article by John Thavis which appeared on February 15, met with an unnamed Yugoslavian bishop to discuss the situation at Medjugorje in light of the recent BCY statement. The pope assured this bishop that the Vatican "would eventually make a statement on the matter." At around the same time, this author contacted Joseph Cardinal Ratzinger at a hotel in Dallas, Texas, and Ratzinger said much the same thing that the pope had. Ratzinger shared the view of the Yugoslavian bishops that nothing supernatural was involved in the events at Medjugorje and stated that the Rome would issue a statement of its own "soon." When pressed to explain what "soon" meant, he simply repeated the word and counseled patience. Later the same year, Ratzinger was asked about Rome's statement on Medjugorje during the question-and-answer session of a conference in Austria. This time he said that Rome was still hoping to make a statement but that the situation had been complicated by the civil war. At the end of April, the Yugoslavian bishops held a three-day meeting during which they hammered out the liturgical guidelines to be enforced at Medjugorje. Again, the bishops seemed to want to have it both ways. The apparitions were condemned but in a way that "is aimed at taking advantage of the spiritual fervor at Medjugorje, while more closely controlling what people are told and taught there."

As in 1986, Rome temporized again, delaying its condemnation because of political considerations. As Ratzinger's statement in Austria indicated, Rome was aware that the political situation during the first half of 1991 was particularly delicate. The Berlin Wall hadn't been down for two years and the whole of Eastern Europe was still in a state of flux. A wrong move might jeopardize the success of the anti-Communist crusade, especially in Yugoslavia. But was Communism really the problem in Yugoslavia at this point in time? Medjugorje tourism had already established de facto freedom of religion and a certain measure of toleration for free enterprise and the private ownership of property. It has also helped foment the rising nationalism that was threatening to tear the country apart. Beginning in March of 1991, the war of words was escalating into war in the conventional sense of the term as armed conflicts between Serbian militias and Croatian police flared up in Pakrac, Plitvice Lakes National Park, and Borovo Selo near Vukovar, where 12 policemen were ambushed and killed. At around the same time, the Serbs drove nearly all of the Croats from the Knin region. In each instance, the Yugoslav army functioned as the military arm of Serbian interests, an act which clearly confirmed the Croat and Slovene resolve to declare independence.

On the other hand, the Serbians were feeling increasingly isolated and paranoid. Deprived of Russian support, they felt that, once again, they were all alone in a world conspiring against them, and from the Serbian point of view, the main forces interested in their defeat usually came from the West, so when they saw the Vatican and Germany eager to recognize the break-away Catholic republics of Croatia and Slovenia, all of the memories of the Ustasha/Nazi terror flooded back and pushed them toward armed conflict.

Like the French generals in 1940, Rome seemed determined to fight the last war. Communism was already gone in Yugoslavia; ethnic civil war was just over the horizon and in many areas had already broken out, and yet Rome persisted in staying with its anti-Communist crusade, even when it fueled Serbian paranoia and made fighting all but inevitable. "The Balkan region," writes Serbian historian Milan Bulajic in his book, *The Role of the Vatican in the Break-Up of the Yugoslav State* (Ministry of Information of the Republic of Serbia, Belgrade, 1993),

> where the Yugoslav state is located, is the Vatican's important "terra missionis," the Independent State of Croatia is " the bulwark of Catholicism." In its liberation struggle, the Serbian Orthodox state—the Kingdom of Serbia—faced the imperialism of Catholic Austria-Hungary, the Vatican's main support in this region. In its struggle against the Yugoslav state, "the Catholic church in Croatia" oriented itself towards Croatian separatism, towards enlarging the differences in relation to the Serbian Orthodox population which was proclaimed hegemonistic and said to have "greater Serbian" aspirations (p. 11).

Bulajic accused the Croatian bishops of "an open attempt to internationalize the crisis in the Yugoslav state, when on February 1, 1991, they sent an open letter "to all the bishops of the world," accusing Yugoslavia of being nothing more than a front for Serbian interests and the persecution of the Church. "The communist ideology," the bishops wrote, "greater Serbian aspirations and military force have found common goals and for this reason they are firmly opposing the western cultural tradition, and the republics with a pronounced West European tradition." As a citizen of Yugoslavia, whose interests were supposed to be neither those of the West or the East, Bulajic felt clearly betrayed by what he considered treasonous statements on the part of his Catholic fellow countrymen.

The bishops for their part accused the Serbs of paranoia as well as imperialism, stating in their pastoral letter that "it is being written and publicly said that the Vatican, the Comintern, the Islamic fundamentalism and the CIA are plotting against the Serbs" and as a result that "hatred towards Catholicism has already flared up among the masses" and it is linked to "the desire of Slovenia and Croatia to become independent."

The bishops then concluded that the only solution was secession:

> We can say, with a clear conscience, that Yugoslavia, every one up to now and also the present one, was a negative experience for the Croats and the Catholics. In fact, since the very beginning, it was improper to be a Croat and a Catholic in Yugoslavia. There were times

when this was a bit less unpleasant, but it never became pleasant. A resolute Croatian orientation was always considered a danger for the state of Yugoslavia. In both Yugoslavias, Catholicism was treated as an alien ideology.

Bulajic then rehashes all of the coincidences surrounding dates in June and May.

> Pope John Paul II received Dr. Franjo Tudjman on May 25, 1991, just as pope Pius XII received the Ustasha leader of the Independent State of Croatia on May 18, 1941. President Tudjman's audience with the pope was formally private because the Republic was not an international legal entity. The Vatican issued no official announcement in regard to the talks between the Pope and president Tudjman...That is exactly how pope Pius XII acted during the "private" audience to Ustashi leader Ante Pavelic, on May 18th 1941, exactly fifty years and one week earlier, because then too, on the basis of positive international law, the Ustashi Independent State of Croatia was not an international legal entity! It was the Catholic St. Jerome Institute in Rome that stood behind the visit of the Croatian Democratic Union's leader to the Vatican, just as was the case on May 18th 1941, during the visit by the Ustashi leader of the Independent State of Croatia, Dr. Ante Pavelic, when Ustashi flags were raised on the St. Jerome Institute and when the coat of arms of the Kingdom of Yugoslavia were taken down. Right after his talks with the Pope, the President went to the Papal Croatian St. Jerome Institute where he stayed for lunch with his escorts. On that occasion he was greeted by the head of the Institute, Mons. Ratko Peric (p. 178).

Serbian paranoia aside, subsequent events substantiate the claim that the Vatican wanted an independent, Catholic Croatia rather than the preservation of Yugoslavia. Rome, along with Germany, against whose expansionist interests Yugoslavia had been formed in the first place, were the first countries to recognize Croatia's independence. A harsh condemnation of Medjugorje at an untimely moment might have strangled Croatia's independence in the cradle. On the other hand, a clear-cut condemnation of Medjugorje might also have allayed Serbian fears of a Austrian/Catholic conspiracy against them. Rome's schizophrenic attitude toward Medjugorje played a crucial role in confirming the Serbs' fears that an international conspiracy was being deployed against them.

"The apparitions," said one source close to the Medjugorje events, "were originally used in defense of the Franciscans against the bishop. There was no talk about an independent Croatia then. It was simply Franciscans defending their turf against Zanic. Not in their wildest dreams did they dream about an independent Croatian. That didn't develop until 1990. They sniffed liberty in '89-'90. In '94 there were a lot of political messages post hoc."

Over the course of events, the "Gospa" never really predicted or anticipated events; she invariably ratified them after they happened with a resounding "I told you so." In the beginning, the Gospa's messages reflected the interests of the Franciscans in the Prusina/Vego affair. Then in the mid-'80s in keeping with the appeal to a much wider audience, the Gospa began saying things like "all religions are equal in God's eyes" and that the holiest person in the village was a Muslim. Then after the war broke out, Mirjana and Petar Ljubicic said they knew it was coming all along. The priests too started to sound much more nationalistic and political as well. In a piece published in Mostar on October 25, 1991, called "Reflections on the War in Croatia," Fr. Svetozar Kraljevic, OFM, major mover and shaker in the Franciscan promotion of Medjugorje, announced that "in the Serbian environment there lives a very different kind of man than the one we know in western society." The statements would get more extreme when war came to Bosnia-Herzegovina six months later. "What appears to be a national and religious revival," Kraljevic continued, "is in reality another tragic spiritual confusion of a nation where practice of faith is conditioned not by inner beliefs but by political interests." Kraljevic is talking about the Serbs here, but his statement has an uncanny application to the Franciscans as well, who now were staring a major defeat in the face as the Yugoslavian bishops first condemned Medjugorje and then deliberated how they could bring the events there under there control, which is to say out of the control of the Franciscans.

Eventually, political events in Yugoslavia overtook the deliberations of the bishops. In early 1991 a Croatian was scheduled to take over the rotating prime ministership of Yugoslavia. When the Serbs blocked his appointment, Tudjman felt he had received his own sign and started to make final plans for a declaration of independence, which he wanted to declare originally on April 10, the same day the bishops issued their statement on Medjugorje, but more significantly the 50th anniversary of the founding of the last independent Croatian state, the Ustasha NDH. Gradually over the winter and early spring of 1991, the Croats and Slovenes increased their demands, threatening secession if they weren't met. In either February or March of 1991, depending on the account, Franjo Tudjman met with Slobodan Milosevic over whiskey and cigars and between the two of them agreed to partition Bosnia-Herzegovina. Croatia was to get the north-western section, Serbia the southeast, and between the two there would be a Muslim buffer zone. Unfortunately for their plans, student riots broke out in Belgrade, forcing Tudjman to postpone his plans. On May 25, he met with the pope, who apparently gave his blessing to Tudjman's plans, as Margaret Thatcher had done in April, and on June 25, 1991, Croatia declared independence. After his meeting with the pope, Tudjman had this to say about the HDZ's cooperation with the Catholic Church. "If, in a specific way the efforts of the Catholic Church and the program of the Croatian Democratic Union hadn't fully coincided, everything that we have achieved in establishing democracy, that spiritual unity and rebirth of the Croatian nation, and which is in a way a miracle, wouldn't have been possible."

On August 17, 1991, the pope celebrated Mass in Pecs, Hungary, and in attendance were 20,000 Hungarian Croats as well as pilgrims from Croatia and various Croatian bishops, including Cardinal Kuharic, the Yugoslavian primate. "I cordially welcome Cardinal Kuharic, the archbishop of Zagreb," the pope said, switching suddenly into Croatian, "and other bishops who have come from Croatia along with numerous believers. Once again I assure you that I am close to your legal aspiration, repeating my appeal to the international community to help you at this difficult moment of your history."

Bulajic found the change in language coupled with the fact that Otto von Hapsburg and his family attended the Mass evidence for his suspicion that the Vatican was conspiring to bring about the dismemberment of Yugoslavia as a way of reasserting Catholic/Austrian hegemony over the Balkans. He cited the interpretation which the Turin daily, *Stampa*, put on the pope's remarks as further evidence. The pope, according to *Stampa*, "has never so far linked in such a direct way the problem of the independence of Croatia and the possibility of visiting that country." Whether Bulajic was on to something or whether he was merely paranoid is in a sense beside the point here. The Church did side with Croatia, and Bulajic's views were not merely his own. They were shared by Serbs at large, and even if they were paranoid, the paranoia fueled the train of unfolding events.

June 25, 1991, was the tenth anniversary to the day of the apparitions in Medjugorje. Our Lady of Medjugorje had not brought peace as the seers foretold, but she did bring independence for Croatia as the Communists had feared, and before too long she would bring chastisement to Bosnia-Herzegovina as well. As to the role Medjugorje played in bringing about the independence of Croatia, Tudjman never let himself be pinned down. In May of 1993, while in Medjugorje for peace talks with Radovan Karadzic and Alia Izetbegovic, Tudjman announced that the Gospa's appearance in Medjugorje (now, of course, officially denied by the Catholic Church) had brought about the "reawakening of the Croatian nation." On May 18, however, while being feted by the Franciscans in the rectory at St. James Church, Tudjman told another story. When Father Pero Ljubicic asked the ex-Communist Tudjman if the anniversary of the apparitions had anything to do with the declaration of Croatian independence, he was told a bit deflatingly by Tudjman that he had already been asked this question and had stated before that the date had nothing to do with the apparitions.

As of May of '91, the "Gospa" seemed more concerned about the bishops' condemnation than the prospects for Croatian independence. On May 25, 1991, Franjo Tudjman met with the pope, who assured him of Rome's support. Tudjman then went to St. Jerome's college and met with its rector, Father Ratko Peric, who in 1993 would become Bishop Zanic's successor as ordinary of the diocese of Mostar. All of this, however, seems to have been far from the mind of the Gospa at the time. On May 5, 1991, the bishops' announcement that that there was nothing supernatural about the occurrences at Medjugorje and the fact that it had been ratified by a vote of 19 to 0, with the only abstention Archbishop Frane Franic of Split, a notorious promoter of things charismatic, made its first official appearance in *Glas Konzila*, the official Catholic paper of Yugoslavia

Twenty days later, on the appointed day for the apparitions, Marija Pavlovic sent Slavko Barbaric, as she usually did, the Croatian transcription of that month's message by fax from Milan, which is where Marija was living at the time. Following the normal procedure involved in the dissemination of the messages, Barbaric gave the Croatian message to Father Philip Pavich, who was responsible for translating it into English. Pavich was having his doubts at the time. He had known about the negative judgment since when it had been leaked in January and so that came as no surprise. Eventually, even after he stopped believing in the apparitions, he would justify his continued presence in Medjugorje by appealing to the bishops' claim, in their official statement, that pilgrims needed spiritual guidance.

Pavich was troubled by something else. For quite some time, he had become aware, primarily though the confessional, but also in the counseling he was doing, that Medjugorje was a major pilgrimage site not only for credulous Catholics but also for devotees of the New Age Movement, particularly in America. As part of his pastoral duties, Pavich would hear the confessions of ladies who had become involved in the occult and now wanted out. As part of their exit strategy, the ladies would leave their New Age books with Pavich, who became over the course of time familiar with both their ideas and their phraseology. Thus, it was with a shock that Pavich read the message of May 25, 1991, the first one to appear after the bishops' condemnation. The

Gospa urged everyone not to get upset about the condemnation but instead to "change negatives into positives." The phrase struck Pavich as both un-Biblical and vaguely familiar. Pavich lived in Jerusalem before he came to Medjugorje and read Hebrew without difficulty, so he knew that the term had not come from the Bible. This drove him to peruse the New Age books the penitents had left behind.

When he got to *Living with Joy: Keys to Personal Power and Spiritual Transformation* (Tiburon, CA: H. J. Kramer, 1986). by Sanaya Roman, he found what he was looking for. Roman, the book's dust jacket announced, had written the book as a "Channel for Orin" ("Or," of course, as Pavich immediately noticed, comes from the Hebrew word for *light* and is therefore related to Lux which is the basis for Lucifer, which means *bearer of light*.) The passage about changing the negative into positive, which Marija Pavlovic cited verbatim in the first message from the Gospa after the bishops' declaration of April 1991 is the title of Chapter Five.

Pavich was saying, in effect, that both Sanaya Roman and Marija Pavlovic were in touch with the same spiritual entity, whose name was most probably "Orin" and not the Blessed Virgin Mary.

"These kids don't read," Pavich said of the seers. "No, what I'm proposing is even scarier. These kids are all in touch with the same being, who is giving them these messages."

A number of things happened all at once during June of 1991. The bishops condemned the apparition, which prompted a message from the Gospa, which convinced one of priests who had supported it for years to change his mind into believing it was now a demonic hoax. At the same time, the political events which had accompanied Medjugorje since the beginning overtook it. On May 18, the Serbs blocked the accession of Stip Mesic to the presidency of Yugoslavia, precipitating a constitutional crisis. One week later, Marija Pavlovic's message provoked a spiritual crisis in Philip Pavich. On May 19, Croatia's 4.5 million people voted for independence; Croatia's Serbs, however, boycotted the election. On the same day, the Bush Administration suspended all economic assistance to Yugoslavia. Schizophrenia pervaded American foreign policy at this time as well. At the same time the U.S. cut off aid to Yugoslavia, Secretary of State James Baker was telling the world that the U.S. would not recognize the break-away republics. U.S. Secretary of State James Baker said that the U.S. was opposed to secessionist moves. He said the U.S. would not recognize Slovenia as an independent country unless that status was achieved through dialogue with the other republics and the central government.

All of the vectors of force surrounding Medjugorje—the political, the military, and the religious—converged during June of 1991 like a number of cars approaching the same intersection at a high rate of speed. On June 17, Bishop Pavao Zanic came to Medjugorje with the pastoral directives which had been promised in the bishop's statement of April 10, 1991, and was now referred to as the obligatory statement. Zanic met with the Franciscans in the basement much as Tudjman would do a few years later. The mood, however, was far from jubilant.

"All the priests knew," one priest would say later, "they're gonna shut this place down."

After the preliminary formalities, Zanic got right to the point, in fact to all three points. The directives were no longer than a paragraph comprising three sentences. To begin with:

> Point number one: Let the visionaries refrain from delivering any public messages. All alleged messages from the Blessed Virgin were to be henceforth delivered directly to the bishop.

> Point number two: the pastor is responsible for promulgating the correct teaching of the church at St. James parish. Nothing is to be said about the supernaturality of the messages and all Marian devotion at St. James is to be in accordance with Pope Paul VI's encyclical *Marialis Cultus*.

> Point number three: all priests and religious associated with the parish are to honor the directive on Medjugorje promulgated by the Yugoslavian bishops.

As Pavich listened to Zanic deliver the directives, he began formulating his response in his mind, haltingly albeit since it would have to be in Croatian and since he now felt that he had one bullet in his gun and was facing a charging rhinoceros.

"I didn't have an AK-47," he said slipping into the rhetoric of the war, "I just had one shot, and so I said to the bishop, 'Why do you want to be stricter than the Church?'"

Pavich was, of course, referring to the second part of the Yugoslavian bishops' statement, which claimed, that "the gathering of faithful from various parts of the world to Medjugorje, inspired by reasons of faith or other motives require the pastoral attention and care . . . of the local bishop." It was, of course, a bit like telling people not to rob banks, but then explaining how to gag the teller and then saying that the robber could count on the Church for help sticking the money in the sack, but that was the statement, and Pavich in his way was trying to live out its implementation.

What surprised him, however, was not the reaction of the bishop but that of his fellow Franciscans in general and of Father Leonard Orec in particular. Instead of joining Pavich in remonstrating with the bishop, the Franciscans all remained silent, leaving Pavich as the only one with an objection. Orec, who was responsible for the construction of the illegal altar just outside the back of the church, and so no stickler when it came to following church directives, quietly took Pavich later and tried to explain the real situation to him.

"This is good for us, Philip," he said, and suddenly Pavich understood the silence of his fellow Franciscans. The conclusion came a bit belatedly but all the more inescapably as a result. The Franciscans were happy with the directives because it was a way of easing the visionaries, who had always been a potential source of embarrassment, out of the picture. Slavko Barbaric, who would learn about embarrassment first hand when he had the Valltorta hot potato dumped in his lap on live TV when Marija Pavlovic told the world that the Blessed Mother had endorsed a book on the Index, told Pavich, "We have our shrine. We have permission for people to come here. Who needs the visionaries anymore." In other words, who cares if the visionaries can't stand outside the Church and make asses out of themselves. Medjugorje had grown beyond them anyway.

A plenary session of the Yugoslavian bishops was scheduled to ratify the directives on June 27, 1991. On June 25, 1991, ten years and a day from the date of the first apparition, Yugoslavia invaded Slovenia as a result of the joint declaration of independence issued by Slovenia and Croatia, and the war, after putting everything on hold temporarily, put the Yugoslavian Bishops' Conference on hold permanently by bringing about the dissolution of Yugoslavia. Now the body respon-sible for any future deliberations on Medjugorje was the Bishops' Conference of Bosnia-Herzegovina, a group comprised of four bishops, all of whom had many other things to think about. The bishop of Mostar, for one thing, had to rebuild the chancery and residence as well as make major repairs to the Cathedral.

The war, in other words, saved Medjugorje. Ratzinger said much the same thing in Austria. Bishop Peric has said publicly that he would welcome Rome taking Medjugorje off his hands, but Rome at this point shows no inclination of doing any such thing. So the whole thing continues to limp along, directed by the Franciscans, who have turned it into a cash cow that is fueling a building boom of convents and monasteries throughout Bosnia. True to form the seers continue to make the sort of outrageous statements one would expect of illiter-ate peasants who became rich overnight. During December of 1991, during the shelling of Dubrovnik, Marija Pavlovic announced that the Blessed Mother was of the opinion that if more people had been fasting and praying that this war wouldn't have happened.

-10-

THE FALL OF YUGOSLAVIA

Nineteen ninety-one would prove to be a crucial year of sorts for Father Philip Pavich. First there was the bishops' statement and more significantly the cynical reaction of his fellow Franciscans, who were by then only too glad to be rid of the embarrassment which the spiritual gaffes and buffoonery of the seers caused. Then there was the growing sense that he was becoming a spiritual lightning rod for every occult guru who wanted to cash in on the crowds of credulous pilgrims passing through Medjugorje. "Lord," Pavich said at one point, "Why am I getting all these books?"

In April 1991 Pavich met a young Australian by the name of Kim Davison, who handed him another book, or at least the manuscript copy of what was to become a significant book on the Medjugorje circuit. Kim was an exotic figure from the homosexual demimonde of Athens. A seller of trinkets by day, a homosexual prostitute by night, and some-time drug dealer, Kim traveled to Rhodes, where he met a woman by the name of Yanula, who had a famous sister, who had a circle of devotees. Vassula was her name, Vassula Ryden, and she was claiming to be not only a seer but someone who got messages directly from Jesus in handwritten form. Jesus would supply the inspiration, and Vassula would supply the handwriting, and between the two of them they came up with a manuscript that had brought about Kim's conversion. Kim gained access to the original notebooks through an itinerant Austrian souvenir peddler by the name of Erwin Schlacher, who volunteered to help Vassula "edit" the notebooks for publication. Now Kim was in Medjugorje to convert Father Pavich to Vassula, and in order to accomplish that he left the original manuscript behind.

Pavich would later compare Medjugorje to a spiritual petri dish that was spreading its occult spores throughout the world. It became more than that. By 1991 it had become a sort of certifying agency as well. If anyone aspired to be a seer in the United States, for example, it was just about *de rigueur* to go to Medjugorje first and have some sort of spiritual experience there with a sympathetic seer or Father Slavko Barbaric. Pavich was evidently being dragooned into that role as well but was reluctant to follow Slavko's example. Over the summer of 1991, Kim evidently became disillusioned with the collaboration between Schlacher and Ryden, concluding that what they were really doing was doctoring and falsifying the originals. As a result, Kim returned again in September, this time with the master copy of Vassula's messages, which included the corrections that needed to be made before the manuscript got printed in book form. Every page that needed correcting had the offending passage marked in red ink and a yellow Post-It note on it for easy reference. Solecisms in the original manuscript like "God has digressed you from the truth," disappeared from the final version of the text as published in *True Life in God*. Theological impossibilities were removed as well. At one point Jesus tells Vassula that the souls in Purgatory could "escape from my foe's claws" with the help of her prayers, evidently not understanding that they had already done so by the very fact that they were in Purgatory. All of the offending statements were excised in notes in red ink in Erwin Schlacher's handwriting. Later, when caught in this deception, Vassula claimed that "God removes from the private notebooks all that should be diffused and re-writes the message in the official notebook." Not knowing Pavich had the original documents at the time, Vassula didn't feel moved to explain how God and Erwin Schlacher wrote in the same hand.

What disturbed Pavich even more was the fact that all of the theological luminaries of the Medjugorje movement, including Father Rene Laurentin and Father Edward O'Connor of the University of Notre Dame, fell over themselves in their haste to endorse Vassula. "What the Serbs did not get done with guns and cannons," Pavich wrote to Father Mitchell Pacwa, S.J. in September 1993, "the Orthodox Vassula has achieved through the very mouths of the 'pillars' of Medjugorje. Rene Laurentin, Archbishop Frane Franic, Ljudevit Rupcic, OFM, Robert Faricy, SJ, etc, etc. ... ." All had endorsed Vassula, and Pavich feared the "wreckage and fall-out this is bringing or will bring."

Before she started getting handwritten messages from Jesus Christ, Vassula Ryden had been a tennis champion as well as a model. Born in Egypt of Greek parents and baptized into the Greek Orthodox Church in 1942, Vassula has long blond hair which upon closer examination revealed itself by the grey roots showing at the part line down the center of her head as artificially produced. René Laurentin has praised her "Nordic beauty," but she looked more like a bleached-blonde Joan Baez. (Both the folksinger and the seer are about the same age.) Her complexion was Mediterranean, an olive like color that clashed with the color of her hair. She wore eye liner, and her face had a puffiness that may have had something to do with fatigue or age. When younger, Vassula got married and then divorced and then remarried a Swiss diplomat and took up residence in the diocese of Fribourg, whose bishop as well as Bishop Heinrich Schwery of the neighboring diocese of Sion, issued warnings condemning her "ecumenical" activities as "too ambiguous."

By January of 1993, however, when she appeared at Father Edward O'Connor's invitation at the University of Notre Dame, she was a well-established fixture on the Medjugorje circuit. In May of 1992 Rev. Brian Harrison, O.S., published an article in *Fidelity* magazine which examined her handwritten messages from Our Lord and Savior as well as the anomalies in her marital status. A few week earlier she had spoken to much larger crowds in California, including one venue at the cathedral of the diocese of Sacramento, where she spoke at the invitation of the local ordinary, Francis Quinn, causing not a little consternation among those who had doubts about the authenticity of her message.

Father O'Connor, who had known Denis Nolan from their association during the early days of the charismatic renewal at Notre Dame, mentioned hecklers at her appearance at Sacramento, while introducing Vassula to the crowd at Notre Dame, but eyewitness accounts disputed this. Alban Rhomberg, who protested her appearance in Sacramento, said later that the only heckling that got done was by Vassula's supporters, who threw holy water and rock salt on the demonstrators outside the cathedral in an attempt to exorcise what they perceived as impious spirits. When Rhomberg mentioned the deletions and contradictions in Vassula's writings, he was told by his interlocutor that she saw Satan in his face.

Vassula's messages came to her in the form of uncontrollable urges, and when she wrote she claimed the handwriting was not her own, but rather that of Jesus Christ himself. "I felt in my body," Vassula wrote, giving her own account of what she did, "a kind of supernatural vibration that was flowing through my hands. I had been writing a shopping list, but my hand began to shake, and the pencil was too strong for me to control."

"It's not automatic writing," Vassula added at another point, almost as an afterthought. If not, it sure sounded that way from her description of it. The disclaimer was not very convincing. Also not very convincing was her repeated editing of her own texts. Since this power comes over her and forces her to write in a hand ostensibly not her own ("my hand began to shake, and the pencil was too strong for me to control") it seems unlikely that she would make many mistakes transmitting what she had to say. However, in studying the history of her books, one is confronted by the fact that page after page of text is littered with the most arrant nonsense and theological error. When something particularly egregious was pointed out, the offending text just got edited out of her book, often by a simple crossing out. Vassula was coming up with consumerist version of Scripture. If it offended, she plucked it out. No explanation was given. For those who believe, no explanation is necessary. For those who are skeptical, one might add, no explanation is possible.

Vassula's arrival on the scene seemed to be confirmation of the fact that the apparition movement was in the grip of a spirit which excluded reason from its deliberations. It was also an indication that one of the primary fruits of the apparition mania was a spirit of division. The psychological dynamics of the movement's followers seemed to guarantee this. The spiritual restlessness (St. Paul would refer to it as "itching ears") among the apparition followers demanded novelty as the effects of a particular apparition wore thin with familiarity. This set up a craving for something new, something a little more shocking than the previous apparition. Once a new seer arrived on the scene, however, there were always those who were reluctant to go along, and the result was division.

Shortly after Vassula's appearance in California, an anonymous open letter entitled "Vassula Ryden: A Free & Clean Instrument of God?" began making the rounds of the various Medjugorje centers. The letter was written by someone who obviously thought that Medjugorje was genuine but just as obviously was having doubts about Vassula, fueled (although this is not stated explicitly) by the fact that Medjugorje luminaries like René Laurentin had endorsed her. "Why," the anonymous Medjugorje supporter wondered (a bit archly), "does [Vassula] reside in Pully, Switzerland—a tremendously wealthy as well as Free-Mason infected town?" "Why," the writer continued in the same vein, "does Vassula track, follow and interfere with the Medjugorje Franciscans' schedules when they travel." The answer: "Those behind her (and here are meant the supra-human beings) and those people around her want HER to get all the attention; and it has been made her mission FOR HER and her texts to attract as much attention as at all possible AWAY from Medjugorje."

Toward the end of the letter, its author intimates that Vassula is a witch, but then quickly backs away from that only to return to it again by claiming that she is perhaps "a basically good person who, possibly even entirely UNBEKNOWNST to herself, has made contact and fell victim to, somewhere in her past, a powerful witch, wizard, or guru who is sending an army of demons upon her—one to control her hand and others to babble into her subconscious mind these texts, misidentifying their true sources in an infinitely arrogant fashion. She might quite possibly be suffering a personal infestation of evil."

How does the writer presume to make such allegations? According to his own account, "The above is a private opinion yet expressed with the permission of the Mother of God to whom this child of Medjugorje remains obedient. Without this permission he would not have written or sent this. The writer is NOT parroting the opinion of anyone else."

No matter how reassuring it was to hear that the anonymous writer ("It is NOT due to a lack of courage that the writer chooses to remain anonymous," we are told, "it is his effort to remain humble and wise before Satan), he was launching this attack only with the express permission of the Blessed Mother, the appeal to this sort of authority was beginning to wear thin in light of so many competing and contradictory voices. What began as an attempt to maintain order in the chaos following the Council, started, after a while, to sound suspiciously like a power struggle in the movement. Either way, the charges and countercharges must have seemed bewildering to the same people, who, not too long ago, saw the alleged messages of Our Lady of Medjugorje as a way out of the confusion plaguing the Church. Now those who chose the Bosnian seers as the way of cutting the Gordian knot of confusion were back at square one. By the fall of 1991, Medjugorje was full of the same cacophony of competing and contradictory claims that had made the movement an appealing alternative in the first place. The anonymous letter writer himself was quickly drawn into internecine politics in the Medjugorje movement: "What kind of behavior is it," he wonders, "when Vassula's spiritual director threatens Canon Law against a Medjugorje Priest for speaking his mind on the subject?"

The anonymous writer here adverts to the stir Father Philip Pavich caused when he questioned the authenticity of *The Poem of the Man-God*, in a fax he sent to Medjugorje centers throughout the world on October 4, 1991, shortly after uncovering the Vassula fraud. Father Michael O'Carroll, Vassula's spiritual director, reacted by writing an open letter denouncing Pavich to the various Medjugorje centers around the world. In the course of his letter he threatened to report Pavich to his superior and, as if that weren't enough, threatened a canon law suit against him.

On June 20, 1987, five days before the day when Bishop Zanic came to denounce Medjugorje and Father Jack Spalding was there filming a segment for Mother Angelica's EWTN, Father Philip Pavich was sitting in St. James Church on a hot afternoon listening to Wayne Weible, the same guy who that week would convince Gianna Bianchi that she too was a seer, talk about a book he found helpful to his spiritual development. It was called *The Poem of the Man-God* and had been written by a lady named Maria Valltorta. The recollection is still hazy in Pavich's mind because, the room being hot and the afternoon being long, he fell asleep and missed the rest of the talk. Pavich began reading New Age/occult material when he learned that just about the entire Medjugorje movement had almost overnight become devotees of Maria Valltorta's *Poem of the Man-God*, a book which had been placed on the Church's Index of Forbidden Books in 1959, when the Church still had an Index of Forbidden books. Pavich saw Valltorta as just another instance of "another Jesus" which Christians are warned against in the Gospels.

"My ostracism began in '91," Pavich would say later, "when I criticized *The Poem of Man-God*. The entity that recommended this book cannot be the mother of God. It had been downloaded from demon World Wide Web. This is spooky. Rome put this book on the Index in September of 1969. They vomited on it. Then Vatican II revoked the index, although they did say that it still retained its moral authority. Suddenly there were no restrictions on private revelations, and the potential for exploitation limitless. It was as if the Food and Drug Administration in the United States suddenly announced that anybody could market any pharmaceutical, any AIDS medicine, without any federal control. There were no more government controls. After the Vatican took off the controls, everything went crazy."

Pavich was now tormented by doubts. He had been in Medjugorje since 1984 translating the messages faithfully from Croatian into English, and all of the inanity and absurdity and mendacity was starting to get to him. Pavich, however, never came to the conclusion that fraud was involved. His involvement in Vassula confirmed him in thinking that the seers were "in touch with an entity."

"That's the scary part," he said. "That's the worst scenario you can imagine."

Pavich got documents on Valltorta from St. James Parish pastor Tomislav Pervan, who had gotten them from Cardinal Ratzinger in Rome, and they confirmed his fears and convinced him that he had to act. He had to warn the Medjugorje groups around the world to drop Valltorta's *Poem of the Man-God*, which had become virtually mandatory reading on the Medjugorje circuit. Armed with what he knew, Pavich wrote a two-page critique and faxed it off to the various Medjugorje centers around the country. The effect of his critique was like dropping a bomb, which unfortunately blew up in his own face. The various Medjugorje centers turned on Pavich for attacking one of their favorite books. Father Pavich was excommunicated from the Medjugorje network for impiety.

Not too long after Pavich's excommunication, in one of the greatest *faux pas* of the movement's entire history, Marija Pavlovic announced on a call-in TV show emanating from New Orleans in the early '90s that the Blessed Mother told her that Valltorta's book was good reading. When someone called in to get Marija Pavlovic's take on *Poem*, she responded by saying, to give her exact Italian words, that the Blessed Mother had said, *"se puo leggere"* or "You can read it." In other words, the Blessed Mother was now recommending books on the Index. Then as if realizing that she had just put her foot deeply into some theological doo-doo, Marija the Seer tossed that hot potato to Rev. Slavko Barbaric, OFM, her spiritual advisor and also a guest on the show, who said rather disingenuously that the TV viewers should consult their local bishops on the Valltorta issue. It was an especially ironic statement coming from the mouth of someone who had been defying his local bishop for years and as of this writing was still engaged in the most flagrant sort of defiance against the new local ordinary of Mostar/Duvno, Ratko Peric.

The Poem of the Man-God incident was not only one of the biggest blunders of the "seers" at Medjugorje, it was also the beginning of the end of Pavich's illusions about Medjugorje. If the voice Marija Pavlovic was listening to was recommending books on the Index of Forbidden Books of the sort written by Maria Valltorta, then it was most emphatically not the voice of the Blessed Mother. This was Pavich's reasoning at the time, but no matter how logical it was per se, this train of thoughts had serious ramifications for Pavich's belief in Medjugorje. Marija Pavlovic wasn't the only seer who had endorsed *The Poem of the Man-God.* The paper trail in America began in June 1989 when Caritas of Birmingham, the same group which had brought Marija Pavlovich to the cow pasture outside Sterret, Alabama, to have an apparition in front of a pine tree where Terry Colafrancesco had mowed the lawn, announced in its bulletin of that month that "Vicka asked Our Lady about the book, *Poem of the Man-God*, and Our Lady is reported to have said, 'It makes for good reading.'"

The alleged reply conjures up a picture of the Blessed Virgin sitting in her room, somewhere in heaven, perhaps looking up from a comfortable chair, reading Maria Valltorta. "It makes for good reading," The Blessed Virgin is said to have said. "Unlike most of what is available to read here," she could have added. Perhaps she wouldn't have said that, but her alleged response to Vicka almost demands it. The vision of the Blessed Mother in her armchair in heaven reading *Poem* sounded suspiciously like a blurb to generated book sales, which since *Poem* was a multi-volume hard bound book generate a significant amount of money, and, sure enough, as was its wont, Caritas announced in the same news bulletin that it would be happy to sell copies of the *Poem of the Man-God* and gave a phone number for ordering with the caveat that "we only accept orders by phone from book stores and Medjugorje centers."

In spite of Pavich's protest, the rest of the movement went along without a murmur of protest, even after Pavich faxed them the documentation from the Congregation for the Doctrine of the Faith. In a letter to Cardinal Siri dated January 31, 1985, Joseph Cardinal Ratzinger, Prefect for the Congregation describes *The Poem of the Man-God* as having already been "examined scientifically and placed in a well-known category of mental sicknesses." "The facts added to the second edition," he continues, "do not change the nature of the work, which evidences being a mountain of childishness, of fantasies, and of historical and exegetical falsehoods, diluted in a subtly sensual atmosphere, through the presence of a flock of women in the company of Jesus. On the whole, it is a heap of pseudo-religiosity. Therefore, also for the second edition, the judgment of the Church to condemn it retains its validity." Ratzinger, in the same letter, maintained that "the Index of Forbidden Books keeps all of its moral authority." As a result, the sale and distribution of the book is "improper."

So much for the Blessed Mother's taste in reading. The sensible reader was faced with one of two conclusions, the most sensible of which was that the seers were not telling the truth when they said that the Blessed Mother endorsed it. When the obvious facts of the case as presented by Ratzinger's office were brought to the attention of the various Medjugorje centers, including Caritas, the spokesmen there attempted to laugh it off as not worthy of serious consideration or claim that there was a mistranslation somewhere along the line.

In his fax of October 4, 1991, Pavich condemned the publishers of*Poem* as "deliberately deceiving the Catholic faithful" by "brazenly . . . distributing these condemned works to a devout but unsuspecting Catholic faithful despite the efforts of the highest authorities of the Catholic Church to warn the faithful that those same laws still retain their moral authority and that the works of Maria Valltorta should be avoided by sincere and conscientious Catholics." Pavich concluded his appeal by citing the statement of the Yugoslav Bishops' Conference (the same one which found nothing supernatural in the events at Medjugorje) to the effect that "a healthy devotion to the Blessed Virgin Mary would be promoted in agreement with the teachings of the Church." "Every sincere devotee of our Blessed Mother," Pavich stated, "will want nothing less. Here is an excellent opportunity to put into practice a true Catholic spirit of obedience and total submission as she would have us do."

Pavich's fax of October 4 remained ambivalent on Medjugorje and makes no reference to the fact that Vicka too claimed that the Blessed Mother saw the book as "good reading." Was it was a sign that he still hoped to salvage some credibility from the apparitions or that he couldn't face up to the contradictions himself? The usual *modus operandi* in embarrassing instances like this was to make a frantic dash for the memory hole. The equally embarrassing admission on the part of Marija Pavlovic in the summer of 1988 that she lied about the Blessed Mother endorsing Father Vlasic and Agnes Heupel's coed religious community was taken care of by simply being ignored.

The simplest damage control on the part of the Franciscans would be to say that Caritas of Birmingham was not reliable, that they had misquoted Vicka, that the translation was faulty, etc., etc. However, that option is not available for the March 1992 EWTN television segment, because both Marija and Slavko Barbaric had been taped on a live call-in show. The words "It can be read," *Si puo leggere*, came out of Marija's mouth as did Barbaric's equally embarrassing recommendation that Bob from Milwaukee, the caller who posed the question, should "ask your bishop what to think."

So there is no claiming any more that the fault lay with mistranslations. Beyond that, Marija admitted, equal damningly that "there are problems with this," which is even more theologically interesting than the fact that the BVM endorses books on the index. Just what she could have meant by this is not clear. Did she mean that the Blessed Mother was lacking in orthodoxy? Did Marija mean that the Blessed Mother was careless in her endorsements? Did it mean that the Blessed Mother didn't really understand what she had been reading up there in heaven? Or did Marija mean that, now that she has put what are obviously absurdities into the mouth of the Blessed Mother, the problems lie with her own credibility?

The problem was spreading. Marija's statement about *Poem* was causing agonizing and consternation throughout the Medjugorje movement. The Rev. Mitchell Pacwa, S.J., was a Medjugorje supporter, but, like Father Pavich, he had written an article exposing the condemnation of *The Poem of the Man-God*. Like Father Pavich, he did not mention the fact that both Vicka and Marija were claiming that the Blessed Mother had endorsed the book. "That can't be Our Lady speaking," he said when asked about Marija's EWTN statement. When asked what the statement said about Marija's credibility, Pacwa admitted that, "It calls it into question." Pacwa finds the seers' statements on the Man-God "self-deluded and foolish," but stops short of saying that they are lying. "Maybe it's not lying," he adds, "but it's certainly an untruth."

. "I think this whole *Poem* thing is going to blow up in their face," Pacwa said referring to the Medjugorje movement. "The people will have to decide whether they are going with the seers or going with the Church."

The effect on the Medjugorje movement was demoralizing, to say the least. Suddenly the group's solidarity was split right down the middle into camps supporting or opposing *The Poem of the Man-God*. Wayne Weible, another well-known Medjugorje supporter dealt with the issue in a way that typified the movement's thinking. First he stopped promoting the book; then in the fall of 1992 he announced in his newsletter that he was resuming its promotion because he found no evidence that it had been condemned, which prompts one to wonder then why he dropped it in the first place. What one saw at work here was a natural selection process, according to which anyone with a modicum of sense or discernment was brutally excluded from the movement the moment he expressed misgivings. This seemed to guarantee that leveler heads would not prevail.

"My assumption," Pavich said later, "was that they would be loyal and would drop it. So on October 4, 1991, I sent a notice to Medjugorje centers that *Poem* had been condemned in 1959. Instead of thanking me, they were outraged that I did this. They were outraged that I could dare contradict the mother of God. If you don't believe in Valltorta, then you don't believe in Medjugorje. That's what they were saying."

Pavich wrote a second follow-up in November 1991, and all hell broke loose again. "A few agreed with me," he said, "but the majority were convinced that I had lost my way. I was duly tarred and feathered for opposing this book. The people selling it were making thousands of dollars. Up to that time I was a more or less respected Medjugorje preacher. After that people just wrote me off and went on promoting Valltorta. Weible had a Quonset hut of full of Valltorta; he held off for a year, then went back to selling them."

If, however, one draws the conclusion that the letter writer who criticized Vassula sympathized with Father Pavich on the *Poem* issue, that is a mistaken assumption. Things are not that simple either. Two lines after criticizing O'Carroll's attack, the letter writer launches an attack of his own, criticizing Pavich for having "badly weakened his own credibility by throwing his highly questionable and unauthorized criticism at Maria Valltorta." This now becomes further evidence of a plot; Pavich's critique showed "perfect timing for those BEHIND Vassula and those around her to think they had won, at least that round." The fact that Pavich opposes both Vassula and *The Poem of the Man-God* seems to have made no impression on the anonymous letter-writer, who was quick to discern plots but not so quick to explain the logical contradictions behind them.

The increasingly bitter denunciations and counter-denunciations traded between the various factions of the Medjugorje movement showed what bitter fruit grew out of the movement's denial of Church authority in the matter. What seemed so simple at the beginning, when all the devotee had to choose between was the seers and the bishop, had now become much more complicated. Ignoring the bishop then seemed like such a minor thing. However, once the proliferation of seers clamoring for the attention of an increasingly lucrative market started contradicting themselves, what then? The inarticulate cry for Church authority to adjudicate between Vassula and her detractors was almost palpable, but it disappeared when the Medjugorje crowd deliberately turned its back on Bishop Zanic. As a result, the seers and their promoters were left to fight it out among themselves, as the spiritual warfare over market share among the competing seers began to resemble in an uncanny way the more conventional warfare that was now starting to convulse what had once been Yugoslavia.

The Franciscans, in the interim, were trying to salvage a solution that would simultaneously distance them from the seers while at the same time allowing them complete control over the "shrine," which they were now claiming had been officially recognized in the Yugoslavian bishops' statement at Zadar in April. In the October/November 1992 issue of *The Mir Response*, Father Slavko Barbaric announced that the Diocese of Mostar now had a new bishop (Bishop Zanic retired); however, it was clear from the tone of his article that the new bishop, Ratko Peric, had the same position as the old bishop. "In an interview," Barbaric writes, "the new bishop stated that the Church's position is clear concerning Medjugorje and all church problems in Herzegovina. This means he is standing behind Bishop Zanic's decision on Medjugorje. We hope his position will change. It is not necessary that he recognizes Medjugorje, but we pray that he will not attack or try to destroy us."

By then, however, it should have been clear that the least of Father Barbaric's worries had to do with the local bishop. Medjugorje was in very real danger of being destroyed 1) by the Serb-dominated Yugoslav army and 2) by the increasingly vicious internal divisions in the movement itself. The competition between the various Medjugorje groups was to have its own natural consequences. A natural-selection process gradually evolved which ensured that only the cynical or the credulous came to the forefront of the movement. As the more rational voices got excluded, the movement automatically became more and more bizarre. Those, like Father Pavich, who refused to step over the next threshold of irrationality got excommunicated, a fact which virtually ensured that those remaining in one of the many splintered groups would become more and more isolated in their mania.

Like the look on Vassula's 51-year-old face, Medjugorje was beginning to show signs of fatigue by the time of its tenth anniversary. The Franciscans were still determined to maintain control, in spite of the seers, if need be, but their strategy had flaws as well. They welcomed the favorable publicity and the effect it had on eroding the authority of the bishop, but as time would show ever more clearly, they had no strategy in dealing with competing seers like Vassula and all of the spin-off seers which would soon proliferate throughout the United States when the war in Yugoslavia cut off tourism. The civil war had put an effective end to the pilgrimage business in a way that the local bishop never could have accomplished on his own. However, the severing of Medjugorje from its most ardent supporters was a lot like the amputation of a real limb. Even though it was gone, the people still felt it was there, and indeed experienced something akin to pain in its absence. Medjugorje had created a huge pool of enthusiasm that was now, with the advent of the civil war and the suspension of pilgrimage tourism, without an outlet. Vassula was an expression of the enthusiasm which had been stimulated by, but could no longer find its outlet in, Medjugorje.

Vassula's arrival on the scene was also a sign that the inner dynamic of the apparition business was working itself out according to its own laws. With each new absurdity, the reasonable people were ostracized for their misgivings, and an atmosphere was created in which the bizarre would be tolerated—nay, demanded—by those who were not going to let reason interfere with their need for a spiritual fix. Vassula, the sympathetic female medium who was ever attuned to telling her audience what it wanted to hear, did not disappoint the people who came to hear bad news. At Notre Dame, she announced that that the end times foretold in the Scripture had arrived.

Evidently this was not news to the audience. There was no reaction from the crowd. Actually this was not surprising. The crowd was evidently suffering from prophecy burnout. And the seers who were doing the pronouncing were suffering from a bad case of diminishing returns. There have been so many dire prophecies emanating from Medjugorje alone, prophecies which, of course, had not come true, that after ten years a certain numbness had set in. In this, the apparitions were a lot like narcotics. Decreasing effect is countered by increasing the dosage. Similarly, the "seers" were faced with the necessity of increasing the rush from their revelations in order to keep their audience's attention.

The apparition followers, so tired of theological and liturgical innovation, found themselves seeking in private revelation the very thing they abhorred elsewhere in the Church. Incapable of arriving on their own at a critique of what is happening, they slipped into the arms of one error while attempting to escape from another. In seeking to flee rationalism, they end up caught up in the occult. Seers like Vassula were simply telling the apparition chasers what they wanted to hear.

In this regard, it is no coincidence that most seers are women, and that most of the people in the audience were women, too. Vassula had the clairvoyance of a medium when it came to picking up sympathetic emanations from her listeners and then re-projecting them back to them as the messages of Jesus Christ himself. It was a parody both of feminine and the feminine consolation they sought from the Blessed Virgin in troubled times. One sensed in personal encounters with Vassula a feminine willingness to accommodate the listener's latent desire for vindication. Vassula has cultivated the ability to tell the disaffected exactly what they wanted to hear. Prophets, in general, were not women, and Vassula, is in this regard, was certainly no John the Baptist. She could articulate the people's frustration, of course, but she could also articulate something uglier as well, a sort of religious consumerism, according to which the people reject sound doctrine and the authority structure of the Catholic Church because it didn't conform to their desires. When it came to private revelations of this sort, the customer was always right, and seers who wanted to increase market share quickly learned to pander to the dissatisfactions of their audience, a strategy which also ended up alienating its audience from the Church as well.

Shortly after describing the end times at Notre Dame, Vassula announced, "The Church is in apostasy." Then, as if to make sure she doesn't get too far beyond her audience, she added by way of explanation that "apostasy means loss of faith." This sort of denigration of the Church was precisely the strategy the Franciscans had pursued in their battle with the bishop, and now that it was being used against them and their own apparition in a subtle way, they were at a loss in how to deal with it. The effect on the audience that had already been pushed to the brink by the ruthless experimentation in liturgy and catechetics of the past two-and-a-half decades was perilous if predictable. Private revelations of this sort were always a challenge to Church authority, and Pavich recognized in what Vassula was doing the emergence of "another Jesus" whose purpose was to lead the bewildered faithful out of the Church in the name of their own excessive piety.

Like the seers, Vassula was surrounded by handlers who ran theological interference for her whenever she came up with something heretical or absurd. When asked about the discrepancy between what Jesus told her about Medjugorje ("My mother is appearing there") and what the local bishop had to say, Vassula said, quite simply, "Bishops make mistakes." Apparently upset that Vassula gave a straight answer to a straight-forward question, one of her handlers at the Notre Dame conference—a good-looking, dark-haired lady—leaned over to say that "she's not saying the bishop there made a mistake." When asked about her statement that "the Church was in apostasy," Vassula answered that she meant " All churches are in apostasy" not just the Catholic faith. By explaining that all churches were in apostasy, Vassula was probably trying to be reassuring in her ingratiating way, perhaps because misery loves company. If Father O'Connor was scandalized by what Vassula had to say, he gave no indication of it in his concluding remarks, even though in a catechism he authored shortly before Vassula's arrival, he explained how the Church will persevere in the truth until the end of time:

"Infallibility is not merely or primarily a papal prerogative," O'Connor had written. "It is in the first instance an attribute of the Church as a whole. . . . Fundamentally, infallibility implies that the Church is not just an association of Christians who do their best to follow their Master but that the Master himself supports and strengthens them in this endeavor as he promised to do.

Father O'Connor went on to cite Christ's promise (Matt. 28:20): "And surely I will be with you always, to the very end of time" as scriptural proof that the Church is not and cannot ever be "in apostasy." Just how O'Connor can say one thing in his catechism and then endorse a lady who says the exact opposite is a mystery whose explication is beyond our powers. It is part of the mystery surrounding the entire Medjugorje phenomenon from beginning to end. O'Connor is an enthusiast, whose desire for private revelation seems to block out his theological expertise. Beginning with the Charismatic Movement, he has supported one supposedly miraculous occurrence after another. He was a supporter of Garabandal; most recently he has been an ardent supporter of Medjugorje. One could say that he supports Vassula because the rest of the Medjugorje establishment does, but he is not simply taking their word on this. According to one source, O'Connor flew to Europe to interview Vassula personally to satisfy his own curiosity, so his approval seems to have entailed some deliberation and effort, yet not enough to see that what she said contradicted what he said in his own catechism. In the end, all one can do is conjecture that desire, of a spiritual sort, overcame reason.

By the time Teresa and Jeff Lopez got married on October 13, 1991, Teresa had laid the groundwork for her emergence as a seer and her efforts were beginning to bear fruit. Using the money she got in her insurance settlement, or what was left of it after she bought her Ford Probe with the vanity plates, she spent, according to Jeff's reckoning, eight or nine hours a day poring over the writings of St. John of the Cross and cutting and pasting excerpts which would appear without attribution in her own books, which would be published by Reck's Riehle Foundation, and after he became disillusioned with her Robert Schaeffer's Queenship Publishing Company would take over its publication. On October 24, 1991, Teresa announced that Our Lady had appeared to her for the first time as Our Holy Mother of Virtues. Even more significant was the place of the apparition, which was now St. Thomas More Parish. Teresa had found her way to a priest that was much more amenable to her messages than the pastor of All Souls, where she and Jeff had gotten married.

Teresa was also making contact with other seers. Right around this time, she met an ex-middleweight boxer from the Ukraine by the name of Josyp Terelya, who was also claiming to be a seer. Jeff Lopez later claimed that Teresa and Terelya agreed "to cover for each other," which is to say that both would assure their respective constituencies that the other was legitimate. In fulfilling his part of the bargain, Terelya announced to a crowd of 7,000 Medjugorje devotees at the Rosemont Horizon outside Chicago that he had had a mystical experience while visiting the Mother Cabrini shrine in Denver, Colorado

"I saw the miracle of the sun and the sun spinning," Terelya told the crowd. "I started to pray. My whole body trembled with such joy I cannot explain it to you. I knelt down, and as I knelt I heard a voice say, 'Josyp, within a year's time, here in this place, very many miracles will take place. It will be a very great pilgrimage center just like Fatima and Medjugorje.'"

They say that all great minds run in the same circles, a fact which must be *a fortiori* true of great minds who are in daily conversation with the Queen of Heaven. Terelya's prediction that Denver would become the Medjugorje of the United States has a more plausible explanation though. The simple fact of the matter is that there were a whole group of female seers all vying for ascendancy at the Cabrini Shrine and after Teresa Lopez found out about them, she initially collaborated with them and eventually superseded them, as the premier seer in the Denver area. Jeff would later tell Tom Doyle, another parishioner, that he had witnessed Teresa plot the entire apparition scheme with Veronica Garcia and Sylvia Gregor, two other seers in the area, also associated with Mother Cabrini Shrine and St. Thomas More parish. The three would eventually become part of a group working out of St. Thomas More known as the 12 apostles, which by the time it had that name had come under Teresa's domination and worked to foster her career. Tom Doyle remembered that the collaboration was not always harmonious. When Veronica Garcia in the parking lot of the Cabrini Shrine heard that another seer was up on the mountain, she said, "Why that bitch, she isn't supposed to be up there now." When Jeff and Teresa would visit the Garcias he would go out back behind their house and smoke dope with Veronica's husband, while the ladies would remain inside and discuss the latest messages from the Blessed Virgin.

One of the seer ladies Teresa met while at the Cabrini Shrine was a woman by the name of Christine Muggridge, who, while at Fatima had received a message about the upcoming significance of the Cabrini Shrine in Denver. Wanting to find out more, Muggridge called Harriet Hamans, a local Medjugorje devotee, in Pueblo. Between then and early 1992, Teresa broke away from the pack as the result first of an article in the local newspaper and then a story on CNN. Then in early 1992 she started getting messages about a bishop. On June 26, 1992, while praying at the Cabrini Shrine, Teresa got the following message: "My dear one, you will travel with the Bishop to see the Holy Father, from there he desires you to travel to Russia. There you and the Bishop shall work towards the triumph of my Immaculate Heart." On January 28, Teresa got another message, "Tell Christine she must come with you." One day later she was told, "The bishop shall clear the way. The time is urgent." On June 30, Teresa and Christine Muggridge sent off an express package to Rome, addressed to a bishop there, Bishop Paolo Maria Hnilica.

The bishop of the messages, it turns out, was Bishop Hnilica. The details are still a bit vague, but according to one source, Harriet Hamans introduced Bishop Hnilica to Teresa Lopez at the Colorado Springs Medjugorje conference in early 1992. On January 23, Teresa called a Father Luciano Alimandi, a priest associated with Hnilica. Shortly thereafter, Teresa had said to Fr. Larry Walsh, the pastor of St. Thomas More parish, "You should invite Bishop Hnilica here." Fr. Walsh was not opposed to the idea and told Teresa that he would go to the Archbishop (then Stafford) and set it up. But Teresa wanted more direct action bypassing the Archbishop and so said, "no, Father. You are to invite the Auxiliary Bishop of Rome to St. Thomas More."

Now, Hnilica was no more the auxiliary bishop of Rome than Teresa Lopez was speaking to the Blessed Mother, but Hnilica was a genius at exploiting the Marian apparition scene for his own financial benefit, and he was likewise aware that the war in Yugoslavia had brought about some fundamental changes in that scene. Hnilica needed another seer, one connected with Medjugorje but not in Medjugorje, an arrangement which would allow him to raise money, for example, for war relief in Yugoslavia from Medjugorje's American supporters who could now no longer travel there on pilgrimage. After making contact with Teresa Lopez, Hnilica was seriously thinking of buying the Cabrini Shrine and turning it into the Medjugorje center for the United States. The course of subsequent events would make that impossible, but the desire to take over the Medjugorje movement in the United States remained. With a goal that clear in mind, other means would propose themselves with time.

On April 18, 1992, Hnilica mailed a fundraising appeal entitled, "Urgent Appeal: From Bosnia Dramatic News," which he said was based on a telephone called from Fr. Leonard Orec, who was calling from the village Makarska, which Hnilica erroneously situated in Bosnia-Herzegovina.

> In the city of Makarska today, as the weeping pastor reported, they have slit the throats of about 50 people including women and children. The populace is going crazy, running through the streets and sending up distressing screams. One can see many children with white hair from being shocked with fear. There is urgent need for pscyho-pharmaceuticals, because for an alternative, many are seeking a solution in suicide. From the windows of the house where the pastor has taken refuge, people can be seen who are being killed on the street like dogs.

To begin with Makarska is on the Dalmatian coast and has always been part of Croatia and never in Bosnia-Herzegovina. Beyond that, it has no strategic significance and was unaffected by the war. In June of 1997, large sections of Mostar were still in ruins from the fighting there in 1993, but Makarska was untouched, not a palm frond out of place, not a mark in the plaster walls, and nothing but quizzical looks on the faces of people we showed the letter to. Hnilica realized that the ban on pilgrimages combined with the atrocity stories in the newspaper and the general ignorance about geography among Americans at large made for a large window of opportunity for fundraising. Jeff Lopez was taken in by Teresa's messages at the beginning but with hindsight came to feel that Teresa's scam was intimately connected to Bishop Hnilica's organization Christian Evangelization Movement-Russia because Hnilica wanted to make Denver a replacement for Medjugorje. Beyond that, both embarked at the same time on a campaign to unite all of competing Medjugorje apostolates under Hnilica's leadership.

Eventually, Teresa would travel with Hnilica to Rome and would meet with the pope, but not in a private audience as she would later claim. While in the line to see the pope in the general audience, Teresa held back to let the line disappear in front of her giving the impression that she was alone with the pope. The main upshot of the trip in terms of Teresa's career as a seer was the surprise announcement that in August of 1993 the pope was coming to Denver for the World Youth Day. The timing of the announcement was purely coincidental, but the rumor spread like wildfire that Teresa's visit was instrumental in the pope's decision, and Teresa, of course, did nothing to quell the rumors.

By December 1991 Teresa was a part of the round of Medjugorje conferences which had taken the place of pilgrimages as a way of giving apparition devotees someplace to go and something to do. Teresa spoke at the Denver conference in December 1991 to 9,000 people, but her notoriety would also lead to her undoing. In the same month she spoke in Denver, the archdiocese appointed a commission to look into her *bona fides* as a seer. Teresa was hardly in a position to weather scrutiny with even a remote chance for approval, so she must have been aware that her earning capacity had a limited shelf life.

She also must have known that the competition was getting pretty intense on the speaking circuit. Teresa attended the Pueblo Conference in October 1991 as a participant; however, she was not listed as one of the conference's big moments in an account written by J. Gary Kuntz, published some time later. "The program was so powerful," Kuntz wrote. "It was like a spiritual Disneyland," allowing the organizers to raise $15,000 at the Sunday Mass alone for refugees and displaced people in Yugoslavia. Father Edward O'Connor, the Mariologist from Notre Dame, got mentioned as saying that if the people who attended conferences like this waited for Church approval, they would "miss out on the present graces." O'Connor also said that the lay people were not bound by the Church's restrictions in the same way that priests were. The lay people at the conference, in addition to listening to the speakers, spent time taking pictures of the sun, and after comparing their pictures with those taken at the Cabrini Shrine began to notice remarkable similarities. An open door seemed to appear on both, at least this is what Kuntz wrote in his account of the conference. Predictably, many of Teresa Lopez's followers suffered eye damage by imitating what had gone on in Birmingham at a much higher altitude.

The high point of the conference involved another speaker, a man, for a change, by the name of Jim Jennings, who, according to Kuntz, was

> an ex-convict who had spent most of his life in and out of jail and was targeted for capital punishment as a habitual, violent criminal, [who] told a moving but humorous story of his amazing conversion. He was leading the life of a "respectable convict" in a New Jersey prison, when after reading Wayne Weible's newsletter, he was "zapped" by

God, who wouldn't leave him alone.

In April of 1988, Jim Jennings was in a cell in a prison in Tennessee, not unfamiliar surroundings for a man who had spent 18 of the last 25 years of his life behind bars for crimes like murder, attempted murder, armed robbery, and assault on a police officer. And those were the crimes he had been caught committing. Having lots of time to kill, Jim and his cellmate rolled themselves a joint and settled down for an uneventful afternoon of TV watching. But something unexpected happened. Jim and his cellmate stumbled across the BBC/Everyman Medjugorje documentary. It may have been the dope or it may have been the video, but Jim sat there mesmerized, and would later claim that he had undergone a religious conversion based on what he had seen.

Medjugorje, thereafter, just seemed to follow him wherever he went. When he was transferred to New Jersey a short time later to do time for other crimes he committed, he ran into a bunch of what he characterized as "little old ladies," who brought religious tracts and articles to the prisoners, one of which was Wayne Weible's newspaper on Medjugorje. Jim was still a bit skeptical, but the coincidences were beginning to form what he considered a pattern, to which he would soon ascribe to divine intent. Helping this idea along was the fact that the chaplain to the New Jersey State Medium Security Prison, Rev. Alfred Hewett, was planning a trip to Medjugorje shortly after Jim arrived in prison in New Jersey. Inspired by stores he had heard, Jim wanted to give Father Hewett something for "Our Lady to bless" so that he could "maybe get an extra oomph of holiness—something different" and so gave Father Hewett an old scapular his mother had given him some years before. Jennings later recounted that even though he didn't get "zapped," i.e., converted, when Father Hewett returned with the now "blessed" scapular, his love for Mary grew.

Jennings later claimed that much of what attracted him to Medjugorje in the first place was its focus on the all-merciful Mother of God, as opposed to the masculine and judgmental father God he felt had threatened to dispatch him to Hell. "Our Lady," he claimed, "just oozed love." God, however,

> is God. You know what I mean? I would go up, and I'd confess my sins. I believed I had to be good. If I'd mess up again, oh man, here come the lightning bolts! But you never heard nothing about Our Lady zappin' nobody. She was a Mom. She would invite the kids [the Medjugorje "seers"], and she'd smile at them, and tell them to wear

something warm on their legs because it was going to be cold the next day. She had beautiful blue eyes.

In March of 1989 Jennings began a novena to St. Joseph so that he might learn how to love and serve Jesus "as he deserved to be loved" and served rather than out of fear. At the end of this novena, he ran across some devotional books by St. Louis de Montfort and ended up making his consecration to Mary on the feast of St. Louis de Montfort a month later on April 28.

In the meantime, to Father Hewett's amazement, Jennings got a dozen or so inmates together to pray the rosary on a regular basis in one of the prison's classrooms and eventually consecrate the entire prison to the Immaculate Heart of Mary on August 15, 1989. All in all, it was an impressive conversion story, and Father Hewett at least was convinced that Jennings was sincere because his behavior wasn't calculated to get an early release, and because it continued after he got out of prison as well. Hewett was so convinced, in fact, of Jennings's sincerity that when Jennings was released from prison on December 17, 1990, Hewett defrayed the expense of putting Jim up in a local motel (at $30 a day) until he could get adjusted to life on the outside.

It could have been an expensive proposition, but it wasn't. Six days after his release, Jim's phone rang. On the other end of the line was Denis Nolan of Queen of Peace Ministries in South Bend, Indiana. It seems that one of the "little old ladies" who had visited Jim in prison was so impressed with his conversion and subsequent devotion to the Blessed Mother that she thought Denis ought to know about him. Denis was so intrigued by the story that he called Jennings at his New Jersey motel and offered him a job. Jim was "ecstatic," according to Father Hewett, and by early 1991 had moved into Nolan's home in Northern Indiana, where he lived for nearly four months with Nolan's wife and seven children.

Jennings got hired as a "janitor" at Queen of Peace Ministry headquarters, a small frame house two blocks east of Nolan's home, but it soon became apparent that Jennings's real value lay more in his witness talks than in his janitorial skills, and he was soon swept up into the Medjugorje speakers' circuit at a time when pilgrimages were on hold and regional conferences were booming across the United States. The war had all but killed pilgrimages to Medjugorje, but it created a boom for the Medjugorje industry in the United States, and Jim Jennings found himself as a result of forces over which he had no control in exactly the right place at the right time.

Jim soon found himself speaking several times a month, and returning with a fairly lucrative stipend from his talks. In addition to the regular stipend, people were often so moved by his talk that afterward they would come forward and ask if they could touch a living saint and in the process of touching him stuff money into his pockets. Since Nolan got the money when Jim returned home, it is not surprising that he began to book him at as many talks as possible across the country. Jennings was soon a Medjugorje superstar, but the role he was playing weighed heavily on his shoulders. Going from zero to sixty, from an incarcerated felon to a religious superstar, a living saint, involved a kind of psychic acceleration that would have un-hinged Mother Teresa, and Jim Jennings was no Mother Teresa. Part of what he brought to the Medjugorje speakers' circuit was a lifetime's worth of bad habits and moral baggage that would have required a life of prayer and asceticism to overcome. What Jim needed as well was a good dose of realism about the limits of human nature, especially fallen human nature wounded by years of habitual sin. Jim was des-tined to learn the hard way that conversion, on the one hand, and dying and going to heaven, on the other, are two different things. And as his star rose on the Medjugorje circuit, it became equally clear that he was not going to learn that lesson from the people who were applauding him as a latter-day saint. Jim had a whole host of bad habits, including various forms of substance abuse that were just waiting to get out of hand when the stress that went with his life as a popular speaker increased.

And this is precisely what happened. In early 1992 Jim moved into a townhouse in the Villa Apartment Complex on the north side of South Bend. Now removed from the constraints of family life imposed while living at the Nolans, Jennings could do pretty much what an ex-con wanted to do. His drinking increased as a result, and then on a spring day, he bumped into a 24-year-old woman living in the apart-ment next to his. Michele Hardman had been living with her fiance for some time, but found herself drawn to Jennings, who was then in his late forties and, although a little scratched and dented from the life he had been leading, by no means unattractive at first sight. What Michele really found attractive, though, was Jim's spirituality. On the first night they met, he invited her to his apartment, where they both watched one of the talks he had given at a recent Medjugorje conference.

"They were very powerful," Michele said later. "I liked where he was coming from."

Michele for her part was coming from a broken family which typified the wreckage the cultural revolution of the '60s spread throughout small towns in the mid-West. Michele grew up in Roseland, a neighborhood bordering a strip of motels and fast-food restaurants on Route 31 north of South Bend. She lived with her father, a Vietnam veteran and his second wife, in a family arrangement that was less than ideal. Michele saw in Jennings, a man old enough to be her father, a number of things she couldn't find in her own father or the other men in her life, most particularly the one she was living with at the time. Jennings fairly radiated spiritual commitment at the time. He was a man who had been down and out, coming from circumstances not unlike Michele's, and by the grace of God he had turned that life around and now was a sought-after speaker, who made money by talking about things spiritual. Michele had been raised a Methodist, which she later characterized as not meaning much of anything. "It's the most laid-back religion there is, " she later said, and in Jim's high-octane Marian devotion, she discovered a religion that was anything but laid back.

Jim's conversion may have been sincere, but the fallen man in him couldn't resist using his new-found spiritual aura as a way of exploiting the sexual possibilities of this new situation. Jim was living by himself at the time and was drinking—if not heavily, then regularly. His loneliness was relieved only by moments of adulation on the speaking circuit, which made a bad situation worse. On the first night after they met, Jennings took Michele to a local hotel, where she says they kissed but "nothing else happened." The next night Jim took Michele to another motel and this time something happened. In addition to his increasingly heavy drinking, Jim Jennings, the living saint on the Medjugorje circuit, was now having sex with his neighbor on a regular basis. As a result, Michele broke off her three-year relationship with her live-in boyfriend, and while keeping her own place, essentially moved into Jim's townhouse.

The growing contradiction between Jim's public and private *personae* seems to have troubled his conscience. Michele remembers waking up in the morning and listening to Jim say that he had to go off to confession. We have no way of knowing what his confessor, Father Edward O'Connor, told him, but we do know that firm purpose of amendment was not one of the things that followed from reception of the sacrament. The very same night, Jim would be back in bed with Michele and the same conscience-driven cycle would start all over again.

In addition to the normal burdens that drunkenness and fornication lay on the human heart, Jim was burdened by the sense that he was a hypocrite. Being hailed as a living saint at Medjugorje conferences across the land only added to the psychic pressure that was building within him. Jim soon started complaining that he didn't like to fly and that he was being scheduled at too many conferences. Since Denis Nolan proved insensitive to his complaints, Jim turned his frustration on Michele. According to Michele, Jim began complaining about the harsh regimen required of those on the speaking circuit. Jim was most probably referring here to the harsh promptings of his own conscience, since being feted at expensive hotels and restaurants hardly seems harsh when compared to life in prison. Jim found himself more and more paralyzed and more and more oppressed by his situation. Unable to live according to the code he preached and equally unable to stand up to Denis Nolan's demands, which he increasingly saw as a kind of spiritual and financial exploitation, Jim sought solace in Michele, and when that didn't work either he began abusing her and seeking something stronger than alcohol to take his mind off his troubles.

Jim had made no secret of his long history of drug abuse. As with any addiction, this one required moral vigilance, and yet the enthusiasm surrounding the apparitions and all of the miracles, which seemed so commonplace, seemed to make that sort of vigilance unnecessary. Father Hewett, Jim's New Jersey prison chaplain, noted how tempting the "I-converted-everything's-okay" attitude was, especially for hardened criminals not used to "needing help" from groups like Alcoholics Anonymous. "Jim," Hewett said later, "didn't take the necessary precautions" to avoid falling back into drug use. This state of mind was especially tempting for someone who had become addicted to the opiate of extraordinary spiritual experiences. Jim believed that he had been cured by some supernatural favor and as a result of that instant cure he felt that the daily struggle against temptations big and small was unnecessary. Jim hadn't taken drugs since he had been released from prison, but he had been drinking heavily since becoming involved with Michele. While he would always dry out for a couple of days before speaking at a conference, the pattern of alcohol abuse remained. Ultimately alcohol wasn't strong enough to combat the stress in his life. At the end of the summer of 1992, Jim started using cocaine again, a fact which Michele blames on Jim's inability to deal with the stress that had come into his life as a result of his career as a living saint on the Medjugorje circuit.

In the fall of 1988 Rick Salbato was on location working as a mechanical engineer on the security system at the American embassy in Damascus and suffering from a bad case of apparition burnout. Although baptized a Catholic, Rick did not practice his faith while growing up. Then, at around the age of 30, he was drawn back to the Catholic faith as a result of his exposure to the then just-burgeoning Charismatic Movement. His experiences with the charismatics ended in disillusionment roughly two years later, experiences which he later described in a book called *Tongues of Satan* published under the pen name The Publican.

Salbato's bad experiences with the charismatics, however, were just the beginning of an odyssey through the strange world of contemporary "apparitions." In the years following his departure from the charismatics, he became a proponent of Portovoce in Mexico, of Frances Klug and the Hill of Hope in California, of Necedah, Wisconsin, and of Garabandal in Spain. He now considers all of these phenomena false and the work of the devil and, beyond that, considers it his apostolate to warn people against the unacknowledged spiritual dangers associated with each of them.

In 1972, Salbato was in New Orleans when one of the Fatima pilgrim virgin statues started shedding tears. What struck him at the time was not the tears, however, but a woman he described as "a raving maniac," who would follow the statue around and try to divert the crowd's attention from it to herself and what she had to say. When a priest at the time rebuked the woman for what she was doing, he was greeted with a torrent of obscenities, which opened Salbato's eyes to two realities: 1) that there was such a thing as false mystics and 2) that these false mystics would inevitably try to attach themselves to something which they considered real.

By the time he reached Damascus in the fall of 1988, Salbato had become thoroughly disillusioned with the paranormal scene on the orthodox right. Just before his arrival in Damascus, Salbato had come from Rocca di Papa, the monastery of Padre Gino. Salbato had believed in Gino too, until he decided to look more closely into the reports of misbehavior he had been hearing. Then he came across the report of those investigating Gino, the "Anecdotal Report Concerning the Group Dynamics of the Oblate Sisters of the Virgin Mary of Fatima," which convinced him that he had been taken in by another religious fraud (See "The Rise and Fall of Padre Gino," *Fidelity*, May 1992, for another account of the same story).

In the course of looking for a place where he could attend daily Mass in Damascus, Salbato discovered an Irish priest working for a group of Italian nuns working in an Italian hospital. The priest had recently been expelled from Iran because of the war with Iraq, and in the course of their conversation, Salbato discovered that the priest was a devout believer in most of the apparitions which Salbato had repudiated. In the course of the next five days, the priest plied Salbato with the messages of various "seers" all over the world and then mentioned that there was one such seer in Damascus.

Salbato overcame his initial skepticism and eventually visited the seer in the Christian district of Damascus who was announcing the messages that came to be known as Our Lady of Soufanieh. Eventually Salbato got to meet the seer, a young mother of two by the name of Mirna (or Miryam) Nazzour. Mirna is a Roman Catholic; her husband is Greek Orthodox, and the messages she allegedly receives concern Church unity. Eventually, Salbato became convinced that this seer was the real thing, as a result of the consistency of the messages with Catholic doctrine, local church approval, the demeanor of the woman herself, and the miraculous occurrences which accompanied her visions. In spite of having been burned in the past, Salbato resolved to promote Mirna's messages. Perhaps because of having been burned in the past, Salbato made a fateful decision with regard to his involvement with Mirna. He decided to promote this apparition and this apparition alone. Salbato insisted that no other apparition be mixed up with the messages Mirna was promoting. The decision was based on his previous experiences. It seems a simple enough resolution to keep, but the decision was to have far-reaching consequences. It was also to cause both Salbato and the group that was founded to promote Mirna's messages, The Messengers of Unity, untold grief.

Salbato left Damascus in late 1988 and went back to Rocca di Papa to write his book on Mirna and the messages of Our Lady of Soufanieh. In the summer of 1989 he was back in California, and Mirna was there too. Crowds started following her; miraculous events started occurring during the prayer sessions with the crowds. Yet as the notoriety increased so did the pressure to associate Mirna with other "apparitions," most notably Medjugorje, which was probably enjoying the apogee of its fame at the time. Salbato found the pressure strong enough to warrant putting up a sign to warn the pilgrims in advance. "Mirna and the Messengers of Unity," the sign announced

> have permission from the bishops of Damascus to announce the messages and the miracles of Soufanieh. We do not have permission to spread information about any other apparition. Please do not talk about or bring literature about any other reported miracle.

The request seemed simple enough, but keeping Mirna free from entangling alliances with other apparitions has proven to be anything but simple. The pressure on Mirna to go along, to scratch the back of fellow "seers," has been exerted by a number of people. Fr. René Laurentin, the eminence grise of the Medjugorje movement, tried in vain to get Mirna to go to Medjugorje. The Little Pebble has written to Mirna asking for an endorsement. The 101 Foundation, John Haffert's (of Blue Army fame) attempt to come out of retirement and get back in the Marian apparition business, asked Mirna to accompany him on their infamous flight to Moscow in October 1992. (Vassula was the star attraction on the 101 flight and pulled down another endorsement from the Medjugorje firmament when Father Ken Roberts came on board the Vassula bandwagon. In addition to Vassula, there were a number of other "seers" on the flight who kept up a virtually non-stop conversation with the beyond. "Seer" Janie Garzia of Austin, Texas, allegedly received a message from Jesus telling the flight's crew members that they had been personally hand-picked [by Him, presumably] for the flight and that He wanted to thank them.)

The real pressure to go along with what was happening elsewhere, however, came from a relative newcomer to the apparition scene. In August 1986 Dr. Antoine Mansour, an Egyptian-educated Arab surgeon residing in Los Angeles, got a call from Tony Hanna, a singer famous in the Arab world, asking him to examine a certain mystic by the name of Mirna, who was residing in Damascus and claiming to have both the stigmata and visions. One year later Dr. Mansour met Mirna again in Hanna's home in Lebanon and accompanied Mirna back to her home in Damascus. One year later in March 1988, Mirna and her husband Nicolas and their daughter Miriam traveled to the United States and stayed with the Mansours at their home in Los Angeles. Mirna was pregnant at the time and gave birth to their second child while in America. Dr. Mansour's wife, Claire, became, in fact, the godmother of Mirna's second child, a fact which frequently comes up in conversation with Mrs. Mansour.

The Mansours were a wealthy couple. In addition to being a surgeon, Dr. Mansour's family owned an Arabic newspaper. Their exposure to Mirna was their first glimpse into a whole new world of Marian devotion as practiced in our time. A number of sources claimed that Mrs. Mansour was more than a little interested in social contacts. If so, the Medjugorje network must have opened before their eyes as a particularly fertile field to explore. Once they saw the clout that the other seers had, it is not surprising that they would come to view their own seer Mirna in a new light. They quickly developed what could be termed a proprietary interest in Mirna. So proprietary, in fact, that Mirna was held a virtual captive in the Mansours' home. When Mirna expressed a desire to go back to Damascus, she got slapped by Mrs. Mansour. The situation eventually got so bad that Nicolas Nazzour, Mirna's husband and a jeweler by trade, was forced to sell Mirna's jewelry to pay for a flight home. When contacted in Damascus, Nicolas was reluctant to talk about the incident. When asked if he and his wife were held against their will at the Mansours' house, he claimed that this was a private matter that he would prefer not to discuss.

Mirna eventually returned to the United States again in the summer of 1989, but this time she did not stay with the Mansours. Between her first and second stay in the U.S., two things happened that would have significance later on. Mirna met Rick Salbato in Damascus and the people who eventually became known as the Messengers of Unity, who dedicated themselves to promoting her message on the condition that they would not have to promote any other alleged apparition—a position best expressed by the already-mentioned sign Salbato put up to deter pilgrims from trying to draw Mirna into commenting on other apparitions.

At the same time that Rick Salbato was making up his mind to promote Mirna on the condition that he could promote her alone, the Mansours were discovering that there was a whole interlocking Marian network out there of alleged "seers" whose primary philosophy seemed to be "you scratch my back and I'll scratch yours." When Mirna and her husband arrived in the U.S. for their second visit during the summer of 1989, the Mansours were visiting in Medjugorje, getting some inkling of just how big this network was. Also in Medjugorje during the summer of 1989 was a certain former tennis champion and Sheraton Hotel model by the name of Vassula Ryden. Vassula was yet to be discovered on the seer circuit, but she was evidently making the same discoveries as Claire Mansour. By 1989 Medjugorje had become very big business. One billion dollars would be invested there by the outbreak of the Yugoslavian civil war in 1991. The hotels and restaurants were already up or on their way up by the summer of 1989. The apparition business was booming.

There is no evidence that Vassula and Claire met in Medjugorje during the summer of 1989, but when Claire returned home to L.A. that summer, she seemed full of enthusiasm for this new-found apparition and was ready to take her own personal seer, Mirna, and work her into the what was a booming Medjugorje/Marian apparition network. There was only one fly in the ointment. Mirna seemed reluctant to cooperate with Claire's plan. When Claire finally got to meet with Mirna in 1989, she was somewhat annoyed to find that Mirna was not staying at her house. Even more annoying, however, was the fact that Mirna seemed now to rely on Rick Salbato for advice. When Claire finally got to see Mirna (at someone else's house), she brought with her two ads which had run in Arabic in the Mansour family newspaper. One featured Claire and Medjugorje, the other Claire and Mirna. When Claire asked Mirna what she thought, Mirna turned to Rick for his opinion, which infuriated Claire. Even more infuriating was Salbato's response. "If you're going to promote Medjugorje," Salbato reportedly said, "I don't want to have anything to do with you."

Mrs. Mansour was a wealthy woman and, according to most reports, accustomed to getting her way in most things. Beyond that, she had just been to the mountain, quite literally, and had seen the possibilities that being plugged into the Medjugorje network might provide her. She had known Mirna before either Rick or the Messengers of Unity had, and now these parvenus had clearly undermined her influence on a seer whom she felt she had discovered all by herself. When she sensed that Mirna was siding with Salbato and the Messengers, Claire exploded with rage and declared a virtual state of war against the Messengers of Unity on the spot. From that moment onward, virtually everything that can be known about Mirna has been strained through the lens of the war which Claire Mansour has waged on the Messengers of Unity in her effort to be declared the sole spokesman for the cause of Our Lady of Soufanieh.

This sort of thing is not unknown among Marian devotees. One need only think of the war fought over the 1984 collegial consecration of Russia between Father Nicolas Gruner and Father Robert Fox. The battle over Mirna, however, makes the Gruner/Fox battle look like a tempest in a teapot by comparison. Because of the Mansours' wealth, the sides are hardly even either. Whenever the Messengers of Unity would attempt to promote Mirna's messages, Claire Mansour would show up on the scene shortly thereafter in a attempt to discredit them. Often she would do it by throwing her money around.

When it became known that Father Fox was going to run an article on Mirna, he received a particularly loathsome letter full of all sorts of insinuations about Salbato and the Messengers of Unity from Bill Reck of the Riehle Foundation, one of the major Medjugorje promoters in this country. At around the same time, Fox received a letter full of the same sort of insinuations from Dr. Antoine Mansour. Enclosed with the latter letter was a check for $250 as well as the statement that Mansour had been a contributor to John Haffert's monumental Fatima film flop, *State of Emergency*, one of the greatest all-time money losers in the history of Catholic apostolates in this country. Virtually everyone who has had contact with Mrs. Mansour claims that her primary apostolate was promoting her own ego; however, even granting that, the ego drama got carried out in a particular way. The battle lines in the war over who got proprietary rights to Mirna's visions were drawn along the lines of other apparitions. The Messengers of Unity wanted nothing to do with other apparitions. The Mansours wanted to be able to link Mirna and her message to the flourishing Marian network out there. And they were willing to use their considerable financial clout to get their way, and getting their way meant, more often than not, undermining the Messengers of Unity whenever they could.

In February 1993 Andree Crehan had just signed on as the new editor of *Mary's People*, Twin Circle Publications' attempt to cash in on the Medjugorje/Marian craze. Andree's predecessor, Ginny Piccolo, was struggling with an article on Our Lady of Soufanieh based on documentation provided by Claire Mansour. When Crehan called the Messengers of Unity for a picture for the story, she found that they had their own version of the apparition, a version which was in her opinion much more cogent and persuasive. Crehan, as a result, decided to go with the Messengers' article, not excluding Mansour's material but adding to it. Mansour, however, became furious at the fact that the Messengers had once more been given a forum for their views and complained to Crehan, who, though willing to add Mansour's material to an upcoming issue, was not willing to rely on it exclusively. Mansour, as a result, went over Crehan's head to Fran Maier, editor of another Twin Circle publication, the *National Catholic Register*, which had also been promoting Medjugorje. Maier, it turns out, would prove to be much more amenable to what Mansour had to say.

"When Fran Maier became aware of the conflict," Crehan would say months later, "he was on the side of the Messengers because they were a center associated with *Mary's People*. He changed his attitude when he was contacted by Claire and she began submitting ads for publication. This occurred after she lied to me about submitting a $1,000 order for copies of the April issue which she then threatened to withdraw. I began to sense that her money was having quite an effect on Fran. He took away my authority to handle the situation probably because I would not act out a 'charade' and because the newspapers were suffering financially."

Rather than give in to what she felt were Mansour's lies about the Messengers, Crehan decided to resign from the editorship of the paper. Crehan now feels that Mansour used her financial clout to influence editorial policy at *Mary's People*.

"She can push you up against the wall," Crehan said about Mrs. Mansour, "and since they [Twin Circle] were having trouble financially, they probably thought they should deal with her so that they could benefit from it. But actually I don't think that they are ever going to benefit from what they did."

What Twin Circle did do was accept Claire as the exclusive spokesman for Mirna, in return for which Claire paid for the ads which she had previously threatened to withdraw. In a letter to the Nazzours and their spiritual advisors, Frs. Zahlaoui and Malouli, Crehan explains why she felt compelled to resign from *Mary's People*. According to Crehan's account, Mrs. Mansour

> began making accusations against the Messengers of Unity, calling them liars and thieves, but it was Claire who was lying. She was determined to have her article appear in the April issue [of *Mary's People*], and at one point even tried to "bribe" me by saying that she was going two withdraw a "$1,000 order." I had never heard of any such "order" and found out that the circulation department had received no such order. Later, Claire even tried to use the picture of Our Lady of Soufanieh to get

special consideration from the advertising department. I kept track of the situation with Claire by writing a memo to Francis Maier, the editor of the *National Catholic Register*, who had hired me for the job as editor of *Mary's People*.

When Claire and I met with Mr. Maier, she again brought up her cruel accusations against the Messengers of Unity. She alleged that there was no worth to their book's imprimatur from Archbishop Barkhash of Damascus and angrily found fault with the book and the videos. From then on, I tried to make Fran Maier understand that he should not allow Claire to be associated any longer with the newspaper in any way. But shortly after I resigned as editor of *Mary's People*, an interview with the Mansours was published in the *National Catholic Register*. In my letter of resignation, I had said that interviewing them would only give the Mansours "another opportunity to undermine the work which the Messengers of Unity have spent three years trying to build up for Our Lady of Soufanieh in this country. I also said that "if Claire is allowed to associate herself with the Centers, I could not in good conscience have anything more to do with her." Even though I loved my work as editor of *Mary's People*, I had to give it up, much as the Messengers of Unity had to withdraw as a Marian center because of Claire's lies and the confusion she created.

On October 12, 1992, Crehan wrote a letter to her successor as editor at *Mary's People*, Gabriel Meyer (previously the Medjugorje correspondent for the *National Catholic Register*), along with documentation which showed that "the Messengers of Unity have been vindicated by Mirna Nazzour (the Damascus visionary) despite all the attempts to discredit them—chiefly through false accusations and ugly insinuations perpetrated by Antoine and Claire Mansour."

Crehan goes on to express regret at the fact that *Mary's People* was included on a list of sponsors for the January 1993 conference which was to sponsor Vassula at both the Sacramento Cathedral and Los Angeles. For her trouble, Crehan, who headed a Marian center of her own, was expelled from the 160 member coalition associated with *Mary's People*. In the letter informing her of her expulsion, Fran Maier accused her of disrupting the unity of the group. Crehan's defense of the Messengers of Unity, a member of the *Mary's People* Marian coalition, was, according to Maier, "fundamentally opposed to the kind of

Marian unity we're trying to build—and we need to terminate it immediately." Which is precisely what happened. In the name of unity, Crehan and her organization, Marian Media, Inc., were expelled from the *Mary's People* network. In the battle between the Mansours and the Messengers of Unity, Crehan still feels that the fault lay exclusively with the Mansours. It was their lies and their manipulation which were causing the disunity. The fact that the Mansours were retained while she and the Messengers had to go is something Crehan found "ironic" in a letter to the publisher at Twin Circle. Ironic, in one sense, but perfectly understandable in another. According to Crehan, *Mary's People* simply chose financial clout over the truth.

There were ironies in abundance here though, and they all revolved around the idea of unity, which was becoming a commodity in short supply in the Marian/Medjugorje movement as that movement rapidly evolved into something more concerned with profit-taking and market share than with disseminating the truth. In the process of elbowing their way to the apparition trough, one orthodox Catholic apostolate after another had been corrupted. The chief fruit of this corruption was disunity. The seers and enthusiasts who scorned the authority of the Church in matters like Medjugorje were now left to battle it out with each other over which seer gets promoted on the apparition circuit. As Rick Salbato said, disunity is the chief fruit of phony seers and apparitions. The rise of someone like Vassula Ryden is simply inexplicable if one ignores the role that credulous (and/or Machiavellian) priests and money play in her promotion. Vassula is a creation of her handlers, and the principles upon which her handlers operate turn out to be, upon closer scrutiny, hardly other-worldly. In fact, "worldly" is the word that comes immediately to mind to describe them.

In the course of this ongoing battle for market share in the Marian movement, something significant happened in Europe as well. In the spring of 1991 Croatia declared independence and plunged what was formerly Yugoslavia into a state of civil war from which it has yet to emerge. As the world looked on in horror, the land of Our Lady Queen of Peace succumbed to the most vicious fighting Europe had seen since the close of World War II. Eighteen thousand people lost their lives in Bosnia alone. "Ethnic cleansing" became a new term in everyone's vocabulary, and 35,000 women, mostly Muslims, were raped by Serbian militiamen. In a BBC video done in the mid-'80s on Medjugorje, the viewer was told that one of the signs of the apparition's authenticity was the fact that ethnic groups in Yugoslavia were finally living in peace. Did then the war in Bosnia revoke the apparitions' authenticity? The Medjugorje establishment was either keeping quiet on this one, or claiming that the war was the result of not heeding the Virgin's call. Either way, the pilgrimage industry in Medjugorje was one of the first victims of ethnic cleansing and, by the beginning of 1992, just as dead as the corpses floating down the Neredva River.

As a result, the Medjugorje industry in this country suddenly found itself all dressed up with no place to go. Ten years of apparitions had whipped the audience in the U.S. into a fever pitch, and suddenly there was no outlet for all this fervor. In an atmosphere like this, a seer like Mirna was suddenly a much more valuable property than before. With a promoter like Claire Mansour behind her, as well as a market full of apparitionites frustrated by the State Department ban on travel to Bosnia, a mega-event was waiting in the wings if Mirna could be brought to the states.

But Mirna was unwilling to come. The reasons given for her reluctance were various. Both Claire Mansour and Nicolas Nazzour claimed that Mirna was unable to travel during the winter. The Messengers of Unity, however, claimed that Mirna was annoyed at being threatened by Claire, who wanted her desperately for the January 1993 extravaganza in Sacramento and L.A. Beyond that, Mirna allegedly claimed that she didn't want to be part of a "circus," i.e., part of a traveling Marian freak show like the 101 Flight. Whatever the reason, Mirna was clearly promising to be a no-show in January , and a gala in the cathedral without her was a bit like filming Ben Hur without the chariot race.

Just when it seemed that a great opportunity to cash in on the apparition market might be lost, the Mansours got a call from René Laurentin, the Marian Svengali. In the spring of 1992, right around the time of the contretemps at *Mary's People* between Claire and the Messengers, Claire got a call from Father Laurentin announcing that an interesting lady by the name of Vassula Ryden was in Arizona and would be spending four hours between planes at the L.A. airport. Would Dr. Mansour, Father Laurentin wanted to know, like to examine her? Since Vassula is not claiming to have the stigmata, it is unclear why Dr. Mansour should render an opinion on her. The only reason that comes to mind is to see if the Mansours would be willing to back her as a seer. If that was the real question, the answer was yes. Claire met with Vassula at the airport for four hours and liked what she saw.

"Usually," Mrs. Mansour said describing her first meeting with Vassula, "myself and my husband we don't fall into things like this. We don't believe immediately. But she was one of the ladies I was really inspired by."

Whether the meeting was orchestrated by Vassula is not clear, but Vassula played it as if she were applying for a position with a prestigious apparition firm. Vassula obviously had her eye on the tour that Mrs. Mansour could arrange for her, and Mrs. Mansour, for her part, was not oblivious to what Vassula had to offer. Here was a lady who, unlike Mirna, could speak English and who, also unlike Mirna, had no scruples about traveling or endorsing other apparitions, no matter how dubious or absurd. Vassula was, in other words, cooperative in a way that Mirna was not. She even was willing to go so far as to say that Our Lord and Savior Jesus Christ told her that his mother was appearing at Medjugorje. This was sure to please the hearts of the crowd that could no longer pour its money into the now defunct Yugoslavian economy.

Vassula was, in other words, Claire's kind of seer, and what she lacked in credibility could be made up by promoting both Vassula and Mirna at the same time. Vassula, in this regard, showed herself to be a quick study. She read all she could on Mirna, and sure enough similarities began creeping into her writings. At the Notre Dame conference, she said that God demanded that the Orthodox and Catholics celebrate Easter at the same time, something which evidently has come about in Damascus as a result of Mirna's messages.

Do the discrepancies in Vassula's messages bother Mrs. Mansour? Evidently not. The worship/veneration switch is explained by the fact that "in Arabic when you say worship, the translation is veneration."

"You mean Jesus is speaking to her in Arabic?" I ask:

"No," Mrs. Mansour responded, "always in English, because she told me its her best spoken language. And He told her that once I speak with you it will spread like wildfire, and it did go."

By the spring of 1992, the apparition movement had taken on a life of its own, and as this great headless body lurched around the country, it became difficult to tell just who, if anyone, was in control.

-11-

THE WAR COMES TO MEDJUGORJE

Anke Blasevic was at one time a Communist. Assigned by the Yugoslav government to be the seers' official translator, she took their messages to heart and converted back to the Catholic faith of her forbears. In April of 1992, Blasevic was in Medjugorje trying now not to translate what Vicka was saying but to calm her down. On April 6, the European Community had recognized Bosnia-Herzegovina as an independent country, and the Yugoslav army, now made up of disgruntled Serbs and Montenegrins, had decided that after their humiliating defeat at the hands of the Slovenians less than a year before, they were not going to retreat any further. In response to the EC recognition announcement, the Yugoslav air force launched air strikes on Siroki Brijeg, killing six people with cluster bombs. Six cluster bombs also dropped on Citluk five kilometers from Medjugorje, but no one was killed. In fact, one of the bombs, which was made up of a metal stem with trays full of hand grenade-like bomblets, failed to go off and was dutifully dragged to Medjugorje and stuck in a sewer grate in front of seer Ivanka Ivankovic Elez's coffee shop and repeatedly photographed as part of the Medjugorje legend about how the village had been spared. Stories would circulate about jets bound for bombing runs over Medjugorje suddenly losing their way and bombs dropping but not exploding and instrument panels mysteriously going white, but the truth of the matter is that Medjugorje was never a target. That fact, however, didn't deter Father Kraljevic from traveling around the United States with an unexploded shell to raise money for war relief. Like the cluster bomb in the sewer it was a macho gesture; Medjugorje was bloodied but unbowed.

Vicka wasn't feeling particularly macho on April 7. In fact, she was in a state that could not be unfairly described as panic. In fact panic was the emotion that characterized the frame of mind of just about everyone at Medjugorje in April of 1992. All of the talk about a chastisement took on new relevance as the prophecy seemed about to be fulfilled at Medjugorje itself. Vicka in fact seemed to indicate that the seers themselves were somehow to blame for the war. "It's our fault," she screamed hysterically, "We should have prayed more." When Blasevic succeeded in calming Vicka down somewhat, Vicka decided on another course of action. Now she wanted Blasevic to get President George Bush on the phone. After she was assured that that was unlikely to happen, Vicka insisted that she and the other seers as well as all the priests contact George Bush by e-mail and ask him to intervene in the fighting and stop the war. Frank Cuccini, an American computer whiz, had set up something called Medjulink in 1990, to propagate the messages, and now the instrument which had been formerly used to broadcast the messages of Our Lady, Queen of Peace, was now turned to another use, asking George Bush for airstrikes against the Serbs. In less than a year, the seers and the Franciscans had gone from worrying about the attacks of the local bishop to worrying about air strikes from the Yugoslav air force. For people used to looking for signs and wonders, this seemed like a sign too big to miss. "War," the Blessed Mother told Lucia at Fatima, "is a punishment for sin."

During the summer of '91, the JNA, or Yugoslavian army, withdrew from Slovenia after being repulsed from their attempt to take over the border posts. Within less than a week, the war was over, and 200,000 JNA soldiers returned to what was left of their country. The Serbs would later complain bitterly that information about troop movements was transmitted to the Slovenian militia by Slovenian sympathizers still within the Yugoslav government. The Slovenians knew in advance that the JNA would not fire on its troops and used this information to bolster a merciless counterattack against the Serb and Montenegrin troops, who now, feeling bitter and betrayed, re-treated back to the borders of what was left of Yugoslavia, a country which at that time included Bosnia-Herzegovina. Half of the troops returned to Serbia, but the other half, about 100,000 of some of the best equipped troops in Europe, took up position in Bosnia-Herzegovina, with time now to lick their wounds and vow that the same thing wouldn't happen twice. It was during this time that the semi-demobbed JNA along with Serb volunteers took up positions on the hills east of Mostar.

During the summer of 1991, the JNA forces were "ideologically" cleansed, which is to say that anyone who had "fascist" inclinations, i.e., all Croatians, were expelled from the army. Tired of hearing his fellow officers refer to him as an Ustasha, Philip Pavich's cousin took a Soviet-built MI Hind helicopter gunship and flew it from Belgrade to Zagreb on September 23, 1991, two days after the Croatians had taken control of the airport, where he was given a hero's welcome, and, thereafter, rewarded by being named Franjo Tudjman's official helicopter pilot. The Croatians were especially happy to get the gunship because—according to some reports, at least— they had no weapons at the time other than a few hunting rifles. That situation would be remedied later when the Croatians broke into the JNA armories in Zagreb and stole the weapons there. Weapons would soon come from abroad as well.

Making use of its tactical advantage in this regard, the JNA, still smarting from its defeat in Slovenia, launched attacks across Croatia, especially in Serb-dominated areas like eastern Slavonia, Banija, and northern Dalmatia. Often the JNA would collaborate with local Serb militias and volunteers from Serbia proper. By the end of the summer, military actions which had begun under the pretext of protecting Serb enclaves soon degenerated into full-scale ethnic cleansing and genocide in Dalj near Osijek and Struge in Banija. As rumors of Serb atrocities spread, refugees swelled into a flood and entire villages like Celije in Slavonia were put to the torch after the Croats deserted them.

On June 30, 1991, the Croatian bishops issued a public appeal for peace, claiming that "Croatia is facing the terrible fate of an imposed war!" By the middle of August 1991, just about every part of Croatia which had a significant Serbian minority population was in the middle of what would have to be called a war. JNA forces entered Croatia from Bosnia-Herzegovina with impunity and opened new fronts in western Slavonia, where the conflict spread to Lika and Kordun. When the JNA occupied Baranja, they expelled just about all of the Croats and Hungarians there, which is to say the majority of the people living there at the time. They attempted the same thing in predominantly Croat towns like Osijek, Vinkovci, and Vukovar. The point of the campaign was to occupy all of the territory east of a line formed by the towns Virovitica- Karlovac-Ogulin-Karlobag. That aim was clearly ethnic cleansing, although the only one honest enough to admit it was the right-wing politician Vojislav Seselj. In September 1991, there was further escalation of conflicts including air attacks on what were then peaceful parts of Croatia. Sisak and Sibenik, which was 83 percent Croat and only 9.5 percent Serb, came under continuous attack for days.

Every political action by the republics that wanted to break away created a violent reaction on the part of the Serbs, who felt they were being backed into a corner by an international conspiracy that was out to destroy them. When Muslims and Croats declared Bosnia-Herzegovina a sovereign republic in September of 1991, the Serbs reacted by declaring the independence of various "Serbian Autonomous Regions," which refused to recognize Bosnia-Herzegovina's borders. Every time the United States or Germany urged their allies to recognize the break-away nations, they pushed the Muslims and the Croats in one direction and the Serbs in the exact opposite.

On September 20, JNA and paramilitary troops took up positions on the hills surrounding Mostar. Within a few days, the JNA launched an all-out offensive against Croatia, designed to split it into militarily unreinforceable enclaves by attacking the predominantly Croat towns of Zadar, Karlovac, and Vukovar, which had already been under siege for three months. The Serbs also launched attacks on Dubrovnik, causing international outrage over the senseless shelling of a town which was known as "the pearl of the Adriatic." Dubrovnik was high on the U.N.'s "World Heritage List," a list of cities which are part of the world's architectural patrimony. It had no known military significance. One report said that the Croats had placed artillery near the hotel housing EC observers to provoke the attack; another said that the Serbs were simply interested in destroying one of Croatia's most significant tourist attractions.

On November 19, 1991, 1,500 Croat soldiers defending Vukovar surrendered to the Serbs after an 87-day siege. Vukovar, one of the easternmost towns in Croatia and the bulwark of Croatian claims in Krajina, would remain in Serb hands until the Serbs gave it back in early 1998. By the time Vukovar fell, Croatia had lost one third of its territory to the Serbs during the four months since it had declared independence. The EC sent observers and wrung its hands but continued on the course it had already established by setting a late December deadline for the recognition of those nations who still wanted to declare independence. Since Bosnia-Herzegovina was the only region left with any interest in independence—Serbia and Montenegro had regrouped as the rump Yugoslavia— and since Bosnia-Herzegovina was even more ethnically diverse than Croatia and had 100,000 JNA troops still within its borders, the EC plan seemed to the perceptive like a recipe for disaster

"The international community," warned a still pretty much unknown Serbian politician by the name of Radovan Karadzic, "above all the ill-intentioned European Community, has taken over all Yugoslav affairs. The result is encouraging secessionist processes." On December 10, 1991, eight months to the day after the Yugoslav bishops announced that she wasn't there, Our Lady of Medjugorje announced through Marija Pavlovic, "Dear Children, I could easily stop this war if there were more people praying and fasting."

The EC, pushed mostly by German foreign minister Dietrich Genscher, was listening to neither the Serbs nor the "Gospa." On January 6, 1992, the European Community granted diplomatic recognition to Croatia and Slovenia, after Germany threatened to recognize the republics unilaterally. Thousands of Catholics showed up at the Cathedral in Zagreb to celebrate a Mass of thanksgiving, and Croatian television showed jubilant citizens carrying signs saying, *"Danke, Deutschland!"* The Serbs for their part were thinking more of the Luftwaffe attack on Belgrade 51 years earlier and feeling like the victim of an international conspiracy. Recognition of Croatia may have led to bloodshed, but it was at least a politically defensible act, if only because just about everyone involved in the conflict agreed that Croatia was a nation. The same thing could hardly be said for Bosnia-Herzegovina, an administrative unit created by the Ottoman Turks, whose population was divided up pretty evenly between groups whose allegiance lay somewhere else. Making up the overwhelming majority of Bosnia-Herzegovina's population were the Croats, who wanted union with Croatia, the Serbs, who wanted union with Serbia, and the Muslims, who were being backed by Islamic regimes in places like Iran, and under Alia Izetbegovic were in the process of creating the first Islamic republic on the European subcontinent. Far down on the list were the "Yugoslavs," mostly people in mixed marriages, who wanted a multi-ethnic country but lacked the ideology and the population to effectively bring that about. Once Croatia became independent, the Croats in Bosnia-Herzegovina had no interest in becoming an independent country. What they wanted was union with Croatia, just as the Bosnian Serbs wanted union with Serbia. The only people who wanted independence were certain Yugoslavians and Muslims, all of whom taken together could not constitute a majority in anything but a few gerrymandered city states. As the EC, dominated by Germany, continued its course, more and more observers saw trouble on the horizon.

Trouble had already reached Medjugorje. The village had been spared the fighting that plagued parts of Croatia, but the war had killed the pilgrimage industry, and now the people who had gone into debt to accommodate it by building hotels could not repay their loans. Milan Lovric, the mayor of Citluk, told AP reporter Mort Rosenblum in early 1992 that people had "invested $1 billion dollars in hotels and businesses, and now they can't pay it back. The area is losing $100 million a year." One unnamed man had borrowed $500,000 to build a hotel, but now "with no guests, the man is ruined."

"It is terrible to see everything go on ice," said Father Philip Pavich. "Both of my parents' birth churches at Lika are now ashes."

On January 13, 1992, the Vatican officially recognized Slovenia and Croatia as independent nations one week after the EC, under

Germany's guidance, had done the same, fueling the sense among the Serbs that they were the victims of an international conspiracy in which Rome and a newly reborn Austro-Hungarian empire were united against them. Writing in the *Christian Science Monitor* on January 29, 1992, Joseph C. Harsh said that the Vatican's speedy recognition of Croatia and Slovenia provided the key to understanding what was going on in the Balkans because aside from the period of the two Yugoslavias beginning in 1918 and ending in 1991, Croatia and Slovenia had been a part of the West for 1500 years, since the time of the Western Roman Empire. Serbia had always been on the other side of "one of the great fault lines in history." From Charlemagne to Napoleon, Croatia and Slovenia had been part of the Holy Roman Empire; from Napoleon to 1918, they had been part of the Austro-Hungarian empire, and now it looked as if they were reverting back to their historical matrix at the urging of a reunited Germany and the Vatican. Yugoslavia was a sort of Wilsonian attempt to blunt German and Austrian and Catholic influence but also a little bit of social engineering. The Americans had been naive enough to attempt an appeal to democracy to paper over one of the great dividing lines of history. History would repeat itself on a smaller scale when the Americans recognized Bosnia-Herzegovina and attempted to create there a smaller version of the entity Wilson had created 74 years earlier.

Germany, however, was doing more than simply cheering on the Croatians and Slovenians from the sidelines. By the fall of 1991, they had become one of the major weapons suppliers for the region, in spite of a United Nations embargo on the sale of weapons. In many ways, the fall of Communism made the war in Yugoslavia, if not inevitable, then a lot easier to stage simply because of all of the weapons, which were now unnecessary for the defense of Europe against the Soviet threat. The DDR, the formerly Communist East Germany, for example, had a completely superfluous arsenal that was scheduled to be scrapped at the same time that the pro-German Croatians needed their own weapons to fight the Serbs. Germany, the country pushing hardest for recognition, was in charge of disposing of those weapons, and so it is not surprising that some of those weapons would appear in Croatia. A number of MiG-21 fighters, scheduled for the scrap heap, ended up landing in Zagreb instead. In March of 1992, the Croatian defense ministry, using a German company as a middle man, purchased 90 military trucks from the now superfluous stores of the French occupying forces in Germany. Hungary, under the guise of helping to equip Croatian policemen, sold the Croatians 10,000 automatic rifles. One Croatian émigré talked about getting phone calls in the middle of night directing them to military bases in Germany where the keys were in the ignition and the papers on the passenger seat and the truck full of weapons. The Cold War had turned Europe into a vast arsenal, whose weaponry was gathering dust or destined to be turned into scrap. Germany had concluded that it was so expensive to scrap Warsaw Pact tanks that it was considering simply dropping them into the Baltic to be used as a breakwater. Why not then sell them to the Croatians? Even fire sale prices were better than dropping them into the ocean. "It's clear," said UN special envoy Cyrus Vance in late 1991, "that the arms embargo isn't working."

On February 29, 1992, Bosnia-Herzegovina conducted a referendum, and 64 percent of the people voted for independence. The Serbs, however, a group comprising a third of Bosnia's population, boycotted the election. On March 3, Alia Izetbegovic declared Bosnia-Herzegovina an independent republic and, ominously, in the same statement condemned the blockades which militant Serbs had set up outside Sarajevo, the new republic's capital. The Serbs were making it increasingly clear that they were not going to back down in Bosnia as they had backed down in Slovenia. The battle over Slovenia was a battle for the abstract idea that was Yugoslavia, since few Serbs actually lived there. In Bosnia, however, the Serbs were fighting for their homes. In responses to Izetbegovic's declaration of independence, Radovan Karadzic, speaking for the Bosnian Serbs, announced that "we are not going to accept an independent Bosnia-Herzegovina." When thousands of peace demonstrators took to the streets of Sarajevo on March 2, Serb militants opened fire. One 20-year-old young woman who watched her unarmed friends get gunned down by Serb militia, immediately volunteered for the Muslim government's defense forces and thereafter put the skills she had learned for use on Yugoslavia's rifle team to use as a sniper, killing Serbs. "I try not to think about it," the lady, who goes by the code name Strijela, or Arrow, answers when asked how many people she has killed. Her target, she said, must be in uniform and must be carrying a gun.

It was clear that the Serbs meant business this time, and as if to underscore that fact, Karadzic announced that EC recognition of Bosnia-Herzegovina would cause civil war. One week later, the United States recognized Croatia and Slovenia, and the stage was set for the worst fighting in Europe since World War II.

On April 6, 1992, exactly 51 years to the day after the Luftwaffe had attacked Belgrade, the European Union recognized Bosnia-Herzegovina as an independent nation. The United States followed suit one day later. In Sarajevo, the number of peace marchers swelled to 40,000, but now the Serb gunman were shooting to kill, and five people died after they opened fired on the April 6 march.

It was the EC/U.S. announcement that brought the war to Medjugorje. The air attacks on Siroki Brijeg and Citluk as well as the partial destruction of the bridge over the Neredva near Citluk were followed by a blockade of the roads leading to Mostar as well as the declaration of a separate "Serbian Republic of Bosnia Herzegovina" and the military forces in the area began exchanging fire. Battles flared in Bosanski Brod, Neum, Kupres, Tomislavgrad, and Banja Luka.

The reaction in Medjugorje was panic. The Church was closed for daily services for the first time since the apparitions began in 1981. On April 7, 1992, Rev. Ivan Landeka, pastor of St. James Parish at Medjugorje, denounced the bombing of Citluk and Sirioki Brijeg. In his letter he claimed that Alia Izetbegovic had sent a telegram to Serb! General Adzic, informing him that an attack on Siroki Brijeg amounted to an attack on all of Bosnia-Herzegovina, including Medjugorje. Izetbegovic reminded Adzic of Medjugorje's importance as a place of pilgrimage renowned throughout the world. Five days later, Ivan Dragicevic, the seer, sent a fax to George Bush, reminding him that "You yourself have said on one occasion, 'Back to the future!' According to the Blessed Mother's testimony, it is the peace itself, which we gain with faith and conversion, that is the future you talk about . So your words: 'Back to the Future!' means back to God who is in Christ 'Our Peace' (Eph 2:14)."

Father Leonard Orec, back from his exile in Germany and now involved in setting up an office that would funnel humanitarian aid to Medjugorje through an office in Split, sent off a fax to George Bush on April 12 as well, co-signing his letter with Father Slavko Barbaric. "We turn to you in the most tragic moment of the history of the Croatian people," the two priests wrote, forgetting for a moment that they were now citizens of a different country, "The war is finishing off our children, old folks, the churches, hospitals schools, kindergartens, mental hospitals, our cities and villages. We turn to you from Medjugorje, the village in which Our Lady is appearing for the eleventh year and is calling for peace....The war is now threatening us with total destruction. We appeal to you to do everything in your power to finish this war, in accordance with your democratic system."

Three days later, Anke Blasevic wrote to George Bush claiming that "complete extermination will happen soon, unless the world does something. As you read this, keep in mind that with every second there is not only one human life violently taken away here, but the number is increasing geometrically." Blasevic concluded her letter by saying that the U.S. and the EC "supported this aggression much more than just participating in it" by its "hesitation and slowness." Not to be outdone by the rhetoric of the rest of the Medjugorje team, Philip Pavich wrote to George Bush too, demanding that he used his office "to mobilize the world for the just cause of stopping World War III!" Pavich felt that the situation in Bosnia was much more serious than

Saddam Hussein's incursion into Kuwait and that it "demanded the appropriate intervention."

Pavich and the rest of the Medjugorje rectory staff then settled down to living under siege. Two small groups of American pilgrims, six from the Chicago area and 12 from Topeka, Kansas, along with English and Scottish pilgrims, were put on a specially chartered bus and sent off to Split. All planned pilgrimages were canceled, and from April 7, 1992, until June 24, the day before the 11th anniversary, the church was locked; the rectory was barricaded with sandbags, and the staff huddled in the basement, listening to the Yugoslav jets flying overhead and waiting for the bombs to drop. Pavich spent the first few nights in the basement, but eventually he began to miss his bed and telling himself and Fr. Petar Ljubicic that the air raid sirens would give them sufficient warning, resumed his normal sleeping habits. The Church, however, remained locked for two and a half months, and it was only a peace march from Humac to Medjugorje staged by a group of brave pilgrims on June 24 that got the Franciscans to open the Church again.

For a long time thereafter, the only people who visited Medjugorje were journalists who wrote stories about how the pilgrims were gone. On August 3, 1992, Lance Gay reported for the Scripps Howard News Service that "the droves of tourists who brought unprecedented prosperity to this valley have stopped coming." Ever the man to see a silver lining in every cloud, Slavko Barbaric told Gay that "there's some message for the world in the fact that that Yugoslavia's civil war started exactly 10 years after that afternoon of June 24, 1981, when six peasant children said they first saw a vision of the Virgin Mary on a hillside outside the town." Did this mean, perhaps, that the Queen of Peace had never been in Medjugorje? No, the meaning was different from that. In fact, the exact opposite:

"Now we have the best argument for the shrine and the apparitions," Slavko continued, evidently forgetting that at one time proof of the apparition's authenticity was the fact that ethnic groups were living in peace. "I think someone who knew something wanted to protect us. God didn't want this war, nor did our Lady. We should have accepted the impulses from the apparition."

During the course of his stay in Medjugorje, some unnamed source told Gay that "Pope John Paul II is backing the children's claims partly from his belief that the Virgin's intercession was responsible for the collapse of communism and partly from the religious revival Medjugorje was spurring." Years later, Philip Pavich would say much the same thing. "The pope supports Medjugorje, but the Vatican doesn't. The Pope is a phenomenologist. He revalidated Sr. Faustina after she had been banned for years. He got her canonized."

After 11 years of daily contact with the Queen of Peace, including prophecies of a great sign, ten secrets, and intimations of chastisement, the seers and their handlers seemed taken completely by surprise when war finally came to Bosnia. It seemed as if they had never listened to their own messages. How else is one to explain the thinly disguised panic that struck all of them? Perhaps the most hysterical response came from Jozo Zovko, who wrote a piece called "Stop Our Pain" in *Sloboda Dalmacija*. The seers did everything but say explicitly that the Queen of Peace was calling for air strikes against Serb positions. And even if they didn't say that explicitly it was the gist of their position.

The outside world, however, showed little interest in following their demands. On April 10, as Yugoslav jets screamed across Herzegovina on their way to targets west of Mostar, General Zivota Panic announced that the JNA would never withdraw from Bosnia-Herzegovina, as it had done from Slovenia, Croatia, and Macedonia, because 65 percent of its industry and military installations were located there. One day earlier, Cyrus Vance, UN special envoy to Yugoslavia, said that U.S. and EC recognition of Bosnia-Herzegovina had damaged the peace process.

The military were not keen on intervention either. In spite of the seers' letters, George Bush announced on July 2 that he was not ready to send U.S. troops to Bosnia. Secretary of Defense Cheney, echoing the views of his boss, said that "the situation doesn't merit a Desert Storm-like coalition. This is an internal civil war." Cheney was of course right, but international recognition of Bosnia-Herzegovina had turned the Serbs into an invading army, transgressing sovereign borders, even though Serbs like Radovan Karadzic and his supporters happened to live in the country they were ostensibly invading. Neo-Wilsonians like George Will could fulminate in his column that "Bosnia, an internationally recognized state, has been invaded," as he did on August 9, 1992, but it was precisely the fact that the Bosnian Serbs were fighting on their own territory for their own homes that gave the military pause when thinking about armed intervention.

As the pressure for military intervention mounted, the professional soldiers were warning that intervention in Bosnia would eventuate in "a quagmire worse than Vietnam." The Serbs, said one analyst "can be defeated but are never beaten," and as proof he indicated the 500-year guerrilla war which followed the Serb defeat at the Battle of Kosovo Pole in 1389. General Lewis Mackenzie, the Canadian who had commanded the UN peacekeeping force in Sarajevo announced in mid-August that it would take at least 79,000 troops just to control, occupy, and dominate all the features around Sarajevo alone. The main difference between Bosnia and Kuwait was the terrain, the characteristic which dominates every military operation. Yugoslavia was one of the most militarized places on earth, thanks to Tito's build-up in anticipation of a Soviet invasion. It was also a nation that had waged a guerrilla war against the Nazis, tying down 30 divisions in the process and contributing to a fatal delay in Hitler's invasion of the Soviet Union. Taking both aspects together, Mackenzie came up with a description of a people who inhabited "classic guerrilla country," and possessed, as well, the will to fight on for a long time.

"You're talking about backing the Serbs into a corner," Mackenzie warned. "And if you read history, it's not a very good idea. You're talking about an organization with a significant capacity to fight and with a significant amount of equipment. Serbia/Montenegro is one of the most densely militarized areas of the world now."

Hitler, Mackenzie reminded everyone, had failed to pacify Yugoslavia with 30 divisions, and so any realistic talk about occupying Bosnia-Herzegovina would require a million troops. The terrain favored mortar and artillery attacks from the heights surrounding the cities, and this sort of weapon was impervious to high tech air attack because it was so small and portable and could be easily hidden and carried around in everything from cars to school buses.

When asked who was to blame for the fighting, Mackenzie was more reticent to assign blame than the press, which was virtually unanimous in seeing Serbia as the villain of the story. "When people ask me whom do you blame, I say, 'Give me the day and the month and I'll tell you.' What the Serbs did three months ago was totally unacceptable," but on the other hand it was in the interest of the Bosnia presidency to "get the Serbs to retaliate in order to convince the international community that intervention is a good idea. So I blame both sides."

What struck Mackenzie the most, however, was the hatred. Mackenzie had served in Beirut and Somalia, but, as far as he was concerned, "You can take the hate from all those previous tours and multiply it by 10" to get a rough idea of the animosity that was fueling the war in Yugoslavia.

At the same time that the generals were saying that there was no military solution to the situation in Bosnia, the first atrocity stories started to trickle out and the term "ethnic cleansing" became part of the general vocabulary. All of this put pressure on President George Bush, the hero of the Gulf War, for an encore, but Bush was in the middle of a feckless re-election campaign against Democratic challenger Bill Clinton, who had no plan of his own but had the challenger's advantage of disputing the status quo. "The president," according to one account published in early August, "clearly has been stung by criticism of congress, including some Republicans, and presidential candidate Bill Clinton, who reiterated yesterday that force must be contemplated."

In the meantime, the parties involved in the civil war, seeing that no intervention was likely, decided to take matters into their own hands. The Croat-Muslim alliance came unglued in early July when Mate Boban, with the help of 30,000 armed followers, declared himself president of the republic of Herzeg-Bosna, the Croatian enclave in southwestern Bosnia-Herzegovina which included Medjugorje, naming Mostar its capital. The unilateral decision on the part of the Croats outraged the Muslims, who were, technically at least, their allies in the war with the Serbs. The Muslims denounced the move as treason, but the incident simply pointed up the chimerical nature of the "nation" of Bosnia-Herzegovina. It was a nation whose population swore allegiance to everything but itself. Boban had simply made explicit what everyone knew, namely, that that section of Bosnia-Herzegovina was really part of Croatia. "The creation of Herzeg-Bosna," according to one news account, "appears to further jeopardize any hope of creating an independent, multi-ethnic Bosnia from the former Yugoslav republic of 4.3 million people, where 44 percent are Muslim, 3 in ten are Serb and 17 percent Croat." Eventually Boban and his troops got their hands on high tech artillery from Germany and drove the Serbs from their positions on the hills surrounding Mostar, but not before some serious damage had been inflicted on the city.

On May 8, Bishop Zanic's palace, which sits prominently on the west bank of the Neredva across the street from the modern cathedral and on the road to Medjugorje at the southern end of the city, came under artillery fire and was destroyed. Zanic was forced to flee and eventually ended up in Rome, where in an audience with the pope, he asked to be relieved of his duties as bishop. As part of the interview, Zanic also asked to name his successor, and the pope, at this moment in no position to refuse a bishop who had been driven from his home by artillery fire, named Ratko Peric as the new ordinary of Mostar. If there was any *Schadenfreude* in Medjugorje over the fact that the bishop's palace was destroyed and St. James Parish untouched, it disappeared with the news that Ratko Peric was Zanic's successor, because Peric had the reputation of being every bit as skeptical as Zanic and more effective administratively in dealing with his critics. This silver lining definitely had a large cloud surrounding it.

One day later, the Franciscan parish of SS. Peter and Paul was also hit by artillery fire and burned to the ground. As a result the Franciscans had no place to celebrate Mass in Mostar. Since building a new church was impossible under these conditions, the Franciscans had to settle for a hall. The location of the hall would be the source of future problems because it lay squarely within the boundaries of one of the parishes where the clergy were loyal to the diocesan bishop.

This fact, combined with the administrative style of the new bishop, was guaranteed to cause problems later on.

While all this was going on in Mostar, half a world away, in Denver, Colorado, Teresa Lopez transferred from All Souls to Thomas More Parish. A month later she would travel to Russia with Bishop Hnilica to bring about that country's conversion. It was the beginning of much travel with the bishop.

Meanwhile, the press, having little to lose, continued to lobby for military action. "The sight of US warplanes and attack helicopters," opined the *Christian Science Monitor*, could have an effect of intimidation on Serb militia men, most of whom undoubtedly have never seen the frightening demonstration of what $25 million can buy in airpower."

Twenty-five million dollars was a lot of money for sure, but it was nowhere near what the war was costing Yugoslavia, up till that time Eastern Europe's most prosperous economy. Dusker Doder, writing for the *Boston Globe,* put the price tag at $40 billion as of June of 1992." There are unconfirmed reports," he continued, "that the Croatians have received soviet-made weapons from former Warsaw Pact members and have recently purchased advanced German artillery pieces, which they are using against Serbian forces in Bosnia-Herzegovina."

The outrage of the Muslims over the creation of Herzeg-Bosna by their erstwhile allies only underscored their impotence in terms of actual power in Bosnia-Herzegovina. Radovan Karadzic, meanwhile, continued to argue for a partition of Bosnia into two parts. "The Muslims," he explained, "are not an ethnic group or a nation in themselves but just a religious group. There is increasing support in Europe for the idea that Bosnia should be divided into two parts. It would be much better for the Muslims to start negotiations immediately."

What the Muslims did have on their side was the sympathy of the New World Order and the Muslim World and the world press, which seemed willing to ascribe anything bad that happened in Sarajevo and environs to the Serbs, in spite of the paucity of corroborating evidence, as in the case of the Water-Miskin Street massacre, that the Muslims perpetrated to blame the Serbs and thereby gain sympathy for their cause. One year later, Ejup Ganic, vice-president of Bosnia-Herzegovina, unwittingly described the situation. "Bosnia-Herzegovina could disappear within a month," he complained, "if the aggression continues and we don't get support." Bosnia-Herzegovina was ruled by people who couldn't control the country. It made Yugoslavia look stable by comparison.

On August 20, 1992, the Holy See recognized Bosnia-

Herzegovina as a sovereign state "with borders set more than 300 years ago," according to Bishop Peric. Seven days later, half a world away in South Bend, Indiana, Jim Jennings wrote a note to Michele Hardman. "I am so happy that we are now formally engaged," he told his new fiancee. "Let this time be holy and prayerful so that our marriage is holy and lasting." Jim had just purchased an engagement ring (on layaway), but his life was anything but holy or prayerful during the late summer of 1992. As Bosnia-Herzegovina descended further into a bloody civil war, the man who was fast becoming Medjugorje's most famous convert in the United States, was experiencing rapid deconversion. There was much wishful thinking in both instances. Calling Jim Jennings a living saint was a lot like calling Bosnia-Herzegovina a sovereign state. The error in both statements would soon become apparent.

Once he started doing cocaine again in the later summer of 1992, Jim Jennings was no longer a reformed criminal. He was what you might call a practicing criminal, now not using Medjugorje as the source of his conversion, but as a front for his even-more-recent deconversion. All of the talk about his conversion, as a result, was more than a little hollow, a fact which he knew better than his audience and a fact which fueled the need for psychic escape.

"Jim," according to Michele, "didn't like giving so many conferences. He felt pressured in that way. Denis was pushing him too hard. Denis wanted more than Jim could give him. Jim felt trapped. Because of what Denis had done for him, brought him into his home and everything, Jim felt like he owed it to Denis. But he hated flying. He felt like he didn't have a life of his own. He wanted his space, and he couldn't have it. He didn't like being scheduled in four and five states in one month. He didn't like flying to conferences, constantly being on and off planes. He wanted more time to himself, and he was like scheduled to do these things without having any say-so in it. It was like he was on a contract or something. That weighed heavily on him a lot."

Jennings was schooled enough in the ways of crime to know that he now needed protection of a more mundane sort than that offered by St. Louis de Montfort's consecration. So, on one of their drug runs, Michele watched as Jim stole a gun when the drug dealer left the room. Jim Jennings was now not only re-involved in criminal activity, he was also armed and dangerous, and especially dangerous to Michele Hardman. As his personality deteriorated under the influence of drugs, Jennings took to ordering Michele around at gunpoint. This included ordering Michele to perform sexual activity which she found repugnant at gunpoint as well. Medjugorje, in addition to being spiritually dubious, was now becoming life-threatening. Jennings may have been driven to cocaine as a confidence booster, since the burden of being a living saint on the Medjugorje speaker circuit had clearly become insupportable, especially since the beginning of his sexual relationship with Michele. Whatever the reason, Michele clearly dates the beginning of the end of their relationship to when Jim started using drugs in the late summer of 1992. During their last few months together, Michele dropped out of college and the two of them would move from one motel to another in and around South Bend. Michele would tie a belt around Jim's arm in an increasingly frustrating attempt to find a usable vein so that she could inject cocaine into his increasingly frazzled system. Before long, cocaine didn't help Jim deal with the psychic pressure either, and Jim in symbolic retribution against the forces that were troubling him went on a drug-fueled rampage in his townhouse, systematically smashing all of his statues of Mary and Jesus, shouting "Come on, Satan."

Denis Nolan would later claim that he was unaware of Jim's bizarre and increasingly violent behavior, an assertion contradicted by Michele Hardman, who remembers Denis and Jim fighting several times over the phone about money and the demanding regimen of talks Jim had to give. "At these conferences," Michele said, "Jim would feel powerful and come back home, [but] here Denis was the powerful one saying: 'Next week you've got to go to Missouri, and the week after that you've got to drive up to Chicago. Jim was being used. It was like a power struggle."

Denis Nolan also claimed that he was unaware that Jim and Michele were living together while he was sending Jim off to speak on the Medjugorje conference speaking circuit, an assertion that Michele contradicted again. "There is no way, " she said that Denis could not have known that she and Jim were living together, since he visited Jim's townhouse when she was there (hiding upstairs, albeit) but with her car parked outside.

Denis Nolan's lack of awareness came to an abrupt end on the night of October 14, 1992, when, now in the throes of his cocaine addiction, and so in need of some cash, Jim Jennings showed up at Queen of Peace Ministry headquarters with a gun and robbed Denis of around $2,000. Jennings was so high on drugs at the time that when he got back to the motel where he and Michele were staying, he announced that he had just shot a drug dealer and that they had to flee. Eventually she got to the truth of the matter, and after telling Jim that he hadn't killed a drug dealer— he had only stolen the money from Denis Nolan—Jim calmed down.

The calm didn't last long. A little over two weeks later, on Halloween 1992, Jim pulled out of the parking lot of the Stevens Motel just north of South Bend and headed south, leaving Michele without a fiancé and without a car. All in all Michele probably got the better part of the deal, but it didn't seem that way at the time. Calling her friend Jim Hassig, a South Bend police officer, for a ride, Michele, Hassig, and Nolan met at the headquarters of Queen of Peace Ministries, where Michele's account of the story, along with sessions of weeping and prayer, were taped for future use. Denis Nolan would later say that he never remembered the robbery, but when pressed admitted that Jim had hassled him because he "had not been taking his medication" for his "serious bipolar difficulty" and that they "ended up praying together." Nolan also did not remember the $2,000, although when his memory was jogged he did say that Jennings had left with "gas money" that night.

Jim Jennings then simply disappeared. Michele, in spite of everything, was still so impressed with Jim's religious fervor and eloquence that she became a Catholic in April of 1993, five months after he left. "I got baptized and became Catholic even though the relationship turned bad. He gave me my faith." Michele still admired Jennings's powerful talks.

"He was so stable in every area of his life, even in his past," she said later. "He was stable in his religion. He didn't back down on what he believed in. He was stable with his conferences. He had a home. I admired him so much. I really did. I didn't see any weakness in him. I think that is what I'm trying to say. He was so strong, and he believed in me. And I don't think too highly of myself, but he brought me out of that. He was a very strong person."

Michele thinks that drugs brought about Jim's downfall, but there are indications that other forces were at work as well. During September or October of 1992, Jennings asked Michele to call a conference in Minneapolis and cancel his speaking engagement. "He was bored," Michele said later. But then she added that he couldn't take the pressure of living up to an impossible ideal. The factors leading up to Jim's downfall were complex enough. He probably couldn't explain them any better than Michele did.

In June 1993 Jim called Michele to tell her that he still loved her, but that he had gotten married, nonetheless, to a woman named Catherine. He told her that she was better off without him, which was true enough, but something he should have thought of in the spring of 1992 instead of the summer of 1993. Jim had dumped Catherine and moved in with Michele, to whom he was engaged to be married on October 2, 1992. Michele had likewise dumped her boyfriend to move in with Jim. Then after leaving town, Jim decided to marry Catherine after all. The feeling of being used, the feeling that Jim had permanently wrecked her life overwhelmed Michele's new-found faith and shortly after the phone call, she attempted suicide.

During the summer of 1993, Jim surfaced in New Orleans, a

hotbed of Medjugorje activity in the United States. For a while he and Catherine lived in the home of Mimi Kelly, coordinator of the MIR Group, the Medjugorje organization which had sponsored Jennings's 1991 talk in New Orleans. Kelly later compared Jennings's deconversion to the type of disillusionment that came over the Medjugorje movement in 1991 when the Church failed to approve the apparitions. "It's kind of like following apparitions and getting so wrapped up in them that the visionary can do no wrong," she said later, "or all of a sudden the Church decided that this apparition is not real and you go, 'Oh my God, well, I'm not going to Church.'" Kelly claimed that Jim was not doing drugs during the summer and fall of 1993, but she failed to mention the fact that by leaving South Bend, Jim had violated his parole agreement and was in effect a fugitive from justice.

He probably could have gotten away with that too if he had kept his nose clean, but on October 9, 1993, Jim lured a man into his motor home and robbed him at knife point. The victim contacted the police, who apprehended Jennings on the same day. Three days later he was released on bond after his wife posted bail. It was only after he bonded out that the local police realized they had released a wanted man.

Again Jim might have escaped if it had not been for his penchant for the limelight. Jim was a compulsive confessor, and once he stopped frequenting sacramental confession and the Medjugorje circuit, he started calling up the talk shows. In early December of 1993 Jennings called into a live television talk show in New Orleans and, according to the show's host, admitted to "being one of the most sinful men on earth," whose derelictions included murdering eight drug dealers. In the course of his confession and a long rambling prayer to the Blessed Mother, Jennings inadvertently gave his first and last names, something which an astute policeman picked up, and on December 8, 1993, the Feast of the Immaculate Conception, Jim Jennings was back in jail again. On March 3, 1994, he was transferred to the Middle Tennessee Reception Center, where he will spend the next 15 years serving out the remainder of his prison term, after which he will return to Louisiana to serve his term for armed robbery. If there were a cautionary tale here, it was lost on the Medjugorje movement, whose insatiable desire for new speakers and new spiritual experiences resembled in an uncanny way Jim Jennings's craving for drugs. Unlike drug addiction, Medjugorje was contagious and spreading by human contact as the proliferation of conferences in the United States rose to meet the demand that was blocked when war shut down the pilgrimages. Michele Hardman wasn't the last person to get hurt in this business. Not by a long shot.

On June 14, 1992, right around the time that Jim Jennings got engaged to Michele Hardman but before he started using cocaine again, the Serbian siege of Mostar was lifted as a result of the combined efforts of the Croats and Muslims. The alliance had lasted since April, but the situation in Mostar deteriorated rapidly once the allies achieved their military goal. In August of 1992, Professor Salih Rajkovic, long-time resident of Mostar and a Muslim, started to notice some disturbing indications that even though the Serbs had been driven back, the war was far from over. Standing on the Splitska street, Rajkovic watched as black-uniformed HOS troops broke into the entry hall of number 17 and rounded up all of its Serb inhabitants. He was told that they were being taken to a HOS prison now housed in a former Yugoslav Army military hospital a hundred meters away. The HOS militia was the military wing of the "Party of Rights" of the same name. Founded by Dobraslav Paraga, it considered itself the true heir of the Ustasha, unlike the wishy-washy folks who belonged to the HVO. Eventually the distinction would become meaningless when the Croats turned on the Muslims and put aside their political differences in the name of ethnic solidarity.

Since the HOS wore uniforms modeled on the uniforms the SS wore during World War II, Rajkovic felt a sense of foreboding for his Muslim compatriots on the east bank of the Neredva River. Soon Muslims started disappearing from public life and the HVO started playing a Croat language version of "Lily Marlene," the famous Nazi song, over loudspeakers aimed at East Mostar. Then Rajkovic remembered his neighbor Milan returning with his face blue with bruises from a beating he had just received at the hands of the either the HOS or the HVO. By this point, as Mate Boban attempted to unify the Croats in preparation for his plan of ethnic cleansing following the declaration of statehood for the Croat enclave of Herzeg Bosna, it was hard to tell the difference. The Muslims, who had collaborated with the Croats, thought that the war ended in June of 1992 and started returning to their homes in East Mostar. What they failed to notice was that few Croats followed them back, even though there were many who lived there before the war.

On May 9, 1993, at 5:00 a.m., the HVO opened fire without warning on the east bank of the Neredva with artillery and heavy machine guns. What followed was a siege every bit as savage as the siege that devastated Sarajevo but one which received next to no publicity by comparison. East Mostar's Muslim inhabitants settled down to a summer in hell in the basements of the piles of rubbles that once had been their homes and businesses. Rajkovic now thinks that the "victory" of June 1992 against the Serbs was in reality nothing more than a strategic withdrawal on the part of the Serbs, who had made a secret agreement with the Croats to partition Bosnia between them. The Croats got the southwest; the Serbs got the northeast, and the Muslims got ethnically cleansed from Herzeg Bosna. As the Muslims on the east bank hunkered down to wait out the siege, those men unfortunate enough to be caught unawares on the west bank were rounded up, put into handcuffs, and marched off to the various Croat concentration camps surrounding Mostar. Rajkovic's uncle was sent to the Heliodrome concentration camp south of Mostar, where he was forced to dig trenches, build bunkers, bury the dead, and do in general any job the Croats felt was too menial. At certain crucial points, the Muslim prisoners were also used as human shields in front of advancing HVO troops.

Rajkovic was aware of Medjugorje for a number of reasons. At one point a group of Muslim prisoners was driven by in buses and told to lower their eyes because they were passing holy ground. Rajkovic, who was reduced to eating grass by the end of the siege of Mostar, kept thinking about the well-fed pilgrims staying in Medjugorje a little over ten miles away. He knew that they were leaving money there for war relief, and he knew that the Muslims were getting none of it. All the Muslims got were rockets from launchers set up near the Anna Maria Hotel in Medjugorje and handgrenades, built in a factory behind a pension on the way into town, and handcuffs. The case of the handcuffs was especially outrageous because they were bought with money raised for war relief by Bernard Ellis, an English steel magnate, convert and a philanthropist who collected money from unsuspecting English pilgrims and diverted it to buy handcuffs for the HVO, who used them in ethnic cleansing against the Muslims. In July 1995 Ellis announced that his Medjugorje appeal had already raised DM 100,000 and was hoping to raise another DM 400,000 in the near future. "The Trustees of this Charity," he wrote, "believe that we are called to show the innocent children of the war in Bosnia and Croatia the meaning of love and friendship, and that by doing this, people all over the world will be united in a desire to find the road which will lead us to peace." By 1997, three of the orphanage buildings for which Ellis had raised money in England had been built, but it was also clear by then that the children there were not really orphans. The most heavily used building in the complex was, in fact, a day care center, where women dropped off their kids and then went off to work in the village's various tourist shops and restaurants. In the fall of 1997, Bernard Ellis was suspended as a trustee of the Medjugorje Appeal.

By 1993, Medjugorje, according to Ed Vulliamy's account in *Seasons in Hell*, had become a junction for the black market and a base for the imminent ethnic cleansing of the Mostar region, a sleazy and disagreeable combination. In the souvenir shops, statuettes of the Madonna were on sale in trays next to others full of Swastikas, Maltese Crosses and other Nazi regalia. The HVO put out a verbal warning that anyone found sheltering Muslims in the Holy City would have their homes blown up (p. 261).

The contrast between what Medjugorje claimed to be and what it was struck Salih Rajkovic even more forcefully:

Refugees [in East Mostar] were with no clothes, food, home—anything. We can never forget the scene when we were sitting in the dark in our homes, and looking at the west Mostar which seemed to be untouched by the war—with electricity, food supplies, water and all other things. I can imagine how it was in Medjugorje, pretty far away from [the] confrontation line and from the war, where much of the aid was brought from the West.

Rajkovic would later say that the only thing the Muslims got from Medjugorje were hand-grenades which got manufactured there and which the HVO lobbed across the Neredva at them.

-12-

MARVIN KUCERA AND THE REFUGES

In October 1992, right around the time that Jim Jennings's career as a Medjugorje speaker was about to crash and burn in a cocaine-intoxicated conflagration, Steve Mahowald got a phone call from a man named Marvin Kucera. In 1990 Mahowald had founded a small apostolate which published a newsletter of limited circulation called *Catholic Commentary*, which dealt with information on the end times, an era whose arrival Mahowald felt was imminent. Wanting to reach a wider audience, Mahowald had taken the pertinent information from the newsletters and put them in a book called *The Great Chastisement*, volumes one and two. In the early summer of 1992, a priest by the name of Gabriel Anderson had picked up Mahowald's book at a local bookstore and, impressed with what he saw, met with Mahowald in person to compare notes about when the end times were going to arrive, a topic on which Anderson had done much research himself.

When Kucera called, he introduced himself as under Anderson's spiritual direction, a fact which made the call seem like something a little less out of the blue. The purpose of the call was to invite Mahowald to speak on Freemasonry and the Catholic Church at what Kucera was calling a "refuge," located in Winterset, Iowa, about 100 miles east of Omaha, Nebraska, where Mahowald lived. Refuges were places where loyal Catholics could go to weather the chastisement when it came. During the end times, which Kucera kept telling people were just around the corner, there would be natural disasters, things like California and Florida dropping into the ocean, but the real end times scenario Kucera was spinning had a lot more to do with the state of the Catholic Church. Kucera converted to Catholicism on Holy Saturday of 1990, and being a quick study, he could see that many people were upset with the state of the Church. The refuge movement was designed to play on those fears. During the final cataclysm, followers of Marvin Kucera could come to his refuges and not have to worry about things like altar girls or the validity of the sacraments as California fell into the sea and the New World Order's police force rounded up loyal Catholics for internment in concentration camps.

Kucera was no stranger to this area of the country. He had been born on a farm near Grand Island, Nebraska, in 1940 and had been back to Omaha as recently as May of 1992 to give a talk. The key to understanding Marvin Kucera's religious cult was Medjugorje. Marvin had gone there in February of 1991, and after returning, as was becoming almost predictable now, he too had begun hearing messages, not just from the Blessed Mother but from Jesus Christ and God the Father and a whole host of other spiritual entities of less exalted pedigree. Kucera had been to Medjugorje less than a month before Teresa Lopez had gone and started having apparitions of her own, so maybe it was in the air or the water. Either way, visions seemed contagious. It might have been the times though, because people who were con artists seemed to sense that at this moment a killing could be made off of frustrated Marian tourism.

Kucera's story was a combination of Teresa Lopez and Jim Jennings. Like Lopez he was having visions, but like Jim Jennings, he told a spiritual-rags-to-spiritual-riches story as well. Like Jim Jennings, Kucera claimed to have broken free of his drug addiction as the result of a spiritual conversion. In one unintentionally hilarious moment during one of his talks, Kucera reached into his pocket for his rosary and pulled out along with it a handful of pills, which spilled all over the floor in front of his audience. Kucera could have ignored the pills or said they were aspirin, but, attempting to regain his composure, he announced to the crowd that, "those are my pain pills," giving some indication that drug abuse was not completely a matter of Kucera's past.

Kucera claimed that he had been molested as a child—by women, he would add, so that he didn't feel comfortable with women—and his molestation, his audience was told, led him to take drugs, and the drugs led him to a divorce and that led him to the streets of San Francisco, where in 1979 he hit bottom. After waking up in a bed full of cockroaches, Kucera decided, "Lord, this isn't how you want me to live," and returned to Nebraska, where he decided to undergo therapy, which eventually freed him of his addiction. Because Kucera's therapy was so therapeutic, he decided to become a therapist himself and was working in that capacity up until 1988. "I was a counselor in 1988," he told his audience in Omaha in May of 1992, "thinking I would be a counselor for the rest of my life, but when the Lord wants you to move on, he kind of nudges you."

Also nudging Marvin at the time was the fact that he was about to be charged with molesting a 16-year-old boy who was under his care as counselor at the time. The sin of having homosexual relations with boys never got mentioned in any of Kucera's true-confessions talks, but the fact was substantiated by Chris Engel, one of his daughters, who also claimed that Kucera had molested her and her three sisters as well. Another daughter, Kathy Mead, told essentially the same story. Kucera, according to Mead, had sexual problems, in particular a fondness for young boys which got him into trouble when he was working at the Mary Lanning hospital in Hastings, Nebraska, in 1988. Rather than face charges for molesting a 16-year-old boy, Kucera simply disappeared, just as he had done when he abandoned his wife and four daughters in the '70s before heading out to San Francisco. Years after his second disappearance, Kucera suddenly showed up in Nebraska to be at his mother's funeral, and at that time he told Chris Engel that he had just gotten back from Mexico, where, according to his view, someone could hide forever, things being so cheap there. Mead also said that Kucera had molested all four of his daughters when they were four or five years old.

Steve Mahowald, of course, knew nothing about Kucera's troubled past when he agreed to speak at the refuge in Winterset, Iowa, nothing other than what Kucera himself had divulged during the talks he gave recounting his conversion and promoting the refuges. He certainly knew nothing about his troubled relationship with his daughters or his penchant for sexual activity with teenage boys. What Steve Mahowald did know, in addition to detailed information about the end times which both men found fascinating, is that he was having family troubles of his own. Mahowald's oldest son Mark, then 14 years old, had been a problem for the family for quite a while. He had a police record and had been diagnosed with Attention Deficit Disorder in April of 1992. After trying everything and after concluding that Mark was a bad influence on their seven younger children, the Mahowalds sent Mark to Boys Town in April 1992. Then in October, six months later, Mark got kicked out and returned home worse than before they had sent him. "We didn't know him when he came back," his father Steve said later, "he was mean, angry, and violent. He was 14 years old and out of control."

Then the Mahowalds remembered that Marvin Kucera's background was in counseling. "When we told him about Mark," Steve said, "Marv came right over that night. Then Mark and Marv went to the adoration chapel. After they came out, Marv said he had a message from the Blessed Mother, who said that Mark was supposed to go with Marv and live at the refuge."

It seemed like a good idea at the time. Father Burns,

Mahowald's spiritual advisor, had no objections. The move would allow Mark to get away from bad companions, at least those his own age, and besides if California happened to fall into the Pacific Ocean or the men in the black helicopters came to put a computer chip in his forehead, Mark would be safe. He could receive the Eucharist without interference from altar girls, and, of course, Marvin Kucera was there to counsel him. Whether he was safe from Marv Kucera was another matter but one that didn't concern either Mark or his parents at the time. When his mother asked Mark what he thought, Mark answered, "Mom, I think I'm supposed to go."

For the next several months, Mark would come home every two or three weeks. Then the visits became fewer and farther in between as Mark and Marvin hit the road to take advantage of the Medjugorje circuit, where he would meet pious middle-aged ladies and convince them that the only place they had a chance of surviving the coming chastisement was one of his refuges. In 1991 Kucera met a 50-year-old woman by the name of Leslie Militti at a Medjugorje conference in Omaha, where he had set up a booth. Mrs. Militti had been to Medjugorje and as a result of her conversation with Kucera, visited his refuge at Winterset, Iowa, where Kucera and his followers were in the process of building a church. Mrs. Militti then gave Kucera $35,000 to help complete the church, and eventually spent another $100,000 building a house on the refuge grounds, known now as the Refuge of the Sacred Heart, where she planned to weather the coming Chastisement. Mrs. Militti would have probably given Kucera a good deal more if her husband, an Omaha stockbroker, hadn't hired a private investigator first.

Right around the time the private investigator showed up at the refuge at Winterset, Mark and Marvin disappeared, claiming that someone was out to kill Marvin. From then on, the Mahowalds would hear reports of Mark and Marvin's travels not from their son but from Mahowald's various contacts throughout the country. "Someone would call and leave the phone number of where they were staying, " Mahowald said, "so I always knew where they were."

The Mahowalds weren't happy, but they weren't overly concerned either. During Easter of 1993, the Mahowalds too went to Medjugorje, where they could hear the Battle of Mostar in the background. It was a time when only the brave or the nutty would go there. While in Medjugorje, the Mahowalds met Sister Shirley and her entourage from Long Island. Mahowald suspects that Sister Shirley was a follower of Veronica Lueken, the "seer" of Bayside, New York, because she and her followers all wore the same light blue berets that the Baysiders wore. In addition to her light blue beret, Sister Shirley wore a nun's white habit under a red leather jacket. Shortly after her arrival,

Sister Shirley announced that she was gong to be transfigured on Good Friday while climbing Mt. Krizevac. Evidently, nothing happened. Eventually she and her followers got kicked out by the Franciscans for staying up all night and howling at the moon like demons.

In July of 1993 Mark was supposed to be in his sister Trish's wedding, and Marv was supposed to play the organ. Neither showed up for the rehearsals, and the family was increasingly concerned about Mark's absence and began wondering whether he would show up for the wedding at all. On the wedding day, the pair did show up finally, but both seemed to be there reluctantly and didn't seem to be part of the celebration. In August of 1993, the Mahowalds went to Disney World. Again Marvin and Mark came but both seemed stand-offish and there under protest. While in Florida, Steve noticed that all of the old anger and violence Mark had demonstrated after leaving Boys Town had returned. Whatever had happened there was happening again, but the Mahowalds still felt powerless to address it. In October 1993, the Mahowalds drove to Winterset to help raise the walls of the new chapel there. Everyone joined in and had a great time. But it was the last time they ever saw their son.

In August of 1991, Marvin Kucera attended the Medjugorje Peace Conference at the University of California Irvine campus. He remembers being so taken by a talk by a Father Steven Barham that he had an uncontrollable urge to go up and touch the man. Kucera was no stranger to uncontrollable urges involving strange men, but this time something unusual happened. Unable to get to the stage by normal means, Kucera would later claim that he had been carried from his seat in the back of the auditorium over the heads of the crowd by angels and deposited on the stage next to Barham.

Robert Stevenson attended the same conference, but he has no memory of a 51-year-old drug addict being borne across the hall by angels. He does, however, remember being impressed by the rest of the conference. Stevenson was 28 years old at the time, recently married and his own boss as head of a modest but adequate-paying business servicing photocopiers. Stevenson was a baptized Catholic, who had a moderately troubled youth. He attended Catholic grade school but began to rebel against his schooling and his family beginning in 8th grade. He attended a public high school for a few years but eventually dropped out and got a factory job. Sensing that the job was leading nowhere, Stevenson got his GED at night and then enrolled at a local technical college. At around the same time, which is to say in 1982, he experienced a conversion back to the Catholicism of his youth. This time around he realized that his training had been woefully inadequate and so started to slake his spiritual thirst by becoming involved in a youth to youth retreat movement sponsored by St. John Vianney, his local parish. It was on one of these retreats in 1987 that he met a young woman, five years his junior, by the name of Suzanne Kozak. Two years later, Robert and Suzanne got married, over the objections of Robert's mother, who felt that the Kozak family was dysfunctional even by California standards. Suzanne's mother had left her husband after 25 years of marriage and moved in with another man, and Suzanne herself had a drinking problem, perhaps as a result of that trauma, but marriage seemed to smooth everything out, at least at the beginning.

The spiritual hunger that brought the couple together at a retreat hadn't abated either. Robert's parents were active in the charismatic movement in Southern California, and so it was almost inevitable that in the late '80s, right around the time he was going to get married, Robert started hearing about a village in Yugoslavia where six children claimed to have daily contact with the Blessed Mother. Robert had attended charismatic conferences, sponsored by the Southern California Renewal Communities, with his family and would eventually get a contract to service their photocopiers, but gradually over the '80s and into the '90s, charismatic conferences became Medjugorje conferences, and in August 1991 at Irvine, Robert made his first contact with the movement.

At first it seemed as if the Irvine conference was just like all of the other charismatic conferences, although in retrospect Stevenson felt that it wasn't as prayerful and was more focused on the speakers and what they had to say. Stevenson remembers listening to Father Ken Roberts and not liking him very much, as well as a priest from Medjugorje whose name he couldn't remember. The war had just broken out in Yugoslavia, although it had yet to spread to Bosnia-Herzegovina, but the fundraising for war relief was moving into high gear.

Suzanne didn't attend the Irvine conference. She was busy getting a degree in nursing, graduating in 1991 and then getting a job at Intercommunity Hospital. At around the same time, Robert's business started taking off, and so the couple borrowed money from his parents and bought a $130,000 tract house in Chino Hills. Perhaps because of her background in nursing, Suzanne decided to become involved in teaching Natural Family Planning with Robert at the parish they attended. On November 30, 1992, the Stevensons had their first child, a girl they named Marie. Although he was worried about his wife's previous drinking problem, Robert was relieved to see her get through the birth without *post partum* depression. As 1993 approached, the Stevensons were a little stressed because of the long hours both of them were working, but the money was coming in, and everything seemed fine.

The spiritual hunger persisted though, and given the times and the charismatic inclinations of Robert's family, it was a sure thing that Medjugorje was going to fill it. Robert had attended the Irvine conference with his father and came home to his wife full of enthusiasm about what he had learned. The war had started in Yugoslavia, but the Franciscan from Medjugorje described how the war hadn't touched the village. Planes would fly over and drop bombs on the Church, but the bombs wouldn't explode. The village had started taking in refugees. The Franciscans needed money to take care of them.

Suzanne was mildly interested in all of it, but too busy with her life to get very involved. Robert, on the other hand, started buying books and making plans to go to other conferences. He wanted to find out everything there was to know about these miraculous occurrences. He remembers listening to Wayne Weibel at one of the conferences and then buying his book and passing it around to all of his friends. The Stevensons then heard about the miracles at Scottsdale, Arizona, and, knowing they were somehow connected to Medjugorje, Robert and Suzanne drove down for a visit. They then bought books on Scottsdale, which Father Jack Spalding was cranking out on a regular basis, and started passing them out to their friends as well. The upshot of all this was the creation of a community of believers which began to have very definite ideas about the signs of the times and the course of future events, all based on some very erroneous premises. The Catholic Church seemed helpless to respond in any effective way, partially because it had been weakened by its association with liberalism. The people who had attended parochial schools with its defective catechesis were now easy pickings for the unscrupulous who seemed to offer a much more fervent alternative. Marian devotion had all but ceased to exist as a part of parish life after Vatican II, and now the repressed was returning with a vengeance. But beyond that, the Church seemed befuddled and powerless to see Medjugorje as a problem. If the pope after all had said that if the people pray, let them go (a fact which was disputed a number of times by the papal nuncio to the United States), then why should parish priests object at these manifestations of piety? Parish priests, after all, were often leading the pilgrimages there themselves.

Before long, the Stevensons were wondering whether they too should go to Medjugorje. Both Robert and Suzanne wanted to go, but both realized that they had neither the money nor the time, and so the idea of a pilgrimage passed. But the curiosity about the supernatural happenings that seemed to have spread to the United States continued to grow.

In 1992 there was a follow-up Medjugorje conference in Southern California, and this time Robert attended with his wife, along with over 15,000 people who packed the Anaheim Convention Center to listen not to just speakers, although Fr. Ken Roberts was there again, this time brandishing a rose that had allegedly been kissed by the Blessed Mother; this time the seers showed up too. Ivan was there, and so was Vicka, whom Robert remembers as smiling a lot. Ivan Dragicevic spoke through an interpreter, and then off in a side room had his vision, which got relayed to the crowd. Medjugorje was really big, bigger now that the mountain had come to Mohammed. Bringing the seers to the United States generated much more disposable income for the people organizing the conferences than did pilgrimages, which had much higher fixed overhead costs in terms of flights and hotel accommodations. The people who ordinarily would have laid out between $1,000 and $2,000 for a trip to Yugoslavia were now not traveling because of the war, and to their numbers were added much larger numbers of people like the Stevensons, who couldn't afford a flight to Yugoslavia but were willing to buy a book or a video.

And Robert Stevenson was buying lots of books. His wife was working 12-hour shifts at the hospital and then coming home to care for their infant daughter and soon-to-arrive infant son at their dreary little tract house with the postage-stamp yard in Chino Hills. Suzanne soon realized that the work was too much. When she started working part-time, Robert took up the slack by working longer hours, but even that didn't dull his appetite for spiritual titillation. One day in 1993 he walked into a local Catholic bookstore and picked up a copy of a book called *Three Days of Darkness*, a depiction of soon-to-happen events, complete with scary demon on the cover that, in Stevenson's words, "scared the living snot out of me." Each book Robert read seemed to up the spiritual ante according to the following dynamic: "So you call yourself a serious Catholic? Do you have your blessed candles ready for the time when blood starts running in the streets and those who don't have holy curtains in their homes will die of fright when they look out their windows?" Playing on the sense of dissatisfaction the devout felt with conventional devotional and liturgical practice in Catholic parishes, the Medjugorje movement would egg them on to acts of supererogation that were leading them subtly out of the church and into the clutches of con men, phony seers, and leaders of dooms-day cults.

"After I read that book," Stevenson recounted later, "I said give me more of that stuff." In retrospect he sees it as a kind of "self torture" as well as spiritually titillating. "It scared me into living my faith more seriously, going to confession more, praying more, praying the rosary." What Stevenson didn't see at the time was that all of the pious exercises he incorporated into his life didn't necessarily lead to a deepening of the faith or closer union with the Church. In fact, they meant the exact opposite. The emphasis in the books on signs and wonders was the exact opposite of faith. Stevenson was following his misguided piety away from the Church.

The substitution of experience for faith is not without its dangers, and anyone familiar with the full sophistication of Catholic thinking on the matter would know that. No one could claim that St. John of the Cross was either a rationalist or a modernist. He was no stranger to mystical phenomena, and yet his writings are full of warnings about the dangers associated with them. Concerning certain "figures and forms of persons belonging to the life to come, the forms of certain saints, and representations of angels, good and bad, and certain lights and brightness of an extraordinary kind," St. John of the Cross is abundantly clear:

> [W]e must never rely upon them or accept them, but must always fly from them, without trying to ascertain whether they be good or evil; for the more completely exterior and corporeal they are, the less certainly are they of God. It is more proper and habitual for God to communicate to the soul, where there is more security and profit than to the senses wherein there is ordinarily much danger and deception; for bodily sense judges and makes its estimate of spiritual things by thinking they are as they feel to be; whereas they are as different as is the body from the soul and sensuality from reason. For the bodily sense is as ignorant of spiritual things as is a beast of rational things, even more so.
>
> So he that esteems such things errs greatly and exposes himself to great peril of being deceived; in any case he will have within himself a great impediment to attaining spirituality. For, as we have said, between spiritual things and all these bodily things there exists no kind of proportion whatever. And thus it may always be supposed that such things as these are more likely to be of the devil than of God; for the devil has more influence in that which is exterior and corporeal, and can deceive a person more easily thereby than by that which is more interior and spiritual. . . . The devil knows how to insinuate into the soul a secret satisfaction with itself. . . . These representations and feelings, therefore, must be always rejected; for, even though some of them be of God, He is not offended by their rejection, nor is the effect and fruit

which he desires to produce in the person by means of them any the less surely received because they are rejected and not desired.

St. John of the Cross is very clear on the matter. Signs and wonders are a danger to faith. They can lead to a kind of spiritual gluttony, and, therefore, "The soul . . . must never desire to receive them, even though they be of God." The Spanish mystic then goes on to enumerate six problems that flow from the desire to receive these extraordinary manifestations of the supernatural:

> The first is that faith grows gradually less. . . . Secondly, if a person does not reject them they hinder his soul so that it cannot soar to the invisible . . . . Thirdly, the person becomes attached to these things and does not advance to true resignation and detachment of spirit. . . . Fourthly, inward spirituality is decreased. . . . Fifthly, the person begins to lose the favors of God since he accepts them as though they were due him. . . . Sixthly, a willingness to accept them opens the door to the devil. . . . It is always well, then, that a person should reject these things and close his eyes to them whenever they come. Unless he does so, he will prepare the way for those things that come from the devil and will give him such influence that, not only will his visions come in place of God's, but his visions will begin to increase and those of God to cease in such manner that the devil will have all the power and God will have none. . . . For by the rejection of evil visions, the errors of the devil are avoided, and by the rejection of good visions no harm is offered to Faith and the soul harvests the fruit of them.

"The devil," St. John of the Cross concludes, "rejoices greatly when a person desires to receive revelations."

Stevenson shared *Three Days of Darkness* with his wife, who told him that she didn't like the "scary stuff," but that didn't deter him on his spiritual quest. At some point during 1994, Robert Stevenson picked up a copy of *Signs of the Times Magazine*, a sort of clearinghouse for apparitions and end-time mumbo-jumbo throughout the world. *Signs of the Times* was published by Ted and Maureen Flynn, who seeing potential in the end-times market, brought out a book of their own, called *The Thunder of Justice*. "I thought it was the greatest book of all times," Stevenson said later. *Thunder* was a mish-mash of all of the contemporary apparitions from Medjugorje to Father Gobbi. It quoted mystics and their prophecies and ladies from South America.

Edward N. (Ted) Flynn had been associated with an earlier religious cult called Apostolatus Uniti, which as Bishop Hnilica would try to do at a later date, aspired to bring all of the Marian apostolates under its umbrella. Apostolatus Uniti staged a conference at which their leader announced that he was getting personal directions from the Blessed Mother, at which point the non-apparitionites in attendance all jumped ship. AU then went belly up when the father-in-law of its director ran out of money. All of this is omitted from the Flynns' web page (Maxkol.org) which got advertised in the neocon journal *Crisis*, whose track record also includes promoting Mother Angelica and Nancy Fowler's phony apparitions in Conyers, Georgia, another Medjugorje spin-off. "Ted," we are told, "has extensive business experience in Ukraine, Belarus, and Eastern Europe. He has managed media ventures and humanitarian assistance projects throughout the world. He has traveled and worked in fifty countries. A graduate of the University of Massachusetts and American University, he has also studied economics at the London School of Economics and the University of Fribourg, Switzerland. He has been very involved in prolife activities for the past 18 years, has studied Marian apparitions for 12 years, and has visited many of the apparition sites."

Sister Philip Marie Burle knew both the Flynns and Mother Angelica and witnessed the effect that the Medjugorje movement and its millions of dollars had on them first hand. She was also on the board of John Downs's Apostolatus Uniti Foundation but left in disgust after it became apparent that he was being manipulated by mystics and squandering his in-laws considerable fortune in the process. "Every time he had to make a decision," she recalled, "he would ask one of his mystics to ask the Blessed Mother what he should do." John Downs is now divorced and living in Baltimore, and in the late '80s and early '90s, Maureen Flynn worked for Downs but wasn't making any money, and Ted was annoyed.

"Then suddenly they had all this money," said Sister Philip Marie. "They were promoting all sorts of shady people, people like Fr. Valentine, who was involved in spiritism, and Vassula." Before long, they had a show on Mother Angelica, but their influence with Mother Angelica went far beyond their own show.

Sister Philip Marie used to be close to Mother Angelica and was a frequent guest on her program, but that relationship came to an end at some time in 1993, right around the time that Robert Stevenson picked up his first copy of *Signs of the Times Magazine*. Sister Philip Marie also used to give retreats at the Monastery connected with EWTN, but around the same time stopped getting invited back and now can't get Mother Angelica on the phone when she calls. Sister Philip Marie used to appear on *Mother Angelica Live* with a priest by the name of Father Michael McDonough, but trouble started when they blew the whistle on Fr. Steven Barham, the man who so impressed Marvin Kucera at the 1991 Medjugorje Conference in Irvine, California. Kathleen Long, who ran the Medjugorje conferences in Chicago, got on his case because of Sue Eck, the editor of *Medjugorje* magazine. Sue Eck felt he was imitating Father Ken Roberts.

Sister Philip Marie, however, had known Barham long before that. Barham, according to her account, was involved with Silva Mind Control during the '60s and '70s. He tried to plagiarize their writings and as a result had to leave the country because they were after him legally. While in Canada he met a Melkite bishop and persuaded the bishop to ordain him without going to the seminary. Barham came from an Assembly of God background and had many full-gospel ministers in his family.

In the late '70s, Sister Philip Marie met Barham, who expressed a desire to accompany her to the Philippines, where she was going to conduct retreats. Sister said that he would have to produce documents; he said this would be no problem. Eventually he showed up at the airport with a broken leg and no documents, ready to embark on the plane. Sister claims that his leg was healed as a result of her prayer, but because of the confusion—he just produced some Xeroxed copies of something or other—he ended up going to the Philippines without papers. While over there he attended only Assembly of God services and because of his failure to produce documents could not function as a priest. Ann Waters, who does Father Ken Roberts's writing for him, felt that Roberts was deceived by him and deceived by Medjugorje in general and thinks Barham's documents were forged, although Melkite Patriarch Maximus V, after getting some money from Barham, eventually issued a statement accepting his ordination.

Sister Philip Marie characterized Barham as the most divisive person she ever met. He was very interested in going on TV; but was not going to Mass at the time. He was a glutton, grossly overweight, something she attributes to a demon. When Sister got back to L.A. in 1981 she reported him to the Archdiocese. After Father George Maloney of the L.A. archdiocese refused to grant faculties to Barham in Los Angeles, Barham then asked him if he would teach him what he should have learned in the seminary. Eventually Barham's desire to be a TV star landed him with Santa Fe Communications, where Harry John, scion to the Miller beer fortune, got taken in by him. Keith Bower, who also worked for Santa Fe Communications during the early '80s, remembers Barham as someone constantly involved in political intrigue as well as the sabotage of TV scripts that were orthodox. Eventually the pope intervened in the Harry John case, and Barham escaped from the wreckage of Santa Fe Communications to the then-rising Medjugorje movement.

In either '86 or '87, Mother Angelica made contact with the rich manufacturer of farm machinery from Holland through Sister Burle. He was interested in evangelization and was a supporter of Medjugorje. Like many other wealthy people, he was taken in by the mystics and their handlers and eventually was declared incompetent by his family after losing a good deal of money.

Another woman who was a close friend of Mother Angelica but then watched the friendship fade as EWTN got more deeply involved in promoting Medjugorje was a Sudeten German émigré by the name of Anna Maria Schmidt. In 1989 both Schmidt and Mother Angelica were in Rome in the midst of trying to get EWTN's short-wave radio station off the ground when they met a Czech bishop who offered to be of assistance. The bishop's name was Paolo Maria Hnilica. Schmidt remembers the bishop as having a split personality. He was fawning to Mother Angelica but overbearing to Schmidt and soon became rude and nasty. It became obvious to Schmidt that his offer to help with the short-wave station, which was then located at Algata outside Rome, was really an attempt to take control of it. Schmidt, who speaks both German and Czech as a result of her Sudetenland heritage, then told Hnilica that he spoke Czech with a Russian accent, at which point he flew into a rage. When Mother Angelica saw his reaction, she concluded that he was not a friend of the Church and decided to have nothing to do with him. Schmidt remembers that Hnilica was in trouble with the law at the time and was claiming that Cardinal Casaroli had bailed him out. She now thinks that he was a KGB agent.

"Hnilica told mother he had been ordained behind the Iron Curtain, but we knew that he spent his time extracting money from people. He is a dangerous man. He was awaiting trial at the time and eventually was convicted around 1992. Hnilica offered to run the station for mother when she was in America. His assistant told Mother that he would like to move in with her two secretaries. I told mother, 'he's trying to get hold of the station.' She threw him out around '92. He goes after every seer. It smells. He's not a priest. He's KGB."

Asked how she knows this, Schmidt replied, "Because of his actions. I've seen the KGB in action, and he's like them. He's a predator. This was in '89 before the wall came down, when there was still a KGB. The short-wave tower's now in Birmingham."

Anna Marie Schmidt also noticed a change in Mother Angelica's attitude toward Medjugorje, but this time the outcome was not so happy. Schmidt remembers the Dutch businessman who supported Medjugorje but can't say if supporting it were one of his conditions for supporting EWTN because she wasn't in on those private meetings.

"Mother originally didn't support Medjugorje, then she changed her mind," Schmidt said. "Mother didn't support Medjugorje in the '80s. When Marija came to Birmingham for her kidney transplant in '88, she told mother to come over and investigate. Mother said, 'no way I'm going down there.' Mother said she had the Eucharist in the tabernacle and didn't need porchlights going on and off to tell her that the Blessed Mother was appearing."

Over the years, Schmidt gradually lost her influence with Mother Angelica. "I wanted to be her friend. I don't know what happened. We drifted apart and she became a different person. I loved her. She was a beautiful and holy woman. Mr. Steltenmeyer is running things now."

"Originally Mother [Angelica] said she would never have anything to do with any unapproved apparition," Sister Philip Marie recounted later, "but then the Flynns got involved and then Michael Brown and then she was promoting Medjugorje."

It was at precisely this point in time that Robert Stevenson made contact with *Signs of the Times Magazine*. Suzanne was curious but uninvolved compared to Robert, who was now taking to going out into their tiny back yard and announcing, "All this is going to be ours." He was referring, of course, to the aftermath of the chastisement, which he and his family, with the help of Ted Flynn's magazine, were going to survive on their way to becoming large landowners. One of the first and most significant effects of the coming chastisement was that the Stevensons, being part of the loyal remnant which would be saved as a result of the holy candles they had stockpiled, would get a much larger back yard.

"I was half serious and half joking," he said later. "It was being embedded in my brain."

It was also having an effect on Suzanne, who was getting tired of just talking. During the summer of 1994, she told her husband that it was time they stopped going to the conferences and start living the messages. It was time, in short, to start getting serious about what they were hearing. Shortly thereafter, Robert was at SCRC headquarters servicing a copier when he stumbled across another book, a little white one called *In the End My Immaculate Heart Will Triumph*. It was co-authored by Teresa Lopez and Bishop Paolo Maria Hnilica.

"This is what did it to us," Stevenson said later. "Perhaps it's a curse. That was the baby that did it. Other people who moved to refuge had done this same book."

Ardie Kronzer did the same consecration at around the same time. It was as if there were a series of steps following a demented logic that led a whole group of people at the same time off the edge of the same cliff. In early 1995, shortly after kneeling down by the bed and doing the 33-day Hnilica/Lopez consecration, Robert Stevenson was poring over *Signs of the Times Magazine* looking for new visionaries, an activity which he characterized later as part of his "stupid hobby" but might be more accurately described as a spiritual addiction or obsession, when he came across a book he wanted to order. While ordering the book, the woman at the other end of the line advised him that the new hot book was something called *My Heart Awaits You* by Marvin Kucera.

The Flynns have since then attempted to distance themselves from Kucera, but the fact of the matter is that they were actively promoting him at the time. The first quarter 1995 issue of *Signs of the Times* has an article entitled, "A prophet for Our Time: A Review of *My Heart Awaits You*" by Marv Kucera, on p. 19, which all but tells the reader to buy the book:

> The Church, Marv is told, will soon split. This split will lead to despair. For God cannot continue to shower his graces in a world that tears His son's body once again. In particular Jesus warns Marv of earthquakes and famine, political unrest and economic collapse.

"But some of the advice is immensely practical," the review continued.

> Marv reports that he has been commissioned by the Lord to set up twelve refuges where the faithful can find peace and security during the time when destruction is unleashed upon our land. Some of these refuges already exist: The refuge of the Sacred Heart in Winterset, Iowa; the faithful and true refuge in North Haverhill, NH; the refuge of the Holy Eucharist in Mineral Point, WI, and the refuge of Juda in Hotsprings , SD. Other refuges are operating, but remain hidden because of their enemies. A few have yet to be built.

The review in *Signs of the Times* endorsed not just the book; it also endorsed the communities described in the book and all but invited its readers to join.

"It is the practicality of Marv's mission that makes it so unique," the review continued. "He is not only describing the evil we see all around us. He also claims he has a role in combating it."

The review concluded by telling *Signs of the Times* readers, "You won't find better marching orders," and letting them know that the book was "available from *Signs of the Times*." A full page ad for *My Heart Awaits You* appeared in the same issue of *Signs of the Times*, informing the credulous that: "The trials will be intense: Earthquakes, tidal waves, and soldiers killing and plundering as in wars past" and then telling them to place an order with their Visa, Master, or Discover card "today."

Which is just what Robert Stevenson did.

"I read it right away when I got that sucker," Stevenson said later. "This book hit me harder than any other one I had read. Spiritually speaking the key factor in our getting duped was the Teresa Lopez book. I was looking for this end times shit. I was sucking this shit in like a vacuum cleaner because I'm looking for it."

But the Kucera book was different, "It spoke of doing something. It spoke of refuges. It gave the impression that the chastisement was real close. I felt I have to be a part of this somehow."

Kucera's book had the phone numbers of the various refuges listed in the back. It was a temptation too great to resist. In early 1995, Robert called the Judah Refuge in Buffalo Gap, South Dakota, and Marvin Kucera answered the phone.

-13-

ETHNIC CLEANSING AND THE GOSPA

In a conversation with Elfried Lang-Pertel, of *Medjugorje Gebetsaktion* out of Innsbruck, Austria, Father Petar Ljubicic made the startling announcement that he had known about the war which was then tearing Yugoslavia apart "ten years ago," which is to say in 1983, because Mirjana mentioned it to him in Tihaljina. "The Mother of God said to me," Ljubicic said relating Mirjana's words to him, "[that] Croatians and Slovenes will be free (and that means Bosnia-Herzegovina too), but first a war will come. Afterwards, they will obtain liberty, and everything which this implicates."

Father Ljubicic's seemingly glib statement raises many interesting questions about things like fate and free will and the responsibilities of those who allegedly have knowledge of the future. If I know for certain that a little girl will be run over by a truck tomorrow in front of my house, what responsibility do I bear in preventing her death? Or does this knowledge prevent any action whatsoever and so leave the person who knows it the helpless victim of fate? And if that is the case, then what point does prayer have? If it cannot change future events, then what is the point of praying?

None of these questions seem to have troubled either Father Ljubicic or Mirjana, nor did their sudden revelation that they had known about the coming war for 10 years have much effect on events which were then just a few weeks in the future. After the Croats drove the Serbs from the heights around Mostar and set up the independent "republic" of Herzeg-Bosna, they then set about to ethnically cleanse Serbs from the surrounding area. The Serb section of Zitomislic, not far from Medjugorje, was completely obliterated and along with it the Serbian monastery there, which in 1986 had a plaque on its wall commemorating the massacre at Surmanci. As a result of the ethnic cleansing, 50,000 Bosnian Muslims moved into the empty apartments and housing in Mostar. By April of 1993, it was clear to just about everyone involved in the area, except Mirjana and Father Ljubicic, that trouble was brewing again. April 5, 1993, was the first anniversary of the siege of Sarajevo, and Germany, so avid to recognize the breakaway republics in '91 and '92, seemed to be having second thoughts now when confronted with the carnage the Serbs had wrought in Sarajevo.

On April 6, Mate Boban, the man who created Herzeg-Bosna, issued an ultimatum to Bosnia (i.e, Muslim) Army forces in southwestern Bosnia-Herzegovina, telling them that they had until April 15 to withdraw from Croat-dominated areas. Otherwise the HVO [Croatian Defense league] would unilaterally impose its authority on Croat regions like Herzeg-Bosna, which had proclaimed Mostar its capital, even though it had a significant Muslim population, which had grown even more significantly in recent months. Since Boban had the backing of Franjo Tudjman, the move was seen as the first step toward partitioning Bosnia-Herzegovina into Croat and Serb enclaves, a move which Tudjman and Milosevic had supported all along. This would of course have meant the end of Bosnia-Herzegovina as an independent, which is to say officially multicultural but unofficially Islamic, country, and so it is not surprising that the decision was followed by a war. The Croats claim that the 50,000 Muslims in Mostar were given explicit orders from Alia Izetbegovic to attack, but news reports at the time made clear that in order to comply with the HVO demands, the Bosnian troops in Mostar would have to abandon their homes, something they found clearly unacceptable. "In a few days there will be a war between the HVO and the Bosnian army," a Croatian electrician by the name of Ivice Antic announced on April 7.

Evidently electricians knew things the Gospa didn't. In spite of knowing about the war 10 years in advance, Father Petar Ljubicic did nothing to warn their countrymen or Mate Boban that war was imminent again, a mere two months in the future. Whatever the reason, by May of 1993 the Croats and the Muslims were involved in vicious house-to-house fighting all along the west bank of the Neredva in Mostar. At this point, Bishop Zanic's residence came under fire again. Three hundred Croatian soldiers were killed in the fighting, which destroyed the west bank area. One can imagine Ljubicic and Mirjana not warning Bishop Zanic, and indulging in a bit of *Schadenfreude* when his residence was destroyed and Medjugorje remained untouched, but what about the 300 Croatian soldiers, a group which would figure significantly in subsequent events in Mostar? Didn't Mirjana and Father Ljubicic have a responsibility to tell the HVO, whose efforts they supported, about the impending battle and thus minimize casualties? Or is there a simpler explanation here?

Throughout May rockets from the copse of trees between the Hotel Anna Maria and the main road out of Medjugorje lit up the night sky as they made their way to the Muslim quarter of Mostar, or as close to its target as missiles of this sort can be aimed. Franjo Tudjman showed up in Medjugorje for peace talks in May and while there announced that the Gospa's appearance in May of 1981 had presaged and ignited the "reawakening of the Croatian nation." The 300 young men who died in the fighting during this period gradually became folk heroes, and their pictures were enshrined in a new church, which the Croatians created out of a meeting hall, a church which did not have the approval of the local bishop.

Eventually the Croats drove the Muslims across the Neredva, and, in one of the cultural tragedies of this war, blew up the eponymous old bridge which gave Mostar its name on November 9, 1993. As the Stari Most, the 400-year-old white stone bridge collapsed into the azure waters of the Neredva River under a barrage of Croatian artillery shells, cheering went up on the west bank. The HVO considered the bridge part of the Muslim influence in Mostar, and no matter how beautiful the rest of the world considered it, they were happy to see it go.

Since the American press and the White House were determined to blame everything bad that happened in Bosnia-Herzegovina on the Serbs, reports to the contrary were few and far between, but gradually word began to emerge about what was happening in Croat-controlled enclaves. In September of 1993 Gradska, a predominately Muslim village near Medjugorje, was ethnically cleansed and most of the buildings were razed. The Franciscans, who used to be supporters of peace when the Communists were in power, were quick to have the Gospa side with the Croatians involved in the ethnic cleansing. "This area was once all Croatian," Jozo Zovko explained to a reporter who traveled to the now pilgrimages village of Medjugorje, "and now it will be again. Gospa wanted it that way."

Reporters who traveled to the home of Our Lady, Queen of Peace, were disturbed by other aspects of the war. The HVO could fight with the more radical right-wing HOS over who deserved the Ustasha mantle handed down from World War II, but it was clear that by 1993, the Croatians had attracted neo-Nazis from throughout the world to fight on their side in the civil war in Bosnia. The HOS had taken to wearing SS-style black uniforms, and HOS leader Dobraslav Paraga was saying the Drina should run red with Serb blood. Journalists who made it to Medjugorje found that the shops which were still selling rosary beads were also now selling swastika pins. On September 26, 1993, Chuck Sudetic, writing for the *New York Times*, reported that "Croatian soldiers in the region often pin rosaries to their uniforms along with Nazi swastikas or symbols of the Ustasha, the fascist movement that ruled Croatia and most of Bosnia during the nazi occupation in World War II."

"That's our tradition here," said one soldier on his way to the front. "It's a sign that this Croatia is a state. Only real Croats wear the Ustasha pin." When asked for his thoughts on the symbols for sale in the gift shops of Medjugorje, Rev. Drago Tolj, OFM, stationed at St. James Parish across the street, plucked a swastika-clutching eagle from the gift shop display case and told Sudetic, "These symbols are a disgrace to Croats everywhere." Tolj, who was the Franciscan superior at Medjugorje, had been asked earlier if Franciscans could be allowed to carry sidearms, and had refused the request claiming that it contradicted the charism of the Franciscans. Not so clear is whether using Medjugorje pilgrimage money to purchase arms, specifically artillery, contradicted the charism of the Herzegovina Franciscans. The Spanish officers assigned by the UN to defend Mostar were always puzzled about the arrival of the high-tech artillery that drove the Serbs from the heights surrounding Mostar in 1992. Other sources claimed the Franciscans were involved in the purchase.

Whatever the explanation, Medjugorje had come a long way from the days when the sign of its authenticity was the fact that ethnic groups were living in peace there. Sudetic visited the ethnically cleansed village of Gradska and opined that "few Croatian officials see a contradiction between the Medjugorje Virgin's message of peace and their drive for territorial control in this Bosnia region."

By the spring of 1993, Jeff Lopez realized that his wife was on the road more than she was home. Teresa was gone nine months of the year traveling with Bishop Hnilica and his entourage. Four of his followers had been ordained priests at Fatima, and one of them, an Italian by the name of Luciano Alamandi, was beginning to show an interest in Teresa that many who saw them together felt was something other than pastoral. Father Hermanagild Jayachandra, an Indian priest who was assistant pastor at St. Thomas More Parish in Denver, saw the seer and her priest embracing at one point. Father Herman was also struck by Teresa's expensive tastes. "Teresa," he wrote in a report of his own, "enjoyed wearing very expensive clothes, European travel on a whim and a very sporty automobile. She had a laptop computer and a fountain pen that alone cost approximately $150. Teresa's philosophy regarding praying the rosary was that one mouths the words and thinks about what one wants. When her theological teaching was questioned, Teresa would become defensive and at times enraged; however, her group would flock to her defense."

Teresa had asked Father Herman to be her spiritual advisor,

but he refused when she asked him to join her on the top of the mountain at the Cabrini Shrine for her apparitions. Other priests would prove more amenable. Father Luciano was overheard at one point saying that he wanted to develop a spiritual union with a seer, and having failed with Christine Muggridge, another Denver seer, finally connected with Teresa, who had assembled a select group of followers, known as the 12 Apostles, to help her fulfill her mission, which was to bring about the conversion of Russia. Teresa would tell her "remnant flock" that the Church was falling into decay, "especially by the Bishops and Cardinals closest to Pope John Paul II." Teresa had also spoken personally to Sister Lucia of Fatima, and it was during this conversation that Teresa learned that her next assignment was the conversion of Russia. At least this is what Teresa was telling her followers at the time. Teresa had gone to Rome to see the pope with Hnilica in early 1992, and although the bishop failed to arrange a private audience for the Denver seer, the pope did announce afterward that he would be attending the World Youth Day in Denver in August 1993, and in Medjugorje circles, this was proof that he was following Teresa's directives.

In March of 1993, Jeff Lopez, who had been trying to track his wife down for months, got a call informing him that she was in a hospital in Rome. Flying over there to bring her back, Jeff ran into Mariologist and expert seer certifier Rene Laurentin. Jeff and Father Laurentin spent time swimming at the pool of Hnilica's villa in Rome, a place Jeff recalls as being luxurious by both Denver and Italian standards. Neither he nor Laurentin spoke much about Teresa, who was in the hospital recuperating from whatever it was that was causing the internal bleeding. "Her clinical history," wrote Alberto Grossi, M.D., in his report of March 18, "was noticeable for hystero-annexiectomy performed in 1990 in United States followed by radiotherapy"

Jeff finally succeeded in bringing Teresa home, but before long she was off again. In June of 1993, Jeff finally tracked her down in Portugal, where she was presumably conferring with Sister Lucia about her role in the conversion of Russia. Jeff ordered her home, but she had no sooner gotten back than both of them were traveling again, this time to a Medjugorje conference in San Francisco in late June 1993.

In the summer of '93, Teresa was a hot property on the apparition circuit and was fast approaching the zenith of her 15 minutes of fame. On July 1, Judy Hill wrote to say that Father Edward O'Connor of the Notre Dame Theology Department had been looking at Teresa's videos and had "a real good impression" from them. O'Connor, according to Hill, "knows you're under attack but urged you to stay with it." On the trip to San Francisco, what Jeff had first sensed in Rome when he brought her back from the hospital was now becoming painfully apparent. As Teresa's fame increased, she increasingly viewed Jeff as a fifth wheel on the vehicle which would make her a superstar on the Medjugorje circuit. Teresa, in spite of her illness, did not want to leave Rome. She also took to wearing a nun's habit, something Jeff found somewhat incongruous when the couple had sex. Jeff hoped that the trip to the San Francisco Medjugorje conference together would revitalize their increasingly attenuated relationship but found instead that Teresa felt that Jeff had become a rock around her neck. Perhaps he reminded her of her previous life as an assistant manager trainee at Wendy's, a life she had no desire to revisit. Whatever the reason, almost as soon as she got back to Denver she was gone with Hnilica and his entourage, this time to a retreat in eastern Slovakia on June 30 with 11 lay missionaries, who along with Bishop Hnilica's Pro Deo et Fratribus community were making preparations for an upcoming trip to Russia.

"She was not happy to leave Rome," Jeff said later. "From the time she came back from Medjugorje she was gone nine months of the year. The madness began once they went international. Teresa was on cable TV and Mother Angelica asking for money. She would never call when she was away, and I think it's because she was afraid that I was going to tell the world what I knew."

Ardie Kronzer also attended the San Francisco Medjugorje conference in late June of 1993 with a new-found friend by the name of Marcia Smith. Smith, who came from the Bay area had been involved in charismatic circles there and had been a lector at the pope's mass in 1987. It was around this time that she became involved in Medjugorje, and, after years of involvement in the pilgrimage scene, she came into Ardie's life in early 1993. Both were involved in planning for the conference, and both women met Teresa Lopez at the conference for the first time. Teresa mentioned her connection with Bishop Hnilica and the CEM-Russia group he had founded with her in Denver. Both women seemed interested in knowing more.

Also attending the San Francisco Medjugorje conference was a young architect by the name of Gary Nolen. Nolen, who came from the same parish in Los Gatos as the Kronzers, was also impressed by Teresa Lopez's talk and approached her afterward, at which time she told him too about CEM-Russia, which was based at her home parish in Denver, St. Thomas More Catholic Church. As an architect, Nolen was interested in rebuilding churches in formerly Communist countries, and so it was with extreme interest that he listened to Teresa after her talk refer to a recently formed group in her home parish in Denver which intended "to provide funding for the rebuilding of churches in the former Communist countries by collecting funds and the establishment of 'sister parishes' which would adopt churches in the former communist countries."

At Teresa's suggestion, Nolen wrote first to Luciano Alamandi on June 28 and then to Bishop Hnilica himself on the same day. Nolen also made contact with Frank and Diane Lyons, two of Hnilica's helpers in Denver. He told them that he had already been working on plans for the rebuilding of Most Holy Mother of God Church in Vladivostok and sent photos as well as the name of the pastor, Father Myron Effing, as someone who might benefit from CEM-Russia's fundraising efforts. It was then that Nolen learned that the fundraising wasn't as straightforward as it seemed when he first heard about it from Teresa. One month later, after hearing that St. Thomas More was interested in becoming a sister parish to Fr. Effing's church in Vladivostok, Nolen got another letter which stated that the CEM board was unable to send any money to help with the restoration of the church in Vladivostok because any funds coming from St. Thomas More had already been earmarked for Bishop Hnilica and his new Pro Deo et Fratribus communities.

Trying not to put him off too much, the Lyons told Nolen that a representative of Hnilica's Pro Deo organization would be in the Denver area at St. Thomas More parish on August 17 and 18, and if he were to come, the Lyons promised to introduce him to Father Paul Gebhard. The meeting was less than auspicious. Nolen was taken aback by Gebhard's attitude, which seemed more interested in the money architects made rather than the buildings they designed. "Can you give us a donation?" Gebhard asked Nolen, who after recovering his composure, informed the young priest that "while I was an architect, I was not a wealthy one and did not have the money to give him a cash donation." Nolen went on to say that his home parish, St. Mary's in Los Gatos, California, was one of the wealthier parishes in the area and that he would be happy to make inquiries there to see if some wealthy parishioners would be willing to bankroll CEM-Russia's efforts.

Father Paul seemed interested. In fact he seemed more interested in Nolen's contacts with wealthy parishioners than he did in his architectural plans. It was then that the name Ardie Kronzer surfaced as a potential benefactor and a very actual rich person from St. Mary's in Los Gatos. Fr. Gebhard listened intently and then agreed to send Nolen color photocopies of pictures which showed the tragic state of disrepair into which Hnilica's Slovakian property had fallen and suggest that Nolen come and see for himself. Eventually the date of their departure was set for October 7, 1993.

"I will always be there for you," Teresa wrote to Jeff in December of 1989, just about ten months before they got married. "I think of your soft brown eyes and your heart-warming smile many times, and it always makes me feel very wonderful. To feel you hold me I know everything will always be okay.

"I know in my heart," she continued, perhaps with marriage on her mind, "I will always love you for better or worse, in riches or poorer, in sickness and in health. You are my life, Jeff, and I couldn't bear to spend a moment without you."

By the middle of 1993 Teresa, now married to Jeff, was spending more than moments without him. She was gone just about all of the time, which was bad enough from Jeff's point of view, but during her long absences from home, Teresa would write to Jeff letters that sounded not as if she missed him but as if she were intent on building a legal case against him by establishing a paper trail. On April 5, 1993, Teresa wrote about unspecified "events that have transpired in the past," which "include violence invoked by you upon me, leading to hospitalization," claiming that such events "can never occur again," and if they did, "I would be forced to file an official written report with the police department." Teresa concluded her letter by informing Jeff that she was planning to give copies of the letter to Father Walsh, pastor of St. Thomas More, and Bishop Hnilica if Jeff's still unspecified behavior continued.

On July 16, 1993, she wrote again to Jeff, this time complaining about his sexual practices, claiming that "in the present state of my health, which is documented at length, I cannot support sexual relations due to the fact that it causes hemorrhaging in me. I ask you not to provoke this by force or intimidation in the future." Teresa then went on to complain about Jeff's "external sexual preferences," informing him that a "perversion of this state is seen by the Church as lawful grounds for divorce on my part."

Teresa, in other words, was planning to divorce Jeff and was busy throughout 1993 creating a paper trail that could be used to bring about this end. "I would ask you," she continued, pursuing the issue of divorce, "to clearly state your intentions for divorce or separation. I cannot go from one extreme to the other. One day you would like us to reconcile and the next day you have no desire to remain and our marriage is over and you see no hope of restoration." Once again Teresa concluded by telling Jeff that her letter "in great confidentiality" was being given to both Bishop Hnilica, "with whom I have entrusted the care of my soul" and also Father Walsh, "who represents the Church." "Please know," she concluded, "this is not a threat but only protection for my own peace of mind."

It was clear that Teresa was spending a lot of time with Bishop Hnilica, but whether she was coming under his spell, under the guise of spiritual direction, or whether both were involved in the same scam is hard to say. "She was obeying a higher command," is how Jeff put it, but it was unclear whether he was referring to the Blessed Mother or Bishop Hnilica. It was clear that both Teresa and Hnilica were using each other to attain ends that they saw as beneficial to them both, and that collaboration involved generating large sums of money. Jeff later claimed that CEM-Russia brought in millions of dollars, and that the money caused dissension in the organization. Teresa got the two things that interested her most, money and fame, and was willing to do whatever was necessary to keep her grip on both—more willing than Christine Muggridge, who bowed out of the seer competition at around this time and returned to the States.

That summer a number of things happened. Denis Nolan staged his peace conference at Notre Dame and began working more intimately with Hnilica, who was now promoting the idea that the various Marian apostolates were in need of unity, a quality which he was quite willing to supply as long as everyone submitted to his leadership. Shortly after the Notre Dame conference, Michele Hardman, perhaps struck by Jim Jennings's absence there, contacted him, found out that he was married, and, after some deliberation, attempted suicide.

In mid-August of 1993 the pope arrived in Denver for the World Youth Day, and many of the Medjugorje followers in the States showed up too. Marcia Smith went to Denver for the pope's visit as did Bishop Hnilica. As part of the festivities, a group of young people put on a dramatization of the way of the cross, casting a young woman in the role of Jesus. Mother Angelica, whose EWTN was covering the pope's visit on a practically minute-by-minute basis, blew a fuse when she heard the news, and, after being specifically asked not to by her then local bishop, went on the air and used the Stations of the Cross incident as a pretext to vent her spleen over everything bad which had happened in the Church in the United States since the Vatican Council. She also announced that as of that moment she was no longer going to wear the updated habit her order had been wearing and promptly appropriated the habit of an order of Carmelite nuns which she found more in keeping with her new views. The video of her *J'accuse* speech electrified the conservative Catholic world in the United States, and many otherwise sensible movers and shakers in that demimonde rushed off to Alabama to kiss her ring and assure her they were on her side. Since Mother Angelica was heavily into promotion of Medjugorje, the apparitions were swept along as a result into the package of what one believed if one considered oneself a conservative Catholic and prided oneself on his loyalty to the Church, even though the Church had condemned the apparitions over two years before. Power in the Church was no different from power in any other sphere of life in the information age. It belonged to whoever owned the TV transmitter, and the bishops in the United States were slowly coming to that realization, to their chagrin, as Mother Angelica's EWTN outstripped the bishops' network in the ratings battle.

Right around the same time that the pope was in Denver, half a world away, Ratko Peric assumed his duties as the new ordinary of the diocese of Mostar by dividing the diocese into four districts, corresponding to the four evangelists and announcing that the Franciscans would have to close down the hall in which they had erected their combination church and shrine in honor of the 300 Croatian soldiers who had died driving the Muslims across the Neredva. Unlike his predecessor, Bishop Peric did not bluster; his strategy was more oblique.

At around the same time that Bishop Peric divided up the diocese of Mostar, Alia Izetbegovic was about to concede that the same thing was going to happen to Bosnia. In the 16 months since they had declared war in response to the EC recognition of Bosnia as a sovereign country, the Serbs had conquered 70 percent of the newly recognized republic, which seemed about to succumb to the political equivalent of Sudden Infant Death Syndrome. The Muslims had lost the war, and agreeing to a partition was the only thing now that was going to save the Muslims from complete annihilation, certainly as a political entity, and perhaps in light of the ethnic cleansing, as a people as well. Izetbegovic said he wanted a multiethnic Bosnia, just as it had existed for 47 years as part of Yugoslavia, but no one believed him other than the people at the State Department and the UN, both of whom wanted the same thing. Both the Serbs and the Croats suspected him of wanting to create an Islamic republic, and so were pressing for partition, and now Izetbegovic had no choice but to go along—at least, not until the aid started pouring in from Iran. On August 31, 1993, perhaps in reaction to President Clinton's repeated claim, "I feel your pain," Father Jozo Zovko published an open letter to Clinton in *Slobodna Dalmacija* entitled "Stop Our Pain!"

By the fall of 1993, it was clear that Teresa Lopez had become an important part of CEM-Russia's efforts in Denver. Energized by the pope's recent visit, CEM-Russia was now planning to hold a tenth anniversary celebration of the March 1984 papal consecration of Russia, which had been requested by Sister Lucia as part of the Fatima message and which many felt had been instrumental in the demise of Communism. Now CEM-Russia was going to do a replay of the consecration in Denver, with plans this time being made by the Blessed Mother herself, who was relaying her intentions to none other than her humble servant Teresa Lopez. On September 16, 1993, Diane Lyons wrote to tell Gary Nolen that "She [i.e., the Blessed Mother] has been very specific in her guidance....The decision has been made to have all the celebration and events surrounding the consecration at St. Thomas More [parish], rather than at a commercial conference area."

As a crucial part of finalizing his plans for 1) the 10th anniversary consecration and 2) the establishment of a shrine to Teresa Lopez's Our Lady of Virtues and 3) his take over of all of the Medjugorje apostolates in the United States under the guise of providing "unity," Hnilica convoked a conference at the Snow Mountain Ranch near Denver from November 5 to November 7 for leaders in the Marian movement in the United States. Its official title was the "Retreat for the Triumphant Victory of the Heart of Mary," and the participants were housed in various hotel-style lodges on the property. There were two qualifications for getting invited. One had to be either a leader of a Medjugorje apostolate and willing to deliver that apostolate over to Hnilica's leadership or one had to be rich. Ardie Kronzer qualified in both regards, but it was clear that her money outweighed her leadership abilities as her primary asset. Denis and Cathy Nolan attended the retreat, as did Brian Miller, who would eventually wrest control of Queen of Peace ministries of South Bend away from Nolan when his involvement with Hnilica deepened to what the board considered a conflict of interest. Jane Sears did not fit the above-mentioned criteria, but she was a journalist who was favorably disposed toward Medjugorje at the time and a friend of Marcia Smith, who was also in attendance. Both Marcia Smith and Ardie Kronzer met Bishop Hnilica for the first time at the Snow Mountain retreat; both had met Teresa Lopez for the first time at the San Francisco Medjugorje conference the previous June. Sears didn't have money or a Medjugorje group to offer, but she could be counted on to write an article favorable to the whole idea of Hnilica bringing unity to the Medjugorje movement. Father Ed O'Connor was also in attendance, as the group's theologian. Gary Nolen was there too, presumably as the group's architect.

Several days prior to the Snow Mountain retreat, Nolen met with Bishop Hnilica, Father Paul Gebhard, Father Luciano Alamandi, Teresa Lopez, and several of her "apostles" to discuss with Hnilica the architectural plans for a lay community and shrine which Teresa Lopez claimed had been given to her by the Mother of God, who was very clear in her instructions that the buildings should be built in the Denver area. At least that is how Teresa put it. Hnilica, although he was not claiming that he was receiving messages, was even more specific. He was of the opinion that the community should be built as close as possible to the Cabrini Shrine, where Teresa had been having her visions, and suggested that Scott White, one of the "apostles," look into the feasibility of buying adjacent land. Evidently Hnilica was reluctant to associate himself with St. Thomas More parish. The reason given at the meeting was an unspecified conflict between Bishop

Hnilica and Archbishop Stafford, the ordinary of the Denver archdiocese, but a more plausible reason is that anything associated with a diocesan parish would come under diocesan control. Money and how it was to be managed were recurrent themes at the pre-Snow Mountain retreat meeting. At one point, Tom Doyle, another "apostle," strongly suggested that all CEM-Russia checks be required to have two signatures to assure better accountability in the dispersal of funds, but his suggestion was vetoed with an admonition about opposing the group's decisions. Nolen arrived at the Snow Mountain Ranch retreat with a sense of mounting frustration. He seemed always to be put in the uncomfortable position of being somehow responsible for raising the money for the buildings he designed. He was also getting the impression that somehow he was supposed to pay CEM-Russia for the privilege of designing their buildings. As always the magnitude of the situation was stressed as the vehicle which made this sound plausible. If something as important as the conversion of Russia were at stake, who could object?

Although Phil Kronzer's name appears on the official guest list, he didn't attend the retreat. In fact he would later claim that he had never been invited. "I don't think Marcia [Smith] wanted me to be there," Kronzer said later. "I wasn't even asked." Jeff Lopez was getting the same feeling. Except for a brief interlude together in Rome and San Francisco, Teresa had been gone the entire year traveling with Bishop Hnilica and his entourage. In early November she arrived in Denver to attend the retreat but didn't tell Jeff, who only found out that she was in town when her painting of Our Lady, Mother of Virtues, a pink, fuzzy monstrosity, got left at the airport and then shipped inadvertently back to the return address stenciled on its container. Eventually Jeff tracked his wife down once again, and he was duly invited to the retreat, but conflict arose almost immediately about the driving arrangements. Teresa, it seems, wanted to drive to the Snow Mountain Ranch with Father Luciano, and Jeff wanted her to drive there with him. As a result, an argument broke out in the parking lot.

By now a pattern was beginning to emerge. Hnilica and his entourage were trying to manipulate both Teresa Lopez and Ardie Kronzer away from their respective husbands. The reasons were, of course, different. Teresa was also a willing participant in the alienation from her husband, who was after all her fourth husband. Ardie, on the other hand, was less calculating in the matter, having fallen more and more under the spell of Marcia Smith. Hnilica's crowd, however, felt that something could be gained by controlling both women, and under the guise of dispensing spiritual guidance, gradually maneuvered them to where they were constantly at odds with their respective spouses. After the retreat, Gary Nolen remembers hearing Father Luciano tell a group of men at the Lyons' house that it was his opinion that Teresa Lopez should leave her husband and seek a legal separation.

Although the goal was the same with Ardie Kronzer—i.e. separating her from her husband so that she could be of more use to CEM-Russia and Hnilica—the method was different. At a certain point during the retreat, Nolen saw Ardie disappear behind closed doors for a meeting with Teresa Lopez and Bishop Hnilica. What happened there is a matter of conjecture, but Phil Kronzer is now convinced that Hnilica staged an "apparition" with the help of Teresa Lopez, who relayed to Ardie a special message from the Blessed Mother, one which indicated the role she would play in the conversion of Russia. When Ardie returned to California after the Snow Mountain retreat, Phil felt that some dramatic change had taken place in her personality. Within a matter of days, they were arguing, causing Ardie to write a letter in which she informed him that while on the retreat she had gone to confession to a priest who had informed her that she no longer had to put up with her husband's temper tantrums. Later Phil would make contact with a nonagenarian in the parish to whom Ardie would take communion. Ardie informed the woman that she had been told by a bishop and three priests that she should separate from her husband, whereupon the woman denounced the men as phonies. In December 1993 Ardie also told a mutual friend, a Father Mike Burns, that she was going to leave her husband. Upset by the change in his wife's attitude, Kronzer left for their house in Carmel. In the past, Ardie would join him and the whole thing would have been forgotten. This time he waited for her for three days, and she never came down.

One day after the Snow Mountain Conference ended, on November 8, 1993, Gary Nolen left with Frs. Gebhard and Alamandi on a flight from Denver to Rome by way of New York. Nolen, as was becoming customary on trips with Hnilica's priests, was paying his own way, a fact that caused embarrassment when, arriving in Rome, Father Gebhard asked Nolen for another $200 so that they could then fly from Rome to Vienna, and Nolen said he didn't have the money.

"I informed Fr. Paul that I could not afford the additional airfare from Rome to Vienna as the cost of the round trip was already a little beyond my financial means," Nolen wrote later, and once again Father Gebhard berated Nolen for not corresponding to the financial status he thought appropriate for an architect. The relationship began to cool perceptibly from that moment on.

When they arrived in Vienna the priests and the architect were picked up by two Pro Deo et Fratribus nuns in Father Paul's personal car, and all drove that evening to Nitra in Slovakia where they spent the night in the convent at the boarding school the Pro Deo nuns were running there for high school students. From there they departed for

Rimiski Sobota with Father Paul at the wheel driving at speeds over 100 mph over snow-covered narrow roads which were barely wide enough for two opposing lanes of traffic. At one point when the police attempted to pull him over, Gebhard stopped until the policewoman got out of her car, and then sped away at his customary high rate of speed, wondering, "Does she think I'm crazy" enough to stop and get a ticket?

When they finally arrived in Rimiski Sobota at 5:00 in the afternoon, Nolen saw that the seminary was in fact a former rectory which the pastor of the village had to abandon because he ran out money—his own—renovating it. The priest had hoped to rent rooms in what was the largest building in the village. His loss, it turns out, was Bishop Hnilica's gain, but the project was not going well because no one involved in the renovation had the faintest clue when it came to either construction or materials. Expensive wood paneling was rotting because it hadn't been sealed against water damage properly. When Nolen brought this up to Father Gebhard, he was told that the materials weren't available in the village, although Nolen found them easily enough, and had to be brought in via the community's Mercedes Benz, which had just departed for Frankfurt, Germany, to bring back a load of plywood.

Everywhere he turned, Nolen saw ostentation and waste. Instead of heating with coal or other available local fuels, Gebhard installed an expensive a high-tech, high-energy-consumption, radiant-heating, electical wall-panel system, which consumed as much electricity to warm the house as the entire neighborhood of single-family units combined. Because it required so much energy, the local government made the Pro Deo people apply for a special permit to install and use it. Fr. Paul appropriated the south side of the building as his personal residence and then installed full window drapes which blocked out the sunlight because it kept the local poor children from looking through his windows. Shortly after they arrived, Gebhard left again, this time to consult with a Dutch mystic in Amsterdam. Left alone, feeling that his professional advice was being ignored, Nolen concluded that it was time to return to California and get on with his life, but not before he began wondering who was paying for all of this waste and extravagance and running around the world.

When he got back home in early December, Nolen called Frank Lyons in Denver and expressed his frustration at his experience in Slovakia. Not only was Father Gebhard not open to Nolen's ideas, the ideas he was proposing for the remodeling were so far from professional standards that the safety of the house's occupants would be jeopardized if they ever got implemented. At this point, Suzy White dismissed Nolen's scruples as stemming from lack of humility. If he were really humble, like St. Francis's brothers, then he would have done what Father Paul asked him to do, no matter how unsafe or wasteful he might have considered it. Lyons then asked him for a copy of his "condition assessment" of Father Effing's parish in Vladivostok so that they might look into funding for that project. A month later, in January 1994, Nolen got a letter from Father Effing informing him that Lyons and CEM-Russia would not be providing funding for the renovation of the church in Vladivostok. They also would not help out with any architectural or engineering conditions assessment studies.

Doing a little research on Pro Deo et Fratribus, Nolen discovered that the priests he had been dealing with had been ordained less that a year before he met them, on December 8, 1992, in Fatima, Portugal, although they had no connection to the diocese of Leira where Fatima is located. Worse still, Nolen learned that Gebhard and Alamandi had been functioning as priests before they had been ordained. The whole order seemed to be run by messages from dubious mystics like Teresa Lopez and the lady from Amsterdam. Was the Church in charge here or not?

In early December Jeff Lopez heard of a job opening in Colorado Springs, and Teresa, in town because of an upcoming major Medjugorje conference, decided to go along for the ride. Nothing got resolved on the trip, which allowed the couple to talk for the first time in a while. When Jeff asked her why she was away so much and why she had gotten so heavily involved in the Marian scene, Teresa turned to him and said, "I can be somebody if I get involved with this."

It was the last time he ever saw her.

On December 18, 1993 Teresa sent Jeff a fax from Pro Deo et Fratribus headquarters in Rome informing him that she wanted a legal separation. Then suddenly aware of her vulnerability because of what Jeff knew about her, Teresa turned to thinly veiled threats.

"I pray you will grant me the favor of the privacy of our personal life," she wrote. "I have not discussed it with anyone fully except the Bishop in great discretion. If you choose to provoke the situation, I assure you I shall be forced to disclose things that would be better left quiet. I have no desire to cause you any harm and I plead with you to allow peace to remain between us. We both know what has transpired between us, and this is no one else's business."

At around the same time, Branomir Tolaitch, former tour guide and translator for the seers, ran into Jelena Vasilj, the locutionary who got into the apparition business, right around the time that Mirjana dropped out. Jelena and the coincidence in dates (if that is what it is) are mentioned in Mary Craig's book: "Four days after Mirjana virtually left the Medjugorje scene, two other young girls made an entrance. From 29th December, ten-year-old Jelena Vasilj claimed to be seeing a vision of Our Lady, 'all in white,' the edges of her gown lined with gold. Her friend Marijana Vasilj began to receive the same gift on the following Good Friday." Branomir and Jelena had become good friends during the time Branomir spent in Medjugorje doing translation for the seers and then later as a principal in his own tour company. Then gradually they became more than good friends, and started talking about getting married "24 hours a day." Eventually the talk about marriage needed to become more than just talk, and Branomir went to Jelena's house to find out where things stood. It was either get married or break it off. The ultimatum was too overwhelming for Jelena, who started crying uncontrollably and then inexplicably, or so it seemed at the time, started talking about Medjugorje and the Gospa. "It sucks," she said, "I hate it. It's the eye of the Virgin. I hate it. You don't know what it's like to have the eye of the Virgin."

That incident marked the end of their relationship. Branomir went back to California, and Jelena eventually ended up with a full-paid scholarship at the University of Steubenville, which she was attending when they met again for the first time in years in late 1993. "Toward the end of '93 beginning of '94 she started wearing weird-ass clothes and a hairdo like Sinead O'Connor. When I told her she looked totally butch, she started crying. I was pissed off. Mate [Ivankovic, son of Marinko] told me she's still in love with me."

Branomir was "pissed off" because of what Medjugorje had done to both of them. He is now convinced that the relationship died because Jelena couldn't face the truth about what she was doing. "She didn't want to lie to me," he said, but she couldn't admit the truth either. He now blames her family for their break up, claiming that the family history indicates a group of people with a genetic predisposition toward this sort of thing. One of the Vasiljs killed a priest's sister and buried her body in a garbage heap, causing a scandal that haunted the village for years. After the apparitions started drawing pilgrims, Zige [Gypsy] Vasilj made money selling crappy wine to credulous Italians by telling them that it had been blessed by the Virgin Mary. "Her father made her do it," Branomir concluded finally. "God will punish them."

Shortly before Christmas 1993, Phil Kronzer's daughter Cindy went shopping with her mother Ardie at the expensive shops in Carmel. Ardie, she remembers, seemed uninterested in getting anything for her grandchildren. Her mind was fixed on one thing. She wanted to buy something for Marcia Smith, and eventually ended up getting her a $200 sweater.

-14-

THE SEER FROM WENDY'S MEETS BISHOP HNILICA

In late 1993 Steve Mahowald got a call from Ted Flynn. "This is Ted Flynn with *Signs of the Times,*" announced a voice on the other end of the line. It was a voice which Mahowald had never heard before and a name which at that time was hardly a household word. Mahowald said later that Flynn seemed insulted that he had never heard of him. Now Flynn was full of bluster and threat. "How dare you write a book with this name," he said, referring to Mahowald's book, *Signs of the Times.* "That's our name. I'm going to sue you."

Mahowald now laughs at the unintentionally comic nature of the conversation. Mahowald had never heard of the man who was claiming to be such a celebrity on the Medjugorje circuit. Eventually he ran into Flynn in person at a Marian conference in Minneapolis. By then, Flynn had gotten over the idea of suing Mahowald, and the book he wanted to call *Signs of the Times* had been published under the less clinched but equally inauspicious title of *The Thunder of Justice.* *Thunder* attempted to jump on the apparition bandwagon by endorsing just about everyone and anyone who was claiming to hear voices, a strategy which carried over to Flynn's magazine, which did end up being called *Signs of the Times.* *SOT* was in many ways more like a catalogue than a magazine. It was a clearinghouse from which credulous apparition chasers could order the latest book by the latest seer. Marv Kucera, whom Flynn endorsed in early 1995, would later say that it was Flynn who boosted his career the most. Flynn in turn was given credibility by frequently appearing on Mother Angelica's EWTN shows. It was in many ways an interlocking directorate of people based on nothing but media exposure within a certain market which operated in flagrant disregard of Church authority.

Over the years, Mother Angelica was developing the same attitude toward the hierarchy that had become common in conservative Catholic circles. It tended to blame the bishops and their liberal advisors for all of the ills in the Church. Flynn probably shared the same views himself, but Mahowald's overwhelming impression at the time was that Flynn was not an idea-driven guy or someone who deeply believed the stuff he wrote in his own books. Flynn, according to Mahowald's assessment, was essentially a secular guy involved in a movement where he saw the opportunity to make a lot of money. Later, someone who ended up at one of Marvin Kucera's refuges as a result of seeing Flynn on Mother Angelica and reading his book remembered a conversation with Maureen, Ted's wife. "If Marv has a problem," Maureen said, "he'll go underground, and we'll do the same."

By January of 1994 the Mahowalds were still not alarmed by their son Mark's absence from home, but they were starting to miss him and began bringing up his coming home in their increasingly infrequent phone conversations. In many respects, Mark Mahowald's silence worked in his favor. A year or so earlier the Mahowalds couldn't have gone 30 days without hearing about Mark from the police. Now they tried to convince themselves that no news was good news. They weren't sure, but they heard that he was going to church regularly, as one would suspect the constant companion of a seer would.

But then the Mahowalds started hearing stories about Marvin's background, and this did little to relieve their distress. In order to allay their fears, they called Father Anderson and discovered to their dismay that Marvin had fired him as his spiritual director. Anderson, nonetheless, told them not to worry. Then Mike Guilfoyle, the private investigator who was trying to get information on Kucera for his cousin Ed Militti so that he could get his wife to stop giving him money, showed up with stories that Kucera was a child molester who had sexually abused his own four daughters and had a penchant for young boys. The Mahowalds dismissed what Guilfoyle said as "nothing he could prove" because they most probably didn't want to believe it and didn't see what they could do even if they were convinced their son was in danger. So they decided to pray about it. "We would pray about it every single day," Mahowald said. "But there were no alarm bells yet."

Then the Mahowalds got a call in March or April of '94 from Ohio. Mark called to say that he had serious dental problems and needed money. Without asking for a second opinion, Steve wired him $500, which was a lot of money for the Mahowalds. Otherwise everything seemed fine, and they talked about other things in a friendly way. Toward the end of the conversation, Steve told Mark that it was time to come home, but Mark said Marv was in danger and that it that wasn't possible.

A week later, Mark called from Flagstaff, Arizona, and talked to his mother, Lois, telling her that he needed money for more dental work." If you need money, Mark," Lois answered, "it's time to come home." When Lois told Mark that they didn't have the money, Mark suggested that she borrow it from Mrs. Linehan, whose house Lois cleaned. "If you need money so bad, it's time to come home," Lois repeated, but feeling she was getting nowhere, she put her husband Steve on. Steve agreed to send them $750, but added "Now I'm telling you under holy obedience to come home." By the tone of the conversation, it was clear to Steve that Mark had reverted to the old angry, bitter, nasty person he had been when he got out of Boys Town. By 1994, however, Mark turned 17 and so could declare himself an emancipated minor. So there was little the Mahowalds could do to force the issue. Not wanting to alienate their son further, the Mahowalds sent him and Marvin another $750 which they could not afford. Kucera's driver's license had expired, so Steve had to rewire him the money. At a Marian conference in Wisconsin, Mark ran into a Father Lemoyne, a family friend, who told him that he was supposed to come home, but Marvin had then gotten a message from the Blessed Mother informing him that it wasn't so.

"We thought of calling the police and saying that he had been kidnapped," Lois said later, "but we felt that if the FBI got involved someone might get killed." The murders at Ruby Ridge had become a luminous event for the circles which the Mahowalds frequented. In fact Kucera's refuges were based every bit as much on militia thinking as much as they were on Marian devotion. The Mahowalds are now convinced that Mark and Marvin were lying about the medical emergencies and exploiting them financially, but they didn't really know what to do about it. Then they started hearing more rumors about Marvin's sexual proclivities, but as before they didn't believe them. "We didn't believe it," Steve said of the rumors, but then as if correcting himself, added, "We didn't want to believe it."

It turns out that Bishop Hnilica had been prescient in not wanting Teresa Lopez's apparitions too closely associated with St. Thomas More parish. In late 1993 St. Thomas More's pastor, Father Michael Walsh received a letter from Archbishop J. Francis Stafford, a letter whose contents he made public on January 1, 1994.

"With regard to the proposed March 25 Marian gathering in a large public area," Stafford wrote, "I do not wish it to be held in the

Archdiocese of Denver. It is too closely associated with the alleged apparitions to Therese Lopez." Stafford had already given a preliminary negative judgment on May 11, 1993, indicating that "there does not appear to be evidence which would indicate a supernatural origin for these alleged events." On February 22, 1994, the diocesan commission concluded that "the alleged apparitions of the Blessed Virgin Mary to Teresa Antonie Lopez are devoid of any supernatural origin." "Anyone," Stafford continued, "encouraging devotion to these alleged apparitions in any way is acting contrary to my wishes as archbishop of Denver." Although the final statement would not appear until March 9, 1994, Stafford had evidently gotten wind of the proposed CEM-Russia conference and decided to warn Walsh to dissociate St. Thomas More parish from any connection with it.

Teresa Lopez had walked out on her husband and family in order to "be somebody" just about two weeks before Stafford's statement put a permanent end to her rise as a seer on the Medjugorje circuit. The timing was spectacularly bad, especially for someone who was in daily contact with the Queen of Heaven, especially since the Blessed Virgin seemed so interested in micromanaging the 10th anniversary consecration, according to Diane Lyons. The decision also threw Hnilica into a panic. Hnilica had big plans for Teresa, and they were connected to Denver in terms of place and March 25, 1994 in terms of time, which meant that he had less than three months to come up with Plan B, in terms of where to have the world's bishops gather to reconsecrate Russia to the Immaculate Heart.

On January 21, 1994, three weeks after Walsh wrote his letter, Hnilica sent a fax to the Franciscans at Medjugorje, asking them if he could use Medjugorje as the site for the reconsecration. The fax gave the impression that Medjugorje was Hnilica's first choice—in fact, the only logical choice for such an event— but the priests at Medjugorje knew better. And if they didn't know better, they were about to be told as much by a group of Medjugorje supporters who were outraged at Hnilica's tactics and his endorsement of Teresa Lopez and what they rightly perceived as his naked attempt to take control of the Medjugorje movement for his own personal gain.

On February 5, 1994, while the Franciscans were mulling over Hnilica's overture 100 miles away, a 120 mm mortar shell exploded in the Central Market of Sarajevo. It was a Saturday, and the market was full of people who were using the opportunity of what seemed like a lull in the siege to get some shopping done. When the smoke cleared, 68 people were dead and over 200 hundred injured in what was the bloodiest incident of the war. The media, true to the biases which they had held throughout the war, immediately blamed the Serbs, but

Radovan Karadzic just as immediately denied their charges, claiming that the Bosnian Muslims had fired on their own people in order to gain an advantage at the upcoming round of peace talks in Geneva, scheduled for February 10.

In retrospect, the evidence seems to bear out Karadzic's claim. The Bosnian Serbs at this point had no reason to commit an atrocity which was bound to turn world opinion against them. They were in control of 70 percent of the country and in the best position possible for the upcoming negotiations. The Bosnian Muslims, however, had their backs up against the wall. Their military was little more than a joke; their population hopelessly divided between the ethnic groups which wanted to carve up the country, and their leader seems to have resigned himself to the necessity of partition and long negotiations which would give the Muslims the best possible deal.

The explosion in the Alimarket on February 5 changed all that. Jumping on the public opinion bandwagon that averred that the Serbs were the root of all evil in the Balkans, the Clinton Administration called for retaliation, and on March 28, less than three weeks later, NATO jets flew their first air strike in the history of that organization, shooting down four Serb planes. The Serbs were then given an ultimatum: withdraw all of their heavy weapons from a 20 kilometer area surrounding Sarajevo. The Serbs, for their part, threatened reprisals against all foreigners in Bosnia.

On March 24, one day before the hastily rescheduled reconsecration of Russia was to take place in Medjugorje, Bishop Paolo Hnilica showed up at the chancery office in Mostar to ask for permission to say Mass on Mt. Krisevac. The upcoming 10th anniversary of the pope's consecration had attracted a whole host of Medjugorje supporters but only one bishop other than Hnilica himself, auxiliary bishop Nicholas D'Antonio, a naive Franciscan from New Orleans. Now Hnilica was having difficulty convincing Bishop Peric to grant him permission. "He told me he was on a special mission from the pope," Peric said later. "So I said, 'Fine, where is your letter of authorization?'" At this point, Hnilica leaned closer to Peric and told him in a confidential tone that the pope had commissioned him in person. There were, in other words, no documents, no letters of authorization, just Hnilica's say-so on the matter. Needless to say, Hnilica did not get permission to say Mass on Mt. Krisevac.

Unsurprisingly, since Medjugorje has never been known to be scrupulous when it came to obedience to church authority, Hnilica went and said Mass without Peric's permission one day later. When the Mass was finally concelebrated on the mountain, the only celebrants were Bishops Hnilica and D'Antonio and Father Leonard Orec, the architect of the Herzegovina disobedience strategy. "It was a miserable showing," said someone who was there.

What the reconsecration lacked in bishops, however, it made up for in the self-appointed leaders of the Medjugorje movement throughout the world, an increasingly bizarre group of impostors, cranks, and eccentrics who were now making a full-time living off the bloated corpse of the apparitions. "Sister" Emmanuel Maillard was there, decked out in her habit, planning to use the consecration formula Teresa Lopez and Bishop Hnilica had concocted in her book *In the End My Immaculate Heart Will Triumph*. Maillard's claim to the title "Sister," which in conjunction with the religious habit she wore, gave the impression that she was a nun, stemmed ultimately from her membership in the French charismatic community Lion of Judah and not from any vows she took sanctioned by the Church. She was also associated with the Beatitudes, a community which had set up a house at Medjugorje without the permission of the local bishop. Kenneth McCall, the Anglican, was there, the creator of Intergenerational Healing, a spiritual exercise that struck one observer as a cross between trafficking in spirits and Chinese ancestor worship.

During the same visit McCall would hold a seance at Bernard Ellis's Peace House at Medjugorje. The Austrian locutionary Maria Simma was also there. Denis Nolan was there as well. Before long the reconsecration was starting to cause consternation among some of the comparatively level-headed Medjugorje crowd. Larry and Mary Sue Eck, editors of *Medjugorje* magazine, were outraged at Hnilca's tactics and the fact that the author of the consecration formula had just been declared a phony by the archbishop of Denver. When they took their protest to Slavko Barbaric, however, they got nowhere, and since they themselves were making a living by promoting something equally bogus and equally condemned by the local bishop, their outrage quickly subsided into acquiescence. Hnilica and Slavko, it was clear, were in this one together. Hnilica's motivation was clear: He wanted to take over the Medjugorje movement, but why Slavko Barbaric would go along with something that was clearly not in the self-interest of the Franciscans or the seers was puzzling. Was it some indication of the service Hnilica had provided in the past, and the power he had in the present as a result? Or were the Franciscans helpless prisoners of the dynamic they themselves had created? Unlike some of the less consistent thinkers in the Medjugorje movement, the Franciscans understood that they couldn't condemn Teresa Lopez for the very thing they themselves were guilty of doing. This would put them in the position of Veronica Lueken, the "seer" of Bayside condemned by the archdiocese of Brooklyn, New York, who announced that the Blessed Mother had appeared to her to say that she was not appearing to the children at

Medjugorje. Not wanting to be in a position where the pot was calling the kettle black, Slavko Barbaric went along with the Hnilica/Lopez consecration and probably hoped that not too many people would hear about it.

One Medjugorje supporter who did hear about it was Charles Toye of Send Your Spirit Publishing of Reading, Massachusetts. Toye had been following the Hnilica/Lopez collaboration since the Snow Mountain Ranch retreat in Denver in November of 1993 and did not like what he saw. Determined to press the issue he called Denis Nolan and asked several times in the same conversation, "Why does Medjugorje need Teresa Lopez?"

"Each time I asked," Toye recounted later, "he fell silent." As time went on, Toye's suspicions began to grow. "Could it be," he wrote in a pamphlet published in June, "that the promotion of Teresa Lopez was an effort to change the direction of Medjugorje spirituality, and to launch a new organization such as "United for the Triumph of the Immaculate Heart announced in May, just before the Conference and founded by Bishop Hnilica and Denis Nolan? Was the this new organization the climax of Denis Nolan and Bishop Hnilica's work?"

In April 1994 Toye faxed an open letter entitled "Clean Up Your Act!" to Denis Nolan as head of the 1994 National Medjugorje conference reminding him that Archbishop Stafford of Denver had condemned Teresa Lopez on March 9 as "devoid of supernatural origin," that the archbishop "speaks for the Church in this regard," and that "one danger of promoting Lopez's material at a Medjugorje Conference is that it might have irreversible negative effects on the credibility of Medjugorje." Toye's letter provided a devastating critique of Teresa Lopez, including the story of how Queenship Publisher Robert Schaeffer scrambled to get a phony imprimatur put on *In the End My Immaculate Heart Will Triumph* so that he wouldn't get stuck with a warehouse full of unsold books.

While most of what Toye said was undeniably true, reading his letter was a bit disconcerting because he seemed completely incapable of seeing that all of his arguments applied *a fortiori* to Medjugorje, whose purity he seemed determined to defend. Toye, however, seems to have discerned the intentions of the Hnilica/Lopez/Nolan crowd fairly accurately in spite of his inability to apply the same lessons to the originators of the Medjugorje phenomenon.

"The new cult of spiritual individualists," Toye wrote, "is attempting to take over the entire Medjugorje movement, not just through its books, tapes and newsletters but also through Marian conferences" like the upcoming 1994 National Medjugorje Conference at Notre Dame. "There is also an attempt by the new cult to make Bishop Paolo Maria Hnilica, S.J., their new leader, and the Conference would launch him in that direction." Toye feared the worst: "The prestige of Bishop Hnilica, combined with the printing power of Queenship Publications and the influence of the National Conference, could devastate the spirituality of Medjugorje."

Then to make matters worse, Nolan announced that Vicka was planning to attend the Notre Dame conference "to support the movement towards unity among Marian Apostolates," which meant that the intent of the 1994 national conference was "to have Medjugorje endorse the new organization and the works of Teresa Lopez." Although Toye was obtuse when it came to the theological difference between Medjugorje and Teresa Lopez, he was particularly acute in understanding why the Lopez phenomenon and all of the other spin-off apparitions were happening. "A trend which began just before the war in the former Yugoslavia," he wrote, "seemed to accelerate when pilgrimages to Medjugorje decreased significantly due to the conflict. Many Medjugorje Centers changed their names to Marian enterprises in order to take advantage of their client's appetites for the world-wide Marian market and the adventure of discovering new apparition sites."

In the weeks before the conference, it looked as if Toye's efforts might bear fruit. "We are constantly receiving telephone calls and faxes from people in the U.S. who are advising us to distance ourselves from the Notre Dame Conference because Teresa Lopez is being pulled into it," Slavko Barbaric said in a fax to Denis Nolan before the conference. "Bishop Hnilica is being presented to us as her spiritual director which, because her experiences have, at least for now, been considered not supernatural, brings him into difficulty. Division has occurred."

Toye was evidently under the impression that the Yugoslavian bishops had approved pilgrimages to Medjugorje and that those who went there were doing so with the Church's blessing. This may have been at least partly the reason for his indignation. If he was expecting support from Slavko Barbaric to preserve the "purity" of Medjugorje, he was bound to be disappointed, however. Eight months after the Notre Dame conference had taken place, Slavko decided to bring an end to the division by telling Toye to shut up. "Bishop Hnilica," Slavko informed him, "really is the 'special delegate of the pope.' What are you quoting of Bishop Hnilica being the 'pope's false delegate'?" The reference here was to an article entitled "The Pope's False Delegate," which Bishop Peric published in the *Glas Koncila* in June of 1994 based on his trip to Rome two days after Hnilica went ahead and did the consecration in spite of Peric's wishes. While in Rome, Peric evidently got to see the dossier on Hnilica the Vatican had compiled, including the doubts about the validity of his consecration as a bishop because of the dubious circumstances under which it occurred in Communist

Czechoslovakia, a fact he would later point out by showing the inconsistencies in Hnilica's entry in the *Annuario Pontificio*. "In the Catholic Church," claimed the author of "The Pope's False Delegate," which Toye had cited in his letter to Barbaric, "Hnilica has no canonical permission and no church authorization that is recorded in the Vatican yearbook which would allow him to regularly act in a functional capacity rather than as a private individual." If Toye had been expecting help from Father Barbaric, he shouldn't have quoted Bishop Peric. "I tell you," Slavko warned Toye, "it is not a good argument."

Undeterred by the dissension in the ranks, Hnilica returned to the United States and made plans to attend the 1994 National Medjugorje conference, where Nolan planned to crown him leader of all Marian Apostolates. Following the conference, a retreat of 185 "American Marian leaders" was scheduled, and Ardie Kronzer and Marcia Smith were scheduled to attend both conference and retreat.

Things had not been going well at the Kronzers' house since Ardie returned from the Snow Mountain Ranch retreat. Phil would later say that she returned a different person. The same person who sat on the boards of five of Phil's corporations, now showed interest in nothing but Medjugorje, and when Phil brought up other things, the conversation seemed to end invariably in a fight. There was a fight at Ardie's birthday party in January. As a way of defusing a tense situation, Phil decided to take his family, including his grown children and grandchildren, to Disney World in April of 1994. The change of scenery, however, did not bring about a corresponding changed of attitude in Ardie. Phil again felt that he couldn't do anything right. While he was off having fun with the grandchildren, Ardie was off by herself, praying or thinking about praying. One day during their stay, she left at 6:00 a.m. to visit a nearby shrine and didn't get back until six that evening and was physically ill when she returned. The shrine was near the house of mutual friends, the Schneiders, who lived in Tampa. While Ardie was visiting with the Schneiders, she told Joanne that she was planning to leave Phil.

In addition to his domestic problems, Phil Kronzer was having problems with his business as well. In March of 1990, attempting to profit from the boom in computer-related sales in nearby Silicon Valley, Kronzer started a company which specialized in customizing floppy disks called Creative Disk. Gradually, the scope of the business evolved into building machinery that processed disks rather than producing the disks themselves. Working with people in the industry, Kronzer and his engineer Sam Montalvo invented a machine that would collate and bag the multiple disks that made up the usual software application. This meant dealing with other companies who supplied the bags and other machinery, but it also meant dealing with the companies that produced and reproduced the software. Gradually, Phil came to realize that these companies were more interested in maintaining exclusive relationships with huge suppliers like Microsoft than in solving logistic and engineering problems associated with production. Phil Kronzer had a product that did the job, but during the course of 1994 he found that he was increasingly unable to sell to companies whose representatives said they needed his machinery. Often companies would take his machines on consignment, only to return them with crucial parts dismantled. Phil began to suspect his own employees of sharing trade secrets with his competitors, who would then use his inventions and freeze him out by paying kickbacks to the large suppliers. CDI would get contracts and then not be able to fill the orders because his suppliers refused to send him crucial parts.

In late May 1994, Ardie Kronzer and Marcia Smith left the bay area to attend the National Medjugorje Conference held at Notre Dame, Indiana. While at the conference, Ardie and Marcia took the stage in front of 7,000 people and did a bizarre little dedication ceremony in front of Bishop Hnilica, during which they dedicated the 12 Bay Area Mir centers, "12 stars in Our Lady's crown," to Bishop Hnilica. Ardie and Marcia stood behind the podium together and began reading their statement simultaneously, until that proved impractical, thereafter reading their parts in turn. What began as jointly given witness, turned quickly into more of a personal testimony from Marcia Smith, who clearly gave the impression of being the dominant member of the pair, as Ardie stood back and listened and spoke only when prompted to do so by Marcia.

"We represent the 12 San Francisco Bay Area Mir centers for prayer and peace," Marcia began, "and we would like to thank Denis Nolan and the Queen of Peace Ministries for this beautiful conference and for the invitation to give a very brief witness about the wonderful work that the Blessed Mother, our Queen of Peace, is doing in the hearts of her children in Northern California. As you can see unity and oneness is why we are all here."

From this point on in the presentation, Ardie, who gave the impression of being either abstracted or sedated, stood back and let Marcia deliver her testimony.

"In 1987," Marcia continued, "Our Blessed Mother as she has done for all of you, called me out of the ordinary circumstances of my life to Medjugorje. In January in the cold rain our Blessed mother became my mother, and I saw the things that you all have seen there as well, the miracle of the sun, speaking and talking with the visionaries, and had the great privilege of being in the apparition room in the very early days, and one afternoon on the apparition hill the Blessed Mother showed me a vision that I did not understand."

Marcia saw the Bay Area in black and then 12 sparks, which got fanned into flames. "Having come from the Renewal of the Holy Spirit in our church," Marcia continued, interpreting her own vision, "I immediately thought those were prayer groups, charismatic prayer groups. And I thought, 'isn't that interesting our Blessed Mother is somehow going to touch our prayer groups.'"

The Blessed Mother then revealed to Marcia that she was to found a Medjugorje Mir Center in San Francisco, something which surprised her since she "was only the second person from the Bay area to ever go to Medjugorje, and nobody knew what Medjugorje was, and it wasn't even on the map." As a result, Marcia prayed, "Mother, you want me to do something like this? You'll have to send the people, I wouldn't know where to start."

It was at this point that Marcia got to the point of her speech. Our Lady had indeed sent the people, and one Mir center was formed after another, but now it was obvious that "these centers like all infants moving into their adolescence were not necessarily in harmony. And we have watched our Mother take her very disobedient children and work a great miracle through Bishop Hnilica, who we first encountered in Denver in November this past year when he taught us that Medjugorje was the fulfillment of Fatima and that if we did not come together and collaborate in the efforts we were making that we would be divided and not unified."

Then as Ardie started reading off the names of the Mir centers, Marcia, *sotto voce*, started ordering people around behind her back until everything was in place for the culminating moment of the consecration. Lifting their arms in the air with rosaries in hand, in a kind of clenched fist salute to the crowd, both Ardie and Marcia then said "Ave Maria to the Triumph" and knelt in front of Bishop Hnilica, who seemed either delighted or embarrassed and hastily blessed both women, placing his hands on their heads.

After the conference ended, Marcia and Ardie stayed on at Notre Dame for a Marian Leaders' retreat. When Ardie called Phil it was to explain that there had been some mix-up in the rooming arrangements. Instead of staying at the retreat center as planned, Ardie and Marcia ended up at a Holiday Inn down the road with two other women. Eventually she made it home in time for Memorial Day weekend, but when Phil and Ardie went out to dinner, Phil was finding it difficult to talk to his wife, feeling that she was being evasive and distant. Phil knew that she had given her talk at the conference in front of 7,000 people and was excited about it at the time, but now Ardie seemed not to want to talk about it. The lack of communication prompted Phil to change the conversation to the topic of their relationship. He wanted to know where Ardie was going from here and whether he was going to be included in her plans. But his questions met with dead silence, both at the latter part of the dinner and in the car on the way home. "I don't want to wait until I'm 70 to find out where I stand with you," he said at some time before the end of the evening. It turns out that Phil got what he asked for, at least as far as an answer to this question. He would not have to wait until he was 70 to find out where he stood with his wife. In fact, he would find out in less than a month, 10 years early, on just about the day of his sixtieth birthday.

At around the same time, Ardie and Marcia were becoming apostles of unity at Notre Dame, Jeff Lopez showed up at his lawyer's office to answer signed interrogatories in the suit Teresa filed requesting a divorce. "The petitioner," Jeff averred in reference to his soon-to-be former wife, "forged my signature on several insurance payment checks and did not use them to pay the medical bills. Arapahoe County credit agency sued for a bad check she wrote. We were both sued for several of these checks. Judgment was made against each of us individually. I paid the judgment against myself.... I discovered that Teresa's problems with writing fraudulent checks and creating bad debts had been the cause of her last two divorces." "I firmly believe," Jeff concluded, that "Teresa attained the $30,000 car accident settlement fraudulently."

Phil's business difficulties reached a head at the Repletech Industry Trade Show in mid-June of 1994 when Phil brought a CDI machine to the show with a new bagger and filed a lawsuit against Automated Packaging Systems, his former supplier, having a process server serve papers at the very same trade show, on June 15, 1994. In addition to the lawsuit, Phil was also occupied at the time with installing six collating and packaging systems at a Microsoft plant in Puerto Rico. As a result, his contact with Ardie during this period of time was mostly by phone, and most of the time he was having difficulty reaching her.

On June 13, 1994, Denis Nolan announced that the movement which was to bring about worldwide Marian movement unity had been, as of the successfully concluded Notre Dame conference, officially launched. He then quoted Bishop Hnilica to the effect that Unity within Christendom

> can never be realized if we do not first attain the true unity within our Catholic Church. Our Lady foresaw this too at Fatima, when she spoke of the evils that were coming into the world and into the Church in our century. The evil with the most disastrous consequences that the devil has raised up to work in our Catholic Church is

precisely division. 'Divide and conquer.' This is the logic of evil."

Three days later, a former football player by the name of O. J. Simpson created the media sensation of the year by leading a phalanx of Los Angeles policemen and TV crews on a low-speed drive down that city's freeways after his wife and another man had been found with their throats slashed.

Toward the end of the month, relations between the Kronzers seemed to be improving. Claiming that they had to go on a picnic somewhere in the hills above Saratoga, Ardie delivered Phil to a surprise party commemorating his sixtieth birthday which 30 or 40 people attended. The festivities, however, did not prevent Phil from thinking that Ardie was nonetheless acting very strange. On the following weekend, Phil went to a golf outing at Pebble Beach Golf Course, within walking distance of their house in Carmel, but Ardie, claiming she had a bronchial infection which the sea air would only aggravate, remained at home in Los Gatos, or at least that is what she said. When Phil returned home on June 30, the actual day of his birthday, he found that his wife had cleared out her closets and had left only a note in an envelope on the bar, which announced that she "had to" leave her husband and that she was seeking legal separation. Ardie assured Phil in the same note that she would never file for divorce because of her Catholic faith, but she had retained a "good Catholic woman attorney" nonetheless, in case Phil decided to file for divorce. If he decided to go that route, Ardie concluded, "you might have to split up your kingdom." At another point, Ardie explained to her children that she was afraid her husband might turn out to be another O.J. Simpson.

Everything that Phil knows about Ardie's actions after her departure had to be pieced together through conversations with people who were mutual friends. In June of 1994, right around the time that Phil was involved in the lawsuit and setting up the collating systems in Puerto Rico, Marcia Smith took Yelka Tolaitch out to lunch and advised her that if Yelka were to leave her husband, the two of them could go into business together. Yelka speaks fluent Croatian and assumed that the business in question involved taking tours to Medjugorje. Two weeks after Ardie left home, she phoned Alice Stadler, a 95-year-old friend from Los Gatos, to whom she had brought communion for 16 years to inform her that she had left her husband on the advice of three priests and a bishop. Alice responded by saying that only a phony priest or bishop would give advice like that. Months later, Father Michael Walsh, Teresa Lopez's pastor at St. Thomas More Parish in Denver, told Phil that he had heard that either Bishop Hnilica or Father Luciano had asked Ardie for $80,000, which sum Phil now thinks was used to finance a trip to Rome and the Holy Land for the bishop and his entourage. Immediately after Ardie's departure, Phil called Marcia Smith who claimed that she was as surprised as he was that Ardie had left and said she had no idea where she was.

Phil now had to carry on with the lawsuit and the business with the added burden of the break-up of his marriage. "I was devastated. I was in shock. The letter from Ardie had a major impact on my life," he said later. In early July, Phil took a business trip to Wisconsin, where he met with a man by the name of Dave McCaffrey, who was then head of a computer firm called Remage. At the meeting, Phil offered to sell his business to Remage for $1.5 million. When he got back home, he hired a private detective.

At around the same time, a story appeared in the German Catholic weekly, *Die Bildpost*, announcing that Bishop Hnilica's conviction for trafficking in stolen goods had been overturned on appeal. Two days later on July 6, 1994, Tomislav Pervan was named provincial *ad instar* to the Herzegovina province of the Franciscans. The title meant that the province was under penalties imposed by Rome. One week later, all of the Franciscans in the province were suspended. Feeling the need for some spiritual guidance, Phil Kronzer decided to make a pilgrimage, but as if somehow sensing that his troubles were associated with Medjugorje, this time he chose to go to Fatima instead.

At around the same time that Phil Kronzer hired a detective and set off for Fatima, Robert Stevenson was at the Southern California Renewal Center servicing a copier where he came across a little white book called *In the End My Immaculate Heart Will Triumph* co-authored by Teresa Lopez and Bishop Paolo Maria Hnilica, consisting of messages which Lopez allegedly received from the Blessed Mother along with the consecration which had been used in Medjugorje that March and a series of prayers for the 33-day-long consecration. When he brought it back to his wife, he was a little surprised by her reaction. Normally Suzanne would just go along with her husband's religious enthusiasm in a vague way, but now she seemed to react differently. "We know what they're going to say," she told her husband without even reading the book. "It's time we stopped going to these things." She was referring to the Medjugorje conferences and the books he would bring home from them, "and time we started living the messages." That night Robert and Suzanne knelt down beside their bed and began the 33-day consecration.

"This is what did it to us," Stevenson said later, referring to the little white book. "The other people who moved to the refuge had done the same thing from the same book." When Stevenson learned that Phil and Ardie Kronzer had also done the same consecration, he said, "This is spooky. Maybe it's a curse."

The Blessed Mother was getting confused too, and given the political situation in Bosnia Herzegovina in the summer of 1994, who could blame her? On August 24, 1994, the Gospa appeared to Marija Pavlovic and announced: "Dear Children! Today I am united with you in prayer in a special way, praying for the gift of the presence of my most beloved son in your home country. I pray and intercede before my son, Jesus, so that the dream that your fathers had may be fulfilled."

Not only was the Gospa getting increasingly nationalistic, she was also having a tough time keeping up with political developments and their geographical consequences in the Balkans. The passage "the presence of my beloved son in your home country" referred to the upcoming trip the pope was planning to make to Zagreb and Sarajevo, which were now in two different countries. On September 7, three days before the pope was scheduled to arrive in Sarajevo, Serb artillery rounds slammed into a mountain less than a mile from where the pope was scheduled to hold his outdoor Mass, bringing about a cancellation of this trip. "The Serbs have a direct line on us," said one local observer. "They watch us and can choose to hit you in the left eye or the right."

The cancellation of the trip had embarrassing consequences for the Gospa, especially in light of her August 24 message. Either she didn't know that the trip to Sarajevo was going to be canceled at the last minute, or she hadn't figured out yet that Croatia and Bosnia were now two separate countries. Telling the residents of Bosnia that Croatia was "your home country" made the Gospa sound more like Franjo Tudjman's press secretary than the Mother of God.

On September 11, 1994, the pope arrived in Zagreb for an abbreviated tour of the Balkans. During the Mass at Zagreb's 12th-century Gothic cathedral, the pope praised Alojzije Cardinal Stepinac as "undoubtedly the most prominent" martyr in Croatia's history.

Terming Cardinal Stepinac a "hero of sacredness," the pope said that "by his work, courage , patience, silence and in the end his death," Stepinac offered himself "as a victim rather than deny his faith" when then-Communist dictator Josip Broz Tito had him tried and imprisoned. After praising the man whom Richard West described as "the major opponent of Slav unity," the pope then spoke of the need for reconciliation among Roman Catholics, Orthodox Christians, and Muslims, locked in war in neighboring Bosnia, rejecting the idea that religion was linked to the "nationalistic intolerance which is raging in these region."

"Has not history created thousands of indestructible ties

between your peoples?"

The Serbs didn't think so. They had been feeling especially beleaguered since they had been blamed for the mortar attack in Sarajevo. NATO airstrikes followed shortly thereafter, and now the Serbs felt that they had their backs to the wall. On August 10, Elizabeth Neuffer of the *Boston Globe* filed a story on how the Serbs planned to battle the world alone. "If NATO attacks us," one 60-year-old Serb bellowed to an approving crowd of fellow Serbs, "we'll attack back and if we all die, so what?" "The Serbs," Neuffer concluded, "would rather die than go back under the Muslims' control. The world doesn't understand what is going on here."

On September 23, 1994, a U.S. A-10 ground assault plane pumped a few hundred depleted uranium rounds into a stationary, unoccupied Soviet-make T-55 Serbian tank on the outskirts of Sarajevo as two British Jaguar jets finished off the job by dropping a 1,000 bomb each on the target. The news story made clear that the tank was singled out "primarily because it would have been difficult to pinpoint" the weapons which were actually responsible for the attack on the peacekeepers the day before. The strategy was reminiscent of the joke about the drunk who was looking for his car keys under the street lamp not because he had lost them anywhere in the vicinity but because the light was better there.

In September 1994, two days after Phil got back from Fatima he found out that Marcia Smith had lied to him. Smith not only knew where Ardie was, under the alias of Ann McCormick, her middle and maiden names respectively, she had leased her an automobile, rented her an apartment, and had a phone installed in Ardie's new apartment as well. The gas and electric service to the new apartment were also listed under Ann McCormick's name. After moving out, Ardie had been in constant contact with the Medjugorje network in the Bay Area, calling Father Ted Shipp, a priest involved with St. Raphael Ministries, which was an integral part of the same network. After Phil shared the information about his wife's whereabouts with his children, Mike and Cindy Hintz, Phil's son-in-law and daughter decided to drop in on her mother unannounced. When they got there they found Ardie, a bit nonplussed by the surprise visit, hoping to engage her in conversation. Before they got very far, Marcia Smith arrived and asked Cindy what was going on. Cindy replied that it was none of her business. Ignoring Smith's pleas, Mike and Cindy jumped off the porch, walked around the house, and followed Ardie into the backyard. Ardie, who was 57 years old at the time, seemed thinner. Later they would estimate that she had lost around 15 pounds; she was also having trouble focusing her eyes and seemed distracted by Marcia, who kept insisting that they had a meeting scheduled with Father Shipp and, prevailing on her, finally got her away from her children and into a car and drove off.

Phil by now had come to the conclusion that the lawsuit with APS played a role in Ardie's leaving. "They convinced her," Phil said later, "that she couldn't take the lawsuit." The women who had urged her to leave her husband, Phil was discovering, also made it as difficult as possible for him to reach her. Jeannie Martin, the DRE from St. Mary's Parish in Los Gatos, picked up Ardie's mail from a post office box, with the result that she only got letters once a week, and then only after the woman who delivered the post had gone over them. Ardie, now freed from the responsibilities of marriage, was swept up into an increasingly hectic schedule of Medjugorje events—conferences, retreats, and prayer groups—which took her to the East Coast and out of the country. In October of '94, Yelka Tolaitch heard that Ardie was in Split and called the seer Mirjana Dragicevic to ask her help in locating her, but soon gave up after it became apparent that Ardie didn't want to be contacted, at least not by Yelka. "Marcia and your wife," Yelka later told Phil, "set up Teresa Lopez." Ardie finally contacted Phil and arranged for a 45-minute meeting at Father Mike Burns's rectory. The meeting led nowhere, and face-to-face contact was soon replaced by correspondence between the couple's lawyers.

In October, Bishop Ratko Peric, ordinary of the diocese of Mostar, traveled to Rome to attend the Synod of Bishops there. During his intervention he brought up the situation in Medjugorje and asked for help in resolving it. "I told them I would be happy if Rome took it off my hands," he said later, perhaps indicating that he was tired of fighting this battle. There was another interpretation as well. If Rome weren't going to take the situation out of the bishop's hands, then he would have to resolved it himself.

In Bosnia, meanwhile, the Muslim-led government was getting a second wind. In October and November, it was finally able to field an army which was able to take ground back from the Serbs. By the end of October, the government forces had captured 60 square miles of territory southeast of the Bihac pocket. By November 1, they had expanded the area they controlled around Bihac to 77 square miles and were on the verge of taking Bosanska Krupa, the first town they had captured during the entire war. Alarmed by the reversal of fortune, Radovan Karadzic vowed to take back the lost ground, which is precisely what the Serbs did over the month of November. The war was clearly headed for a stalemate. The Bosnian Muslims, in spite of a huge infusion of arms from Iran, one-third of which went to the Croats for the courtesy of letting their planes land in Zagreb, were unable to consolidate the "country" of Bosnia-Herzegovina by force of arms, and the Serbs and the Croats couldn't partition Bosnia-Herzegovina into chunks of territory belonging to Serbia and Croatia respectively because NATO and the United Nations wouldn't let them. By the end of November, U.S. Defense Secretary William Perry was intimating that the Bosnian government had lost the war, and Sir Michael Rose, the commander of the 24,000-man UN peacekeeping force was suggesting withdrawal if the situation continued to deteriorate. Meanwhile, the Serbs put the villages they recaptured around Bihac to the torch.

"Bihac," said Kemal Kurspahic in the *Boston Globe* at the end of November . . . is really the first chapter of post-Cold War history. All the institutions that were supposed to keep some international order and provide leadership have failed." The Muslim government, Kurspahic continued from his offices at Harvard University, where he was spending the year as a Nieman fellow, is "defending certain values on which this civilization was supposed to function. Not only their lives and their wives and their children, but the ideal of tolerance and multi-ethnicity." The war in Bosnia came down to a war between two competing world views. The Muslims were being paid by NATO and the UN to represent abstractions of the sort the West had been fighting over since the French Revolution proposed "Liberty, Fraternity, Equality" as the universalist credo that would both negate and provide a substitute for the ties which nation, family, and Christianity had proposed in the past. The Serbs, for their part, were fighting for blood and soil. They and their families made up one-third of the population of Bosnia and occupied one-half of the land. Woodrow Wilson had carried his crusade for abstraction, then under the banner of democracy, to this part of the world by creating Yugoslavia in the aftermath of World War I. Now that Wilson's legacy had collapsed, the people who believed in the abstractions were determined to do the same thing all over again on a smaller scale. Bosnia, now a smaller version of Yugoslavia, had become the bulwark of multiculturalism in the Balkans, and rump Yugoslavia was now Greater Serbia, and now even the *New York Times'* s Roger Cohen was having second thoughts about Wilsonian country-making by fiat, even if it were being done on a smaller scale, terming the recognition of Bosnia-Herzegovina in April of 1992 "as close to criminal negligence as a diplomatic act can be. Indeed, international recognition and the outbreak of the Bosnian War were simultaneous: The world put a light to the fuse."

The West was having a tough time articulating its own principles. If, in other words, it was okay to violate the sovereign borders of the old Yugoslavia by recognizing Bosnia-Herzegovina as a sovereign state, why were Bosnia's borders, which its own government had never been able to control, then so sacrosanct? Bosnia, in other words, made no sense as a country, but the people who ruled the world had long ago decided that their political will was reason enough. They had the power and so, therefore, they could create countries by fiat. The Serbs, believing in the primacy of blood and soil over abstractions, no matter how powerful the countries which proposed them, were cast in the role of villain in a neo-Wilsonian crusade which now seemed bent on making the world safe for multiculturalism. Leveler heads, which claimed that the goal in Bosnia should be a workable peace and not borders which never corresponded to political reality, were shouted down by people like Jim Hoagland of the *Boston Herald* who announced on December 12 that "if flattening Belgrade is what it takes to get Serbian acquiescence to a withdrawal that increases the Muslim war-fighting ability, flattening Belgrade would be justified in this context." On December 20, Jimmy Carter flew to Sarajevo to meet with Radovan Karadzic and intimated that Karadzic was justified in claiming that "the American people have heard primarily one side of the story," only to be corrected by Dee Dee Myers, who set the record straight by announcing from the White House that "the Bosnian Serbs are the aggressors in this war." The Clinton Administration then hinted that Carter was being manipulated by Karadzic, who, they intimated darkly, used to be the psychiatrist for the Sarajevo soccer team.

On November 8, 1994, Father Stefano Gobbi, creator of a worldwide network of "cenacles" known as the Marian Movement of Priests, which were in turn based on what he claimed were locutions from the Blessed Mother, appeared on *Mother Angelica Live* and announced that "all secrets" would be revealed by the year 2000, hoping to cash in, in his own way, on the apocalypse fever that was afflicting certain segments of the Catholic population in the United States. When a TV viewer called in to ask if this included the secrets of Medjugorje, Gobbi claimed, "I do not know about Medjugorje. Our Lady has only appointed me to be the head of this movement." The statement implicated Gobbi in two lies. To begin with, the Congregation for the Doctrine of the Faith would eventually rule that there was nothing supernatural about the messages which appeared in his book *Our Lady Speaks to Her Beloved Priests* and would eventually force him to delete all references to the Blessed Mother in the title, reducing it to the slightly incoherent title, *To Her Priests*.

But beyond that Gobbi lied when he said, "I do not know about Medjugorje," because the "Blessed Mother" had mentioned it to him in one of his messages. Actually, the situation was more dramatic than that. Gobbi's book was full of dramatic messages, but the message of July 3, 1987, was an "urgent message," so urgent in fact that the MMP felt obliged to print up what must have been millions of fliers announcing that "already during this year, certain great events will take place concerning what I predicted at Fatima and have told, under secrecy to the children *to whom I am still appearing at Medjugorje*." Just what happened in 1987 is not clear. Had Gobbi sent out the same dire message two years later, he might have laid claim to predicting the fall of the Berlin Wall and the collapse of the Soviet Union. As it was, he not only came up empty in 1987, he also put himself on record as saying that the Blessed Mother was appearing to the children at Medjugorje, claiming that he heard this from the Blessed Mother's mouth. The statement was to prove especially embarrassing in 1991, when the Yugoslavian bishops, speaking for the Church, announced that the Blessed Mother was not appearing in Medjugorje. Not to be outmaneuvered by the course of events, Gobbi chose the Soviet solution to his problems. The offending passage was simply stricken from all editions of his book beginning with the 1991 edition.

One day after Gobbi lied on Mother Angelica, Ivan Dragicevic married Loreen Murphy, the former Miss Massachusetts, in a Catholic ceremony in Boston. Ivan always claimed that the Gospa had a plan for his life. As of 1994 that plan included flunking out of two seminaries, taking an oath of allegiance to an officially atheist communist government to serve in their military, and now marrying a beauty queen and acquiring homes and expensive cars and furnishings on two continents. A little less than two weeks later, while the Dragicevics were still on their honeymoon, Teresa Lopez's divorce from Jeff was finalized on November 21, 1994. A little over a month later, on December 25, 1994, Ardie Kronzer was spending Christmas Day with her daughter Cindy and her family in California. Standing at the sink in the kitchen, Ardie suddenly burst into tears and began apologizing for being such a terrible mother. Cindy tried to comfort her mother, but Ardie seemed inconsolable and couldn't stop crying. When Phil heard later about his wife's behavior, he became convinced that the Medjugorje group under Marcia Smith had such a hold on her that some physical intervention might be necessary to keep her from going back to them. "We had the opportunities," he said.

Two weeks earlier, CNS reported that "the slow-moving wheels of Italian justice" had stymied Italian prosecutors from hauling Bishop Hnilica back into court ever since his conviction for receiving stolen documents had been overturned on procedural grounds. They indicated that as soon as they found out why the court decided in Hnilica's favor, they would consider reopening the case.

-15-

THE BISHOP GETS KIDNAPPED

In June of 1994 Father Philip Pavich was in the middle of a months long stay in Rome when he happened to see Joseph Cardinal Ratzinger, prefect for the Congregation for the Doctrine of the Faith, walking across St. Peter's Square on the way to his office. Pavich wanted to talk about Medjugorje in general but about Vassula in particular and the connection between the two as well, and so, throwing protocol to the winds he simply walked up to Ratzinger and asked, "Can I see you?" After Pavich stated the reason for the meeting he was proposing, Ratzinger gave him a knowing smile and quickly wrote a note saying he should contact instead a Father Gian Franco Girotte in his office. Evidently Girotte was already at work on the same project. On January 3, 1995, Pavich finally met with Girotte, and over the next few months, Pavich and Girotte collaborated on the Vassula project, a collaboration which culminated in the CDF condemnation of Vassula in October of 1995. Pavich was convinced at the time that Vassula was a trial balloon for Medjugorje; however, the idea raises more questions than it answers. If the Vatican could deal with Vassula, a spin-off of Medjugorje, with relative dispatch, why had they still not said anything on Medjugorje, other than reiterating whatever the Yugoslavian bishops had said?

Pavich had no answers, other than that the pope was protecting it, but by January of 1995 he had had enough. Within the space of a little over 10 years, Pavich had gone from a devotee to someone who was convinced that Medjugorje was sort of a spiritual bug zapper which attracted both the credulous and the spirits who feasted on their demise and the middle men who facilitated the exchange while making profits for themselves. While in Rome Pavich had requested permission to be transferred back to his home province in Chicago. In

January, he returned to Medjugorje to pick up his effects, but then something unexpected happened. Tomislav Pervan, formerly the pastor at Medjugorje, now provincial *ad instar* for the renegade Herzegovina province, called him into his office. Pavich was quite aware of the irregular nature of the ecclesial situation there but had hung around in the hope that his activities might bring about some reconciliation. By January Pavich had dismissed any idea of reconciliation as the result of actions on his part as futile. The rebellion had been going on for almost 20 years, and it had been institutionalized, camouflaged, and nurtured through the apparitions, and nothing he could say would change that situation, so it was with a cold resignation that Pavich met with Pervan. Pervan's meeting, however, turned into the pastoral and psychological equivalent of hot and cold showers. At first Pervan berated Pavich for disloyalty to the Croatian province because of his trip to Rome. Then he berated him for all sorts of pastoral irregularities in his ministry; finally, Pervan pulled out a sheaf of letters written by English-speaking pilgrims from all over the world praising Pavich's pastoral care, and suddenly reversing his previous approach, Pervan asked Pavich to stay on at Medjugorje because he was so popular with the pilgrims.

The abrupt about-face on Pervan's part can be interpreted in any number of ways. The most plausible is that the Franciscans had come to see Pavich as a threat to Medjugorje, but that the best way of dealing with the threat was keeping him under close scrutiny, which meant keeping him at Medjugorje. That was the simple part of the story; the complex part involved coming up with an explanation of why Pavich agreed to stay because that is what he did. Instead of moving back to Chicago, Pavich unpacked his bags and continued his ministry as chaplain to the phony apparitions, an assignment which continued to afflict him with a bad case of ambivalence. On the one hand, Pavich viewed the apparitions as a clearinghouse for the occult being run by a renegade bunch of Franciscan Mafiosi. On the other hand, he got to minister to the troubled refugees from the "Am-Church," which is to say the modernist morals, theology, and liturgy afflicting the Catholic Church in the English speaking world since Vatican II while at the same time preventing them from going to the enthusiast extremes the normal reaction to this sort of thing all-too predictably created. The crucial enabling device in Pavich's ambivalence was the equally ambivalent 1991 BCY statement on Medjugorje, which called for the care of pilgrims coming to the shrine where the Blessed Mother had not appeared and was not appearing. In many ways, Medjugorje was the Marian equivalent of deconstructionism: The shrine was a sign of the Blessed Mother's absence. Likewise Pavich was often afflicted with doubts about his role there, feeling on bad days that he may be lending credibility to the very thing he was trying to oppose. As of early 1997, he was still agonizing over what to do. In March 1997, he was planning to do a novena for guidance. The last day of the novena would coincide with the pope's visit to Sarajevo. If bitterness could be poured into a cup, then Pavich's cup would run over if he were to explain his education at the hands of the religious freak show that made its way to Medjugorje to bow down before the idol which Pavich characterized as "another Jesus."

In January 1995, around the same time Father Pavich was meeting with Father Girotte in Rome, Phil Kronzer contacted a number of exit counselors and finally hired a guy from Philadelphia. Exit counseling has fallen on hard times lately. The same government which declared Bosnia an independent country also declared Scientology, with about as much justification, a religion, and thereafter decided that people who tried to remove family members from what they considered abusive cults could be charged with kidnapping. The so-called Church of Scientology, whose highest spiritual state was taken from the clear button on an adding machine, profited from Caesar's largesse in creating religion by fiat and had fought a series of court battles which resulted in a victory over one of its major foes, the Cult Awareness Network, which ended up going out of business because of a large legal judgment against it. CAN also lost all of its files to the very group that was trying to put it out of business, creating a chilling effect among the beleaguered group of people who tried to get friends and relatives out of cults.

Throughout his battle to restore his marriage, Phil Kronzer found himself swimming against powerful currents which dictated the terms of the discussion. Religion was deemed by the legal system as *de facto* bizarre, and so no one could claim that Scientology, invented by a science-fiction writer in the '50s, was any different from Roman Catholicism, which had been around since the beginning of the Christian Era. Similarly, the man who fought to restore his marriage was to some degree *de facto* suspected of wanting to restrict his wife's freedom to be herself. Finally, all of the cultural arrangements in California seemed to favor divorce over marriage because there was a large network of people, mostly feminists, who profited handsomely from wrecking marriages. The lawyers made out well, as did the real estate agents, who profited every time one of California's multi-million dollar homes went on the block. Often the two groups worked hand in glove.

Given the circumstances, Phil was involved in an uphill battle, which is probably why he felt moved to contact an exit counselor. It seemed like a simple solution to a problem that was becoming bewilderingly complex. Phil had decided on an intervention for some time in February, feeling that with three days of unhindered access and the help of the exit counselors, he could break the hold that the Medjugorje crowd had over his wife. The counselors suggested a remote place in the mountains, and so Phil rented two cabins near Truckee. Ardie would be abducted during a meal that was planned for a Sunday night. Two days before the dinner date, however, Ardie called to say that she had developed a bronchial infection and couldn't make it. Perhaps she had been warned. At any rate, after that, the meetings between Ardie and her family became fewer and farther in between. At this point, Phil began to feel that other people were somehow privy to his plans in a way that he didn't understand.

At around the same time that Phil Kronzer was making plans to have his wife deprogrammed, Robert Stevenson called the Juda Refuge in Buffalo Gap, South Dakota, and had a long conversation with Gwen and Eben Johns, who were living there at the time. They had come to Kucera's refuge by way of Lubbock, Texas, where they had seen some miraculous photos—Mary of the Diamond, or something like that coming down from heaven and into the church there. Robert was so enthusiastic about his initial phone call that he decided then and there to donate a photocopier to the refuge. Just what role a photocopier was to play during the coming chastisement was not clear then or now, but before long Robert's wife was calling the Johnses at the Buffalo Gap refuge on her own, and before long, the two were making plans to travel there in person. The Stevensons had become, in fact, so convinced that they were being called by God to move to the refuge that they had their first garage sale before they flew out for their first visit. As an omen foretelling something about the upcoming trip, the Stevensons in addition to the usual detritus that gets offered at garage sales put the presents they had received at their wedding up for sale as well.

As part of the restructuring of the diocese of Mostar into four parts, Bishop Peric had given the Franciscans a deadline of March 12, 1995, to vacate the hall that housed the illicit St. Anthony's CIM parish. By March 26, the deadline had not only come and gone, the supporters of the Franciscans in Mostar had become so enraged by the actions of the bishop that they were now organizing protests against him. Denied an audience, the Franciscans and their supporters took to the streets.

At around the same time, a woman in California by the name of Mary Doe (not her real name) was trying to put the pieces of her life together. The mother of two children by two different men, Doe had undergone a conversion and had persuaded the father of her second child to marry her in the Church. Then inexplicably he up and left her.

As part of her conversion, Mary had gotten involved in prolife work, and then Marian devotion, and then, after helping her father build an easel for the soon-to-arrive image of Our Lady of Guadaloupe, Mary had been handed a copy of Ted Flynn's magazine, which at the time was heavily promoting Marvin Kucera as the spiritual flavor of the month. Mary had seen Flynn on Mother Angelica and felt that he was, therefore, approved by the Church. Since Flynn was promoting Kucera, Kucera, she reasoned, must be approved as well. Later, after Mary's involvement in the refuges deepened, Marvin told her that the proof of his authenticity was his acceptance by the Flynns. "You have to be really authentic to be accepted by them," he said.

Mary got a copy of *My Heart Awaits You* in March of 1995, and with the sense that her life of raising two kids with no husband was not doable without some kind of divine assistance, she began reading Kucera's book with an eye open for clues about the future and the sense that she had to trust the Lord wherever he was leading her. At the back of her copy were the same phone numbers that Robert Stevenson had found in his book, and so in April of 1995, thinking that this was where the Lord was leading her, Mary gave Marv Kucera a call.

Mary had undergone a conversion experience in October of 1991. After going to confession and deciding to pray the rosary on a regular basis, Mary soon noticed that getting serious about the Catholic faith in California at that time meant getting involved in a phony apparition. People started coming to her to turn her on to false apparitions, something she found confusing because she had only received an 8th grade education in the Catholic faith, and the schooling hadn't been particularly good either. Right around the same time, her oldest sister gave her a book on the alleged apparitions in Scottsdale, Arizona. Going to Catholic bookstores, Mary became so annoyed at all of the material on Medjugorje and its spin-offs that she made the owner of the Catholic Footsteps bookstore in Hesperia, California, an offer: She would buy up all his Medjugorje material and put it on her VISA card if he would promise not to restock it. Victor, the owner, did not take her up on her offer. "There are people who would get very mad at me if I did that," Victor told her, referring to either the store's backers or its regular customers.

In October 1991 Mary finally went to Scottsdale, Arizona, because the apparition thing "wouldn't leave me alone." Mary knew that Scottsdale was intimately connected to Medjugorje, and she knew that she didn't like Medjugorje, but one day she went to her parent's house, and her mother informed her that they were going to Scottsdale, and Mary took this a sign from heaven that she was supposed to go. When she got there with her family, Mary went to Maria

Goretti parish for Mass, confession, and the rosary and met no visionaries but did meet Fr. Jack Spalding, the priest who created the Scottsdale spin-off apparitions, who blessed something or other for Mary. At around this time, Mary's parents bought land in Arizona.

In February of 1993 the whole family had made contact with a visionary from Piru, California, by the name of Sadie Heronimo. Sadie was involved with Father Gobbi's Marian Movement of Priests and had been getting visions herself of a catastrophe which was to strike California imminently, something like an earthquake. Before long, Sadie came up with the day and the hour, and so Mary's family dutifully bought RV's and trailers. Her father was wealthy, and so buying this sort of thing was no problem for him. On March 19, 1993, the feast of St. Joseph, they all ended up in the parking lot of St. Joseph's Church in Nepomo, California, waiting for the chastisement to occur, with the permission and tacit approval of Father James Cadera, the pastor of the church.

Needless to say, nothing happened. Sadie the visionary would periodically go off to a fairground nearby, where other visionaries were waiting, to consult with her peers, to find out what was holding up the chastisement. "She told us a bunch of garbage," Mary said later, but in spite of the garbage, no disillusionment with the phony seer business set in. In fact, when Mary got back home she became even more heavily involved in apparition chasing, in particular with the MMP, whose imprimatur (which she later discovered was a fake) calmed her fears about its legitimacy.

Although Mary seemed to weather each successive fake apparition without serious disillusionment with the Catholic faith, the apparition chasing was starting to take a toll on her marriage. Mary had married an abusive alcoholic in 1982. The marriage lasted five months and ended in divorce but not before she conceived a child, Tiffany, who was born in 1983. In 1984 Mary met Pat Doe, born in 1957, who had been raised in Minnesota, one of ten children from a Catholic home. Neither Mary nor Pat were practicing the faith at the time and so because she had not gotten an annulment, they got married in front of a justice of the peace in 1984.

In 1988 Mary kicked Pat out of their home for being unfaithful. He was spending nights away from home with no good explanation. They separated in 1988, and the divorce became final in 1991. However, they never really broke off the relationship totally. In October 1991, Mary began annulment proceedings against her first husband. By then she had two kids, one by the first husband and one by the second, Kaitlin, born in 1987.

In the summer of 1993, Pat and Mary decided to get remarried in the Church, something they did on July 3, 1993, with Father Cadera officiating at the same parish in whose parking lot they had awaited the end of the world—or at least the end of California—that past March. Perhaps because of the embarrassing experience of the previous March, Father Cadera was having a change of heart about apparitions. Cadera had just been to Ireland and when he came back he kicked all the Medjugorje people out of the parish. When Rene Laurentin heard about this, he came to see him to demand an explanation and was told, "I have been enlightened by E. Michael Jones," referring not to an encounter with the man in person but rather the reading of his book, *Medjugorje: The Untold Story*. Pat and Mary became involved with Santa Maria, another apparition, after they picked up a book on it with an imprimatur by Msgr. Rohde, who had examined the seer with the assistance of Rene Laurentin, seer certifier extraordinaire. Rohde was also responsible for the phony imprimatur on Teresa Lopez's book.

After their remarriage, Mary returned home with Pat and became involved in home schooling, going to mass every day and dabbling in various apparitions—a regimen not untypical for the Catholics of the time who considered themselves serious about the faith. In June of 1994 she invited a priest to her home to enthrone the Sacred Heart there. In the course of his visit, Mary told him that her husband hated sacramentals, to which the priest said it was because of something in his personal life. In spite of what the priest said, or perhaps because of it, Pat continued to resent the faith. He didn't like the rosary or prolife work or home schooling. When he arrived home on February 25, 1995, and Mary started talking about her prolife activities, he responded by saying that he had had enough. He then went up to his room, packed his stuff, and left. Mary is now convinced that he was having an affair at the time.

A little over two weeks later, on March 13, 1995, the missionary image of Our Lady of Guadaloupe was scheduled to arrive in town. Mary and her father had built an easel for it and had then gone to Barstow, California, to deliver it . While there a fellow apparition chaser gave her a copy of Marv Kucera's book. At the time, she was particularly vulnerable. Her husband had just walked out on her, she had no car, and she was praying to God, "What am I going to do?" When she got Kucera's book, the thought immediately crossed her mind, "God wants me to move to the refuge." As a result she called Kucera in April of 1995

Marv called back a few days later and suggested that she come to Prescott, Arizona, to meet him. Pat called around the same time, and the two decided to go meet Marv together along with Mary's daughter Tiffany, who was 13 at the time. Marv was looking for land near Prescott, Arizona, to start another refuge. The meeting with the Does, however, did not go well. Of the three members of the Doe family who drove to Arizona that April, Mary was the only one who didn't develop an immediate dislike for Kucera. Pat said immediately that Marv was a phony. When they got back home, however, Marv contacted Pat, who went back for a short visit in spite of his initial negative reaction.

In the meantime Tiffany's dad found out about the trip to the refuge and began legal proceedings to get custody of Tiffany based on the plan to move there. While in the RV park in Arizona where her parents were staying, Mary woke up at 3:33 a.m. after a horrifying dream in which her daughter was taken from her. She then went to her parents and told them she had to return to California immediately and then left in their car and got back to California in five hours. When she went to her ex-husband's house, he wouldn't let her in and informed her that she had missed a custody hearing the previous day at one p.m. and that her daughter wasn't coming back.

Mary couldn't get her attorney on the phone. Pat came over and both got on the phone with Marv, who said he would pray for them. He also added oddly that her daughter had made her decision and that Mary would therefore do better to drop everything and come back to the refuge. Marv had talked Pat into reconciling and now wanted both of them to come back to the refuge because Pat was an electrician and handy with other machinery as well. The judge, in the meantime referred the matter to family court. Kucera was named in the court papers, along with his book, *My Heart Awaits You.*

Once the custody hearing took place, the judge almost immediately gave Mary custody of the child again feeling that the whole thing was obviously a trick on the part of her first husband. The husband then persuaded Tiffany to say that Mary had been beating her, whereupon the judge reversed the order. Marv was still pressuring Mary to move to the refuge, but she now told him she wasn't going anywhere until she got Tiffany back. Eventually, Tiffany recanted before the judge, and Mary got custody again, but not before Marv in his opportunistic way took credit for Mary regaining custody. Marv pulled strings with the Almighty—at least this is what he was claiming after the fact. In the meantime, Pat decided to leave his wife and family once again, and so when Mary got her daughter back in June 1995 along with permission to move wherever she wanted, she took it as a sign that she and her daughter were supposed to move to one of Marvin's refuges.

Two years after the house-to-house fighting in Mostar in May 1993 had resulted in the deaths of 300 Croatian soldiers, the families of those soldiers and their Franciscan supporters showed no sign of acceding to Bishop Peric's request that they close down St. Anthony's

CIM Church hall and return to their diocesan-appointed parishes. The March 12, 1995, date appointed by Bishop Peric had come and gone, and the protests, instead of abating, grew more intense. On April 2, 1995, Bishop Peric was at home in his new makeshift residence in the modern cathedral building across the road from the bishop's palace, which had been destroyed two years earlier in the battle during which the Croats had driven the Muslims out from the west bank across the Neredva into eastern Mostar. On March 26, the same group of people had marched to the bishop's residence and demanded an audience and had been refused. This time they weren't going to take no for an answer.

After setting up a microphone in the plaza outside, a mob of thugs and women sympathetic to the Franciscans demanded that Peric come out and meet with them. When Peric failed to appear, the mob became angry, broke into the residence, and searched it from room to room until they found Peric, at which point they dragged him out to the microphone and demanded that he give the Franciscans permission to continue running their illicit church. Standing there with diocesan Vicar Luka Pavlovic next to him, Peric again refused and then went on to say that just as Jesus Christ had to suffer, so he as Christ's representative for the diocese of Mostar would have to suffer too.

The speech only enraged the mob even more, and at this point they surged toward him, tore off his pectoral cross, ripped off his cape, and punched him in the stomach. at which point he reminded them that the ecclesial penalty for assaulting a bishop was automatic excommunication. The mob, however, in no mood to hear lectures on canon law, dragged both Peric and Pavlovic to a waiting car and drove them to the CIM church hall, at which point he was directed to get out of the car, enter the hall, and light a candle in front of the 300 dead Croatian war heroes, whose pictures adorned the wall inside. Peric, however, refused to get out of the car, and so he and Pavlovic sat there for the next ten hours, while the crowd outside taunted him by shouting that his mother was a Serbian and that there were plenty of guns in Mostar, presumably which could be used on him. The Franciscans, who could have dispersed the mob at any time during the long day of protest and standoff, pretended not to know what was happening.

At 10 p.m. the situation was critical. The mob surrounding the bishop's car had convinced itself that the bishop was guilty of some insult to their dead, and it was only a matter of time because they took action which they considered appropriate to that affront. At this point Father Ivan Sevo, the superior of the Franciscan monastery, showed up with Ico Skoko and the mayor of the city of Mostar. Between them, they persuaded the mob to disperse. Then as everyone was going home, the mayor tried to hustle Peric and Pavlovic off into a waiting taxi, but Peric refused again to get out of the car insisting that he be taken home in the same car which brought him.

By 11 p.m., Peric was back in his residence. In May 1995 he published an account of the kidnapping incident in the diocesan newspaper; however, he didn't have to wait that long for a response. The next day his fax machine started smoking with letters of condolence and outrage from the various church officials who had heard about the incident. On April 3 he received a fax expressing support from Cardinal Tomko, Prefect of the Congregation for the Evangelization of Nations and formerly associated with the CDF. On the same day, Peric got a letter of support from Rev. Herman Schalueck, OFM, the general of the Franciscan order, who apologized for the behavior of those under the spiritual guidance of the Franciscans, "who respect neither you nor me." Eventually, the church hall got shut down, but the Franciscans continued to whip up the local population against the bishop in other ways.

In April of 1995, Ardie Kronzer, going back on what she had written about marriage and her Catholic faith in her good-bye letter to her husband, filed for divorce. Phil now thinks the issue was money. The people who were advising Ardie felt that they weren't getting at the Kronzer money in a way that justified their efforts. Divorce meant that Ardie would get 50 percent, according to the laws of the state of California, and the people functioning as Ardie's spiritual directors already had plans for the money. In the summer of 1995, Gary Nolen, now disillusioned with the Hnilica crowd, ran into Ted Flynn at a Medjugorje conference in Colorado Springs. When Flynn learned that Nolen was from Los Gatos, California, he exclaimed, "Oh, you must know this lady from Los Gatos who is doing all of this wonderful work for the triumph!" When Nolen mentioned Ardie's name, Flynn responded, "Yes, that's her. I understand that she is donating millions to the cause."

The fact that millions of his money had been earmarked for Hnilica's organization could not have pleased Phil Kronzer at the time. In the spring of 1995 he was already involved in one legal battle that wasn't going particularly well. In March Phil and his lawyers had worked out a statement from Brad Weisse, the man who had been keeping Phil abreast of APS tactics against him, and sent it off for him to sign. When they hadn't heard from him in five days, Phil contacted him, and Weisse said he had a problem with the cover letter. When Phil told him to ignore the cover letter, Weisse admitted that he had just gotten a phone call from APS attorneys and that he wasn't prepared to sign the statement they had worked out over the phone. Weisse subsequently changed his testimony completely when APS took his deposition in May 1995 and was now on the other side in the case.

As a result, it became obvious to Phil and Sam Montalvo, his engineer, that they had to do something quickly to turn the situation that their company faced around. Based on their successes with the Microsoft supplier in Puerto Rico, Phil and Sam knew that they had the best disk-packaging system on the market. However, based on the information Brad Weisse had been feeding them, they knew as well that they were being frozen out of the market. They also knew that in two months, Microsoft was planning to launch Windows 95, an operation that entailed the bagging of millions of disks. CDI needed to get its machines in place in order to meet the huge increase in demand that Windows 95 would create. In order to break the impasse, Phil and Sam decided to do a mailing about the CDI bagger/ collator to certain key personnel at Microsoft.

Just as the initial phone calls in response to the mailer started trickling in, Sam got a call from a Liz Johnson, the lady in charge of world-wide commodity sales at Microsoft. Ms. Johnson was irate to begin with, telling Sam that he had to stop sending letters to Microsoft, but became outraged when Sam intimated over the phone that people were lining their pockets at Microsoft with kickbacks that sabotaged production and the efforts of small companies like CDI. In response to Sam's statement and repeated mailings, Ms. Johnson came up with the classic Hollywood line. "If you don't stop mailing," she told Sam, "I will personally go to Bill Gates and make sure you never do business with Microsoft again."

On June 2, 1995, Captain Scott O'Grady of the United States Air Force was flying his F-16 just south of the Bihac pocket in northwestern Bosnia to enforce the UN mandated no-fly zone when his radar indicated that a missile was heading in his direction. Nine seconds later his just-refueled plane started to come apart around him in a ball of fire but not before he reached for the lever of his ejection seat and shot himself safely out of the disintegrating plane. O'Grady landed safely and spent the next five days on the ground eating bugs, drinking rainwater, and avoiding Serbian paramilitary forces. On day three of his ordeal, Our Lady of Medjugorje appeared to him, or at least he thinks she did. O'Grady had met a friend of his divorced mother in Las Vegas who had been to Medjugorje, which was in the southern part of the same country where he was now. The story came back to him while hiding out from the Serbs. "It's hard to put this into words," he said later, "but I saw the vision through feeling it, and the feeling was very warm and good."

On June 17, 1995, the chancery of the diocese of Mostar issued a document entitled "Falsehoods on Film," in which they condemned a newly released film entitled *Gospa*, starring Martin Sheen as Father Zovko and Morgan Fairchild as his sister the nun. The film, which was produced by a group of four Croatians, one of whom was the former maitre d' for the Four Seasons Restaurant in New York City, never got distribution in movie houses, but it did end up being promoted by the archdiocese of Los Angeles, in spite of the fact that the Church had already gone on record against the apparitions. What especially attracted the attention of the diocese of Mostar was the film's portrayal of Bishop Zanic, who is, interestingly enough, the only character in the film who doesn't go by his own name. Known as Petar Subic in the film, Bishop Zanic is portrayed as a cowardly opportunist who collaborates with the Communists in suppressing the apparitions out of fear of government reprisal against the Church. "You know, Petar," the evil commissar says to "Bishop Subic," "I'm not an evil man, anymore than you're a holy man. We both want to survive." The chancery rejected this portrayal of Zanic as "untrue":

> Not even a shadow of cowardliness or easing-off of the bishop before the communist authorities was ever in question, let alone any type of collaboration with them, as can be concluded by watching the film. Instead, the bishop always behaved in a courageous and dignified way.

"Falsehoods" then cited the letter Zanic wrote to State President Sergej Kreigher on September 1, 1981, defending Jozo Zovko and condemning "all these irresponsible slanderous attacks against myself and my priests." For his pains in defending Zovko, Zanic was portrayed as a craven collaborator. "Falsehoods on Film" concluded by bringing out the incongruity at the heart of the film. In a land where hundreds of Catholic priests were martyrs for the faith, *Gospa* chose to celebrate the life of a priest who had been deprived of his faculties in 1989 because of repeated sexual harassment of female pilgrims. One actor involved in the film evidently shared the bishop's low opinion of it, if perhaps for other reasons, dismissing it as "a Catholic propaganda film."

In July of 1995 Microsoft released Windows 95, which was collated at all of its assembly plants without the help of CDI, now known as Autodisk, collating systems, and Phil Kronzer hired a detective to stake out Ardie at her new apartment in Foster City. Phil was planning another intervention for the last week in July, and then the date was postponed to August 15. The detective, masquerading as a jogger, was to abduct Ardie and take her to a place where Phil could convince her with the help of exit counselors that she had fallen under the influence of a religious cult. Once this became clear, Ardie would return to her husband, and Phil's troubles would be over. Unfortunately, Ardie got wind of Phil's plans, and once again the attempt to get her de-programmed failed. This time there was talk of her going to the FBI.

On August 19, 1995, Robert Stevenson turned 32 and as a birthday present, he and his wife Suzanne decided to visit Marvin Kucera's Juda Refuge, a former ranch in the Black Hills near Buffalo Gap, South Dakota, just south of Rapid City. Compared to their tract house in Chino Hills, the refuge seemed "like heaven," at least for a while. Robert remembers the main house as surrounded by pine trees and hills from which one could see for what seemed like hundreds of miles down the valley. The Stevensons had always talked about doing missionary work, and now, with Suzanne being a nurse and the world about to come to an end, it seemed as if their dreams were about to come true. The time of persecution, after all, was right around the corner. When Robert called Marvin and told him he was calling from California, Marvin said in no uncertain terms, "Get out of there right away." At the time there was only one house at the refuge, to which two mobile homes had been added to house the newcomers. In addition to that, there was a barn, a Quonset hut, and a tack shed to take care of the animals—the cows, pigs, chickens, and a horse—that were to allow the refuge to operate independently of the outside world.

One of the families already there when the Stevensons arrived was Gwen and Eben Johns, who had come there from Texas. When the Stevensons arrived, Marvin was also there, along with a young man by the name of John Mark, whom he introduced as his son, although it became clear that was not the case when Marvin later told the Stevensons that John Mark was a juvenile delinquent he had picked up on his travels. Robert felt that there was something effeminate about Kucera's behavior and suspected that he was a homosexual, but these initial impressions somehow got lost in the overwhelming impression the refuge was making on him and his wife. On their first day there, they climbed the hill behind the house up to the life-size crucifix at its crest and were already thinking about moving. They were excited about the idea of doing something for God.

After a brief conversation with Marvin, the Stevensons spent most of their time with Gwen and Eben Johns, asking them what it was like working there and getting a sense of what they believed. What they heard encouraged them. The Johns shared many of the Stevensons' beliefs, as did many of the people who traveled in those circles. They practiced NFP; they did home schooling, and they believed, as a result of listening to the swarm of phony seers whose messages percolated through the Medjugorje network, that the world was shortly coming to an end. So far so good. But in addition to all that, the Johns were fervent followers of the Old Mass, and this was a new wrinkle for the Stevensons and a bit hard to swallow since they had come to the apparition scene by way of the Charismatic Renewal in California, which most definitely was not promoting the Tridentine Mass. Sensing that they might be turning the Stevensons off, the Johns decided to drop the Old Mass stuff and took them instead to the newly laid foundation for the Refuge chapel, where they pointed out the rooms where they were going to hide priests in the basement of the chapel when the persecution came.

After staying for about a week, the Stevensons climbed the hill with the Stations of the Cross one last time on Robert's birthday, praying the rosary as they went. When they reached the top of the hill, Robert looked up and saw a cloud in the shape of an angel with its arms outstretched to embrace them. This was finally the sign they had been looking for. When they got back down, they told Marvin, who didn't seem surprised. In fact Marvin told the Stevensons that the angel's name was Sebastian and that he had been given that information in a recent locution. Impressed at the seeming coincidence of all of these miraculous signs and wonders, the Stevensons made up their mind on the spot. They were moving to the refuge. That, however, was not how it worked, Marvin informed them. They couldn't just invite themselves; in fact, even Marvin couldn't just invite them to move there. They had to let the Holy Spirit invite them. When Robert expressed a willingness to put down $3,000 on a lot, it was proof enough for Marvin that the Holy Spirit had invited them. Robert, of course, didn't have that kind of money, but his business did, and for a moment he seems to have suffered a twinge of conscience by the prospect of using his business capital in this way. But, what the hell, he thought, it was only a matter of days before California dropped off into the Pacific Ocean anyway, and after that happened what good would it do to have a business servicing photocopiers? Three thousand dollars poorer, the Stevensons returned to California and started selling everything they owned.

Robert's parents thought the plan to move to South Dakota was a terrible idea. Suzanne's father, however, thought that any plan to move out of California was a good idea and supported them. Robert as a result contacted Marvin about buying a house and put his business, which was then assessed for between $60,000 and $70,000, up for sale. Robert's inventory alone had a value of $20,000, and when he hadn't found any takers during his first month back from South Dakota, that is what he sold the entire business for, to a friend, in September of 1995.

Suzanne, in the meantime, had been going around to all of their friends, informing them of the imminent move, all but bragging about it while at the same time asking their friends for prayers. During a charismatic prayer meeting with their friends Donna and Dave, Suzanne had a series of visions. She saw her family as a group of five dandelions floating along in the wind. Troubled for a moment by the fact that there were only four people in her family as of that time, Suzanne closed her eyes and tried to change the number, but the vision persisted and along with it the sense that "God is going to plant us elsewhere." Robert had a vision himself, of the Star of Bethlehem, and after a while it was clear that no matter what happened to them at the time, it would be interpreted as a sign that they were supposed to do what they had decided they wanted to do anyway, and nothing that their friends or a priest who warned them about the dangers of private revelations could say was going to dissuade them. "We were only looking for people who approved," Robert said later. Suzanne was even more excited than Robert. She was eager to get out of California and eager to get away from Robert's family, who, she felt, had never accepted her because of her mother moving in with another man, because of her drinking, because of her general lack of feminine skills.

There was only one small problem left once the Stevensons had ignored the warnings of their friends and Robert's family. They couldn't sell their house. Real estate had taken a plunge in California since they had bought the house for $139,000. Now it was assessed at $109,000, and they still owed $123,000 on the mortgage. Again, as they did whenever an obstacle stood in the way of their dreams, the Stevensons decided to pray about it, and as a result of their prayers, Robert got a vision, this time of a house floating in the ocean. A debt was a debt, he told himself in his more rational moments, but the vision was just as clear. California was going to fall into the ocean, and the bank was going to lose it anyway, so why not just walk away from the house? Which is precisely what the Stevensons did, destroying their credit rating in the process. Robert simply signed the house over to a finance company, which would assume the debt and rent it to the increasing number of Californians who could no longer afford homes.

Having burned that bridge behind them, the Stevensons drove out of town on October 19, 1995, heading east in a Ryder truck full of what was left of their belongings and a van. Suzanne drove the van and Robert the truck, and the two of them talked with each other the whole way back east to South Dakota over the CB radios they had purchased for the trip.

Before they had left, the Stevensons had sent Marvin $10,000 to buy them a mobile home and then another $1,500 to have it hooked up to a sewer system. Instead Marvin hooked up both the Stevenson's trailer and the one next to theirs, which belonged to a woman by the name of Wally Gorman, to the same septic tank, probably making $500 as a result. Kucera also made money on the trailers. When Robert arrived, Marvin handed him a $9,000 receipt for his $10,000 mobile home and now feels that since it was an old metal model from the '70s that Marvin probable paid less than $8,000 for it and pocketed the rest after getting a doctored receipt. The Stevensons arrived just in time for the first snowstorm of the year, and Suzanne, who claimed to be allergic to the cold as a result of living in California, shivered in the mobile home whose roof leaked as the wind battered the metal box unmercifully. In spite of the cold, or perhaps because of it, the Stevensons conceived their third child on the night of their arrival at the Juda refuge. Now the fifth dandelion in Suzanne's vision had been accounted for. It was taken as a sign that God was with them on this one and that they had made the right move.

By this time, other people were moving in, convinced of the same things that had brought the Stevensons to Buffalo Gap. In addition to the Johnses, who, the Stevensons found out shortly after their arrival, were having marital problems, there was Wally, with whom they shared the same septic tank, and the Fitches, and a mean-looking stock broker from New Jersey and his wife. Robert said the "stockbroker" looked more like a Mafia hit man. His wife, he remembers, was heavily involved in Medjugorje, but then that wasn't all that unusual since everyone there believed in Medjugorje. In addition to that, just about everyone at the Juda Refuge was a regular reader of Ted Flynn's magazine, *Signs of the Times*, which is also not surprising, since all of the people at the refuge were there because they heard of Marvin through the magazine. Some of the residents were into Nancy Fowler's phony apparition, another Medjugorje spin-off, out of Conyers, Georgia. The stockbroker's wife was also involved in promoting Betania, an apparition site in South America. But just about everyone there was familiar with all of the apparition sites, just about all of which were traceable to Medjugorje in some way, and a large part of the conversation at the refuge was devoted to interpreting the various messages. Not that there was a whole lot of conversation. Robert would later claim that Marvin had all of them working at the refuge like slaves. Suzanne was doing housewife-type work, but Robert was soon spending long hours outside in the cold learning how to run heavy equipment—he learned how to run a backhoe while he was there—and tending the farm animals, milking the refuge cow, and feeding the refuge chickens. The long hours of working meant, at the beginning at least, that there wasn't a lot of time for prayer, which was confined to a short morning prayer and the rosary on Wednesday nights. That, however, would change soon.

In November 1995, Mary Doe arrived at the Juda Refuge alone, after leaving her two children with her parents in California. While there she met the Stevensons, who she learned had also just moved from California. Mary remembers Suzanne Stevenson as a nice young mother. Suzanne seemed to be coping fairly well with the rigors of life on a ranch in South Dakota, but she had been there less than a month when Mary arrived. While at the refuge, Mary was answering the phone, and one day she got a call from Maureen Flynn in Virginia. Marvin wasn't at the refuge when Mary arrived. He, she was told, was staying in Virginia with the Flynns, who she was also told were having marital problems at the time. Since Marv was known to have counseling experience, he had no trouble insinuating himself into the marriages of the people at the refuges and elsewhere and would usually leave the marriages, if they existed at all after his ministrations, worse off than they were before. Asking Marvin Kucera for marriage counseling was like asking Dracula to do blood work, something the Johns and the Does and the Stevensons would find out first hand. John Mark, another beneficiary of Marvin's counseling skills, was in Virginia too, working on the Flynns computers. John Mark, they would later learn, was to computers what Marvin was to marriage counseling.

The prayer regimen at Juda changed dramatically, however, in December of 1995 with the arrival of a man by the name of Richard Irwin. Irwin, a man in his early fifties, came from St. Paul, Minnesota, where he claims he was once an executive with 3M, at a job which he lost because of his heavy involvement with Operation Rescue, the attempt to shut down the abortion industry in the United States through non-violent blockades of abortion clinics. Irwin was also a devotee of the phony apparitions of Mary Ann van Hoof at Necedah, Wisconsin. Necedah was in many ways the mother of all phony apparitions in the United States. On October 7, 1950, 100,000 people showed up at an out-of-the-way farm in central Wisconsin to watch the sun spin and listen to an illiterate woman, whose mother happened to be a medium, announce, in the words of the Blessed Mother that, "The enemy of God (Communism) is creeping all over America. . . . Alaska is the first stepping stone."

Mary Ann van Hoof eventually got so many phone calls from apprentice seer Veronica Lueken, the lady behind the phony apparitions at Bayside, New York, that she had to have her number changed. On June 17, 1955, Bishop Treacy, ordinary of the diocese of Lacrosse, within whose boundaries Necedah was located, issued a statement condemning the van Hoof apparitions as a fraud and warning the faithful to stay away. On March 29, 1975, Treacy's successor, Bishop Frederick Freking, after experiencing years of disobedience, quarreling, trafficking in spirits, and general spiritual terrorism emanating from the Necedah shrine, put Mary Ann van Hoof and the seven leaders of the shrine under personal interdict. On March 18, 1984, at the age of 74, Mary Ann van Hoof died and went wherever phony seers go for their eternal reward. According to Bishop Freking, she had not been reconciled with the Church at the time of her death, nor had she expressed any desire of the sort. On June 24, 1985, Freking's successor, Bishop John Paul, issued a formal statement extending "the penalties applied to the principals named in the decree of interdict to all those who publicly associate themselves with the shrine."

Ten and a half years later, Richard Irwin showed up at the Juda Refuge in South Dakota, commissioned by Marvin Kucera to run it in his absence, and began to implement his obsession with Necedah under the guise of intensifying the prayer life at the refuge. The recitation of the rosary was moved back one hour to 8:00 p.m. to coincide with the recitation of the rosary at the same time at Necedah. The Rosary was now going to be recited seven nights a week as well, in addition to which Irwin instituted prayers every afternoon and stations of the cross every Friday. When some of the people complained about the increasingly onerous burdens of work and prayer at the refuge, Irwin exploded at them and told them they didn't deserve a leader of his spiritual caliber.

Pretty soon the marriages of the people at the refuge started to buckle under the strain. Eben Johns was 40 years old. His wife Gwen was 38. He was a carpenter by trade and had five children, but soon found out that he was expected to work like a slave at the refuge for no money. Gwen once had to go to Marvin to ask for money to buy a bra, and Eben was growing sick of the financial and spiritual exploitation that was the regime at the refuge. Before long he was sharing his misgivings with Robert Stevenson. When word got back to Richard Irwin, Eben was kicked off the refuge and banished to a hotel in Rapid City. In his absence, Irwin had another man move in with Eben's 38-year-old wife. In the meantime, Marvin called Eben's father, a medical doctor, and asked him to prescribe tranquilizers for his son, whom he accused of various psychiatric disorders, including child abuse. Almost immediately after getting the call from Kucera, Dr. Johns called his son at the hotel in Rapid City and told him that he was in a cult and should do everything within his power to get himself and his wife and children out. This involved regaining the trust of his wife, who was rapidly falling under Irwin's spell, so Eben returned, apologized abjectly, and then made his plans to escape. Marvin, knowing he needed a carpenter on the refuge, allowed Eben to come back if he agreed to submit himself to an exorcism. Acceding to Kucera's demands, Eben came back, borrowed $400 from the Stevensons, and on February 9,

1996, the Johns, on the pretext that they had things to do in Texas, left the refuge for good. When Richard Irwin found out they had left and were in Texas, he paid the Johns a visit and told them that their desertion of the refuge was a "desecration," for which they would be punished. God, Irwin informed them, would punish them. God would cause each of them to fall over dead and their children would all starve to death. By then, Eben was no longer under Irwin's spell, but he still couldn't believe that the man who was the godfather to one of his children would say something like that.

-16-

TWENTY YEARS OF REBELLION

At around the same time that Gwen and Eben Johns dropped out of the Juda Refuge in South Dakota, Phil Kronzer received notice that his divorce from his wife Ardie had been finalized. Although it had the air of finality about it, the divorce, far from meaning that the battle for the Kronzer fortune was over, meant that the battle was just beginning to intensify. Every effort that Phil made to reconcile with his wife had not only failed, it seemed beyond that to intensify the desire of the forces working with Ardie to dismantle his assets one chunk at a time. The biggest item at the moment was the Kronzer house in Los Gatos, which was on the market at $1.6 million and not selling.

On February 7, 1996, Phil hired a woman by the name of Regina Moore to work for Autodisk. Moore's expertise was in computers. In September 1995, she had been hired to teach computer skills at St. Mary's parish in Los Gatos. As one of her first projects, she decided that, since October was prolife month, she would help the students design and print prolife bumper stickers. When one of her seventh-grade students objected, the principal of the school took his side and told Moore to cancel the assignment. When Moore refused, she was fired.

At around the same time Moore got hired at St. Mary's in Los Gatos, Phil Kronzer hired a man by the name of Darryl Monda as a consultant to Autodisk. Monda's job was to re-establish the company's reputation in the computer industry after the beating it had taken as a result of the APS lawsuit, which in early '96 had blossomed into a countersuit for libel as well. Phil needed someone who knew his way around the industry, someone who could tell him who was intent on sabotaging his operation and why. As one of the first things he did, Monda flew out to a seminar in Boston where he met with Doug Taylor, the man at Microsoft who was in charge of all of Windows 95 production. Gradually, Monda began to get a grasp of the magnitude of the forces arrayed against his boss. He found out there was an approved supplier list which determined who got in the door to sell product to Microsoft. He found out that APS had a reputation for threatening people, and that this reputation for intimidation spread throughout the industry and above all to the people that Phil needed as witnesses in his lawsuit. It was around this time that Brad Weisse told someone that he felt bad about the Phil Kronzer situation, but APS had "put a gun to my head." It was around this time as well that Phil began to notice what seemed like a series of uncanny coincidences. Six days after Ardie filed for divorce, Bernie Lerner filed his libel suit. It seemed that Phil was always fighting a battle on two fronts. It seemed that the people involved in the civil suit knew what was happening in the domestic case and vice versa.

After dying down in Mostar after the abortive kidnapping of Bishop Peric in April of 1995 and the subsequent closing of the St. Anthony CIM church hall, the Franciscan rebellion against the bishop of Mostar flared up again, this time at St. Francis parish in Capljina, five kilometers in the other direction from Medjugorje. On May 12, 1996, Father Jure Bender was appointed pastor of St. Francis Church in Capljina. When he and three associates arrived to take up their duties at the parish, they were met by another mob. One of the priests was knocked from his motorcycle, and all of them withdrew after their lives were threatened. On the same day, the Herzegovina province went into what one observer termed "the ecclesial equivalent of cardiac arrest." From that time on, the Franciscans could perform no legal sacraments and what was more troubling—to them at least—they could receive no new novices until they agreed to hand over the church in Capljina to the bishop's priests. Faced with even these draconian measures, the Franciscans refused to give back the parish.

As a result, on July 14, the entire Herzegovina province was suspended. The pastor in Capljina, Boniface Barbaric, was also assistant novice master for the province. Because of his disobedience, he was now seen as unfit to form new Franciscans, and by July it was clear that his truculence over the Capljina parish was threatening the existence of the entire province. But, as in the past, the Franciscans saw more disobedience as the only course justifying past disobedience. In the middle of July a delegation of parishioners went to the newspaper in Capljina and announced that they would not allow Mass to be said at St. Francis until the Franciscans came back. On July 20, 1996, an article on St. Francis parish appeared in the local newspaper along with a picture of the parishioners cinderblocking the front door shut. On either side of the now-blocked front door, the parishioners hung banners proclaiming in four languages that when the church was returned to its rightful owners, i.e., the Franciscans, the door would be unblocked. From then on the Franciscans continued to say Mass, but the parishioners entered and left by the church's side door.

On May 14, 1996, Phil Kronzer was in Seattle taking depositions for the APS lawsuit when he got a call from Regina Moore. Since May 1, Moore, Kronzer, and Monda all occupied offices in the rear of the K & K building in Campbell. Now Moore was calling to say that she had just received a letter in the mail which she needed to discuss right away, and not in the office and not at home either. When Phil got to the restaurant, he could see that Regina Moore was, in his words, "terrified," so terrified in fact that she wouldn't show Kronzer the letter, which by now he had figured out, contained unspecified allegations against him and threats against Moore.

"I can't help you, if you don't show me the letter," Kronzer pleaded. But he got nowhere. Moore had talked to her spiritual advisor, Father Robert Finnegan, who had helped out in the investigation of Teresa Lopez, and Finnegan had advised her just to walk away from her involvement with Kronzer and his problems. At that point Phil said that he was going to subpoena the letter, which seemed to leave Moore relieved of any personal responsibility in divulging its contents.

Phil was now staring a July 1 trial date in the face and watching helplessly as first his star witness and then the woman who was doing his secretarial and computer-base legwork got scared into abandoning him. Then, it seemed, that everything was happening at once. Two days after she got the letter, Regina Moore resigned. Not long after that Phil noticed the literature which she had prepared had been changed in a few crucial parts to give a fundamentally inaccurate picture of the machine he was trying to sell. When he confronted Darryl Monda about the changes, Monda said in a voice mail message that Sam Montalvo had authorized them. When he played the message for Sam, Sam, in his words, "went ballistic," convincing Kronzer that Monda and Les Radobald, the salesman he hired, were working for APS and not for him. At this point, Kronzer called a locksmith and had locks changed to all of his offices. When the locksmith reported back to him, however, he told Phil that two of the locks had already been changed. What he tried to do to Monda, Monda had already tried to do to him. Just why became apparent when at around the same time Ardie's attorney, Sherrol Cassady, filed a petition to hold Kronzer in contempt of court. At the end of May, Phil was negotiating a loan he needed to keep his business empire running. When Cassady heard about it, she claimed that money belonged to Ardie and that Phil was diverting assets. Phil is now convinced that Monda knew about the contempt citation and was convinced that Phil was going to jail. Once Phil was in jail, he planned to take over the company and put an end to Phil's lawsuit and his attempt to break into the disk-packaging market. Phil luckily came up with a large sum of money and narrowly avoided going to jail. Monda and Radobold got locked out, and by June had signed agreements separating themselves from Autodisk.

In June, however, APS's lawyers sent Kronzer's lawyers its list of witnesses, and Phil was surprised and dismayed to find Ardie's name on the list. Wondering what that was all about, he drove to a golf outing at Passa Tiempo Country Club he had already arranged with Dave McCaffrey, formerly of Remage, a computer supplier in Minnesota. After the round of golf was over and Phil had explained as best he could what he thought was happening to him, Dave McCaffrey said, "Based on everything you're going through, I'm going to write down a name and a phone number. I recommend you call this guy. He's the best in the business."

The man in question was a private investigator from Minnesota by the name of Fernandez. Three or four days later, Phil gave him a call and Mr. Fernandez told him that he worked undercover for the FBI. He would periodically, so he said, go off payroll, get the goods on some criminal, and then go back on payroll to apprehend him. Before Mr. Fernandez would agree to work for Phil, he wanted to do some investigating on his own. Two days later he called back and told Kronzer, "Boy, somebody is really after you." Based on that phone conversation, Phil flew to Minneapolis with two suitcases full of documents and a large check. Over the next few weeks, Fernandez would call Phil six to eight times a day, always it seemed on the verge of a big breakthrough. It turned out, or so Mr. Fernandez claimed, that Phil wasn't the first victim of Marcia Smith. Then he was about to have a grand jury convened, at which point the FBI would become involved, at which Phil would be free of any more legal expenses because the state was going to prosecute her in a criminal suit. Fernandez assured Phil that he would personally put the handcuffs on Marcia Smith when his investigation was concluded. This went on for about six weeks. Then Fernandez was supposed to fly to Boston to get Brad Weisse's declaration, the one he had refused to sign in March. When Phil hadn't heard from him in a few days, he called Fernandez's wife Lisa—$65,000 of the money he paid Fernandez ended up in Lisa's account— who told him that he was in Wyoming buying an RV. That was the last Phil heard from Mr. Fernandez, who disappeared in late July 1996. Fernandez is now being sought by the FBI for making false claims about being one of their agents.

In July of 1996, Phil Kronzer's lawyers served Regina Moore

with a subpoena and got a copy of the letter she had received two months earlier. Just before she handed the letter over to Kronzer's lawyers, however, Moore also got a letter from Ardie's attorney, Sherrol Cassady, telling her to ignore the subpoena. Why, Phil found himself wondering at the time, would Ardie's lawyer be interested in defending "William J. O'Brien," the author of the letter? When he finally got a copy of the letter, the answer became a little clearer.

"Dear Ms. Moore," the letter began, "This letter comes to you in the spirit of love that binds Mary and Jesus' children to the Spirit of Truth." The letter was purportedly from "a committee of Concerned Catholic Laity from the Diocese of San Jose" writing "in defense of the Church, our Bishop, and, in this instance, the Pastor and the Parish staff of St. Mary's in Los Gatos."

"We are a large group," the pseudonymous Mr. O'Brien continued, "represented by a prominent Canon lawyer from the Vatican, as well as a civil attorney from Dallas who works exclusively for the United States Catholic bishops. We are preparing to expose the truth about Mr. Phillip Kronzer's 'pretended righteous' attacks on the Bishop and St. Mary's as well as others in the local Catholic Church."

The letter wasted no time getting to its main point, which was a personal attack on Phil Kronzer, who, it intimated, was a "desperate crank with a personal axe to grind." By the end of the letter, the intimation became more explicit. Kronzer was a "fiery angry person" who "has an extremely dangerous, vindictive agenda for denigrating the Bishop and destroying St. Mary's Pastor and parish staff."

"His anger over his divorce," "Mr. O'Brien" continued, "and futile attempts to blame others in the Church for the breakup of his marriage, motivates him into a pretense of saving unsuspecting people from his own fate, as well as from random internal evils."

"Many of us in the San Jose Diocese, who have known the Kronzers for many years" the letter continued in its insinuating way, "are sadly aware that Mr. Kronzer's drinking problem, and all that is related to it, is the cause of his divorce....It is no secret in this Diocese, and elsewhere, why Mrs. Kronzer finally had to leave a very difficult and hurtful marriage, which she heroically coped with for many many years in an attempt to protect her children."

Interestingly, what followed was an attack on Father Finnegan, specifically the role he played in Stafford's condemnation of Teresa Lopez. Whoever "Mr. O'Brien" was, he was evidently a supporter of Teresa Lopez, something which contrasts sharply with his professions of obedience to bishops in the rest of his letter.

The purpose of the letter was clear. "Mr. O'Brien" and his friends wanted to intimidate Regina Moore because "a significant number of us on this Committee...know very well that Mr. Phillip

Kronzer is incapable of writing the kind of letter, with the educated sentence structure, informed Catholic vocabulary and the ultraconservative agenda that you, or perhaps Father Finnegan, have been preparing for his signature."

There were other reasons as well. Monda's change in Autodisk literature could only take place when Regina Moore was no longer in charge of copy and the computer files that were the basis for the mailer to Microsoft. Either way, the purpose of the letter was to get Moore out of the picture, and thereby cripple Kronzer's ability to communicate.

"Very soon," the letter continued, "unless you determine otherwise by separating yourself form Mr. Kronzer's angry agenda, many Catholics in this Diocese, including St. Mary's Parish, will know who Mr. Phillip Kronzer's ghost writer and computer expert really is. It will be out of our hands. Is this the mark you wish to leave behind you, as someone who has been paid to do someone else's dirty work as his revenge against others, because he refuses to accept his own responsibility for his divorce? Is this what your future employers in Ireland would consider a good recommendation?

"At this point you are being given the opportunity to separate yourself from any further contamination. We shall pray that the Holy Spirit guides you and protects you in this very short window of grace. For when the legal action begins and all of Mr. Kronzer's personal records and database, as well as all those who have assisted him are subpoenaed, hopefully, you will no longer be involved, and can plead ignorance."

After meeting with Moore in May, Kronzer asked Darryl Monda to contact the Campbell Police Department to see if an investigation was warranted and eventually charges could be pressed, but the officer in charge, at least according to Monda's testimony at the time, said the letter did not warrant a criminal investigation, although Kronzer might want to investigate the possibility of filing a civil suit. Phil then had his lawyers subpoena the police department's records and again Sherrol Cassady sent them a letter telling them to ignore the subpoena.

On June 25, 1996, the fifteenth anniversary of the "apparitions," Jose Carreras, one-third of the three most famous tenors on the planet, arrived in Medjugorje to sing at a benefit concert with tickets priced at between $60 and $100 a piece. The concert eventually took in $900,000. Also at the concert was Croatian president Franjo Tudjman, who arrived by helicopter without bothering to inform the authorities of the sovereign state of Bosnia-Herzegovina that he was coming, much less ask their permission to make the visit. Conspicuous by its absence during the ceremony was the Bosnia-Herzegovina flag, in place of which the Croatian flag was flown, a fact which caused more anger among the Bosnians. Tudjman's actions were seen as part of the pattern of gradual annexation which Croatia had been exercising toward this part of Bosnia ever since it had declared independence. Tudjman's statement that "what happened in Medjugorje is exceptionally important for the whole Croat nation" didn't help diplomatic matters much either.

Reporters on hand to cover the concert developed a severe case of cognitive dissonance, noticing the incongruities between the messages of Our Lady Queen of Peace and how they got implemented by the Croat ultranationalists who lived there. John Pomfret of the *Washington Post* noticed that at the gift shops, "Nazi-inspired souvenirs — swastikas and German iron crosses — lie next to figures of the Madonna and T-shirts reading: 'It's cool to know the Lord' and 'I love my mother.'" He also found out that "Croat militiamen from the town played an active role in first incarcerating and then expelling tens of thousands of Muslims from nearby villages during the 1993-94 war between Croats and Muslims in Bosnia."

The Franciscans at Medjugorje contributed significantly to the aura of schizophrenia surrounding the shrine:

> Priests in the town blessed Croat fighters bound for the front and lauded their attempts to carve a purely Croat state out of the southwestern corner of Bosnia. In an interview, Father Rupcic, the Franciscan, seemed to encapsulate the town's Jekyll and Hyde character. Pointing out his window at the crowd around the formidable twin spires of St. James Church, which dominates Medjugorje, he exulted in the communion of different races and ethnic groups. "We are creating a United Nations," he said. "But this is the real United Nations, brought together by her message." Yet when asked about Bosnia's Muslims, Rupcic's tone turned less neighborly. "They are nothing but Islamized Croats," he said.

On June 15, 1996, Mary Doe packed her belongings and her two children into a Ryder rental truck and drove from her parents' home in California to Marvin Kucera's new refuge in Snowflake, Arizona. Because her parents had property in Arizona, Mary had the opportunity to visit with Kucera a number of times before she made the final decision to move to the refuge. She had been there on May 2 with her children, staying at a hotel. At that time, Kucera was still looking for property and so Mary looked with him, along with Moira Noonan and Helen Jobe, two wealthy California women who were considering moving as well. Jobe, a tall, thin woman with dark eyes, married a rich California farmer right out of high school, and after he died of multiple sclerosis a few years later, she inherited an estate worth over $10 million. Both Helen Jobe and her brother Paul Bergman were heavily involved in the apparition scene, and since Marvin Kucera was the hot item on the Medjugorje circuit at the time, it is not surprising that their paths would cross. The middle man in this transaction was a woman by the name of Ariel Fauley. In early 1993, Fauley joined the Holy Rosary Church and Dominican Priory parish, whose pastor, Father Bartholemeu de la Torre, OP, would later testify that Fauley was not, as far as he knew, a Hare Krishna, even though one year before she moved there she was identified as such in a West Virginia newspaper story. It seems that Fauley was living down the street from the Hare Krishna national shrine in a house which was described as owned by the group when one of its members got killed there.

Father Bart de la Torre, it turns out, is Helen Jobe's cousin. At some time during the mid-'90s, either he gave Helen a copy of Marvin Kucera's book or Ariel Fauley, who had founded what she termed a religious order and was traveling the Medjugorje circuit selling expensive rosaries which she made, introduced Helen to Kucera's book. Either way, Helen was now in Marge Thornberry's real estate office in Arizona, and it was clear that she was going to bankroll the purchase of the land that Marv needed to start his refuge. It was also clear, at least to Mary Doe, that Kucera and Fauley were locked in a battle over who was going to control Jobe and her money. Thornberry, the real estate agent handling the deal was a local Medjugorje enthusiast. While the group was sitting in Thornberry's office listening to Marvin tell the story of his conversion, the phone rang and the owner of a ranch, which was previously off the market, decided to put it up for sale. This was taken by all as a sign from God. Eventually, Marvin bought five separate non-contiguous properties, including the above-mentioned 110 acre ranch for $800,000. The name of the refuge was to be Our Lady of Guadaloupe refuge and the chapel, to be built on the grounds, the St. Therese chapel. Marv got this information directly from God. Eventually, Jobe would give Marvin $1.6 million dollars before he disappeared. In May he was more interested in telling her what she wanted to hear. When the topic of Veronica Lueken and Bayside came up, something which Helen viewed favorably, Marvin tried to be diplomatic, claiming that Veronica Lueken was "okay at the beginning" but then her messages "got out of control." During her visit, Mary Doe continued to have negative feelings and yet still continued to make plans to move. When she finally arrived on June 15, things started going wrong immediately. The kids were having a horrible time; no one got along, and Marvin complained that she had arrived a day early. On June 16, Mary went to Mass with Helen and her brother Paul, whom she could see was really excited about moving to the refuge.

Helen had a flight out of Phoenix that day, and so Mark Mahowald drove her to the airport with Mary's daughter Tiffany. Mark, Mary remembers, was interested in girls, but got in trouble with Marvin whenever he found them together. While in the car Tiffany heard Ariel tell Mark that she was in charge of Helen's money, but that they needn't worry because Ariel was going to use her influence to help build the refuge. Ariel Fauley, she remembers, had "far out ideas"; she told Tiffany that the Blessed Mother picks her nose, causing Mary to think, "This lady's nuts." When Mark and Tiffany returned from the Phoenix airport, the group ate dinner at the big house where Mark and Marvin lived. All that Marvin could talk about during dinner was how much he hated Ariel Fauley. "This," Mary thought, "is not Christian behavior." It was clear, however, that Ariel needed Helen more than Helen needed Ariel now, and Marvin continued to exploit the situation, doing everything to separate Helen from Ariel so that he could get control of the money. It was also clear that Marvin didn't like Mary and didn't want her at the refuge. The only reason she was there was because Mark liked her, and evidently her daughter too. Marvin's antipathy toward women in general caused Mary to wonder if he were a homosexual.

On June 24, Mary got a phone call from Pat, saying he was out of work and needed help. Mary said, why not move up here, why not talk to Marv about it. Marv knew that Pat was an electrician and that he could run heavy equipment. At 6:00 p.m. Mary got a call from Pat, "I'm in Showlow [a town nearby]; come pick me up." To Mary's surprise, Pat proceeded to move in not with her and their children but with Mark and Marv in the big house. The next thing Mary knew, Marvin was knocking on her door. After telling Mary to send the children into the other room, Marvin then said, "Pat told me all about you. You remind me of my ex-wife." Marvin then asked Mary to leave the refuge, but when she told him that she had nowhere else to go, Marvin left. Mary was now wondering if her husband had become sexually involved with Marvin.

Mary later recounted how Marvin once told her, "Your husband is bisexual" after asking her questions about Pat. At around the same time, Marvin told Mary he could tell whether someone was homosexual or not because of the fact that he had been molested when younger and could pick out certain tendencies in other people. When Mary asked Marv if he were a homosexual, he said no, something her daughter Tiffany disputed. Whenever Marv would call on the phone and Tiffany would answer, she would always tell her mother, "he sounds gay."

Under the guise of being a counselor, Marvin continued to gather personal information from couples on the refuge as a way of breaking up their marriages. He told Mary more than once that her marriage was invalid. Just as Marvin never wanted Mark near girls, he also never wanted Pat near Mary. Pat, however, seemed under his spell, giving him at one point both his credit cards and the owner's card for his truck.

Pat, Mary concluded, got on so well with Marvin because he was a con man himself. When her father came for a visit, he told Mary that Pat would take care of her. Hearing this, Mary hugged her father and then burst into tears. She knew Marv was a phony, and now she knew her husband was involved in the same scam, and here was her father being supportive in a way that left her vulnerable to these men's predations. Faced with such unconditional support, Mary was simply at a loss what to do.

On July 8, Marv returned from one of his mysterious trips to Denver just in time to meet with Helen Jobe. While Marvin was away, Mary remembered, Pat would play with their children. When Marv got back, he ignored them. When Marvin got back, he was eager to have Helen meet the new chaplain for the refuge, a Father Ryan Scott, who was coming to enthrone the refugees' homes to the Sacred Heart. In the meantime, it was business as usual at the refuge, which meant administration by apparition. Marvin and Ariel and Helen would all go off and have their separate apparitions and if they all got the same message it was a sign to proceed. Before long Ariel was out of picture, reduced to sending indignant faxes from Oregon, which Mary would read when she did cleaning at the big house. Feeling that she had to warn Helen, Mary called her a number of times to express her misgivings about what Marvin was planning to do. After one phone conversation, Marvin came running down to Mary's mobile home. "I heard you call me a phony," he said, causing Mary to wonder if he had been listening in on her phone conversation.

"You think I'm a phony, don't you?" Marv said.

"You weren't there. How did you know I said that?" Mary answered

"Jesus told me," Marv responded.

Because she had money and was willing to give large chunks of it to the refuge, Helen was to be taken seriously. At one point, Helen started talking about UFOs at the big house, and Marv was quick to agree with everything she said. When Mary turned to her husband Pat and rolled her eyes, she realized that he was going along with Marvin on this one. "He was either Marv's lover," she said of her husband later, trying to explain his behavior, "or he was in it for the money."

In spite of Marvin's assertion to the contrary, Mary became convinced he was listening in on her phone conversations and doing his best to monitor the thoughts of everyone at the refuge. His main instrument of control, however, was dividing married couples against each other, and Mary began to feel the effect of the strategy first hand, as Marvin extended his control over her husband Pat. Marvin's aversion to Mary grew over time. In part it stemmed from his antipathy to women in general, but it grew with Mary's refusal to succumb to his control. On July 10, Father Frank Chicoine came to the refuge to enthrone the Sacred Heart in Mary's mobile home, something which Marvin wanted Father Scott to do. During his stay Fr. Chicoine refused to talk with Marvin. In the meantime, Pat told Mary one day that Marvin confided in him that he was a homosexual before his conversion, and then went into considerable detail about what he used to do, something which convinced Mary of the truth of the statement but also caused her to wonder again about her husband's relationship with Marvin. Throughout their stay at the refuge, Marvin would use every opportunity to come between Mary and Pat. He would claim that the two weren't validly married, and soon Pat was saying that he didn't have to pay attention to what she was saying because they weren't really married anyway. Marvin, usually under the guise of counseling, would tell Mary that she was a terrible mother. Then during one session, he broke off what he was saying, took out a Bible and placing his hand on it, swore that he would not report her to Arizona state's child protective services, which Mary interpreted as a threat to do just that. By July 12, Marv and Mary couldn't be in the same room together, nor would she allow either of the girls to be alone in his presence.

When she first arrived at the refuge, Mary used to handle the phone inquiries from people who would call from all over the country wanting to join, until she got tired of lying to people, and then she decided to make all her calls from her husband's phone. One day while trying to erase the messages on her husband's answering machine, she stumbled across a message to Pat from some unknown woman. "Pat," the woman's voice asked, "where are you? What's going on with you? I need to know where I stand with you." It was clear that this was a message from Pat's girlfriend. In February 1995, Mary had confronted Pat. "Is there someone else?" she wanted to know. Pat had denied having an affair then, but now Mary had evidence. Since Pat was living with Marvin at the time, Mary went up to the big house to confront him. Putting the answering machine down on the table, Mary said, "Hey Marvin, listen to this," and pressed the play button.

"You lied to me," she said to her husband.

Pat continued to deny the affair, but Marvin just played stupid.

Finally, Pat decided to take another tack.

"You're not my wife," he said, "I don't have to answer to you."

Marvin still seemed shocked. "Pat," he said, "I can tell you're lying. I used to do the same thing."

At that point, Marvin left the room. Mary, however, didn't keep the revelation a secret and went around telling everyone at the refuge what had happened. What ensued was a huge argument between Pat and Marvin, after which Pat walked around like a dog with its tail between his legs. At this point, she decided that enough was enough, that it was time to leave, but in spite of everything she still wanted to leave with Pat. When she went to him with the suggestion, however, Pat refused. "I'm not leaving the refuge," he told her. "This is the best thing that ever happened to me."

One day after Mary made up her mind to leave, on July 24, she encountered two local men who were working on her mobile home, adding a room. When she went inside, she smelled drugs. She mentioned it to Marvin, who just shrugged the whole incident off because, she now feels, he was using drugs himself. His eyes, she remembers, were always glassy; his face was always flushed, and he sweated profusely. When it was clear that Marvin had disappeared, the residents of Juda in South Dakota went through his room and found thousands of dollars in $20 bills along with drug paraphernalia and amphetamines. After prayer on Thursday, Mary announced that she was leaving. Marv's reaction was to turn to Tiffany, Mary's 12-year-old daughter and say, "You don't want to leave, do you?"

Mary soon began to feel that her life was in danger. At about this time, she received a phone call from a woman who had stayed with her in the same mobile home with her fiancé, a man by the name of Dale Mann, who claimed that he had worked for the CIA. Mann had cancer and so needed to take naps in the big house. One day, when everyone thought he was asleep, Mann overheard Marv say to Pat, "We have to get rid of Mary before Helen Jobe gets here."

Not needing to wait around for further proof, Mary filled her car with the clothes and the stuffed animals they had brought and drove back to California. Two months later, Pat called to talk to Kaitlin. As soon as she left, on July 26, 1996, Mary called Ariel Fauley and then Helen Jobe, who was still planning to move to Snowflake permanently, to tell her what she had learned and warn her not to go, but like Mary herself, a few weeks earlier, Helen refused to listen.

One day before Mary Doe drove away from the refuge in Snowflake, Arizona, Suzanne Stevenson gave birth to a baby boy by the name of Joel at the Rapid City hospital. Robert Stevenson's joy at the birth of his third child was tempered by the increasingly grim nature of his situation at the Juda refuge at Buffalo Gap. It wasn't so much the long hours of work without pay, although that was certainly a factor. It was rather the constantly repressed realization that he, as the head of this young family, had made a big mistake, one which he couldn't admit to himself. Then there were the people he was living with. They were certainly serious about religion, but he was starting to realize that they weren't Christian. He was also starting to worry about his wife's state of mind. She had become disillusioned as well, and by the summer of 1996 it was impossible to ignore the change. As the pregnancy proceeded, Suzanne was getting more and more depressed. It might have been hormonal, but more probably, the mood swings had to do with the hopelessness of their situation. They were being psychologically ground into powder by a cruel exploitative cult which had lied to them and bilked them of their money, but the most psychologically debilitating aspect of the whole thing was that they couldn't summon up the courage to admit that they had made a big mistake.

Gradually during the late summer of 1996, rumors of problems at the other refuge in Arizona began filtering back to South Dakota. Robert heard that Marvin had brought a priest to the refuge at Snowflake, but that after he had performed a marriage and some baptisms and had celebrated Mass for them, the community was divided over whether he was in fact a priest or not. Robert had heard about Helen Jobe's millions, but he also heard that because of the phony priest scandal, she had backed off and had gone back to her farm in California. He also heard that Helen had given $100,000 to Ted Flynn to produce a video.

Suzanne was in an even more vulnerable position than her husband. She had just had a child by a man who had delivered her over to what amounted to a religious slave labor camp. Feeling that she had never been accepted by her in-laws, she was even less psychologically prepared to admit that she had made a mistake than her husband was. Whether it was the rumors or whether it was postpartum depression or the general hopelessness of the situation, Robert hardly recognized his wife when she returned from the hospital. She seemed cold and callused, put the baby on the bed and told her husband, "you can deal with this," and then at the end of her first week back, she announced to her husband, "Honey, I'm seeing the Blessed Mother." A few days later, she announced that she had had a vision. "I don't know how to tell you this," she said in an emotionless voice, "Our son is going to die." After that she spent most of her time away from the house, neglecting the infant, leaving milk from a breast pump so that Robert could feed him, so that she could spend more time in prayer, presumably in close conversation with the Blessed Mother.

"This was a side of her I had never seen before," Robert said later. "She would leave the house in the middle of the night and go up on the holy hill or down to the prayer house, which had just been completed at the time. She would talk to other people at the refuge and would leave and wouldn't come back. Then she told me that she felt that I didn't believe her."

What Robert didn't notice at the time was that much of her time away from home was now being spent with Richard Irwin, who evidently did believe her and spent long hours with her conferring over her alleged messages and giving what he considered spiritual guidance. In retrospect, it seems that Suzanne had come to the conclusion that there was no turning back, that her husband was not going to protect her, and like an inmate in a concentration camp, Suzanne decided to make friends with the sadistic commandant. Or perhaps she was more ambitious than that. Recognizing that private revelations were the collective Achilles heel at the refuge, Suzanne most probably decided that having apparitions of her own was the only way to improve her social status in an otherwise hopeless situation. Whether Richard Irwin was taken in by Suzanne's claims or whether he wanted to get close to this woman almost 30 years his junior for other reasons remained to be seen.

In the meantime, the situation in Snowflake continued to deteriorate. On August 5, Paul Bergman moved to the refuge permanently, and his sister, Helen Jobe, accompanied him on the move. Five days later, Helen returned to California, planning at that point to move back to Snowflake permanently on September 7, 1996. Within a week of moving to the refuge, Bergman started quarreling with Kucera over the way he was spending his sister's money. "It seemed," Bergman said later, "that [Kucera] was very wasteful with it." In response, Kucera replied, "Once the money is donated, I have the final say on how it is spent." Kucera's abrupt response led to frequent phone conversations between Bergman and his sister, which, given Mary Doe's experiences, were most likely monitored. On August 21, Paul Bergman informed Kucera that his sister wasn't going to send any more money. When he heard this, Kucera became furious and told Bergman, "I wish I had never heard of your sister or taken any of her money."

On August 24, Kucera arrived at Snowflake with about 45 people from other refuges and his newly appointed spiritual director, Father Ryan Scott, who was introduced as coming from the diocese of La Crosse, Wisconsin, where he was associated with something called the Holy Rosary Abbey. Scott had brought a tabernacle and altar with him which were to be used in the newly completed chapel, where on the day of his arrival, Scott said the Tridentine Mass. Two days later, on August 26, Scott said another Mass and blessed the marriage of a young couple living at the refuge. But Paul Bergman's doubts were beginning to grow. After the Mass, he made his usual call to his sister Helen and found that Father Bart was there with her. Perhaps in response to Bergman's questions, Father Bart asked whether Father Scott had permission from the local bishop to have the wedding and the baptism and where both were to be recorded. Unable to answer his cousin's questions, Bergman rejoined the group and soon found himself in the middle of a heated discussion over Father Scott's credentials. "How do we even know that this guy is a priest?" Bergman blurted out after someone suggested that the marriage might not be valid.

One day later, after Mass had been celebrated by another priest at the refuge, Margaret Reger announced that she had called the Diocese of La Crosse and had spoken with Father Michael Gorman, the diocesan Chancellor, who informed her that Scott was not a validly ordained Catholic priest. Gorman then gave Reger the phone number of "Archbishop" Erwin Krouse, leader of something called "the American Catholic Church" headquartered in Desert Hot Springs, California. Krouse then told Reger that Scott had been ordained a priest in the "American Catholic Church" two years earlier but had since then been excommunicated for, among other things, being a "homosexual, a con artist, and a habitual liar," who "bounces from place to place" and had stolen money via computer and altered check vouchers from Krouse's organization. Krouse also told Reger that Scott had been sentenced to jail for fraud in 1994 and was currently on probation. He also gave her the phone number of Scott's probation officer. In the meantime, Bergman also learned that the Judah Refuge in Buffalo Gap, was "not sponsored or approved" by the diocese of Sioux Falls, South Dakota, which was telling people to be "very careful and not get involved" and that Bishop Chaput was keeping an eye on them. After conferring with the Regers, Paul Bergman decided to approach Kucera with the information.

When Bergman confronted Kucera with the information he had gotten from the diocese of La Crosse, Kucera started to scream, claiming that "ever since you have been here you have caused nothing but division and trouble by complaining about how the money is spent. You are doing the work of Satan," Kucera said, glaring at Bergman with what he remembers as "a look of utter hate and evil in his eyes."

What followed was a lot like the theological version of comic opera without the music; the refugees tried their best to adjudicate the situation according to the code of canon law. When Paul Bergman attempted to read the canon about Mass in a private chapel, Scott asked him what edition he was using. When Bergman responded that he had the 1983 edition, Scott responded that only the 1984 revision was valid. When Bergman continued to read from his edition, Kucera shouted, "I will not allow that to be read at this meeting since it is not the current issue." At another point, Kucera shouted, "This is not a democracy. I am in charge here." Kucera then demanded that another edition be brought in, but when it arrived it turned out the be the same one Bergman was citing.

"Since you claim to be a canon law expert," Bergman continued, addressing Scott, "where does it say that you don't have to have permission from the local pastor to have a baptism."

There was complete silence for about two minutes when Ryan finally said that he would "need the rest of the seven or eight volumes of commentary to answer that." Bergman then asked if it were possible get some independent verification of Ryan's ordination, something besides his own paperwork, and Kucera answered that it was impossible because Scott "was being blackballed and persecuted by Father Gorman." Beyond that, Kucera continued, the Roman Catholic bishop who had supposedly ordained Ryan at the bishop's sick bed had died. Marvin continued by saying that it was impossible to verify Scott's credentials because "the Church lies to cover up the truth, and the only good bishops there are, are part of the underground church, and these bishops will deny everything to protect the underground church." Going Kucera one better, Scott then told the assembled refugees that he had been raped by 12 priests in a locked cathedral and then sworn to silence and then blackballed anyway.

Bergman was by now "really disgusted" and "wondered what my sister and I had gotten into." A day later he stopped by to visit with the Regers, only to be informed that no one on the refuge was allowed to talk to him. On August 30, Paul Bergman was about to get into bed when he heard a knock on the door. Marvin Kucera was there with four members of the Board of Elders and an ultimatum.

"We are here to ask you to leave," Kucera said. "You have one week to get out. Your sister's money will not buy you a place on this refuge."

On Tuesday, October 1, 1996, Bergman, his sister Helen, and the Regers each received a certified letter from Marvin informing them that they had until October 19 to vacate the premises or he would be forced to start legal action to have them evicted. On October 3, 1996, Bergman learned that Marvin Kucera had left town. No one has seen him since. Helen Jobe eventually regained title to the property for which she had paid an inflated price, but Marvin and Mark disappeared with the $1.6 million she had given them to buy it.

After she got out of Snowflake in August, Mary Doe spent the next few months trying to warn people about the dangers associated with the refuges. When she called Helen Jobe to warn her, Helen said "Marv has put me on the checking account." But Mary responded by saying that if she had not been made an officer of the corporation, she had no control over the money.

Mary then started thinking about Ted Flynn and his connection to Mother Angelica. Ted Flynn was a major promoter of Marvin, the only visionary who was in so deep with the Flynns. Marv was their star visionary. Marv and Mark used to write articles for *Signs of the Times* magazine. Mary now feels that Ted Flynn was getting kickbacks, and that Ted Flynn knew Marvin was a fraud. "You'd have to be an idiot not to," she said later. But she still has a number of unanswered questions: "Who are Ted and Maureen Flynn? This is big business to them. How did they get into the conferences?" Then there is the matter of Ted Flynn's relationship with Mother Angelica. Mary knew that Ted was on *Mother Angelica Live* promoting *Thunder of Justice*. Ted Flynn was not only mentioned on *MAL*; he was a regular on EWTN.

Alarmed at the potentially large number of people who might be taken in by the same scam, Mary called Sister Raphael at EWTN and told her that it was crucially important for her to pass the information Mary had on Ted Flynn on to Mother Angelica. Mary was hearing them all the time on the programs there.

"One of the reasons I believed that Marv was genuine," Mary said later, "was because I heard Ted Flynn on EWTN. Taken together, they gave Marv credibility."

Sister Raphael later confided to Mary that she and Mother Angelica had read *Signs of the Times* magazine and had concluded that a bunch of the messages could not be from God. When Mary then asked Sr. Raphael why EWTN kept promoting Flynn, the nun said nothing. Mary continued her attempts to reach Mother Angelica because she felt she needed her help in exposing " the phonies."

"Ted and Maureen were dirty," she said, and then went down the list. "Marv was dirty; Fr. Spalding was dirty. The light was coming on now."

Mary told Sister Raphael to stop promoting Ted and Maureen Flynn and that Mother Angelica would only be lending credibility to their fraudulent scams if she continued to do so. She also mentioned Ryan Patrick Scott, the phony priest who was supposed to be Marvin's spiritual director. At the time, Doe thought that Mother Angelica was being duped. In November 1996, Mary sent Mother Angelica a letter documenting the case against the Flynns, Marvin Kucera and Ryan Scott, along with copies of *Signs of the Times Magazine*, with ads and articles promoting Kucera.

Mother Angelica never responded to her letter.

Beginning in August of 1996, Suzanne was spending more and more of her time with Richard Irwin and less and less of it with her family. Joel, the Stevensons' newborn infant, was now competing with Richard and a newly arrived visionary by the name of Chico, who was competing for Richard's attention and his time and his skill in interpreting their visions.

"It was her way of being upwardly mobile," Robert said later. "Richard was the head figure there, and delusionaries will fall in love with people in higher status and then try to keep it secret. Suzanne may have some mental disorder. When she was drinking she once told me that Mary Magdalen had to become a sinner for Jesus to love her. Whether she was doing the same thing all over again, I don't know. But I do know now that her main problem is never being able to admit that she was wrong. People with deep insecurities project their problems on someone else. She would never apologize for anything that she did."

Robert found Suzanne one night standing outside Richard Irwin's door shaking and muttering to herself, "Robert doesn't believe me." Richard, however, was more than happy to oblige the new visionary, who was now relieved of the concentration-camp labor regimen the rest of the refuge was subjected to as Richard and Chico and Suzanne spent hours poring over their latest revelations, pondering what they could mean. Both spouses remained oblivious to what was happening. In spite of the house being a total disaster and his kids crying all the time, Robert was in a way proud of his wife and her newly discovered spiritual gifts. When his parents arrived for a visit, they noticed that his wife was hardly ever there, and treated them coldly when she was, but they said nothing, even if they suspected that something odd was going on.

Richard's wife, Sharon, a woman older than Richard, which is to say at least in her late fifties, who had already been married once before, was even more oblivious than Robert. "The lights were on, but no one was there," he said later describing a situation which she probably felt she couldn't cope with if she admitted it and so, like the rest of the refuge, retreated into illusion.

By September, rumors about the problems at the refuge in Snowflake, Arizona, had become too widespread to deny anymore. In early September Kucera arrived at Juda with "Father" Ryan Scott, and both conferred behind closed doors. When they weren't conferring together, Kucera was parading Scott before the refugees at Juda as the paradigm of a new breed of priest, the kind that was going to be persecuted for being part of the underground church, whose arrival was fast approaching. In an uncanny way, all of these predictions would come true soon enough, at least for Marvin who would "go underground" after Helen Jobe filed her lawsuit against him. The vision of the end times, the chastisement, the underground church, the persecution, it turns out, constitutes among other things a pretty accurate picture of how a criminal views the world. Add to that fact that Kucera and Scott were also part of a homosexual conspiracy, and you have the Rosetta Stone which gives the best interpretive key to their visions of coming apocalypse.

Sensing that Marvin was soon going to be gone and that a vacuum at the top of the refuge power structure would ensue, Richard Irwin started taking the spiritual reins of the community more and more into his hands, holding forth in long rambling lectures that tied together the incidents at Ruby Ridge, Waco, the Oklahoma City bombing, and various things he had read in *Spotlight Magazine*. At one of these gatherings, he asked Robert what he would do if soldiers came onto the refuge and tied him to a tree and then raped and killed Suzanne in front of his eyes. Robert was dumbfounded by the question. "Look at what they're doing in Bosnia," said Richard in response to Robert's silence, almost taunting him in front of his wife. "This is what we have to look forward to."

That night, Robert woke up and discovered that his wife was not in bed with him. Getting up and looking around, he found that she wasn't in the house either. Eventually he found her in the refuge house of prayer kneeling in front of one of Jozo Zovko's Our Lady of Tihaljina statues, which Helen Jobe had purchased on one of her trips to Medjugorje for $5,000 and then donated to Juda. Robert knelt down next to her. "What's wrong?" he said.

At that point, Suzanne related her latest vision. She saw a scene of soldiers coming on to the refuge and breaking into the house of prayer where she was kneeling as she was then in front of the Medjugorje statue. The soldiers then grabbed Suzanne, dragged her to floor, raped and then killed her. Suzanne's visions, it turns out, were remarkably similar to Richard Irwin's fantasies. "It shocked the living snot out of me," Robert said later, "but I didn't react."

In October 1996, Richard Irwin suggested that Robert accompany him on a trip to Snowflake, Arizona, where, as a result of the lawsuit which Helen Jobe filed, Marvin was auctioning off the community's property—the trucks, the backhoe, and all of the rest of the equipment he had bought with Jobe's money—to raise money to fight her in the lawsuit. Richard, almost as an afterthought, asked Robert to bring his wife along "because," he said, "she could guide us with her locutions." After they arrived, Suzanne would stay up until the small hours of the morning conferring with Richard about the messages she had just received from the Blessed Mother. It is at this point that Robert began to suspect that his wife was sexually intimate with Irwin.

Eventually, the auction took place, in spite of Paul Bergman's efforts to stop it. Bergman stood at the driveway of the property holding up a sign warning prospective buyers that the property was under litigation and gave himself credit for the fact that equipment but no property got sold that day. The refuge took in about $30,000 that day, but Bergman later claimed it cost them $22,000 to do it. Going through the refuge property in preparation for the auction, Robert found a 9mm handgun and an envelope full of cash, both of which belonged to Marvin. At the same time, Suzanne continued to have visions. Now after her sessions with Richard Irwin at the big house, she would wake Robert and tell him she had visions of babies crying in the night. "The Blessed Virgin wants us to pray for the crying babies," she would tell Robert. But there were no babies crying, at least none that he could hear.

Finding the gun and the money had brought Robert slowly to the realization that Marvin was a fraud, a suspicion he decided to share with Richard Irwin. The refuge empire was clearly falling apart. Marvin was gone, and evidently had taken so much money with him that he could afford to be careless about the thousands of dollars he had left lying around in envelopes. In his usually wary way, Richard was coming to the same conclusion but decided to use the information to his own advantage. The best way to figure out what was going on was to conduct an impromptu investigation of "Father" Scott. This would allow them to get to the bottom of the Kucera mystery. Scott's monastery was in Viroqua, Wisconsin, and Irwin decided that the most logical thing to do given the circumstances was to drive up there and find out what was going on. What Irwin failed to tell the Stevensons was that Viroqua was near Necedah, and that he was using the investigation of Scott as a pretext to bring the Stevensons there.

In October of 1996, the rebellion of the Herzegovina province of the Franciscans against the papal decree *Romanus Pontificibus* was more that 20 years old and showing no signs of abating. In early October, Boniface Barbaric made plans to celebrate a Mass of protest on the piazza in front of the bricked-up doorway of St. Francis Church in Capljina. Shortly before Mass was scheduled to begin, on October 4, Barbaric received a fax from Herman Schalueck, the general of the Franciscans, explaining that no Franciscan could take part in the liturgy. In spite of the warning, 13 Franciscans concelebrated the Mass with Barbaric, thumbing their noses at the general.

On November 15, 1996, the general came to Mostar to the

cathedral crypt church to celebrate Mass as a first step in defusing the crisis. When he got there the church was packed with local supporters of the Franciscans bearing banners with slogans arguing their case against the bishop. The Franciscans, as had become their habit in the increasingly tense Herzegovina case, wanted to use the locals to make their point. When he saw the crowd and got the gist of what the signs were saying, the general refused to proceed, "This Mass," he told them, "will not go on until the banners are removed." At that point, 30 Franciscans took of their albs and stoles and refused to say Mass with the successor of St. Francis.

On March 19, 1997 the general wrote another letter explaining that if St. Francis parish in Capljina was not handed over to the bishop, the Herzegovina province would lose its right to receive novices as well as the ability to allow their minor seminary candidates to proceed to ordination. That meant that they would have no ordinations, and that meant that when the current group of Franciscans died, the province would die along with them. To give some indication of what this meant, the Herzegovina Franciscans had more seminarians than all of the other Franciscan houses in Western Europe combined. The Franciscans were to hand over the parish before the pope arrived in Sarajevo in April 1997.

On November 6, 1996, the Most Rev. Raymond L. Burke, Ordinary of the Diocese of LaCrosse, Wisconsin, sent out a notice to all bishops on NCCB/USCC letterhead, informing them that "an individual named Ryan Patrick Scott (born Randall Dean Stocks) has been attempting to raise funds for the 'Holy Rosary Abbey,' which he has established near Viroqua, Wisconsin." Bishop Burke went on to claim that Scott was not now nor had he ever been a Roman Catholic priest, although it was reported that he had "simulated the celebration of the Mass and other sacraments." Scott, according to Burke's account, had been ordained by the "American Catholic Church" also known as the "Reformed Catholic Church in America" and had been recently arrested and charged with violating the terms of his probation for a previous felony conviction.

By November it was clear that Marvin was gone for good and that the lawsuit which began at the Snowflake, Arizona, refuge was now threatening to spread to Juda in South Dakota, leaving the prinicipals of the corporation there liable for Marvin's malfeasance. As a result, Richard called a meeting of the remaining refugees and announced that he was going to leave. On their way back to South Dakota from Arizona, Irwin and the Stevensons stopped off in Necedah after checking out Ryan Scott's credentials (or lack of them) in nearby Viroqua. While at Necedah, which Robert Stevenson described as a swampy clearing in a forest and one of the creepiest places on earth, Suzanne had a vision of the Blessed Mother blessing Father Peters, the priest in residence at the interdicted shrine. Father Peters had once had faculties in the diocese of La Crosse, until one day the diocesan auditor noticed something unusual about his bookkeeping methods. Shortly thereafter, Father Peters showed up at the Necedah Shrine and made a contribution of $187,000 to go toward the building of their new chapel. Father Peters had been there ever since, saying illicit Masses for the followers of Mary Ann van Hoof. Father Peters, in addition to irregular accounting practices, had other unusual personal habits as well. He would spend most of his time during the day sitting around naked, and when the spirit moved him, he would occasionally drink a glass of his own urine.

Richard, now sensing that he was losing control of the Juda Refuge as a result of Kucera's disappearance and Ryan Scott's exposure as a phony priest, announced that he was moving to Necedah. The refugees panicked when they heard the news. Irwin may have been a nut case, but he was their nut case. He may have been a running a concentration camp, but it was their concentration camp, where they were safe from the predations of the above-ground Catholic Church with its altar girls. When the refugees heard the news, many of them offered Irwin money if he would stay on. They were afraid that things were going to fall apart without a leader. Eventually Irwin settled on Les Cox, an articulate young convert, as his successor. Les and his wife Mary used to call the Stevensons just as the Stevensons used to call the Johns. It was the Stevensons who convinced them to move to Juda, and now the Stevensons were about to hand over the ignition keys to the Titanic to the Coxes.

Suzanne decided that Robert should move on ahead of them to Necedah to find a job there, an arrangement which of course left her pretty much alone back at the refuge with Richard Irwin. At the same time, Irwin, under the guise of scrutinizing Suzanne's messages from the Blessed Mother, had been going over Robert's faults with her one by one. Robert wasn't watering the cows; Robert was lazy. Missing from Irwin's denigration of Suzanne's husband was the fact that he had to spend much of his time at home caring for the children which Suzanne had all but abandoned once she started getting messages from the Blessed Mother. Ever the considerate husband though, Robert did go to Necedah, but failed to find a job and so in December he was back at the refuge, cutting huge amounts of firewood, which he would never get to burn, wondering what was going on. In response to his wife's nagging he agreed to go back and look for a job once again after Christmas. In the meantime, he and Suzanne accompanied Irwin on a trip back to Minneapolis for Thanksgiving dinner with his family.

Phil Kronzer's suit against APS did not go to trial in July; in fact six months later, APS lawyers were still deposing witnesses. In October 1996 Darryl Monda and Les Radobold were deposed. Phil listened as they denied knowing people he knew they knew. The suit was not going well. On November 14, 1996 the case went into mediation, and, as Phil put it, APS "didn't offer us a dime." At the same time, Sherrol Cassady was putting pressure on Phil to the get the Kronzer family home, which had been on the market for 18 months, sold. Cassady then had someone she knew appointed real estate agent and pressured Phil into dropping the price to $1.5 million. On December 16, Phil got a call asking if he could be out of the house in a week. In late January he was out of town when he got a call informing him that the house had been sold. Closing was on January 24. Still out of town, Phil called Ray Moses and told him to move his stuff out.

In late November 1996 fliers began appearing in Catholic parishes in the Denver area. "Jesus is Coming to Colorado" said the headline, and then reading smaller print, one learned that Vassula Ryden was coming to Denver on December 8, 1996. In spite of the Vatican condemnation of Vassula in October 1995, the flier went on to claim that "permission," presumably of Vassula's appearance had been "given by Cardinal Ratzinger" on "May 10, 1996." In addition to that an "Apostolic Blessing" had been "given by Pope John Paul II on August 11, 1996."

-17-

"THE HAZARD OF IMMINENT SCHISM"

By the beginning of January 1997, Robert Stevenson was running out of options. In addition to the $130,000 house they had walked away from in California, he and his wife had invested over $10,000 in the mobile home Marvin had bought for them, and that figure didn't take into account the long hours Robert had put in on both the home and the other buildings on the Juda Refuge. Now he was unsure of how to proceed. It made sense to stay until they sold the house, but Marvin was now on the run, and those left on the refuge threatened to be dragged down by the lawsuits his malfeasance had spawned. The one option which neither Robert nor his wife seems to have entertained at the time was returning to California because that would have meant admitting that they had made a mistake in front of their families, an option Suzanne found particularly repugnant because it would have meant losing face in front of her in-laws. So instead of facing reality and admitting that they had made a mistake, Suzanne seemed determined to press on farther into the unexplored interior regions of the land of illusion. Suzanne, now just about completely under Richard Irwin's control, decided that the family should move to Necedah, where they would live on the grounds of the "For My God and My Country" Shrine of the now-deceased seer Mary Ann van Hoof. Although it antedated Medjugorje by some 30 years, Necedah had been drawn into Medjugorje's orbit. Ray Scheffl, the man who ran the Necedah bookstore, told Robert that Nancy Fowler of Conyers, Georgia, was referring people to Necedah because she saw the book on Necedah which someone had left with her light up. Fowler got into the apparition scene shortly after she returned from a trip to Medjugorje in the late '80s.

Robert, it was decided, should move to Wisconsin in early January and spend his time there looking for a job. Suzanne would remain at Juda with her children and, of course, Richard Irwin. Plagued by indecision, still not convinced that he had been the victim of a hoax, ordered around like a slave at the refuge, Robert had effectively lost his authority as head of the family and had difficulty opposing his wife's obsessions. Of course, the more he acceded to his wife's bizarre demands, the more he lost his authority and the more she held him in contempt and, in a strange but understandable way, the less she trusted him to make decisions. If he were willing to go along with his wife's bizarre demands, his wife reasoned, then she certainly couldn't put any trust in his judgment, and what followed, of course, were more increasingly bizarre demands, hatched in collaboration with Richard Irwin. The apparitions would also help chart their course. If he found a job, Suzanne reasoned, it was a sign they should go.

It took him two weeks, but eventually Robert found a job in LaCrosse in a machine shop for $9 an hour, a sum he felt was demeaning compared to what he had been earning in California as head of his own business. Once the sign had been granted, the Stevensons pulled up stakes in South Dakota, once again walking away from a home they had bought, and arrived in Necedah on January 27, 1997. On their last trip to Necedah, shrine leader Ray Pritzl told the Stevensons that they could move into a large six bedroom house on the grounds, near Father Peters' house so that Suzanne, being a nurse, could take care of him. Richard and his wife Sharon were to move into another house on the compound. When he finally got his family to Necedah, Robert found that the arrangement had changed once again. The Stevensons and the Irwins were going to live in the house that had been promised to the Stevensons alone. One week later, the arrangement changed again when Father Peters move in with them, on the same day, it turns out, that Robert started his job in LaCrosse with the long commute that went along with it. Suzanne, thereafter, was left to spend her days with a psychotic defrocked priest who was functioning as the chaplain to an interdicted shrine and Richard Irwin, who spent his time now indoctrinating Suzanne into his theories about the end times and how the Jews had taken over the world.

This is not to say that Richard Irwin wasn't as psychopathic as Father Peters. Soon the long hours Richard and Suzanne were spending together started to have their effect. Two weeks after he started his job in LaCrosse on February 3, Robert was sitting across from his wife, when she announced, with what he later termed a diabolical smirk, that their marriage was over. What followed was a torrent of abuse, most of which Robert had heard at one time or another coming out of the mouth of Richard Irwin: Robert was lazy; he treats his wife like shit; their marriage has been shit from the beginning; all he wanted from Suzanne was sex. When she finally upbraided him for not agreeing to counseling, Robert seized at what seemed like the only opportunity left to him and agreed to go to meet with a priest recommended by Richard Irwin.

In spite of being recommended by Irwin, the priest eventually told Robert and his wife that the Necedah shrine was under interdict and that they should separate themselves from it as quickly as a possible. Feeling that Richard was coming between Robert and his wife, the priest also recommended that Richard move out while his wife was in St. Paul visiting relatives. After agreeing to the new arrangement in principle, Irwin flew into a rage when Robert informed him that Ray Pritzl had found him a room at a local hotel.

"You did what?" Irwin started screaming when Robert told him that he had just gotten him a room. "Nobody tells me to leave my house," Irwin screamed, now shaking uncontrollably as well. "I ain't gonna go. This is my house."

Taken aback by Irwin's rage, Robert started backing away from him, which evidently emboldened both Irwin and Robert's wife. At that point she started screaming at him as well in front of their children, who then started crying, adding to the general din in the house. Perhaps because Robert had been fasting for days as well as sleeping three hours a night and working a full-time job in a machine shop, his reaction was general befuddlement. Maybe, he began to think, I made a mistake. It was the same psychological dynamic that had eroded his authority at Juda. The more he backed off, the more his wife felt justified in questioning his authority, and the more she did that, the deeper she fell into the clutches of the man who was determined to destroy their marriage. Meanwhile, Richard Irwin was working himself up into a psychopathic rage. His shaking was augmented now by a frantic pacing back and forth. Talking to himself or to no one in particular, he was now threatening to call 911 or to get a gun and kill someone.

That night, the Stevensons went to counseling again, this time to a Fraternity of St. Peter priest from a nearby parish. This counselor, independently of the first, reiterated what the first priest had said. Necedah had been condemned by the Church, and the people who lived there were under interdict. The priest had even heard of Ryan Scott and relayed the LaCrosse diocese report on him. Once Suzanne and Robert got back to the shrine grounds, Richard undid whatever good the priest had done, using, of course, the arguments about the corruption of the Catholic Church and its clergy that Marvin Kucera had perfected as part of the recruiting strategy for the refuges. Ryan Scott could not be a phony priest, Irwin argued, because once while on the Necedah shrine grounds he had had a vision of Mary Ann van Hoof in heaven wearing three crowns, a fact which also proved that Mary Ann had been right all along and the bishop wrong, Mary Ann being in heaven and all. Wherever the discussion started, it always ended up somehow with an attack on the bishop and either Marvin or Richard claiming that the bishop and his priests couldn't be trusted. This was the most basic, if unwritten, law governing Necedah and the refuges before it. If the bishop could be trusted, the whole necessity for the refuges collapsed like a house of cards. Then, as if to strengthen his case one final time, Irwin launched into a description of how Bishop Burke had beaten up Father Peters, shortly before he had found asylum at Necedah.

The statement was preposterous enough to push Robert over the edge. Suddenly the whole explanation upon which he had based his life for the past two years collapsed under the weight of its own absurdity. Suddenly it was easier to believe that the Catholic Church and the local bishop were what they said they were than it was to believe one more preposterous story from the mouth of Richard Irwin or Marvin Kucera. Just to make sure, he asked Father Peters himself if the bishop had ever beaten him up. When Father Peters said, "No," the scales fell from Stevenson's eyes. When he confronted Irwin with the evidence, Irwin went into one of his psychotic shaking fits, pacing up and down, threatening to call 911, etc., etc. Robert knew now that he was in a cult, but he also didn't know what to do about it. The most perplexing thing about his predicament was how he had gotten into it in the first place. He had ended up in something very evil while all the while thinking that he was doing something good. "My heart was pure," he said later. "We taught NFP; we prayed the rosary every day; we were prolife. St. Louis de Montfort said you would never be deceived if you prayed the rosary. We were living the messages of Medjugorje, going to Mass and confession, fasting once a week. How did this happen then?"

Two days before the Stevensons arrived in Necedah, an interview with Bishop Peric appeared in the French journal *Present*, conducted by Yves Chiron, biographer of Paul VI. In it, Peric reiterated that what he had said before about Medjugorje, strengthening his position at some points and at others meeting the new claims that the Franciscans were making head on: "It cannot be claimed in any way whatsoever," he told Chiron, "that there has been a 'recognition of the cult' or that the parish church at Medjugorje has been recognized as a Marian sanctuary on a diocesan, national, or international level." When asked if his authority over Medjugorje had been superseded, Peric almost regretfully said that it hadn't but that he "would very happy if the Holy See would reserve to itself the inquiry on the events at Medjugorje, forming its own commission and arriving at a definitive judgment." Peric concluded by saying:

> There are many disorders there. There are Franciscan priests there with no canonical mission; religious communities have been established without the permission of the diocesan bishop, ecclesiastical buildings have been erected without ecclesiastical approval, parishes are encouraged to organize official pilgrimages, etc. Medjugorje, considered as a location of presumed apparitions, does not promote peace and unity but creates confusion and division, and not simply in its own diocese. I stated this in October 1994 at the Synod of Bishops and in the presence of the Holy Father, and I repeat it today with the same responsibility.

Toward the end of February Robert began to realize that Suzanne was spending most of her time with Richard Irwin. She had even started sleeping upstairs in his bed. When Robert confronted her demanding that she sleep downstairs with her husband and her children, Suzanne claimed now that she was afraid of Robert, fearing that he was going to rape her. Fearing that he was losing his mind, Robert decided that he needed to talk to some normal people.

Eventually he made contact with Father Gorman, a priest associated with the diocese who was familiar with both the Necedah story and the Juda Refuge story, as well as the Ryan Scott story. After listening to Robert describe the situation at the house at Necedah, with Father Peters wandering around the house in the middle of the night and drinking urine and Richard Irwin ranting about calling 911 or killing someone, Father Gorman told Robert that his family was at risk and that he had to get them out of Necedah as quickly as possible. He also said he would give Robert the diocese's dossier on Necedah, which he had sent to his office at work rather than to where he was living. After the meeting, that night while his wife was praying the rosary back at the shrine, Robert went to church and renounced Marvin Kucera and all the craziness that went along with it; he felt, he said later, "as if a truck had been lifted from my back." When he finally got a copy of the diocesan report on Necedah, Robert made copies and sent them to various family members. He also kept a copy in his car.

One night when he got back home, he found Suzanne upstairs in the overheated house with Richard Irwin, listening to him rant about how the Jews ran everything. What began as a theological disagreement with what Richard was saying soon escalated into another full scale battle. "Jesus was a Jew," Robert told Richard, and before long he was telling Irwin that it was time for him to get out of their marriage. It was time to "stop talking to my wife behind my back." Then turning to his wife, Robert added that Irwin was trying to control her, and he understood now that they had fallen into a cult. "You're a cult leader," he said to Irwin.

"This is a sacrament," Stevenson screamed at Irwin, feeling that the crisis had arrived and that it was time to act. "This is my wife, and me and my wife are getting out of here."

Robert at that point turned to his wife, who looked at Irwin and then looked at him and said, "I'm not going anywhere with you."

Suzanne then went to the phone and called 911 and told the police that her husband had guns in the house and was threatening to kill her. "Oh shit," Robert said and sank into a chair holding his head in his hands, trying to understand why his wife would do this to him. "She took my heart and trampled on it," is how he put it a few months later. In the meantime, Irwin slipped into one of his psychotic fits. "You messed with the wrong guy," Irwin said over and over again, shaking and pacing the floor. When the police arrived, Robert started yelling, "I'm in a cult. Help. I'm in a cult." Given the bedlam in the house, it's a miracle no one got shot by the police, who, reacting to what was going on as a generic domestic disturbance, ordered both Richard and Robert out of the house. Robert ended up in a motel in LaCrosse, where, his ulcers bleeding and unable to sleep, he called an attorney and made plans to get as much of his family out of Necedah as quickly as possible.

On February 2, 1997, one day before Robert Stevenson began his short-lived career as an assistant machinist in LaCrosse, Wisconsin, Mirjana Dragicevic started having apparitions again. Mirjana was the seer who had started it all; she was the first to get all ten secrets; she was also the first to drop out of the apparition business, an exit she accomplished gracefully if a bit abruptly on December 25, 1982, when she handed the secrets to Father Petar Ljubicic and went back to life as an agronomy student in Sarajevo. Her abrupt reappearance on the apparition scene caused some comment but little surprise from those who knew the situation. One of the tour guides who knew Mirjana personally felt that her reemergence as a seer had an economic explanation. "Marko [Soldo] chased away Mirjana's boyfriend," he said, "married her, built a house, and as a result, got into financial trouble. They needed the cash and so she started to have apparitions again. Now Marko is selling diesel cars from Italy. He's on radio ads in Croatia selling used cars."

A priest who knows her has a slightly different explanation, first of all of why she wanted to get out and then of why she wanted to get back in again. Mirjana's desire to leave is bound up with the village's sexual code, which prohibits intercourse with the Blessed Virgin while at the same time engaging in sexual intercourse, even in marriage. So the two original seers, Mirjana and Ivanka, checked out of the apparition scene early on, but then Mirjana, seeing herself superseded by Marija Pavlovic and seeing what she and the other seers were capable of getting away with, started to have second thoughts. After all those years of living in the poverty to which Yugoslavian agronomists are condemned, Mirjana decided to get back on the apparition track, this time with a big house with lots of rooms, which could be rented out to pilgrims, who by the late '90s had become jaded with the usual tour and now wanted to sleep, if not with the seers, then under the same roof at least. "She can now," the priest continued, "bring in $100,000 a year from the pilgrims because she is having a vision every second of the month. All of the seers but Jakov have hotels in Medjugorje. Now Mirjana wants back in."

"Nothing sticks on these kids," he continued. "They're made of Teflon. As a result they soon realized that you don't have to quit if you get married. So Mirjana got back into the apparition business after she realized you could pretty much get away with anything. Once she did that, it became open-ended, and they all basically became lifetime visionaries. The first two have announced that they are going to have visions for the rest of their lives. All of them are now getting some kind of monthly allotment. Mirjana was the oldest. They called her the *Pankerica*, their word for punk. There is no soda fountain here, no place where can you go when you've got to get a way from your parents, if you want to have a smoke, for instance—not dope, just cigarettes. You don't do this sort of thing in front of your parents, if you're a 16-year-old girl; no, you get away, and then when they were up on the mountain having a smoke, they saw something, a high-wattage spirit guide, Oren , the Cosmic virgin, a deceiving entity."

Ever since the Catholic Church decided that nothing supernatural was going on in Medjugorje, the question of just what the "seers" were seeing became more problematic. Bishop Zanic, who had the advantage of talking to the seers firsthand in their native language, felt that the apparitions of Medjugorje were a joke that got out of hand. The initial interviews which Jozo Zovko conducted with the seers bear this interpretation out. The two girls who started the whole thing told Zanic they had gone up the hill to tend sheep. When Zanic reminded one of them, Ivanka Ivankovic, that it was a sin to tell a lie, she almost immediately recanted and said they went up to have a smoke. Just what they were smoking at the time was a source of contention as well.

Mirjana Dragicevic, the other original seer, was known as a big city "*Pankerica*," and her reputation in the village was associated with the big city, Sarajevo, and drugs. The charges never got resolved one way or the other. The children were never tested to see if they had taken drugs, and in the end the accusation of drug use got dismissed as heavy-handed Communist propaganda of the sort this sort of person would mount against saints.

But the "seers" are far from being declared saints by the same Church which declared them liars. So the questions remain. What exactly did they see on that day in June in 1981? Or did they see anything at all?

In late October 1989 Ivan Dragicevic, the Medjugorje "seer," was a long way from home. He was in San Francisco in fact, and having survived the biggest earthquake in recent memory on the day of his arrival, he was standing in the back yard of a Croatian emigré by the name of Joe Tolaitch, having a cigarette. Joe Tolaitch was part of the Croatian Diaspora living in the Bay Area. He had grown up in Metkovic, a few kilometers down the Neredva from Medjugorje, and had in fact been one of the first people to arrive in Medjugorje as pilgrims during the summer of 1981. Joe's attitude toward the Blessed Mother had a distinctly practical bent. Faced with the prospect of having a seer who had daily contact with the Blessed Mother in his own home, Joe asked Ivan if the Virgin Mary might divulge during one of her visits her favorite six numbers, so that Joe could put them to good use in the state lottery. Perhaps Joe had become skeptical because of Ivan's lifestyle. Whatever the reason, he never got an answer to his question, which prompted him to ask Ivan on that evening while he was having a cigarette in his back yard, whether Ivan was really seeing the Blessed Mother. Ivan's answer was something less than reassuring to the pious. "Joe," Ivan replied after taking a drag on his cigarette, "I'm seeing something."

Evidence from other sources close to the seers corroborates Ivan's testimony. Mirjana once described a vision in which she saw the Virgin Mary appear, only to be replaced by a second virgin, who told her in a different voice, "You see even the devil can come dressed as me." In a second encounter, Mirjana saw a beautiful young man standing in the doorway to her room who told her that even the devil can come as a beautiful being. The possibility that the seers were seeing a spiritual entity which was not the Blessed Mother was mentioned explicitly by a priest who has been associated with the apparitions for over ten years and during that period has gone from being an avid believer and promoter to a confirmed skeptic. After years of hearing confessions and assembling a library of New Age material from penitents, it became clear to him that Medjugorje was a major stop on the New Age circuit. Before long, the Blessed Virgin even started talking like a New Age guru. The first message to issue from the lips of "Our Lady of Medjugorje" after the bishops' condemnation was that her devotees should turn "negatives into positives," a turn of phrase which struck this priest at the time as totally unbiblical, a feeling which received dramatic confirmation when he found exactly the same phrase coming from the lips of New Age guru, Sanaya Roman, "Channel for Orin." "*Or*," the priest remembered, was the Hebrew word for light. The Latin word is *Lux*, whose genitive is *lucis*, which is the root of the name "light-bearer," or "Lucifer." The passage about changing negatives into positives which Marija Pavlovic cited verbatim as the first message from the Gospa after the bishops' declaration of April 1991 is the title of Chapter Five of Sanaya Roman's book, *Living with Joy: Keys to Personal Power and Spiritual Transformation.*

Somewhere between the hypothesis that Medjugorje was a joke that got out of hand and the theory that the kids are talking to demons, I begin to descry a third possibility, based on its geographical and historical context and their relationship to the massacres at Surmanci just on the other side of apparition hill. The "seers," according to this theory, saw a ghost. Ghosts, to begin with, have a psychological existence, whereas demons are ontological. Demons are actual beings; they are pure spirits, or angels who have chosen to rebel against God and live in a state of eternal separation from Him. Their only consolation comes from making other rational creatures, who were created to share happiness with God, share their misery instead. Ghosts, on the other hand, are a function of the mind which beholds them. They are traditionally seen as the souls of men who have not gone to hell but rather to purgatory, whence they escape periodically to admonish the living about some still unfinished business.

Like the monster in horror fiction, ghosts represent the return of the repressed. Ghosts, as in the case of Hamlet's father, represent an unrighted wrong. They are an indication that an event in the past has failed to achieve closure. As a result of repression, usually caused by guilt, the ghost frequently re-presents itself at moments usually associated in some way with an anniversary of the event that needs to be repressed.

To give a typical example, women who have abortions generally relive the guilt and anguish associated with the death of their child on the anniversary date of either the abortion itself or on the day the woman has calculated as the child's birth date. The aborted child rises ghost-like on the anniversary of his death and accuses the mother in much the same way that Banquo's ghost accuses Macbeth and the ghost of Hamlet's father reproaches Hamlet.

Reduced to its simplest form, Medjugorje was this: Two girls saw something on the other side of the hill where the Surmanci massacres took place, on the fortieth anniversary of the massacres, at a time when Tito had been dead for a little over a year and all of eastern Europe was aflame with the nationalism that the Polish labor union Solidarity had inspired in the subject nations of the Soviet empire. Father Zovko tried to deflect attention from Surmanci, claiming that it was absurd "to offload on Medjugorje all the guilt for wartime atrocities that even we older ones hadn't heard of; and as for the children, they weren't even born," but the Serbs remained unconvinced. Belgrade papers satirized an Ustasha terrorist Madonna with a large knife between her teeth and a caption proclaiming, "The True Face of the Blessed Mother."

In Medjugorje the "anniversary reaction" was collective as well as personal, and collective in a way that involved the Serbs. Hence, the coincidence of dates. Our Lady of Medjugorje appeared at virtually the same time that the Serbs erected the plaque commemorating the atrocity at Surmanci at the orthodox monastery at Zitomislic, and both of those events occurred forty years to the day after the massacre itself. Ghosts always represent an unrighted wrong. The recognition of the wrong is triggered by some related event, like an anniversary, or the dislocation of the established order. In 1980 the sense that the established order was coming to an end in eastern Europe was in the air. In order to maintain order in an ethnically diverse country riven by atrocities during World War II, the Communists literally fashioned a lid out of concrete and placed it over the opening where the genocide of the Serbs had taken place at Surmanci. If repression can be represented by a lid placed over unwelcome memories and the emotions they generate, then the death of Tito and the election of a Polish pope and the rise of Solidarity meant that the Communist lid was about to be removed from Yugoslavia, and the first thing that rose into consciousness in Herzegovina after the communist repression was removed was the guilt over what the Ustasha terrorists had done during the war. In 1989, as a hint of the nationalism that was to follow, the Serbs literally removed the lid and took their dead home. But as in horror movies, so in real life. The guilt is re-presented in a form that is less threatening. Instead of a monster representing the Enlightenment gone wrong, the Herzegovisti were confronted by a warning Mother, a figure of radical ambivalence in which consolation is always a thin veneer over catastrophe, which will follow if her instructions are not carried out.

What the children saw, of course, became irrelevant by the third day of the apparitions when the Franciscans, specifically Jozo Zovko, became involved and turned the seers into foot soldiers in their war against Bishop Zanic. The deal with the children was cut as payment for not denouncing them as a hoax and exposing them thereby to the ire of a local population that wanted to believe that their deliverance was just around the corner. *Vox populi, vox dei* applies here in an uncanny way. It is the people who make a phony apparition, not God or the Blessed Virgin. They fashion it into the idol of their desires, and so it is not surprising that Medjugorje should take on a nationalistic cast at this place and time. The Virgin was simultaneously the ghost of Croatian sin and the sign of Croatian nationalist hope that the old order was ending, and because the fall of communism seemed like a possibility in the summer of 1981, the Virgin was conjured up by an oppressed Croatian nation to bring it about. The times were propitious. Tito had died in 1980; all of Eastern Europe was in turmoil caused by the picture of Solidarity workers kneeling in front of the Gdansk shipyard praying the rosary to the Black Madonna. If the Madonna could save the Poles who prayed to her at Czestochowa, why couldn't the Gospa save the Croatians who prayed to her at Medjugorje?

Although it was modeled consciously on Lourdes, with a little bit of *Garabandal* (the warning, the chastisement, the permanent supernatural sign) thrown in for good measure, Medjugorje itself was more like the equally bogus apparitions in Marpingen in Germany, which for a brief moment in the 1870s outdrew even Lourdes, upon which it too was based. By the beginning of the nineteenth century, apparitions had taken on the form which they still retain to this day. They happen to children of oppressed minorities or neglectful parents in borderlands during times of momentous social change. Medjugorje and Marpingen fulfilled both criteria. Marpingen took place in part of Germany which had changed from one country to another, and at the time of the alleged apparitions was suffering under Bismarck's attempt to crush the Catholic Church, that subsequently came to be known as *Kulturkampf*. In his classic study of the "apparitions" of Marpingen, David Blackbourne paints a picture which has remarkable similarities to Medjugorje:

> The struggle in Prussia between state and church, known as the *Kulturkampf*, had already heightened denominational tensions and created fear among a substantial proportion of the Catholic minority; and by 1876 the economic recession that had begun three years earlier was causing serious distress and prompting calls for remedial measures....It was in order to gather bilberries—"Waelen," in the local dialect—that, on the hot Monday of 3 July, a number of young girls found themselves in the Haertelwald, a hilly wooded area that contained many

rocky gullies and lay a few minutes away from Marpingen to the south-east....Within less than a week thousands of pilgrims were streaming to Marpingen. Reports spoke of 20,000 in the village, with up to 4,000 at the apparition site singing, praying, and taking away foliage or handfuls of earth from the spot....the civil authorities closed off the area, the three visionaries began to claim apparitions in the school, in the graveyard and the church....Marpingen became a *cause celebre*. Journalists, priests, and the sellers of pious memorabilia descended on the village, as well as pilgrims from Germany and abroad. Supporters and opponents of events there dubbed Marpingen 'the German Lourdes,' even 'the Bethlehem of Germany.'... There is no doubt that modern apparitions were commonly triggered by larger events: periods of wartime or post-war stress, political conflict, socio-economic crisis. It is also plain that many apparitions had an impact in turn on contemporary political conflicts, above all in helping to foster Catholic identity against the claims of the state or the challenge of anticlericals.

Blackbourn feels "there is overwhelming evidence... of the link between the apparitions and a combination of political persecution, material distress, and social change. That is true not only of the original events in Marpingen, but of the revitalized apparition movement in the twentieth century" (pp. xxi-xxvii).

Bosnia Herzegovina, it should be remembered, is the ultimate borderland for Europe. It marked the border between the East and West in the Roman Empire, between the Catholic and Orthodox lands of the Middle Ages, between the Austrian and Ottoman empires after that, and until most recently the western most rim of communism's confrontation with the West, in the twentieth century's version of the schism between East and West. The children who began both Marpingen and Medjugorje had been influenced by Lourdes, Mirjana reading a book on it in the period between June 6 and June 21, 1981. The children represented an oppressed Catholic population looking for release from Prussian Protestantism or Communism respectively. Unable to achieve relief by either political or intellectual means or by force of arms, the oppressed population turned to popular Marian piety as an expression of protest. In both instances, it was the expectation and suppressed aspiration of an oppressed Catholic people, given leadership by the local priest, which brought the crowds and became the driving force behind the apparition. The priest became as well the mediator of the intense psychological pressure that public scrutiny would bring to bear on the children as the crowds increased in size and expectation. In exchange for protection from exposure, the children became the pawns of the priests, who, especially in the case of Medjugorje, used them for their own political ends, first as a weapon against the local bishop, and secondly and increasingly as a weapon against the Communists as the tide of nationalism rose to fill the vacuum created by an ideology no one believed in anymore.

Mirjana was always characterized as the most "sensitive" of the seers. She cried a lot. Mirjana read a book on Lourdes at some time in early June and then, reflecting on her situation as part of a persecuted Catholic minority in a borderland area neglected by the regime because of its Catholicism, which was linked inalterably in the regime's mind with atrocities committed against the Serbs, she "saw something" on the mountain, and her people were energized by a local instance of events that seemed to be moving the entire world. One month after an attempt was made on the life of the pope, the Virgin came to offer consolation and warning. As one woman who heard about the apparition within a matter of days while watching TV in Split put it, "It had to be true."

On January 10, 1983, Father Tomislav Vlasic interviewed Mirjana and then transcribed the tape, which was later published in severely edited form in books by Svetozar Kraljevic and Robert Faricy/ Lucy Rooney. Rev. Ivo Sivric summarizes the profile of the seer which emerges from the interview:

> Reading the interview with Mirjana, it is evident that she hears voices. Mirjana is quite frank in her conduct and about her interior disposition; at one time or another, she has suffered "terribly depressive moods," she has behaved so strangely at school in Sarajevo that her peers considered her crazy. She is seized by sudden onsets of tears, as well as by "unexpected laughter"; she "cries for no reason"; she "is too sensitive"; etc. When the visions began, Father Zovko asked Mirjana if she were exhausted. She replied: "I would like just to sleep." Like Vicka, she complained only once of a "fit of tears." But she had these "crying fits" from the very beginning of the visions. It seems that she liked to cry. I have the impression that she is vulnerable.

One of the passages that got excised from the original interview, probably because it might cast doubt on her mental stability, is Mirjana's description of purgatory. "There are souls in Purgatory," she tells us,

> who pray a lot to God but nobody here on earth prays for them. There are other souls in Purgatory who do not pray at all, but some people on earth pray for them. These prayers are not applied to those souls in Purgatory for whom the prayers are offered but rather to those who pray. For the souls [in Purgatory] who pray a great deal, God allows them to communicate with their people here [on earth]. There was a woman whose two daughters were killed and they appeared to their mother in a dream and petitioned her to pray for them.... I then asked the Gospa what that meant, and she replied that they are in Purgatory and are in need of a little hope to get them into Heaven: they begged their mother to pray for them while they prayed for themselves. There was another woman who lived in a house and something kept constantly knocking on her window. Later on, this very same woman got an apartment way up on the sixth floor and again something kept tapping on her window. I questioned the Gospa about what it was. She replied that the souls in Purgatory were doing so because she has forgotten to pray for them, and they are demanding her prayers.

There is no simple Sherlock Holmes explanation of the entities who come and tap on Mirjana's window. This mystery is not going to be solved by the Enlightenment's detectives or its scientists but only by someone who can understand the psychological and religious needs of the people who collaborated on establishing the meaning of the event. Mirjana may very well have divined in some mediumistic way the psychic forces driving the region, and then, as if shocked by what she uncovered, she tried to get out from underneath the burden by progressively involving more people as collaborators. First she involved the other kids, then Marinko Ivankovic, then Jozo Zovko and the Franciscans, then the Croatian people, then Catholics from abroad, and finally the forces trying to destabilize communism.

The best metaphor is more predatory than that. There was no conspiracy here—at least not at the beginning, not until the Franciscans took it over, and even after that it was always a case of big fish eating little fish. As soon as any one person could assemble a certain number of people in one place who were willing to throw X amount of D-marks into a hole, that person was a candidate to be eaten by someone more powerful than he. Once the crowds became significant enough in size, Zovko was motivated to take it over from Marinko Ivankovic, and the same process has been happening ever since. Big fish eat little fish; they open their mouths and bite 'em; little fish eat littler fish and so on ad infinitum.

The same thing could have happened on the spiritual realm. Fr. Guerrero in his book on Medjugorje recounts the story of Sr. Magdalena of the Cross, the false Spanish mystic who fooled her congregation with her mystical powers up till the moment of her death, when she confessed that she had made a pact with the devil, confessed, and died. When Sister Magdalena first started seeing these apparitions she thought they were genuine, but then after she had gotten hooked on the spiritual pleasures associated with them, the devil revealed himself as the true figure behind the entity she had been seeing and made her an offer she couldn't refuse. The same possibilities apply at Medjugorje and also help explain the changes that have taken place in the seers' lives; for things have changed there without a doubt. Ivan was not driving a BMW in the late '80s, nor was he married to a beauty queen. If a deal was cut, it seems to have been cut some distance down the road from the first apparition. At least the pay-off came later.

Even granting the authority and the solace and protection that the priests offered, the psychological pressure on the seers was enormous, and given the fact that she orchestrated it at the beginning, it is perhaps not surprising that Mirjana Dragicevic would be the first to crack under the pressure. On Christmas day 1982, 18 months to the day from the first apparition, Mirjana announced that the apparitions had stopped. Before departing, however, the Blessed Virgin gave Mirjana ten secrets, which would be revealed to the world after three warnings, in the form of three dire events, which would take place just before the visible sign would appear from heaven. Once the great sign appeared, if the world did not turn to God, it would suffer a terrible punishment.

"As for the tenth [secret]," Mirjana warned the world, "it is terrible, and nothing can alter it. It will happen."

As of early 1997, it looked as if Mirjana were planning to weather the chastisement—now a bit long in coming—in style. Mirjana now lives in a German mansion right across the street from Ivan's German mansion. Both buildings would hold their own in a well-to-do suburb of Karlsruhe or Stuttgart, which came to symbolize the promised land for Mirjana's generation whose fathers were often away from home laboring as *Gastarbeiter* in the *Bundesrepublik*. Both houses have lawns, which require frequent watering, something in short supply in a place like Medjugorje.

By March 1997 Suzanne was being nicer to Robert, but his ulcers would start bleeding every time he got near the house where Suzanne was living with Irwin, and so he was staying away more frequently, usually in a local hotel. While away he continued to make phone calls and was turning up more evidence on Richard Irwin and how he operated. Gwen Johns, recently escaped with her husband and family from Juda and now living in Texas, told Robert during one phone conversation that Richard Irwin had paid for their expenses to travel to Necedah in 1991. The trip didn't have its desired effect though. The Johns thought it was the creepiest place on earth. Gwen, who, like Irwin, was born and raised in St Paul, also told Robert he had broken up his best friend's marriage.

In the meantime, Robert was also circulating the diocesan report on Necedah to family members, something which came to Suzanne's attention when she found a copy on the front seat of Robert's car. After asking Robert what the report was doing in his car, Suzanne went on a counter-offensive, calling her parents and other relatives, telling them that she was not in a cult and that Robert was being controlling and manipulative. At one point Gwen Johns called her at work and told her to get her children "the hell out of there," but Suzanne used the opportunity to turn the whole situation around, bringing up the $400 the Johns had borrowed to make their escape but had never paid back. "Anyone who talked to my wife," Robert said later, "became intoxicated with hate poison." In order to defend her position, especially her position of keeping the children at Necedah, Suzanne had to turn on her husband and conduct a campaign of character assassination and disinformation in order to counter the dossier that he was circulating from the chancery.

Eventually Suzanne called a meeting of the Necedah people as a way of reining in her husband. In attendance were Tom McNally, the shrine's lawyer, Father Peters, the Irwins, and the Stevensons. Robert handed around copies of the dossier and said that they should be obedient to the bishop. "If you can't trust this bishop," he said, "you can't trust anybody."

Tom McNally, whose fees were being paid from the shrine's trust fund, was the first to object.

"You're just regurgitating the same old shit I've heard for years," McNally said.

Then Robert brought up the issue of the Father Peters' money and where it had come from. Father Peters had donated $187,000 toward building the shrine prayer house. He still had another $300,000 in the bank, plus something or other in various safe deposit boxes, and on top of that he had just bought a brand new Plymouth Voyager. Where, Robert wanted to know, did all the money come from?

"I saved it," said Father Peters.

Now there were three explanations. The shrine was saying that Fr. Peters had won the lottery; Father Peters was saying that he saved around a half a million dollars from his salary as a priest, and the diocese was saying that he embezzled it. Both the bishop and Father Gorman had come to the shrine to plead with Father Peters to come back to the Church. In the course of the conversation, Fr. Peters said that he was at the shrine because a psychic had told him to go there, a fact which had a certain plausibility to it since the back door of the house was covered with lottery numbers he had gotten from psychics.

Faced with the three explanations, Robert told the assembled shrine members, "I'm going with the bishop's explanation. This whole organization stinks."

"What business is where he got his money to you," Suzanne responded, and at that point Robert realized that she had been corrupted by the money too, since her salary was coming from the same trust fund.

Two days after the meeting, the domestic turmoil and the sleepless nights took their toll. Robert was laid off from work. When he arrived to tell Suzanne the news, he noticed that she had packed a suitcase and was in the process of putting it in the car. Robert tried to engage her in a conversation on trust. She countered by saying that he was spying on her.

"I can't take this verbal abuse any more," he said. "Suzanne, I'll do anything for your trust."

Suzanne put the suitcase in the trunk and slammed the lid down.

"If you want my trust," she said, radiating the hatred which had become familiar to him, "You better stop doing what you're doing. You've been a Judas to your own wife."

With that, she drove off, nearly running over Robert's foot.

Easter was approaching, and Robert, in spite of repeated calls to his parents, didn't know what to do. He was scared, just generally scared of the evil that seemed so powerful; he was afraid for his kids, of what might happen to them if they continued their association with the shrine. On Easter Sunday, he showed up at the shrine with a bouquet of flowers for his wife. He was there for the shrine Easter egg hunt for the kids but reasoned to himself, "Maybe if I bring my wife flowers, I can get to her heart. Flowers never fail," he thought.

When he got there, Joel was asleep, and Suzanne wore the glassy-eyed look he had come to associate with the evil spirit which had taken possession of her soul.

"I got some flowers," he said, offering his wife the bouquet he had brought.

"I don't want them," Suzanne responded. Then as if thinking that the flowers were too good to waste or perhaps softening somewhat to her husband's overtures, she said, "I'll go down to the church and give them to the Blessed Mother."

Suzanne mentioned the "sacred spot," and Robert immediately thought in reply," You mean the cursed spot?"

His attempt at reconciliation once more rebuffed, Robert brought up the custody of the children.

"Honey," he said, "I've got to see my kids." After some more verbal skirmishing, Robert arranged to have them spend the night at his house that coming weekend. After picking them up from the shrine on April 4, he got in the car and drove straight through the night to Denver, Colorado, where he got on a plane and flew to Los Angeles, where his father picked him up at the airport.

On April 16, 1997, the deadline the Franciscan general had given to Boniface Barbaric to hand over St. Francis Church in Capljina to the bishop's priests, the pope finally arrived in Sarajevo. The date for the transfer of the parish had come and gone, and the front door of the church still remained sealed with cinderblocks, but the pope in the course of his homily made brief mention of the "shrine of Our Lady Queen of Peace in Bosnia where pilgrimages never stopped." The statement was a back-handed slap at Medjugorje, which had been shut down for two and a half months with its staff cowering in the rectory basement during the late spring of 1992. It was only a group of pilgrims marching from Humac to St. James that persuaded the Franciscans to open the church up for services again. The pope was in fact referring to the offcially recognized Marian shrine at Hrasno, 40 kilometers southeast of the Medjugorje, which had not shut down during the war. Perhaps stung by the pope's criticism, Slavko Barbaric went up to Cardinal Kuharic after the Mass and demanded that Medjugorje be recognized as an official shrine. Kuharic said that was impossible, but this didn't stop the Franciscans from doing just that in their promotional material. On July 5, 1997, the pope sent Bishop Peric a telegram expressing his best wishes for the twentieth anniversary of the shrine of "Kraljica Mira" at Hrasno, calling it, in contradistinction to Medjugorje, a "*vero centro di devozione Mariana.*"

The night before the pope's arrival in Sarajevo, a bomb was discovered under a bridge on the road the papal motorcade was to travel. Just who planted never got resolved, but the people associated with Medjugorje blamed the Muslims. As far as diplomacy went, the trip was less than a success. The Serbian representative boycotted the ceremony welcoming the pope; Alia Izetbegovic showed up in a military uniform as a way of insulting the pope, and making it clear that he didn't want him to come. Not all Muslims felt that way though. Salih Rajkovic said that many Muslims cheered the pope during his visit and saw it as a gesture of peace. While in Sarajevo though for the pope's visit, Rajkovic heard many Croats complaining that the pope had snubbed them by not visiting Medjugorje: "He," the Croats said, referring to the pope, "did not come to us, but to Muslims. He is not our pope because he avoided Medjugorje."

When Suzanne Stevenson realized that her children were no longer in Wisconsin, she took the next plane to Los Angeles, drove to Robert's parents' house, and with the help of her mother's boyfriend, broke down the back door to the house. She then flew back to Wisconsin with the kids and filed for divorce. By being the first to file, she got a legal advantage over her husband who had no contacts in Wisconsin. She, on the other hand, had the legal and financial resources of the Necedah Shrine behind her. Now Robert has to live in Wisconsin if he wants to see his children and if he wants for fight for custody. The courts always favor the mother; the courts likewise favor any group which calls itself a religion, no matter how bizarre its beliefs or practices, by claiming that it cannot interfere in its affairs. The result is a system which favors the destruction of family ties in Robert Stevenson's life every bit as much as it favored the same thing in Phil Kronzer's life. The only difference is money. Robert has no money, and so once he had been deprived of his children, the courts, the lawyers, and the real estate agents will leave him alone to ponder how or why his wife would exchange two months of Necedah and six months of Richard Irwin for years of a marriage that both of them considered a non-revocable sacrament.

All of that love has now turned to hatred in an alchemy that Robert still doesn't understand. Suzannne and Richard, he now says, "are massively obsessed with each other," and spend their time conspiring to hurt him even more by depriving him of access to the children.

"She thinks I'm weak," he said at one point. "She even called me a wimp."

Because she hurt him, Suzanne has to hate him because unless she can see him as the villain of the story she will have to grapple with her own culpability in the break-up of their marriage.

"You corrupted me," Suzanne said to her husband the last time they talked. "I wanted to be a nun. I wish I had never met you."

When Robert reminded Suzanne that the last three times they had sex, it was her idea, she abruptly changed emotional gears. "I just used you to get off," she said.

"Now," he concludes, "she has guilt galore and is projecting all of her guilt on to me. She probably thinks that I could never love her again if she admitted that she had an affair." As of now, Robert has effectively lost his children to Necedah. "I can't touch them now," he said. "In their formative years, Satan has them."

On June 23, 1997, Phil Kronzer decided to make one more pilgrimage to Medjugorje. The once-booming tourist attraction in Herzegovina was still struggling to shake off the effects of the war. The buildings which had been left half finished now had workers on them once again. The seers seemed determined to help the villagers recoup their losses. All of them showed up with their spouses for a private Mass celebrated by Father Ivan Landeka. The only seer who didn't show up for the Mass was Marija Pavlovic Lunetti, who decided to sit out the sixteenth anniversary in Italy.

Phil's reason for coming back to Medjugorje was simple. Phil had met Mirjana and her husband during one of their trips through California. They had stayed at his house at Los Gatos, and for an even longer period of time at the Kronzers second house in Monterery, and had even told Phil that their second child had been conceived there. Phil's plan was simple. Phil wanted his wife back, and he wanted Mirjana's help in getting her back. His reasoning seemed plausible enough. If Ardie left him because of Medjugorje, what better way to get her back than have one of the Medjugorje seers arrange their reunion. Mirjana could even say that she had talked it over with the Blessed Mother, a statement no less implausible than the ten secrets, which the average Medjugorje enthusiast had no trouble believing.

When Phil arrived at the Soldo house, on the afternoon of June 25, Mirjana was busy inside instructing pilgrims. After Phil re-intro-duced himself to Marko, Mirjana's husband, she finally appeared at the door but did not invite him in. Phil had been there the day before and had given his name to a group of pilgrims at the door, some of whom he recognized from his wife's prayer group in California. Now he suspected they had gotten to Mirjana.

It took Mirjana a while to get to the door, and once there it became clear that the encounter was going to be brief. Mirjana was heavily made up; her hair is frosted and she spoke with the low voice of someone who smoked heavily, still smoking after all these years. Phil recounted his story as best he could feeling a bit like a Fuller brush salesman, and getting just that sort of response from Mirjana.

"I need your help to get my wife back," he pleaded.

"I'm sorry. I can't help you," she answered either anxious to get back to the pilgrims or anxious to get away from Phil. Whenever Phil came up with another way of asking for help, Mirjana repeated the same answer. When Phil offered to return later, Mirjana terminated the meeting by saying she was busy, and without further ado, walked back into her house to instruct her pilgrims further in the messages of Our Lady Queen of Peace.

Later the same day, Phil ended up in the orange shipping container that is Father Philip Pavich's office just outside the rectory at St. James Parish. There was little that Pavich could do by then other than listen to Phil's story. He had been blacklisted in his way by the very group of Franciscans that wanted to keep him there. In January of 1997 Pavich had given an interview to a reporter from *The Stars and Stripes*, the newspaper for the U.S. Army, in which he blasted the seers for their greed and for trafficking in spirits. After the article appeared the reaction from his fellow Franciscans was so intense that Pavich wrote an abject letter of apology to the newspaper accusing himself, in the manner of defendants in Communist show trials, of lack of Christian charity for what amounted to telling the truth. After making his novena in April, Pavich inexplicably decided to remain in Medjugorje.

When Kronzer brought up his reception at Mirjana's house, Pavich commiserated for a bit and then talked about how the seers are involved in the occult. The villagers read tea cups; Mirjana dabbled in spiritism in Sarajevo. That in combination with the 600 murdered Serbs on the other side of the mountain was enough to draw down an evil spirit bent on more mischief. The villagers are also big on the devil, an aspect of peasant life that makes its way into the messages which mention Satan more than they mention God. The same attitude toward hell and the devil makes its way into everyday speech as well. "F*** Jesus," Pavich says, "is a common expression here, along with "F*** Mary," and cursing, as in calling on demons to consign a person to Hell."

Vicka, he continued, used to keep a picture of a headless Christ on a crucifix between two horses rearing up on either side at one of her houses. Before long, a group of pilgrims staying at her house complained that they were being oppressed by the picture, but she refused to remove it, saying that it was just something that someone had left there. Then things got worse at the house. The rooms turned freezing cold, and the pilgrims found that their rosaries would get tangled around their throats and start to strangle them, until finally all the pilgrims fled, full of some uncanny fear.

"If I were Satan," Pavich continued, warming to a topic that had been on his mind so long, with so little opportunity to discuss it, "this is how I would get at the pious. Take something that is not only not on the level of divine revelation, but a lie as well, and then get all these pious people to promote it to the status of a divine oracle, and then get them to clobber the fellow who disagrees, even the bishop, get these seemingly pious people to offend against charity by attacking anyone who wants to preserve the integrity of divine revelation. The devil gets the pious to tell anyone who disagrees with them, 'You're doing Satan's work by opposing me.' This is the essence of schism."

The two Phils, whose lives have been changed forever by coming in contact with Medjugorje, swap stories; they commiserate, and then it is time to go. There is nothing more that can be done by hanging around the now-bustling shrine, as it readies itself for the gala anniversary Mass at the pavilion behind the church. Bishop Hnilica is a concelebrant, in his first appearance at Medjugorje since the consecration debacle in March of 1994. Almost as an afterthought, Father Pavich brings up a name that might be helpful—Jane Sears, a journalist from California. Pavich scrawls her number on a piece of paper. For six months during his travels in search of the key combination of information and contacts to get his wife back, Phil carried the name in his head, if not in his pocket. Then in December of 1997, he finally met with Sears, who informed him that she had typed the "William J. O'Brien" letter to Regina Moore, as someone dictated it to her at her apartment. The person doing the dictating was Marcia Smith and present at the time was Phil's wife Ardie. What Phil now had in hand was the basis for a lawsuit. The downside of the revelation, of course, was that Ardie was a willing tool in the destruction of her own marriage. Jane Sears later indicated that the pressure Phil was putting on the Medjugorje group was beginning to show in Marcia Smith, who at one point told Jane that if she had it to do over again, she would never have taken Ardie out of the house in Los Gatos. In addition to finding out that "William J .O'Brien" was Marcia Smith, Phil learned that Darryl Monda had made phone calls to Smith's apartment, something which explained how material from his divorce kept showing up in his civil suit.

Meanwhile, hemmed in by ecclesial sanctions which prevented them from administering the sacraments at the barricaded church in Capljina, the Franciscans edged closer to schism by bringing in an anonymous "bishop" to administer the sacrament of confirmation at St. Francis Parish on October 5, 1997. The Franciscans were now clearly on the road to schism, and the Bishop Peric was both aghast and furious:

"To such 'shepherds,'" he wrote in an article entitled "The 'Confirmation' in Capljina and the 'Charisma' of Medjugorje,"

> Jesus would say: "Truly, truly, I say to you, he who does not enter the sheepfold by the door but climbs in by another way, that man is a thief and a robber" (John 10:1).

The anonymous guest in Capljina did not enter the Church through the main doors, because for 15 months now, a brick wall has been built up in front of them blocking the entry of the legitimate pastors of the church. This guest jumped in from the other side, rejecting every Christian tradition, all norms of courtesy and neglecting the specific law of the Church. They say he even carried the signs of the bishop's office, a mitre and crosier, which no normal bishop of the Catholic Church would ever do on the territory of another diocese without the express permission of the local Bishop.

The anonymous bishop, if he were in fact a bishop, refused to give his name to the congregation; he refused to say were he came from, other than it was from "a far away, yet beautiful country" that was "more than a thousand miles away from your lovely country and your beautiful city," but he did mention that the reason he was there was because he was a frequent visitor to Medjugorje, a fact especially galling to Peric because the Franciscans kept insisting on the importance of separating the Capljina affair from the Medjugorje affair. Now it turned out that there was a connection after all. Peric, in fact, saw a connection between the two incidents that went back 15 years:

> The unlawful "Monsignor" of Capljina...initially inspired by the spirit of Medjugorje with "peace and happiness," and later on with sadness and great unhappiness, upon seeing that things are not going the way he and those who invited him would like them to go, is now working against unity, peace and order, against the regulations and canons of God's Church, and he's also abusing the sacrament of the Holy Spirit. Medjugorje transmitted the first "messages" 15 years ago when in January 1982, the so-called "Madonna" through one of the "seers" got involved in a question of the jurisdiction of the local Church by defending some disobedient Franciscan chaplains and rebuking the local Bishop Pavao, that he made a "reckless decision." The "seer" used an even harsher word in her description! And now, Medjugorje has spiritually inspired an unlawful "minister of confirmation" who goes to Capljina to dissolve Church unity and to deceive hundreds of candidates for confirmation.

At around the same time, an article appeared in *Ckrva na Kamenu*, Mostar's diocesan newspaper recounting the story of how Vicka, with Slavko Barbaric's collaboration, claimed that the Blessed

Mother requested that a 100 bed hotel be built in Medjugorje and how the message was used to attempt to shake down a large amount of money from a Dutch religious community. When the money wasn't forthcoming after he initial request, Vicka wrote again on March 19, 1995, reminding the potential benefactors of just who they were dealing with:

"I have already written to you by my friend N. N. and his family," Vicka wrote, "and I write you again, because perhaps you didn't understand me well, and in the same time I am in a certain sense a little amazed that you are asking also other messages beside those of the Madonna, the Mother of God."

Vicka then quickly gets to the point:

When the Madonna, the Mother of God, approves and insists to start with the work on the building, then I don't understand why you are doubting and asking any other message and the approval from common people.

On October 2, 1997, Ratko Peric responded to a letter from Thierry Boutet, secretary general of Famille Chretienne of Paris, explaining that he had changed his mind about Medjugorje:

On the basis of the serious study of the case by 30 of our "studiosi" [academics who have taken part in three commissions], on my episcopal experience of five years in the Diocese, on the scandalous disobedience that surrounds the phenomenon, on the lies that are at times put into the mouth of the "Madonna," on the unusual repetition of "messages" for over 16 years, on the strange way that the "spiritual directors" of the so-called "visionaries" accompany them through the world making propaganda of them, on the practice that the "Madonna" appears at the "fiat" (let her come!) of the "visionaries," my conviction and position is not *non constat de supernaturalitate* [the supernaturality has not been proven] but also the other formula *constat de non supernaturalitate* [the non-supernaturality is proven] of the apparitions or revelations of Medjugorje."

On November 12, 1997, Mother Angelica appeared on her *Mother Angelica Live* TV show and blasted Roger Cardinal Mahony, ordinary of the archdiocese of Los Angeles, for a pastoral letter on the Sunday liturgy which had been promulgated in the archdiocese. Mother Angelica claimed that the letter either ignored or deliberately downplayed the real presence of Christ in the Eucharist and announced as a result that "my obedience in that diocese would be absolutely zero, and I hope everyone else's obedience would be zero" too. Two days later, Mahony wrote to Mother Angelica complaining about what he considered a wrong-headed reading of his document. He pointed out that mention of the real presence was in a footnote because its truth was taken for granted. This only fueled Mother Angelica's fires, and on her *MAL* show on November 18, she deepened her criticism of both Mahony and the document. Mahony responded again on December 1, this time demanding that Mother Angelica read a public apology on the air at least four times between December 1 and December 25. What made it onto the air did not constitute and apology, according to Father Gregory Coiro, director for media relations for the archdiocese. Mahony was so outraged by Mother Angelica's defiant attitude that by early 1998 he was looking for more than just a retraction. In an article which appeared in the January 30, 1998 issue of the *National Catholic Reporter*, Father Coiro announced that Mother Angelica had violated Canons 753 and 1373, which forbid inciting disobedience against a bishop. One of the penalties provided for by these canons was interdict, and Father Coiro made it clear that Mahony was not ruling that penalty out of the question as he took his case against Mother Angelica to Rome.

Two days before the article appeared, Mother Angelica staged what many saw as a counter-attack of her own by announcing that she had been miraculously cured of a back ailment that had kept her in a brace and special shoes for 40 years. The miraculous healing took place as a result of prayers offered by an Italian mystic, whose name was not being released, and, lest anyone fail to see the connection between the healing and the Mahony controversy, the Italian mystic announced that Jesus and Mary appeared to her and told her that they "were pleased" at what Mother Angelica "was doing for the Church." On the same show in which she announced her healing, Mother Angelica also said she was not going to submit to medical examination. Cardinal Mahony later announced his own interpretation of the healing. "God did it for me," he said, "so you can't accuse me anymore of attacking this crippled nun." Either way, it was just one more episode of the seer vs. bishop conflict that had dogged Medjugorje from its inception. In late March of '98, Mother Angelica was back on the air, announcing that she had gone to Garabandal, the phony shrine in Spain, to thank the Blessed Mother for her miraculous cure. Cardinal Mahony was traveling during the month of March too. He gave an address to the plenary assembly ofthe Pontifical Council on Social Communications on March 18 asking, "Who Speaks for the Church?"

On February 25, 1998, Phil Kronzer met with Bishop Peric in Mostar. This time he had with him the film crew which had filmed *Visions on Demand*, Mike Grimes and Maurice Alexander, as well as a journalist from Liverpool by the name of Jeff Pickett. Kronzer's plan was to take Peric's *non constat* letter to Thierry Boutet to Rome, where he planned to ask that the Vatican issue an official, unambiguous condemnation of Medjugorje, before any more marriages got destroyed. Peric also gave Kronzer other documents, including a photocopy of Ivan's testimony in 1982 that a great sign would appear in June and an article which appeared in *Slobodna Dalmacija* which announced that Tomislav Pervan and Jozo Zovko, both of whom had taken vows of poverty as Franciscan friars, were now major shareholders and trustees in a new bank which is to provide quality banking service to the entire area, including pilgrims to Medjugorje.

Kronzer's plan proved simpler in plan than in execution, perhaps because his plan also involved making a movie which would be the sequel to the *Visions* video. At around 6:45 p.m. on February 27, Picket and Grimes set out by car to Medjugorje where they hoped to photograph Vicka or Ivanka as well as the hand-grenade factory. As they approached "Millionaires Row," their term for the road in Bijakovici where seers Ivan and Mirjana lived, a dark Mercedes forced them off the road, and the driver and his passenger then ordered Grimes and Pickett out of the car at gunpoint. Grimes obliged and had his camera confiscated; Pickett remained in the car until the passenger side window was smashed in, whereupon he was dragged out of the car and held at gunpoint and watched as Grimes was knocked to the ground and beaten. Pickett was then beaten, sustaining a number of broken ribs. The two then abandoned their car and escaped their assailants by running up apparition hill, where they hid for that night. Eventually they were picked up the next day when the police found them walking along the main road to Mostar. When they arrived at the police station at Buna 27 hours after they left, Grimes went into shock and had to be taken to the hospital.

Phil Kronzer, in the meantime, found that the Hotel Ero would no longer take his credit card, even though they had accepted it when he stayed there in June of 1997. As a result he was forced to have a wire transfer sent to the new bank, whose trustees included Fathers Pervan and Zovko. The bank then either lost or deliberately misplaced the transfer, forcing Kronzer and his party to spend an extra week in Mostar, but by then, they had been advised to move to the east bank or Muslim section for their own safety. By the time he got back to California, Kronzer was threatening to sue his children, who had refused to send him the money he needed to get out of Bosnia. He was also threatening to sue his main business partner. He also said that he was no longer interested in getting his wife back. Instead, he was planning to sue her for $2.7 million.

Over two hundred years earlier, another pope, Prospero Lambertini, then Pope Benedict XIV, wrote another book called *De Servorum Dei beatifactione et Beatorum canonizatione*. Lambertini's book on canonization is also one of the seminal works on the evaluation of private revelations as well. And beyond that it has a lot to say about the dangers associated with them as well. Lambertini's book possesses a sophistication when it comes to things spiritual that this age would do well to heed, explaining that evil spirits "have at times recommended that which is good in order to hinder a greater good, and have encouraged persons to do a particular act of virtue that they may the more easily deceive the unwary and in the course of time lead them by degrees to commit most horrible sins." It turns out that the unwary turn up the places one would least expect them, in the highest office of the Catholic Church, for instance. Lambertini mentioned the example of his predecessor, Pope Gregory XI, who lay on his death bed, clutching the Eucharist to his breast and warning those around him "to beware of both men and women who under the guise of religion speak visions of their own heads." For Pope Gregory XI, Lambertini continued, "seduced by such, had neglected the reasonable counsel of his friends and had dragged himself and the church to the hazard of imminent schism."

It is the type of warning that even a pope should heed.

BIBLIOGRAPHY

Aarons, Mark and Loftus, John. *Unholy Trinity: How the Vatican's Nazi Networks Betrayed Western Intelligence to the Soviets.* New York: St. Martin's Press, 1991.

Anderson, Walter Truett. *The Upstart Spring: Esalen and the American Awakening.* Reading, MA: Addison-Wesley, 1983.

Associated Press. "Bishop Doubts Visions by Virgin of Woman," 11/30/88

Beljo, Ante. *Yugoslavia: Genocide a Documented Analysis.* Sudbury: Northern Tribune Publishing, 1985.

Bellant, Russ. *Old Nazis, the New Right, and the Republican Party.* Boston: South End Press, 1988.

Berelson, Bernard. *Reader in Public Opinion and Communica tion.* Glencoe, IL:
Free Press, 1950.

Bernstein, Carl, and Politi, Marco. *His Holiness.* New York: Doubleday Press, 1996.

Blackbourne, David. *Marpingen.* New York: Vintage Books, 1995.

Blanshard, Paul. *American Freedom and Catholic Power.* Boston: Beacon Press, 1950.

"Bosnia-Herzegovina: Ousted Commander: Izetbegovic Plans Pure Muslim State." Tanjug, 10/25/97.

Bulajic, Milan. *The Role of the Vatican in the Break-Up of the Yugoslav State.* Belgrade: Ministry of Information of the Republic of Serbia, 1993.

"Burglary Charge Filed in Marshall Shooting Episode," *Times-Leader,* 1/17/92, p. 5B.

Burtchaell, James T. Philemon's Problem. Chicago: Foundation for Adult Catechetical Teaching Aids, 1973.

Chiron, Yves."Medjugorje: The State of the Question," inter view with Ratko Peric. *Present,* 1/25/97

Cornwell, Rupert. *God's Banker*. New York: Dodd, Mead & Company, 1984.

Craig, Mary. *Spark from Heaven*. Notre Dame, IN: Ave Maria Press, 1988.

Dragnich, Alex N. *Serbs and Croats: The Struggle in Yugoslavia*. New York: Harcourt Brace Jovanovich, 1992.

Dvorchak, Robert. "True Believers Find Visions of Mary at Far-Flung Locations."Associated Press, 10/15/94.

Finnegan, Rev. Robert. Report. 4/96.

Flynn, Ted. "A Prophet for Our Time: A Review of *My Heart Awaits You* by Marv Kucera *Signs of the Times*, First Quarter1995, p. 19.

Galot, Jean. "Le apparizioni nella vita della Chiesa." *Civilita Cattolica*, 4/6/85, pp. 19-33.

Gay, Lance. "Pilgrims Gone in War-Torn Nation, but Famed Shrine Survives." Scripps Howard News Service, 8/3/92.

Gospa. Produced and directed by Jakov Sedlar. New York: Wayne Films.

Hall, Brian. *The Impossible Country*. Boston: David R. Godine Publishing, 1994.

"Hnilica Pope Report." *Queen of Peace*, Special edition, Pittsbugh Center for Peace. Spring 1995.

"Italian Judicial Process Keeps Bishop out of Court," CNS, 12/11/94.

Janz, Dennis. "Debunking Medjugorje," *Christian Century* vol 107, May 30-June 6 1990, p. 563-64.

Jones, E. Michael. *Medjugorje: The Untold Story*. South Bend, IN: Fidelity Press, 1988.

Laurentin, Rene, and Lejeune, Rene. *Messages and Teachings of Mary at Medjugorje: Chronological Corpus of the Messages*. Ohio: The Riehle Foundation, 1988.

Luburic, Ante. "What Kind of 'Fruits' are These?" Diocese of Mostar, May 16, 1997.

Knox, Ronald. *Enthusiasm*. New York: Oxford University Press, 1950

Kwitny, Jonathan. *Man of the Century: the Life and Times of Pope John Paul II*. New York: Henry Holt and Company, 1997.

Manuel, David. *Medjugorje Under Siege*. Orleans, Mass.: Paraclete Press, 1992.

"Master Plan for Tourist Development in Medjugorje intro duced," Nick Schinker, NC News/*The Catholic Herald*, 12/29/88, p. 7.

Mazza, Michael. "The Deconversion of Jim Jennings." *Fidelity* May 1994, pp. 18-28

"Medjugorje Dispute Continues," National Catholic News
Service, 3/20/88.

Meek, Richard. "Visionary Discusses Apparitons of Mary."
Catholic Chronicle, 9/25/92, p. 3.

Meyer, Gabriel. "Medjugorje Sparking New Communities of
Faith," *National Catholic Register*, 10/14/90, p. 1.

O'Danaos, Timmy & Ferentes, Donna. "Bishop Hnilica Goes on
Trial." *Fidelity,* February 1993.

O'Grady, Scott, with Coplon, Jeff. *Return with Honor*. New York:
Doubleday, 1995.

Paris, Edmond. *Genocide in Satellite Croatia, 1941-1945*: A
Record of Racial and Religious Persecutions and
Massacres, translated from the French by Lois Perkins,
The American Institute for Balkan Affairs, 1961.

Pavich, Rev. Phillip, O.F.M. *Consecrating Our Hearts to Mary.* A
plus videos, 1990.

Peric, Most Rev. Ratko. "Criteria for Discerning Apparitions"
from *Prijetolje Mudrosti* (The Throne of Wisdom),
Mostar, 1995, pp. 266-86.

Randall, Jonathan. "Historic Feud Simmers among Catholic
Priests in Bosnian Hamlet." *Washington Post*, 4/13/97, p.
A27.

"Ratko Peric on Rebuilding Bosnia's Church." *National Catholic
Register*, 3/26/95.

Ratzinger, Joseph. *The Ratzinger Report*. San Francisco:
Ignatius, 1985.

Reck, William A. *Dear Marian Movement, Let God be God.*
Milford, OH: The Riehle Foundation, 1996.

Rubin, Elizabeth. "Souvenir Miracles." *Harper's,* February '95,
pp. 63-70.

Schaeffer-Duffy, Scott. "Mary, Queen of Peace, Missing Amid
MedjugorjeNationalism." *National Catholic Reporter*,
February 11, 1994.

Schutz, Will. *Here Comes Everybody*. New York: Harper & Row,
1971.

Schutz, Will. *Joy: Expanding Human Awareness*. New York:
Grove Press, 1967.

Simpson, Christopher. *Blowback: America's recruitment of Nazis
and its effects on the Cold War.* New York: Weidenfeld
and Nicolson, 1988.

Simpson, Christopher. *Science of Coercion: Communication
Research and Psychological Warfare 1945-1960*. New
York: Oxford University Press, 1994.

Sivric, Rev. Ivo, OFM. *The Hidden Side of Mejugorje*, edited by

Louis Belanger, translated by Suzanne M. Rini. Quebec: Les Editions Psilog Inc., 1989.

Spalding, Jack. "Story of Scottsdale: St. Maria Goretti Parish," given in St. Louis, St. Thomas the Apostle Church, Florissant, MO, April 25, 1990.

Stehle, Hansjakob. *Die Ostpolitik des Vatikans: 1917-1975* . Munich: R. Piper & Co., 1975.

Sudetic, Chuck. "A Shrine in Bosnia Is Now Illuminated by Rockets," *New York Times*, 9/26/93, Sect. 1 p. 20.

St. John of the Cross. *Ascent of Mount Carmel*. London: T. Baker, 1889

Thavis, John. "John Paul II Meets Bishop, Discusses Events at Medjugorje." CNS/*LA Tidings*, 2/15/91.

Thavis, John. "Pilgrims Should Stop 'Deluding Themselves' about Medjugorje." CNS/*Denver Catholic Register*, 2/1/89 p. 10.

Tolstoy, Nikolai. *The Minister and the Massacres*. London: Century Hutchinson Ltd, 1986.

Tudjman, Franjo. *Nationalism in Contemporary Europe*. New York: Columbia Press, 1981.

Vulliamy, Ed. *Seasons in Hell: Understanding Bosnia's War*. New York: St. Martin's Press, 1994.

"War and a Piece." *Spy Magazine*, Vol. 9 Issue 4, Jul/Aug 1995, p. 50.

Weingarten, Paul. "Thousands Gather in Texas to Await Miracles," *Washington Post*, 8/16/88.

West, Richard. *Tito and the Rise and Fall of Yugoslavia*. New York: Carroll & Graf Publishers, 1994.

Wooden, Cindy. "Vatican Spokesman Says Pope Has No Plans for New Marian Dogmas," (CNS), *Sooner Catholic*, 9/7/97.

"Yugoslavia Finds Tourist Gold at Site of Alleged Apparitions," National Catholic News Service, 4/18/88.

INDEX

L

La Dolce Vita 140
Laborem Exercens 95
Lambertini, Prospero 371
Landeka, Ivan 236, 364
Lang-Pertel, Elfried 265
Laurentin, Rene 54, 73, 78, 94, 102,
    106, 114, 115, 117, 118, 125, 126,
    165, 196, 198, 220, 227, 269, 307,
    xiv
Lefebvre, Archbishop Marcel 145
Legion of Decency 20
Lena, Giulio 112
Leo XIII 13
Levine, Joseph E. 18
Little Pebble 220
Ljubic, Marijan 73, 75, 88
Ljubicic, Petar 105, 189, 191, 237, 265,
    266, 350
Loftus, John 11, 21, 30
Long, Kathleen 260
Lopez, Jeff 158, 174, 208, 211, 268,
    269, 292, xiii
Lopez, Stephanie 160
Lopez, Teresa 159, 174, 179, 209, 210,
    241, 250, 262, 270, 274, 275, 276,
    283, 284, 288, 300, 325, xiii
Lourdes 355
Lovric, Milan 233
Lubbock, Texas 150
Lucia, Sister 129
Lueken, Veronica 64, 252, 286, 317,
    328
Lunetti, Marija Pavlovic, see Marija
    Pavlovic 364
Lyons, Diane 274, 284
Lyons, Frank 278
Lyons, Frank and Diane 271

M

Mackenzie, Lewis 238, 239
Macmillan, Harold 8
MacNutt, Francis 42
Magnum Crimen xvi
Mahony, Roger Cardinal 368
Mahowald, Mark 251, 282, 329
Mahowald, Steve 249, 251, 281

Maier, Fran 223, 225
Maillard, Emmanuel 286
Maloney, George 260
Manda 47, 49, 77, 96, 114, 115
Mann, Dale 332
Mansour, Antoine 220
Mansour, Claire 220, 221
Manuel, David 2
Marcinkus, Paul 96, 103, 104, 109
Marija 203, 262
Marpingen 27, 62, 84, 86, 355
Martin, Jean-Louis 117
Martin, Jeannie 297
Massamini, Tony 41
McCaffrey, Dave 294, 324
McCall, Kenneth 286
McCarthy, Senator Joseph 22
McClory, Robert 31
McCormick, Ann see Marcia Smith
    296
McDonough, Michael 260
McGrath, Archbishop Marcus 133
McKenna, Sister Briege 51
McManus, Bishop William 133
McNally, Tom 360
Mead, Kathy 251
Medjugorje 2, 25, 33, 53, 60, 65, 66,
    67, 68, 69, 73, 74, 76, 77, 94, 105,
    107, 124, 127, xii, xv, xvii, xx
Medjugorje Gebetsaktion 265
Medjugorje: The Untold Story xiii
Mengele, Josef 106
Mesic, Stip 192
Messori, Vittorio 65
Metkovic xx
Meyer, Gabriel 225
Mihailovich 8
Mikulic, Brando 91
Militti, Ed 282
Militti, Leslie 252
Miljus, Branko xvii
Miller, Brian 275
Milosevic, Slobodan 69, 170, 189
Mindszenty, Joseph 11
Mirjana 78, 79, 81, 105, 106, 107, 189,
    265, 266, 357, 364
Mirna 220
Misic, Aloysije xv, xvii